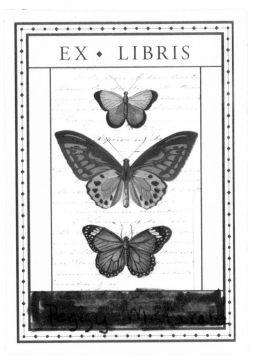

# EX · LIBRIS

Peggy McCauls

D1271150

PASTORAL
CARE IN
HISTORICAL
PERSPECTIVE

# COMMENTARY

"This is the most important book on pastoral care to be published in several years. It performs precisely and imaginatively and readably the function promised in its title — to set the ministry of pastoral care in proper historical perspective."

Seward Hiltner, D.D.

"This book is a timely and significant resource in the 'identity crisis' which grips the pastoral ministry today. It is a reminder that self-understanding is a dialogue with history as well as rigorous self-examination here and now."

Charles R. Stinette, Jr.

By WILLIAM A. CLEBSCH and
CHARLES R. JAEKLE

# PASTORAL
# CARE IN
# HISTORICAL
# PERSPECTIVE

New York • Jason Aronson • London

*To Two Virginians:*

Betsy Birchfield Clebsch

Ann Murden Jaekle

**New Printing 1983**

ISBN: 0-87668-717-6

Library of Congress Catalog Number: 84-45113

Manufactured in the United States of America.

# PREFACE

This book's reception in seminaries and divinity schools and by members of the pastoral and healing professions as a manual for advanced training and retraining in the pastoral arts, has gratified the authors. In addition, we are grateful for the frequent quoting and excerpting of the interpretive essay in works of scholarship and anthologies on the cure of souls, under secular as well as religious auspices.

Seven years after the second edition appeared, we see another use for the book, one that surpasses our original intention. Our historical perspective and the materials we have viewed from that perspective render the book a record—admittedly sketchy—of the major transformations of the Western personality, particularly in its spiritual dimension, throughout the Christian era. This perspective brings into sharp focus the modern, self-conscious, critical, voluntaristic personality of our own time. It is just this new personhood that has become the bafflingly versatile object of attention for the secular healing arts as well as for the contemporary practice of pastoral caring.

Perhaps most emphatically in the area of marriage and family therapy, this modern personality finds new ways of hurting and needs new ways of being helped. In a sense, the contemporary healing arts deal with clients and techniques both of which transcend the bounds of our book. However, we must understand the earlier transformations of Western personhood if we are to comprehend its more diffuse manifestations today. Only thus can we measure how significant is the fact that psychotherapy's central role in the healing arts now changes swiftly in response to new occasions and new opportunities.

This new edition of a possibly dated book is nevertheless timely. Pastoral care, viewed historically, touches interests that run both wider and deeper than the church and the ministry it sponsors. Therefore, the book portrays human griefs and appetites that persist today, even if they now take new forms not precisely outlined in documents drawn from past eras. Timeliness, in this case as in many others, is a reward for taking the past seriously.

The first five exhibits in Part 5 show how Christianity assimilated and transmuted the Stoic personality of the later Hellenistic period. Were we to revise the exhibits to make this portrayal more fulsome, surely there would be a reading from Boethius' *Consolation of Philosophy,* to show how Christian ideals reshaped and uplifted the Stoic life-style. The four steps of the pastoral function of sustaining were ministered by Lady Philosophy to the imprisoned consul, under sentence of death, who thus learned that bad fortune was more instructive than good because the latter implied a false promise of happiness on earth. The pagan Stoic personhood had steeled itself to do what could be done in matters over which humans have some control, and had left everything else to fortune or fate. The profoundly (if only implicitly) Christianized Roman personality in Boethius, reflected emergingly in our first five exhibits, learned the transitoriness of all things under our control, and lived with this ambiguity by drawing hope from faith in a providential deity who would bring to fruition everything beyond our control.

The next group of readings, numbered six through twelve, portrays the explicitly Christian personality of the Latin Middle Ages. This form of human life understood itself as the prize in a for-keeps battle between the forces of spiritual good and those of spiritual evil. Being human became an exciting contest lasting until death sounded its inevitable knell—or even thereafter. The chief human strengths and weaknesses came to be neatly identified and classified, and the minor virtues and vices were placed securely in relation to them. If one could only identify one's own besetting sin, then specific virtues could be practiced to offset it. Every evil could be cured by a kind of allopathic discipline. To sharpen the picture of the medieval personality we might propose a reading from the later Roman penitentials, especially those that distinguish between attrition, in which the soul regrets its evil deeds out of fear of punishment, and contrition, in which the spirit rues its sins out of regard for the worthiness of others—especially the divine Other—who were offended by the misdeed. Such an exhibit would show how the Latin Christian form of personhood turned human sinfulness into a platform from which to levitate the soul to the purifying love of God.

Readings numbered thirteen through nineteen point to the personality of the Enlightenment, with its emphasis on identifying the special faculties of each individual person. These propensities were taken to be refinable toward virtuosity by dutiful practice and exercise. Good nominees for further readings about this personality are too many to enumerate, but we might have been clearer about the difference between the spiritual virtuosity that cultivated the religious feelings and the virtuoso who practiced benevolence—the one liking duties toward God and the other emphasizing duties toward neighbor, the one a John Wesley and the other a Jeremy Taylor.

Finally, the appearance of modern personhood—self-starting, self-examining, capable of living serially in many dimensions and moods and attitudes, genuinely "polypolitan"—might have been depicted more elaborately than is done by the book's two last readings. But, after all, the writings of Nietzsche and Freud are readily available!

To consider the book a sketch of the development of the Western religious personality is by no means to undercut its emphasis on the pastoral and other healing arts, which still flourish today in their traditional patterns and at the same time are assuming novel and variegated forms. There remain recent (and by now conservative) patterns based on psychoanalysis and client-centered therapy. There are recovered forms such as meditation, body movement, and breath control, and there are really novel types such as love massage, bioenergetics, transactional analysis, existential analysis, and primal therapy. Pastoral or religious cure of souls today involves all these techniques and more. This proliferation of therapies has been germinated by a culture that is increasingly open to exploration and invention regarding the style and character of humanness. And this variety yields instances of personhood that hurt and hope in ways as yet hardly described, but recognizable in novels, plays, posings, paintings, fantasies, and many other projections of unmapped areas of human experience.

When this book first appeared, the landscape occupied by helping professions was still dominated by medical psychiatry or its conservative variants such as client-centered therapy, reductionist analysis, and other techniques of restoring normalcy and achieving adjustment. Modern pastoral care, especially in the form of counseling, developed under the tutelage of one or more of these classical medical and psychiatric systems. Clergymen given to specializing in the pastoral arts did their clinical training in established institutions of health and welfare, under recognized therapists whose views toward pastoring ranged from suspicion to supportive curiosity. Pastors who became expert in counseling or psychotherapy received nurture at the hands of benevolent psychiatrists, toughening by hostile psychiatrists, advice from friendly psychiatrists, and treatment from talented psychiatrists.

Today things have changed. Clergymen specializing in pastoral therapy may well contract for supervision from an Esalen encounter leader, a Gestalt psychologist, a family process-therapist, or a practitioner of Rolfing—all of whose work is far removed from the medical models that taught and nourished earlier pioneers in the pastoral counseling movement.

The classical psychiatry in the context of which the readings in this book were selected is rooted in the mechanistic science of the late nineteenth century, and it relates psychiatrist to patient in ways reflecting the authoritarian nineteenth-century physician's stance toward his physically ill and medically ignorant patient. The physician, socially sanctioned and professionally trained, was taken to be objective. He had not only the tools but also the wisdom of his ancient trade. If the patient would only place himself under doctor's care and follow doctor's orders his migraine headaches, gastric complaints, phobias, depressions, or other ills might be relieved. So it remains, provided the patient still views his trouble in a perspective that requires diagnosis and treatment by a medical practitioner.

It is at the point of the patients' sense of the nature of their troubles that the most profound changes are occurring. Increasingly, men and women bring to therapy ailments that do not easily fit the nosology of classical psychiatry; nor do they resonate to a pastoral counseling informed by it. The helping professions are highly reactive. For, after all, the healer's first task is to get the patient to hurt in ways the healer can alleviate; if those ways of healing are taken to be objective and to arise from a body of traditional lore, however esoteric or exoteric, then the hurting must be brought into the orbit of that lore. When new forms of hurting—much more, when new forms of human personhood, present themselves—the very exploration of them suggests that new means of helping are needed and are clued by the patient as much as, maybe more than, by the healer. In our day the florid growth of new and sometimes bizarre therapies is a social index of the hunger for variety and individuality that pervade contemporary life. It is common wisdom that we live at a time when traditional values no longer either nourish or justify our current life-style. Thus our behavior labors to reflect a value referent. Personal fulfillment becomes self-fulfillment. The purpose of living becomes self-direction, not "calling" *(Beruf)* but "occupation," or even self-occupation. Hedonic, privatized, self-actualizing personhood may be deeply troubled not by some specific hurt but simply by a sense of directionlessness. For the entire Western Christian experience down to our time, men and women went to their pastors when they *felt bad.* They were sick and they sought healing. Or they suffered a loss or disappointment and they wanted solace and sustaining. Or they were perplexed by decisions *sub specie aeternitatis* and they looked for guidance. Or they were estranged from fellow or deity or both by some presumably identifiable deed, whether of commission or omission, and they needed reconciliation.

Today clients in swelling numbers seek therapy not because they feel bad but because they *do not feel good.* The helper, to be sure, may uncover hurt beneath or beside aimlessness, or pain hidden in ennui, but the contemporary client is ready for more than cure, more than recovery of a status quo ante. We today suffer from lack of spiritual "weight" and purpose for our lives, and we would gladly embrace hurting if to do so brought increased meaning and significance. We quest not for restoration but uplift—literally, "relevance"; we thirst not for knowledge but for wisdom; we hunger not for adjustment but for fulfillment.

Nowhere in our society are the novel demands on pastoral care for contemporary personhood more manifest than in the new patterns, new strains, new expectations, new woes attending family life, especially marriage. In fact, one datum of the newness of the situation is that this book, first published only ten years ago, includes no specific treatment of marriage counseling. The complexity of modern marital and family relations, to be sure, showed themselves with ever greater clarity (indeed, publicity) during the decade. And that complexity is so impressive today that we would belie it were we to tack on a token exhibit or chapter by way of remedying this deficiency. The function of reconciling, we contended then and still think now, is in the foreground of pastoral care and is the likely means of addressing pastoral insights to marital and familial problems. To do so will require extension of the notion of reconciliation from putting back together to finding new and fulfilling relations.

To be sure, the church's record in marriage counseling is, overall, not impressive. Long periods until the Protestant Reformation produced little but homilies and other commentaries dealing with constraints on monogamy (including from time to time warnings against an overly enthusiastic attitude in the marriage bed) and restraints against divorce and remarriage (serial henogamy). During the Protestant era devout physicians and clergymen aware of the antics and pains to which married spouses were prone wrote about them and offered their prescriptions and advice, sometimes pointedly. In 1619 the Reverend William Whatly published a treatise called *The Bride Bush: Or Directions for Married Persons,* in which he tells us:

> Most men enter into this estate and being entered complain thereof. They should rather complain of themselves. It is an unfit thing and a fruit of ignorant pride to cast the blame of our grievances upon God's ordinances. It had been happy (saith one) had I not married. Oh, that I had not married.

Whatly goes on to admonish and chastise his dissatisfied parishioners:

> For shame keep silence. Thou are indeed married to an ill companion. Thy wicked flesh, that body of death, that only husband—sin.

Canons of privacy about what went on between husband and wife may well have prevented a detailed record of the marriage therapy done by skilled physicians and clergy—as also with the practice of hearing confessions and assigning penance (see pp. 64-65). If marriage is among the most sorely troubled of our society's institutions and among the most difficult of all human relationships, it may also be the most widespread area of Westerners' traditional experience about which we know the least.

Of marriage today we know that no other human relation reflects so quickly or so decisively the currents and surges inside the two persons who compose it. The stakes are high in terms of potentiality for both joy and woe. The protective sanctions are eroded by means of avoiding pregnancy and by attitudes countenancing deviations or even normlessness. Every aspect of marriage is fragile. The act of marrying may range from viewing the bonds as divinely tied to arranging a casual roommating; yet the initiation of any such relation is a moment of intensity. Traditionally, "till death do us part" gave temporal symbolism to the implication that human mating calls upon the whole of two persons. Traditionally, the acceptance by two persons of a single name and the symbolism of the ring(s) underlined the seriousness of the decision as mutual pledges to share entire lives with one another as with no others. Today, many eschew these traditional symbols and undertake explicitly temporary alliances by poetic avowals of affection and love. A powerful modern mood reflects that men and women ought to relate "naturally," that is, with commitments that are tentative and private. Who knows what tomorrow may bring: what new configuration of attraction or appetite? What new sense of who one is? Yet, lovers continue to find high voltages in their life together. One cannot be at once committed and casual, and relationships without commitment lack substance. Hence, the anguish and the perils of marriage are not extinguished in the new mood. One discovers that the deliberate absence of symbols does not dispel the demands symbolized.

Longevity is such that many marriages today might survive physically far beyond the golden anniversary; can a marriage remain satisfyingly alive as long as lengthened life expectancies endure? Divorce beckons as an end to marital troubles, and introduces new and often more perplexing difficulties. The values and meanings of earlier generations become less viable for present realities, and marriage becomes problematic for most and meaningless for many. As marital partners in earlier times discovered the pains as well as the joys of the connubial state, they might have sought from family physician and pastor advice concerning the sins and confusions attending their intimacy. But today both the design and the purpose of the relationship is under fundamental questioning. Fixed meanings frustrate people in rapidly changing circumstances; yet biological drives issue in acts that plumb deep significances of human experience. Men and women bearing modern personhood seek ever new meanings; does not that quest imply new partnerships?

In these and many more ways marriage stands as a paradigm of problems that reach to the bone and marrow of contemporary personhood. How can one belong to or with another? From the standpoint of individuality we moderns can see our lives as artistic creations and ourselves as artists. One is responsible for the texture, contours, colors, and structure of one's own life, and it is his or her responsibility to make it worthwhile. Can two artists paint a single picture for two individualities? How and with what commitment and intensity does one person belong with another? In short, a decisive struggle is being waged as to whether the traditional forms of marriage have any future. Perhaps commitment to another is a *sine qua non* for any selfhood with heft and muscle. Without it, modern life with its alternatives, choices, and capacities for detachment may be experienced as alienating, fragmented, isolated. Without commitment there is no belonging and without belonging we tend to feel crowded and harassed and finally depersonalized.

We raise these questions not to answer them but to use marriage as an example of the predicaments and possibilities of modern personhood, the understanding of which is the implied task of a book displaying former types of personality through the portal of pastoral care. To care therapeutically for the modern personality involves philosophic as well as historic wisdom. Indeed, it is emblematic of our day that psychotherapy as various professionals practice it leads from the comfortable confines of technical and strategic considerations of good craftsmanship into the arenas of uncertainty known as philosophy and ethics. Some psychotherapists—and some of the most talented—have embraced this fate and become gurus speaking the language of prophecy, myth, and dream. For their clients search as insistently for enlightenment as once clients sought adjustment. Therapists, like pastors, today rely on sharing with their clients great convictions about what is ultimately significant and worthy of ultimate commitment. Modern practitioners of the healing arts indeed are reactive to an emergent, hitherto unknown personhood.

But other new personhoods, as this book demonstrates, have appeared before. And the functions of pastoring that have been adapted to them in the past are serviceable, with adaptation, for today—certainly for pastors and not unlikely for therapists whose great convictions lack, or seem to lack, specifically religious content. The four functions of the pastoral art, sustaining, guiding, healing, and reconciling, are powerfully operative today. These activities do not merely record the dimensions of therapy done by clergymen long ago and far away. Rather they signalize what is happening, updated to be sure, here and now. Maybe whoever reads this book can share the authors' astonishment in viewing the contemporary scene and in realizing at the same time how much of what is done today by therapists is recognizable in what has been done before by pastors. Maybe we can marvel together at the durability of human woes and the inventive triumphs of human aspirations, at the temptations and the wonders of being human, and at the ingenuity by which the helping professions can convert some of those woes into triumphs, some of those temptations into wonders.

Yet the past is for helping us to see the present more clearly. When we realize how our forebears came to experience the humanness they were given, we still as moderns must realize that we go further than they in creating the humanness we enjoy—or, maybe, despise. And it is this humanness, as it rises to new joys and sinks into new despairs, with which the pastoral and other therapeutic arts must deal. The practitioners of those arts, both religious and secular, shall learn from the history of Western personhood and the history of Western pastoring if they are to help us stretch the human capabilities. Otherwise, we shall ignorantly groan in the old predicaments instead of trying to find fulfillment in the new ones.

WILLIAM A. CLEBSCH
CHARLES R. JAEKLE

# Contents

## PART 3    32

# THE FOUR PASTORAL FUNCTIONS

## PART 4    67

# PASTORAL CARE PAST AND PRESENT

# PART 5

## EXHIBITS

# PART 1

# THE SHAPE
# OF PASTORAL
# CARE

## 1. Introduction

The Christian ministry of the cure of souls, or pastoral care, has been exercised on innumerable occasions and in every conceivable human circumstance, as it has aimed to relieve a plethora of perplexities besetting persons of every class and condition and mentality. Pastors rude and barely plucked from paganism, pastors sophisticated in the theory and practice of their profession, and pastors at every stage of adeptness between these extremes, have sought and wrought to help troubled people overcome their troubles. To view pastoral care in historical perspective is to survey a vast endeavor, to appreciate a noble profession, and to receive a grand tradition.

Although only a tiny fraction of the total activity of pastoral care has been recorded, the range that is documented is overwhelming. The records, even when only sampled, reveal immediately two features of soul care under Christian auspices. First, the richness and inventiveness of pastoral ingenuity defy all efforts at complete comprehension, so great is the variety of ways that troubled people have been helped pastorally. Second, each intimate and unique act of pastoral helping in the past stands discrete within its own specific conditions—human, historical, personal,

1

cultural, and ecclesiastical. Paradoxically, then, nothing proposed today as a novelty in soul care is really new, yet each pastoral act is, as each has always been, fresh, distinct, and unrepeatable.

Any historical review of pastoral care, therefore, however cursory, at once will heighten appreciation for the vast treasures that lie in the tradition, and will sharpen one's sense both of the uniqueness of human troubles that now arise and of the ever-novel ways in which soul care can be exercised. Much that past pastors have done was indeed ingenious, contemporaneous, rich, and creative, and becomes fresh and exciting in recollection. Each opportunity for the care of souls today presents itself as novel and unique and demands ingenious and creative ministering.

Christian pastoral care, being by its very nature no simple cumulative skill, defies neat classification and systematization. To learn *about* the tradition of pastoring, grand as it may be, guarantees no increase of pastoral proficiency. Pastoral knowledge cannot be transmitted in objective, non-personal terms. Pastors are persons representing the wisdom, resources, and authority of Christian faith as that faith helps troubled individuals. Pastoral proficiency is therefore acquired within the pastoral relationship, and the student who would learn from this tradition must find a way to enter into the actual pastoring of the past. No amount of chemical analysis of paint and stone makes a Michaelangelo, yet a Michaelangelo would know the great tradition of painting and sculpture that preceded him as his genius emerged, and he would sense in that tradition the genius of many worthies contributing to his own. So the analytical and historical study of pastoral care that is proffered by these chapters merely opens the door to a magnificent trove of lore that is the habitat of every pastoral act. Subsequent exhibits allow for a possible vicarious participation in traditional pastoring. This lore must galvanize the attention of all who would engage today either in pastoring itself or in another of the specialized helping and healing professions. Pastors, physicians, psychiatrists, counselors, lawyers, and social workers will discern, in the present samplings of a vast literature, facets and fascinations that perchance go beyond the notice and comments of the editors. Granting all that, we nevertheless dare to edit, to analyze, to systematize, to comment, and to classify.

For ours is a day in which pastoral care is everywhere challenged and stimulated by fresh insights into the problems of being human, insights developed by behavioral scientists and by those adept at the healing arts no less than by philosophers and theologians. Pastoral care today is undergoing a swift and sweeping transition. This transition begs a necessity to appropriate and appreciate the lore of a long and fruitful experience of Christian pastors in helping troubled people. To their methods and aims we are no more bound than we are able actually to re-enter their particular circumstances. Yet history knows no absolute discontinuities, and much that we might take to be new methods of soul care we may learn to be mere variations upon time-honored approaches to the task. Ours is indeed a time of transition, but it is not the first such time. Others before us have faced new insights from the behavioral sciences and healing arts, from the philosophies and theologies, of their day. Others before us have labored to learn the lore of the pastoral art, even as they resolved to practice that art inventively. As we attempt to define the pastoral posture and the pastoral functions, and to describe the many modes and means of soul care, we must remember that, while ours is a time of change, other transitional times have occurred again and again during the centuries.

In all the literature about pastoral care under Christian auspices, there is no writer of greater importance than Gregory the Great. A Benedictine monk, Gregory in A.D. 590 became bishop of Rome and richly developed the papal office. At the end of the sixth century he wrote his remarkable treatise, *Pastoral Care*, in response to his elevation to the episcopacy. It quickly became an exceedingly influential book, even to the extent that it became customary for newly ordained bishops to receive a copy of this work along with the Canons of the church. A large part of the influence of Gregory's rule is accounted for by the fact that he lived in just such a transitional time as our own. Summarizing the classical tradition of the Church Fathers, Gregory strove to codify soul care into a work applicable to his own day. He stood at the beginning of a new era when the church was pressed and stretched by the task of Christianizing the Teutonic and Slavic folk who had recently occupied the European continent. For the church's achievement in molding the whole of European culture Gregory's treatise became a chief resource, establishing the patterns, the vocabulary, the aims, and the methods of soul care. It has been claimed with accuracy that Gregory's *Pastoral Care* furnished for secular priests a pattern of conduct just as the *Rule* of Benedict did for the western monks.[1]

Gregory was moved by the changes and challenges of his time to set forth some concise definitions of pastoral care. Pushing the simile no farther than that, our time of transition begs that we attempt the same. Unavoidably and not undesirably, definitions demand exposure of points of view. Against certain recent trends in pastoral (or "practical") theology, we regard pastoral care as only a part—to be sure, a dignified and indispensable part—of the total work of Christian ministering. Therefore, we distinguish pastoral care, on the one hand, from all the many ministerial roles that involve leadership of groups (such as the conduct of worship, church administration, preaching, teaching, community relations, and the like), and, on the other hand, we distinguish it from

---

[1] See Henry David, S.J., ed. and tr., *Pastoral Care*, by St. Gregory the Great ("Ancient Christian Writers," Westminster, Md.: The Newman Press, 1955), p. 10.

many helping services and healing arts such as those rendered by lawyers, physicians, psychiatrists, counselors, social workers, and the like, even though at times ministers may render services similar to those rendered by other helpers.

General definitions and distinctions, however necessary, are inept vehicles for the appreciation and assessment of the vast lore of pastoral care known to contemporary Christians. A representative sample of this lore is provided by the exhibits that comprise the larger part of this book. These readings will at another place be set in their historical contexts. Here we first state concise definitions. Then we shall review briefly the history of pastoring in the Christian tradition, pointing out its major past trends. Next we shall present a rather detailed analysis of the four functions of pastoral care and shall illustrate how each of these functions has developed throughout Christian history. Finally, this introductory exposition will suggest how certain historic features of pastoral care may enrich the practice of soul care today.

2. Definitions

The ministry of the cure of souls, or pastoral care, consists of helping acts, done by *representative Christian persons*, directed toward the *healing, sustaining, guiding,* and *reconciling* of *troubled persons* whose troubles arise *in the context of ultimate meanings and concerns*.[2]

I. *Representative Persons.* First and most simply, pastoral care is a ministry performed by *representative Christian persons*, persons who, either *de jure* or *de facto*, bring to bear upon human troubles the resources, the wisdom, and the authority of Christian faith and life. Such representative persons may or may not hold specific offices in a Christian church, although theirs is commonly the office of authorized pastors. They may be called "elders," "ministers," "rectors," "priests," "presbyters," "bishops," "deacons," "confessors," or many another name. They may hold no churchly office whatever. Yet to perform pastoral care, they must in some way possess and exercise, or be taken to possess and exercise, the resources of the Christian faith, the wisdom distilled from Christians' experiences, and the authority of a company of Christian believers. It is to be noted that Gregory's *Pastoral Care* was written by a bishop— a pope, in fact—in order to guide other bishops in the heavy responsibility of shepherding souls. In the seventeenth century, Richard Baxter, a presbyter, wrote a handbook for presbyters called *The Reformed Pastor*. Exhibit 3 is drawn from a very early Christian pastoral handbook written especially to guide bishops—the *Didascalia Apostolorum*. However, un-

---

2 Healing, sustaining, and guiding have been delineated and discussed by Seward Hiltner, *Preface to Pastoral Theology* (Nashville: Abingdon Press, 1958), pp. 89–172. Although indebted to Hiltner, we have developed our own meanings for these terms.

ordained and officially uncommissioned persons can also bear the authority of the Christian faith to troubled persons. One of the following readings is from a tract telling late medieval Catholics how laymen can be pastors to one another in the crisis of dying [SEE EXHIBIT 10]. It is noteworthy that, while the Christian tradition yields abundant literature showing how ordained persons should function as pastors, pastoring by unofficial persons has undergone relatively little thoughtful analysis, although its continual exercise cannot be doubted. In all these cases, some form of the Christian confession of faith becomes an essential ingredient in the helping act of pastoring, for the pastor is, or is taken to be, a representative person who confesses Christian faith and brings Christian meanings to bear upon human troubles.

II. *Troubled Persons.* Second, the ministry of pastoral care is directed to troubled persons and is aimed at supporting and helping them as individual persons. To be sure, Christians ancient and modern have given the name "pastoral letter" to pronouncements by bishops stating policy for all the believers under their care. Such a pastoral letter might in modern times direct that racial segregation weigh heavily upon the consciences of believers. Before proper pastoral care may arise in this circumstance, however, some person must apprehend that he is involved in the matter of racial segregation; thus, *a* trouble becomes *his* trouble. Pastoral care begins when an individual person recognizes or feels that his trouble is insolvable in the context of his own private resources, and when he becomes willing, however subconsciously, to carry his hurt and confusion to a person who represents to him, however vaguely, the resources and wisdom and authority of religion.

Since soul care always deals with troubled persons, the pastor finds himself necessarily ready to support the individual against the claims of institutions and groups. Often between individual needs and institutional claims no antipathies arise, yet it is unrealistic and may even become cruel for the pastor to assume that they are always in harmony or are capable of being harmonized. Frequently pastoral care seeks to introduce an individual into a group in order to relieve his hurt or even in order to place him in the way of finding relief. When that introduction is undertaken, however, *for the sake of the group, pastoral care ceases* and some other ministry, perhaps that of evangelization, begins. Such a shift may be, either consciously or unconsciously, quite necessary. Sometimes a severely disturbed person must be restrained not only because restraint might benefit him but also in order to protect society. In this manner, or in others, soul care may lead to an act of social responsibility, and perhaps only after the discharge of the latter may the former be resumed. Nevertheless, the proper ministry of the cure of souls cannot be dictated by managerial, institutional, or societal rights and needs, for it finds opportunities for its exercise only to the extent that the welfare of the individual person can remain the paramount interest.

III. *Meaningful Troubles.* Christian men and women, of course, in innumerable instances help other individuals in neighborly or charitable ways, without being taken to be representative of the spiritual resources of the Christian religion; thus, Christian doctors and lawyers frequently exercise vital ministries of healing and guiding troubled persons. But only when personal troubles evoke profound concerns and raise questions about fundamental meanings, and only when the troubled person is ready to accept help from a representative of Christian faith as it bears upon such concerns and offers these meanings, does true pastoral care arise. It is, of course, quite possible for a lawyer and his client to approach a problem with complete seriousness and as involving significant issues of right and wrong; but their act becomes Christian pastoral care only if that seriousness and those issues are understood and interpreted with reference to Christian affirmations. In modern times it has become patently clear that Christianity has no monopoly on issues of ultimate meaning. Out of the background of philosophical existentialism and of his own shattering experience during imprisonment by the Nazis, a philosopher-psychiatrist has written:

> In my opinion and according to my personal convictions and experiences (be they clinical or metaclinical ones), the first and foremost aim of mental hygiene should be to stimulate man's will-to-meaning and to offer him concrete meaning potentialities. . . . Thus, we can understand the wisdom in the words of Nietzsche: "He who has a *why* to live for can bear almost any *how*." In these words I see a motto for all psychotherapy and education. This is also why logotherapy calls upon man's will-to-meaning and tries to evoke it whenever it is hidden in the unconscious or is repressed.[3]

Thus, a specifically non-Christian (which is not to say un-Christian or anti-Christian) concern for helping troubled persons is seen in our day to border closely upon Christian pastoral care as we have defined it. Moreover, Frankl has perceived that most—if not all—human troubles point eventually to issues of ultimate meaning, even though they may be "hidden in the unconscious" or "repressed." Thus, every attempt to deal with human trouble may implicitly engage the meanings and concerns that Christian pastoral care explicitly engages.

Pastoral care calls forth questions and issues of deepest meaning and highest concern, for it is exercised at a depth where the meaning of life and faith is involved on the part of the helper as well as on the part of the one helped. Gregory's treatise, previously cited, earnestly warned

---

[3] Viktor E. Frankl, *From Death-Camp to Existentialism*, tr. Ilse Lasch (Boston: Beacon Press, 1959), p. 103. Reprinted by permission of the Beacon Press, © 1959 by Viktor E. Frankl.

"Logotherapy" designates a form of psychotherapy which takes man's search for meaning and purpose more seriously than the more familiar psychoanalytical systems and behavioral psychologies have done.

against persons who, while pretending to be pastors, concentrated upon worldly or transitory matters. He exhorted pastors to be concerned for both the inward and the outward affairs of persons in trouble. Gregory, like other spokesmen of the long traditions of pastoral care before and after him, perceived that, while the troubled person's hurt or difficulty called for amelioration, the helping act, when pursued in depth, inevitably involved such problems of the soul as the issues of meaning or futility, of obedience or disobedience, of faith or doubt, of humility or pride. Of course, there are many instances in which personal troubles raise or seem to raise no concerns bearing upon the profoundest meanings of life, and often representative Christian persons deal with individuals in terms of these more superficial troubles. But the particular posture of pastoral care is called into being when the troubled man or woman senses, however dimly, his need to work out his problem with specific reference to his ultimate concerns, and wishes to bring those concerns into engagement with Christian affirmations.

IV. *Other Helping Acts.* A plethora of helping acts stands in adjunctive or contiguous relationships to pastoral care but nevertheless do not belong properly to that specific ministry. On many occasions works of charity, of welfare, of education, of binding up wounds, of giving ethical counsel, and so forth, have come to be closely associated with the Christian ideal of love for the neighbor. These acts may well display one or more features of the pastoral posture. They may help individual persons, they may be done by representative Christian persons, they may aim at a certain healing, guiding, sustaining, or reconciling, and they may involve crucial questions of meaning. Yet, unless they involve all these ingredients in intimate association with one another, they do not rightly belong to pastoral care. In the mid-second century, a devastating plague swept the Mediterranean coasts, becoming particularly terrible in Egypt. Most of the populace fled the cities and towns for the sake of their lives. In Rome, and especially in Alexandria, there remained behind many Christians who at great danger to themselves charitably nursed the sick and buried the dead. Lacking from this generous activity was any special representation of Christian faith to troubles eliciting ultimate concerns. Helping acts in this instance, however admirable, were hardly pastoral. Pastoral care is not synonymous with acts of mercy, or with works of love and charity, or with neighborliness, or with recruiting church members.

Theologically one may be convinced that all good things come of God, but the solution of human trouble is not always recognized by the blessed as involving God in any way. A crude but interesting case in point is the healing in the name of Satan in which partly Christianized persons of medieval Europe engaged. Finding no relief for their illnesses in the sprinklings, anointings, exorcisms, and masses by Christian ministers, these persons sought sorceresses, returned to the half-remembered household deities and fairies and elves who remained part of their folk-lore, and, in many cases, there found healing.[4] Yet the fact that individuals who called themselves Christians were healed in the presence of others who called themselves Christians furnishes no ground for considering this an example of the ministry of the cure of souls.

More subtle distinctions are called for when we turn to acts by persons engaged in the modern helping professions who are recognized by our communities both as professional men and women and as professing Christians. They heal, sustain, guide, and reconcile as doctors, undertakers, lawyers, psychiatrists, social workers, and so forth. Ordinarily their helping proceeds from their unique professional postures and draws upon their special professional resources. While these men and women may be persons of profoundly felt and consciously exercised Christian vocation, their helping remains outside the ministry of pastoral care unless they come to act as persons who represent the Christian religion's resources, wisdom, and authority. Conversely, the same thing must be said of a vast range of activities by professional ministers who utilize official status in their churches in order to perform works of mercy, community welfare, education, relief, and so forth; professional competence should enable them to distinguish these acts from the circumstances in which they engage in the cure and care of souls.

Our definition of Christian pastoral care is indeed a de-finition, for it sets certain limits and readily acknowledges that much helping activity falls outside the proper realm of pastoring. Professional ministers delude themselves and abdicate their pastoral responsibilities when they assume that, since all ministerial acts are, at least by intention, helpful, therefore all these acts are pastoral. On the contrary, pastoral care comes into its dignity as its definiteness is recognized.

V. *Functions of Pastoral Care.* Each special function of the cure of souls calls for brief description.

A. HEALING is that function in which a representative Christian person helps a debilitated person to be restored to a condition of wholeness, on the assumption that this restoration achieves also a new level of spiritual insight and welfare. Pastoral healing, thus, involves recuperation from a specific ill, but it is distinguished by the fact that it regards cures as advancements in the soul's ability to reckon on illness and health as experiences fraught with spiritual significance. Pastoral healing may take place by means of the impartation or application of curative agents and actions, or by means of the elicitation of spiritual attitudes and actions from the person seeking to be healed.

B. SUSTAINING consists of helping a hurting person to endure and to transcend a circumstance in which restoration to his former condition

---

[4] See G. G. Coulton, *The Medieval Village* (Cambridge: at the University Press, 1931), pp. 262ff.

or recuperation from his malady is either impossible or so remote as to seem improbable. The sustaining function normally employs the means of compassionate commiseration. But it goes beyond mere resignation to affirmation as it attempts to achieve spiritual growth through endurance of unwanted or harmful or dangerous experiences. Perhaps the commonest form of sustaining is found in the pastoral ministry to bereaved persons, whose loss is indeed unredeemable but whose experience opens up the significant spiritual implications of death as confronting the bereaved and as having confronted the deceased.

C. The pastoral function of GUIDING consists of assisting perplexed persons to make confident choices between alternative courses of thought and action, when such choices are viewed as affecting the present and future state of the soul. Guidance commonly employs two identifiable modes. *Eductive guidance* tends to draw out of the individual's own experiences and values the criteria and resources for such decisions, while *inductive guidance* tends to lead the individual to adopt an *a priori* set of values and criteria by which to make his decision. Perhaps the most familiar modern form of eductive guidance is that commonly known as "client-centered therapy,"[5] while inductive guidance classically appeals to the long tradition of Christian moral theology and casuistry.

D. The RECONCILING function seeks to re-establish broken relationships between man and fellow man and between man and God. Broadly speaking, each of these horizontal and vertical relationships has been understood as inescapably involving the other. That is to say, while we may distinguish between broken or restored relationships with God and with neighbor, only very rarely has Christian pastoring dared to separate them. Reconciling employs two emphatic modes of operation, which we call forgiveness and discipline. Classically, Christian pastoral care has employed the mode of *forgiveness* in the sacramental acts of confession and absolution, both of which aim at amendment of life and the restoration of right relations with God and with neighbor. *Discipline*, on the other hand, has classically served as a mode of the reconciling function by placing alienated persons into situations in which good relationships might be re-established.

It must be remarked that in various times and places the *means* which have been employed by these various functions, even in their various modes, have changed and shifted greatly. *Healing*, for example, has employed such instrumentalities as prayer, oil, herbs, medicines,

---

[5] Carl R. Rogers has become a widely known spokesman for this type of therapeutic counseling, which recently has exerted an almost normative influence upon pastoral counseling in American Protestant circles. See Rogers, *Client-centered Therapy* (Boston: Houghton-Mifflin Co., 1951); Seward Hiltner, *Pastoral Counseling* (Nashville: Abingdon Press, 1949), esp. pp. 47ff.; and Carroll A. Wise, *Pastoral Counseling; Its Theory and Practice* (New York: Harper & Brothers, Publishers, 1951).

relics, shrines, words of exorcism, vows, and so forth. *Sustaining* has also
used prayer, holy objects, regulations, and so on, and in the Christian
tradition has elicited a vast literature designed to show persons how to
endure the inevitable hurts of life and death. *Guiding* has employed
many different techniques of counseling, and has appealed to various
codifications of virtues and sins, manuals of advice, and the like. *Reconciling* has employed various sacramental, ritual, and personal means.

Finally, it must be noted that our distinctions between the functions, the modes, and the means of pastoral care are devised for the sake
of classification and do not represent sharp separations. Obviously, several functions, modes, and means have been employed in a single "case"
of pastoral care, not only in our own society but generally throughout
the Christian tradition. For example, an unmarried pregnant woman
might engage the pastoral relationship with an injury that seeks the
restoration and advancement of healing; with a condition, at least temporarily inevitable, that must be endured until its termination; with a
perplexity over possible courses of action, such as abortion, confinement,
or "giving up" the baby for adoption; and with broken relationships with
her family and loved ones and a sense of broken relationship with God.
In such a complex, though not unknown, case, all the functions of
pastoral care might appropriately be employed in all their various modes
and by utilizing a variety of means.

In summary, when pastoral care is viewed in historical perspective,
it is seen to be a ministry of helping of a quite specific character.
Troubled persons who at least implicitly sense that their troubles involve
the basic issues of human existence are dealt with pastorally in terms of
their own, individual circumstances. Christian pastoring is a helping act
performed by persons who represent the resources, wisdom, and authority
of Christianity in one or another of its versions. Healing, sustaining,
guiding, and reconciling are the four distinct pastoral functions. Each
function uses more than one mode and a multitude of means. These
definitions are keys, by which the history of Christian pastoral care may
be unlocked to yield its rich treasures.

# PART 2

# HISTORICAL EPOCHS
# OF PASTORAL
# CARE

## 1. A Rich Treasure

The vast data recording the history of Christian pastoral care represent, of course, only a tiny sample of the total pastoral activities that have gone on in actual practice. In the broad view, the vast range of Christian pastoring may be plotted without undue misrepresentation in some eight sections, provided we remember that we produce only a map. A map may show that here there are pines, there oaks, there maples, and so forth, but in truth the lines drawn on paper do not exist in the forest, for clumps of oaks may appear in dominantly maple areas. Even so, the epochs into which the history of pastoring may be periodized are not tightly sealed from one another. Moreover, when the history of Christianity is periodized in terms of the cure of souls, the epochs may differ considerably from perhaps more familiar divisions of the history of Christian doctrine, just as the lines of a modern road map will not always coincide with those on a topographic chart.

Periods of pastoral practice nevertheless make interesting divisions of the history of Christianity. To be sure, in each pastoral epoch, Christian ministers healed and sustained and guided and reconciled perplexed persons; in each epoch all these pastoral func-

11

tions have been practiced. Yet each specific period reveals one or another function, or mode of performing that function, to have been practiced so pervasively or with such fascination that the era may be characterized by it. In any one era, a single pastoral function, healing or sustaining, guiding or reconciling, polarized all the others around itself. These leading emphases in the history of pastoral care captured the imagination of pastors because they proved to be viable for new cultural and personal conditions. Rather more for the sake of clarity of presentation than for the sake of precise and exhaustive description, our historical perspective on pastoral care will lead us to discern and discuss one major, polarizing function for each of eight major periods. Clear examples of the exercise of these functions within the circumstances of the epochs may be found in the Exhibits, which are arranged in chronological order.

The novelty that recurrently appears in the Christian cure of souls springs mainly from the power of some mode of one or another function to polarize the ways of administering the other functions. Rarely has the novelty arisen from the invention or discovery of new modes of healing, sustaining, guiding, and reconciling troubled individuals. For example, guidance in the early Middle Ages was mainly inductive, but in modern America it is largely eductive. In the early Middle Ages it became necessary to convince persons in rather uncivilized circumstances that certain acts were wrong or hurtful while other deeds were right or helpful. In our own times of cultural pluralism and individualized values, the eductive mode has come to dominate the pastoral guiding function in a remarkable way.

While the four basic functions of pastoral care have been exercised throughout the entire experience of Christian folk, each function has operated from time to time through various modes and by a variety of means. In the early Middle Ages, catechetical training in basic Christian ethics, along with elaborate penitentials classifying sins and their appropriate penalties, was the dominant means of guiding people. Frequently the means employed by the various pastoral functions have been so attuned to the time and place of their use that they seem to us strange and sometimes even bizarre; for example, the naming of healing potions for particular saints, or public and detailed confession of individual sins. Such means often have fallen into disuse without due regard for their continuing therapeutic value. The noted American psychologist of religion, William James, advocated public over private confession on therapeutic grounds, but this procedure remains generally unused, since it violates the modern preference for the fundamental privacy of religion. Therefore, our historical survey will notice pastoral practices that were once extremely beneficial and appropriate but are now all but discarded. Before dismissing them as interesting only for their antiquarian quaintness, however, their value and the possibility of reapplying them in our own time merit attention. Just as the means of anointing for healing became, in the Latin Catholic tradition, "extreme unction" for sustaining persons facing death, so other means have undergone transmutation and reapplication and may do so yet again and again.

## 2. Periodization

We shall delineate and briefly describe eight epochs of the history of Christian pastoring, and shall point out which function was dominant during each epoch. It may be helpful first to summarize these periods.

I. *Primitive Christianity.* The first era of Christian pastoral care lasted until circa A.D. 180 and was characterized by an emphasis on sustaining souls through the vicissitudes of life in this world, believed by the early Christians to be running swiftly toward its end.

II. *Under Oppression.* In the era of persecutions, from about A.D. 180 through the end of the reign of Diocletian (A.D. 306), the function of reconciling troubled persons to God and to the church became more important than the function of sustaining. During these decades, pastors labored hard to codify major sins and their appropriate penalties.

III. *"Christian" Culture.* A third period, characterized by guiding persons to behave in accord with norms of a newly Christian culture, ensued when Christianity became a legal religion under Emperor Constantine the Great, and continued in Eastern Christianity through the flowering of the great Byzantine culture.

IV. *The "Dark Ages."* In the West, the church's encounter with the Teutonic peoples of northern Europe quickly polarized soul care around inductive guidance.

V. *Medieval Christendom.* The era we commonly call the high Middle Ages brought about a codification of pastoral care around a well-defined sacramental system, designed to heal all maladies which beset any segment of the common life.

VI. *Renewal and Reform.* The rise of individualism in the Renaissance and Reformation thrust reconciling into a prominence unknown before or since that era; the Reformation era, with regard to soul care, belongs with this Renaissance period, for, in fact, the Reformation's great upheaval in doctrine and in ecclesiology never generated a corollary revolution in the cure of souls.

VII. *Enlightenment.* During the Enlightenment, Christian pastoring focused sharply upon sustaining souls as they passed through the treacheries and pitfalls of a threateningly wicked world.

VIII. *The Post-Christendom Era.* New circumstances of the late eighteenth- and early nineteenth-century revolutions against the Christendom societies of earlier times, and the concomitant voluntaryism and pluralism of modern Christianity, brought with them an array of pastoral work that has been largely oriented around a type of guidance that educes values and norms from personal convictions and value systems.[6]

Since the dawn of a new awareness of man, traceable to seminal thinkers of the nineteenth century like Dostoyevsky and Freud but fully articulate only in our own era, we have witnessed the rise of non-pastoral professions capable of healing, sustaining, guiding, and reconciling troubled individuals. In this circumstance, the ministry of pastoral care has fallen into the position of a junior partner to many other helping professions. The reaction to this circumstance of pastoring has been to raise serious questions about its own validity while at the same time borrowing techniques from psychology, law, medicine, education, and social work. These questions and borrowings indicate that ours is indeed a time of transition, and that as yet no new pastoral pattern has emerged with sufficient strength to warrant designating our time as a new epoch.


3.  Sustaining in the Primitive Church

Two characteristics mark Christian pastoral care in the earliest epoch: extreme diversity of functions and modes and means, and a general pervasion of this diversity by a concern to set all helping acts within the context of the supposedly brief period of time until history met its end. That concern naturally led pastoral care to emphasize the function of sustaining.

From the chrysalis of first-century Judaism, itself exhibiting enormous religious variety, Christianity emerged only at the end of the second century as a patently separate religion, identifiable as such not only by its adherents but also by the custodians of Hellenistic culture. There developed during this time strong centers of Christian activity at Jerusalem, Antioch, Alexandria, Ephesus, and Rome and in southern Gaul. Each center rather independently produced its distinctive customs, ministries, liturgies, scriptures, traditions, theologies, and pastoral practices. Since these religious communities were on the whole isolated, both from one another and from the cultural enterprise of ordering the Mediterranean world under the *Pax Romana*, the Christianity of the day exhibits very

---

[6] Of a vast literature on the history of Christianity, perhaps the most useful single volume in English is Williston Walker, A *History of the Christian Church*, revised by C. C. Richardson, W. Pauck, and R. T. Handy (New York: Charles Scribner's Sons, 1959); its bibliographical suggestions (pp. 549–568) provide ample descriptions of the religio-cultural history of these eight epochs. Few studies have been made, however, of the history of Christian pastoral care; *The Ministry in Historical Perspectives*, ed. H. R. Niebuhr and D. D. Williams (New York: Harper & Brothers, 1956) contains valuable material, and the most thorough modern study, John T. McNeill, A *History of the Cure of Souls* (New York: Harper & Brothers, Publishers, 1951), deals mainly with pastoral discipline.

little standardization. Perhaps the one most notable common attitude among the early Christians was their expectation of an imminent return of the Lord and a concomitant termination of all earthly, historical existence [SEE EXHIBIT 1].

Pastors, who in many places were carefully distinguished from prophets, evangelists, teachers, missionaries, administrators, and other church functionaries, dealt, to be sure, with a wide range of personal problems, such as sickness, death, bereavement, sin, marital strife, and the like. Yet the expectation of the *parousia* galvanized all pastoral helping, for these individual problems were conceived as circumstances to be endured briefly until the cataclysmic vindication of the hopes of the faithful. Thus, pastoral records show that slaves were exhorted to continue patiently in slavery, widows in widowhood, virgins in virginity, and so forth, while human history ran its presumed short course. To be sure, healings occurred by way of imitating the curative thaumaturgy exercised by the Lord himself, but these healings were valued rather as they displayed the power of Christ and his followers than as they ameliorated the plight of the sick and the maimed. The function of guiding involved primarily eschewing evil until the end—an avoidance deemed to be achievable by faithful, baptized Christians. Reconciling exhibited greater concern for the purity of the congregation than for the binding up of broken relationships.

The warning that the time was short and the end near rings through most of our records that tell of the life and thought of the primitive Christians. "Watch therefore; for ye know not what hour your Lord doth come," warned the evangelist (Matthew 24:42, Authorized Version). After citing that verse, one old Christian writer exhorted believers to "be frequently gathered together seeking the things which are profitable for your souls, for the whole time of your faith shall not profit you except ye be found perfect at the last time"; so wrote the author of *The Teaching of the Twelve Apostles*, possibly as early as the end of the first century.[7]

Since divine forgiveness had been received by the baptized believers in Christ, it was expected that they should lead blameless lives with respect to one another and to the world around them. By the middle of the second century, the problem of post-baptismal sin arose, in the congregation at Rome and presumably elsewhere, with such force that in the capital one Hermas composed a fascinating document, *The Shepherd*, dealing with this problem. The book recounted the author's vision of an angel of penance in the form of a shepherd, who imparted the message

---

[7] *Didache* XVI:2, *The Apostolic Fathers With an English Translation by Kirsopp Lake* (2 vols., "The Loeb Classical Library," London: William Heinemann Ltd., and Cambridge, Mass.: Harvard University Press, 1912), I, 333. By permission.

that forgiveness was available to those who sinned after baptism, but that this kind of repentance would avail but once, and in that instance only for certain less grievous sins. Claiming the authority of the Lord, *The Shepherd* urged that pastors regulate repentance and penance. So popular was the writing that it was considered Scripture by some of the famous fathers of the church, such as Irenaeus, Tertullian, and Origen. Hermas taught that God forgave sins because God was merciful and men were weak. Before baptism, sins sprang from ignorance; in baptism, the believer was cleansed and made holy, gaining a new knowledge and a new condition enabling him to live in purity and righteousness. But since such persons in fact did commit sins, Hermas posed the practical answer that after baptism there might be one more opportunity for repentance and mercy, provided the believer showed clear proof of true repentance and made payment for his error.

After the Shepherd had enjoined Hermas to keep all of God's commands, the following interesting exchange was recorded:

> "I will yet, sir," said I, "continue to ask." "Say on," said he. "I have heard, sir," said I, "from some teachers that there is no second repentance beyond the one given when we went down into the water and received remission of our former sins." He said to me, "You have heard correctly, for that is so. For he who has received remission of sin ought never to sin again, but to live in purity. But since you ask accurately concerning all things, I will explain this also to you without giving an excuse to those who in the future shall believe or to those who have already believed on the Lord. For those who have already believed or shall believe in the future, have no repentance of sins, but have remission of their former sin. For those, then, who were called before these days, did the Lord appoint repentance, for the Lord knows the heart, and knowing all things beforehand he knew the weakness of man and the subtlety of the devil, that he will do some evil to the servants of God, and will do them mischief. The Lord, therefore, being merciful, had mercy on his creation, and established this repentance, and to me was the control of this repentance given. But I tell you," said he, "after that great and holy calling, if a man be tempted by the devil and sin, he has one repentance, but if he sin and repent repeatedly it is unprofitable for such a man, for scarcely shall he live." I said to him, "I attained life when I heard these things thus accurately from you, for I know that if I do not again add to my sins I shall be saved." "You shall be saved," said he, "and all who do these things."[8]

Prominent as became the ministries of guidance and reconciliation in light of the early Christians' worries over post-baptismal sin, even these functions were exercised in the context of the pervasive attitude of waiting for the coming of the Lord. As the decades passed, that expectation

8 *The Shepherd of Hermas*, Mandate 4, III, *The Apostolic Fathers With an English Translation by Kirsopp Lake*, II, 83, 85. By permission.

eroded and the church found itself in open and enduring enmity against the dominant culture and its approved religion.

## 4. Reconciling During the Persecutions

Although sporadic and local oppression of Christians by the Roman Empire occurred as early as the reign of Nero (A.D. 54–68), only near the end of the second century did the church come to understand itself generally as radically opposing the religious claims of the imperial culture. Even so, Christians found their religion conformable to many of the proximate values of Hellenistic society. From the standpoint of the Empire, Christians were valuable citizens only if their allegiance to imperial aspirations was unqualified. Where such allegiance took the form of participating in the state cults, Christians frequently refused it. Thus, from the well-known persecution at Lyons and Vienne in Gaul in A.D. 177 until the abdication of Diocletian in A.D. 306, broad and often explicit enmity prevailed between Church and Empire, punctuated by several epochs of relative peace. Recurrent and persistent, though not continual, as were the persecutions, each generation of Christians was prompted by official threats to renounce their faith by enlisting their religious allegiance to emperors. On these occasions many Christians compromised. Throughout this era, the unavoidable pastoral problem was to determine what degrees and kinds of renunciation of Christianity were forgivable. The leading pastoral function soon came to be that of reconciling apostates to the church, steadfast believers to the once lapsed, and factions within the church to one another. Earlier, one occasion of forgiveness of post-baptismal sin had been allowed only if that sin were less grievous than the cardinal evils of adultery, idolatry, and murder [SEE EXHIBIT 2]. Now even idolatry in some degree and, by extension, the other major sins, were deemed not unforgivable.

The Decian persecution of the middle years of the third century, which was administered broadly over the whole Empire, demanded that standard practices for readmission of lapsed Christians be discovered and applied. Through the influence of Cyprian, bishop of Carthage [SEE EXHIBIT 3], the role of the bishop as the definer of church membership, and thus the work of the bishop as the chief Christian pastor, arose out of the circumstance of persecution. Even as the pastoral work of reconciling was standardized and localized in the office of the bishop, many Christian pastors revolted at the very idea of admitting lapsed persons back into fellowship with the church. Therefore, this era bristled with repeated controversies between moral and pastoral rigorists, such as Tertullian [SEE EXHIBIT 2] and Novatianus and Hippolytus, on the one hand, and what came to be the major party of more lenient pastors and moral theologians on the other. Many rigorists, including Tertullian, were expelled from the church as schismatics, specifically because of their refusal to follow the dominant episcopal policies in reconciling lapsed Christians with the church.

Novatian, a presbyter at Rome who had written a major book on the doctrine of the Trinity, had sided with Cyprian in wishing to restore to the church persons who had compromised with paganism during the persecution under Decius. But when the very liberal Cornelius became bishop of Rome in A.D. 251, Novatian by reaction became a rigorist, received consecration as the capital city's rival bishop, and advocated a strict policy of expelling lapsed Christians from the church for life. Among his contemporaries was a bishop, whose name is unknown to us, who wrote a scathing denunciation of Novatian and his followers for their presuming to judge the souls of men—a judgment that, as the bishop argued, the Lord reserved for himself. He wrote:

> O impious and wicked as thou art, thou heretic Novatian! who after so many and great crimes which in past times thou hadst known to be voluntarily committed in the Church, and before thou thyself wast an apostate in the family of God, hadst certainly taught that these might be abolished from memory if well-doing followed. . . . For the sins which he has committed shall be abolished from memory by the good deeds which succeed. Thou reconsiderest now, whether the wounds of the lapsed who have fallen, stripped bare by the devil, ought to be cursed; *dashed down, as they are.* . . . Nor indeed ought we to wonder why this Novatian should dare now to practise such wicked, such severe things against the person of the lapsed, since we have previous examples of this kind of prevarication. Saul, that *once good* man, besides other things, is subsequently overthrown by envy, and strives to do everything that is harsh and hostile against David. That Judas, who was chosen among the apostles, who was always of one mind and faithful in the house of God, himself subsequently betrayed God.[9]

With great vigor the church began to claim that bishops were authorized to readmit lapsed persons into the full fellowship of believers, asserting that these officers therein exercised a mercy similar to that displayed by Christ.

In this period of persecutions there flourished a literature of forgiveness in which some church leaders advocated the severe procedure of exomologesis, or public confession and penance [SEE EXHIBIT 2]. Of course, pastors also worked to sustain the courage and faith of believers condemned to imprisonment or to death, and, similarly, the pastoral functions of healing and guiding continued apace. Yet circumstances tended to galvanize various pastoral concerns and activities around the matter of working out the theology and procedure for restoring persons

---

[9] "A Treatise Against the Heretic Novatian by an Anonymous Bishop," §14, *The Ante-Nicene Fathers*, ed. A. Roberts and J. Donaldson (9 vols., Buffalo: The Christian Literature Company, 1885–96), V, 661.

of feebler faith to full communion with the church after they had compromised under persecution. Their compromises involved various devices, such as purchasing forged certificates of imperial religious loyalty, fleeing to avoid persecution, hiring substitutes to make obeisance to the imperial genius, and the like. Very subtle distinctions were developed in certain localities so as to determine what devices constituted genuine apostasy, and, naturally, different degrees of disloyalty to the church demanded different penalties and procedures for reconciliation. Pastors sought to guide persons confronted with significant decisions in connection with persecutions, but even this function took its lineaments from the main endeavor of reconciling, or avoiding the necessity of reconciling, lapsed persons with steadfast congregations and with God.

## 5. The Prominence of Guidance in the Imperial Church

When the Christian religion, long regarded by emperors as a stubbornly dissident force in Hellenistic civilization, found itself thrust suddenly into the role of providing a new principle for the unity of that civilization, the cure of souls, like doctrine, liturgy, polity, and other ecclesiastical affairs, was rapidly and radically revolutionized. From the time of Constantine's accession to power early in the fourth century down through the golden age of Byzantine culture under Justinian I and his successors, Christianity's prominence as unifier of society continued and grew, despite a brief punctuation by the short reign of the anti-Christian emperor Julian, and despite governmental and social upheavals such as that represented by the barbarian conquest of the western provinces.

Classical Christendom placed upon the church the heavy burden of dogmatic unanimity and ecclesiastical uniformity, for the unifying agent must itself exhibit fine unity. As it had been costly to be a Christian, it became equally costly not to be one. Sudden favor from populace and imperial throne riveted pastors' attention to the enterprise of guiding perplexed persons to interpret and construe their decisions and actions as involving at once cultural significance and Christian meaning. As the theologians adapted reigning philosophies to assist in setting forth church dogma, and as liturgists adopted the pomp and circumstance of official ceremonies for Christian worship, so pastors, while acting as semiofficial educators, as dispensers of state welfare funds, and as leaders of an imperially endorsed religion, sought to put a Christian interpretation upon troubles that beset people. The great court preacher John Chrysostom adroitly loaded the regnant Stoic psychology with Christian meanings and starched popular morality with Christian theological and religious sanctions [SEE EXHIBIT 5].

Probably in the first or second year of his career as a preacher in the

city of Antioch, Chrysostom delivered a series of sermons aimed at the
moral reform of the city. A characteristic passage from one of these
sermons shows how confidently he educed Christian virtues from the
reigning values of the culture:

> In order to know that it is a good thing to exercise temperance, we need
> no words, nor instruction; for we ourselves have the knowledge of it in
> our nature, and there is no necessity for labour or fatigue in going about
> and enquiring whether temperance is good and profitable; but we all
> acknowledge this with one consent, and no man is in doubt as to this
> virtue. So also we account adultery to be an evil thing, and neither is
> there here any need of trouble or learning, that the wickedness of this
> sin may be known; but we are all self-taught in such judgments; and
> we applaud virtue, though we do not follow it; as, on the other hand, we
> hate vice, though we practise it. And this hath been an exceeding good
> work of God; that He hath made our conscience, and our power of
> choice already, and before the action, claim kindred with virtue, and be
> at enmity with wickedness.[10]

Fusing Christianity and classical civilization into Greek-speaking
Christendom emphasized the pastoral function of guiding—indeed, a
particular kind of guiding which sought less to inculcate given principles
of Christian tradition than to educe from the civilization standards and
norms that opened themselves most readily to Christian sanctions. While
the spread of orthodox dogma required careful catechizing to convey such
subtle christological distinctions as councils of bishops recurrently drew,
the cure of souls sought to deal with the vast range of personal problems
presented by a church membership that was coterminous, after Theo-
dosius' Edict of Thessalonica in A.D. 380, with citizenship in the empire.
As doctrine took its leads from the precisionist theology of an Athanasius,
pastoring built upon the confidence that imperial favor toward Christianity would inaugurate a thoroughly Christian society. Eusebius Pam-
philius and Lactantius Firmianus dilated that confidence into a full-
blown theology. The end of church-state enmity won from most clergy
unbounded enthusiasm for the new commonwealth and enlisted them as
quasi-public officials dedicated to the welfare, temporal and eternal, of
all citizens. Although the conduct of public worship became the chief
clerical occupation, pastors also assumed important roles as arbiters of
social and personal morality. Many pastoral functions became formalized.
The ministry of healing concentrated upon anointing with holy oil, and
the ministry of reconciling became largely a matter of administering and
enforcing standard church policies. Since the world in which Christians

---

[10] John Chrysostom, *Concerning the Statues*, Homily XIII. 8, *A Select Library
of the Nicene and Post-Nicene Fathers of the Christian Church*, First Series,
ed. by Philip Schaff (14 vols., Buffalo: The Christian Literature Company,
1886–90), IX, 428–429.

lived, as the late Professor Cochrane noted, had been made "safe for Christianity,"[11] the ministry of sustaining focused upon specific personal troubles like bereavement and incurable ills. All of these buttressed the central function of guiding. Perhaps no subsequent era of soul care has so strongly emphasized guiding as did the era of the Imperial Church, and in no other epoch has the function of guiding been cast so completely in its culturally eductive mode.

## 6. Inductive Guidance for the European Peoples

In the western or Latin portions of the classical empire after the beginning of the fifth century, the church was confronted with the herculean task of drawing into itself the hordes of rude peoples who swept over the territory we know as western Europe. Previous experience at eductive guidance in the era inaugurated by Constantine proved apt preparation for the pastoral task of persuading barbarian folk to accept Christian descriptions, diagnoses, and remedies of their troubles. The church, as custodian of classical Roman civilization and of a formal Christian religion, raised up an elite class in the form of Benedictine monks to transmit this culture and interpretation of life. For an intellectual picture of its prominent role in society, the church relied upon the work of the theologian Augustine of Hippo, who had portrayed the one ecclesiastical body as representing the kingdom of God upon earth and as heaven's only gate. Kings and emperors utilized the church's monasteries, bishoprics, and parishes to extend their civilized rule over crude and unsettled peoples.

The cure of souls found useful in the monasteries became the standard for pastoring common folk as well. The monastic ideal—to purge the desires of the flesh not only out of the fear of God but for the love of God—evoked precise schemes of spiritual development that would kill pride by promoting humility. Incorporated into the prominent monastic rule of St. Benedict of Nursia (A.D. 529) was a twelve-step ladder of humility that began on the rung of fear and ended on a life of love. The faithful monk would: (1) constantly fear God, remembering that hell awaits those who hold God in contempt and heaven those who fear Him, and that all human actions are reported hourly to God by angels; (2) neither love his own will nor delight in his own desires; (3) submit in total obedience to his superior; (4) endure in silent patience all obstacles, and even injuries, that beset his path; (5) hide neither his evil thoughts nor his secret sins but in humble confession reveal them to his abbot; (6) be content with lowliness and regard himself as a bad and worthless worker in all that he is assigned to do; (7) not only acknowledge himself

---

[11] Charles Norris Cochrane, *Christianity and Classical Culture* (New York: Oxford University Press, 1944), p. 197.

inferior to all others but believe it in the depths of his heart; (8) do nothing unless authorized either by the monastic rule or by the example of his superiors; (9) keep silence until asked a question; (10) never be easy or quick to laugh; (11) speak gently, without laughter, humbly and gravely, in a few reasonable words; (12) exhibit his lowliness to all who saw him and in all his deeds. Thus would the monk achieve the pure behavior of neighborly love and be enabled to keep the church's precepts naturally—not through the fear of hell, but through the love of Christ and through a delight in virtue.[12]

In setting forth his ladder of humility, Benedict was paraphrasing and rearranging steps of humility that had been devised a century earlier by the great authority on eastern monasticism, John Cassian[13] [SEE EXHIBIT 6]; only the first and last steps were Benedict's own original contribution to the scheme.[14] The monastic ladder of humility that set the standard for Western Christendom's morality thus incorporated insights won during the time of Constantine and his successors. In the form given it by Benedict, the ladder imbedded itself in the imagination of medieval life, and by the twelfth century it had permeated popular as well as monastic piety. Early in that century, Saint Bernard of Clairvaux [SEE EXHIBIT 8] wrote a lengthy treatise elaborating the steps of humility and showing its opposite in a descending ladder of pride. This scheme of spiritual and moral living he employed as an accompaniment to his own four-step "ladder of love": man loves himself for his own sake, then proceeds to love God for man's own sake, then loves God for God's sake, and finally (in heaven) loves himself for God's sake only.[15]

These schemes of spiritual growth and ladders of Christian devotion were of enormous importance for pastoral care not only of monks but of common, secular people. While the elite spiritual class took the whole progression as their ideal, secular folk were to be guided by their pastors into achieving at least the first three steps of the ladder of humility. In Benedict's rescension, that meant first to fear God, then to purge one's desires, and finally to obey the church. For the application of this scheme to the common life, concrete and detailed rules were set forth under ecclesiastical sanction, and these elements of "moral theology" pastors

---

12 See Benedict, abbot of Monte Cassino, *Regula Monachorum*, vii, text and translation in *The Rule of Saint Benedict*, ed. and tr. Justin McCann (Westminster, Md.: The Newman Press, 1952), pp. 36–49.
13 See Cassian, *Institutes*, IV.xxxix, in NPNF:2, XI, 232.
14 See Paul Delatte, *The Rule of Saint Benedict, A Commentary*, tr. Justin McCann (London: Burns Oates, 1950), p. 103.
15 See Bernard de Clairvaux, *The Twelve Degrees of Humility and Pride*, tr. Barton R. V. Mills (London: Society for Promoting Christian Knowledge; New York and Toronto: The Macmillan Co., 1929), esp. pp. 6ff.; cf. *Saint Bernard on the Love of God*, tr. Terence L. Connolly (Westminster, Md.: The Newman Press, 1951).

were to apply to the daily life of their people. Thus, guidance was inductive in that people were persuaded to interpret their own lives by the
norms of Christian rules for living that were carefully devised, rigidly
administered, and strictly sanctioned. This device was elaborately designed to lead the rather uncivilized and zestful peoples of Europe during
the early Middle Ages into Christian living.

Pope Gregory the Great at the end of the sixth century codified,
regularized, and stressed the work of pastors as that of guiding troubled
people into Christian belief, the Christian cultus, and Christian morality.
Facing a vital and undisciplined society, pastors proliferated sacramental
rites and practices to cover every crisis of the common life of individuals
and groups. Thus, pastors taught disturbed people to lay their troubles
before the church for identification and for relief. The Teutonic and
Frankish peoples whom the church encountered of course brought their
own folk culture into Europe with them, providing the raw content and
energy which, under church auspices and directions, built European
civilization. On the whole, this folk culture was earthy, virile, familial,
and loyal. Pastoral ministrations focused strongly upon matters of sexual
morality and upon the disciplining of other natural appetites, and applied
Christianity as a brake on the nature-paganism of the barbarians.

Throughout the early Middle Ages, pastoral care therefore centered
on guidance in its inductive mode. The means used by the guiding
function, and by the continuing but now subsidiary functions of healing,
sustaining, and reconciling, proliferated vastly as the rich lore of traditional Christianity mingled and merged with the rich lore of barbarian
paganism. The latter demanded objectivization of spiritual realities—a
demand readily met by sacramental elaborations. Raw and rough peoples
were taught long lists of specific sins and the penalties involved in committing them; for example, the penitential of Halitgar [SEE EXHIBIT 7]
distinguished three degrees of sinful kissing and provided appropriately
graded periods of fasting for each. The ancient practice of confirmation
came to be applied to the life-crisis of puberty and adolescence as a gift
of grace administered when the young person had reached the age of
discretion and had demonstrated his knowledge of elementary Christian
teachings. The early medieval pastor's kit was amply furnished for all his
various functions, but everywhere and always he sought to guide troubled
persons into viewing their perplexities as the church viewed them, and
into accepting the answers and remedies that the church proffered.

## 7. Medieval Christendom and Sacramental Healing

By the end of the eleventh century, the Catholic Church had permeated the common life of European society. Religious conformity became the foundation on which social cohesion was built, and the uni-

versality and unity of Christian Europe found twin symbols in popes and
Holy Roman Emperors. The cure of souls in these circumstances centered
upon the power of divine grace to heal both the inherent and the accidental deformities of human existence. Ministers imparted this healing
by means of objective, sacramental embodiments of that grace. The
medieval parish became the compact, inclusive geographical-social entity
in which lived men and women of every sort and condition, to whom the
parish priest dispensed divine medicines as they were needed for bodily
or spiritual health. The sacrament of ordination empowered these men
to diagnose and cure men's ills. Baptism, universally administered, restored sinful persons to a pristine spiritual condition by overcoming the
generic malady of original sin. Other sacraments provided healing grace
on the occasions of the great risks to human welfare: confirmation on the
occasion of puberty and adolescence, holy matrimony at marriage, extreme unction at death, and penance at repeated occasions of actual sin.
The Mass provided grace more generally for times of temptation, disease,
demon possession, moral frailty, important decisions, anniversaries,
agrarian procedures, economic ventures, journeys, bereavements, and
every occasion of perplexity, joy, or woe.

Sacramental grace not only served to restore medieval men and
women to an assumed prior condition of health, but also granted power
for spiritual growth toward the universal desideratum of eternal bliss.
The sacrament of unction, to be sure, performed also a sustaining function; a codified moral theology guided decisions; important reconciling
functions were carried out through the system of spiritual indulgences
that, from the time of the Crusades onward, remitted the temporal
punishment of the soul after death in purgatory; nevertheless, these latter
pastoral functions were subordinated to a pervasive emphasis upon sacramental healing.

One prominent medieval manual for pastors revealed by its very
name the healing emphasis that pervaded the period: *Corrector et
medicus*. The treatise comprised Book XIX of a long manual on church
administration compiled by Burchard, bishop of the important see of
Worms between A.D. 1000 and 1025. Burchard explained:

> This book is called "the Corrector" and "the Physician," since it
> contains ample corrections for bodies and medicines for souls and
> teaches every priest, even the uneducated, how he shall be able to
> bring help to each person, ordained or unordained; poor or rich; boy,
> youth, or mature man; decrepit, healthy, or infirm; of every age; and
> of both sexes.[16]

---

16 "The Corrector of Burchard of Worms," *Medieval Handbooks of Penance*,
tr. John T. McNeill and Helena M. Gamer (New York: Columbia University
Press, 1938), p. 323; the excellent translation of *Corrector et medicus* fills pp.
323–345 of this invaluable book. By permission.

Indeed, Burchard made good his immodest claim by diagnosing a vast range of spiritual diseases and prescribing their specific remedies.

After the emergence of the new sociological phenomenon of town life and the new economic factor of an artisan and bourgeois class, the neat arrangement of the inclusive medieval parish underwent significant upheavals. These new circumstances called into being the great orders of mendicant friars, Franciscans and Dominicans, who kept the church in fruitful contact with persons uprooted from the familiar agrarian, manorial life. These orders came into being at the apex of ecclesiastical power under Pope Innocent III. During this period, the church codified the sacramental system by designating and defining the seven official sacraments of catholicism. A concomitant thrust toward standardization of pastoral care may be seen in the fact that the Fourth Lateran Council (1215) sought to eliminate the highly popular but locally variant penitentials by which diverse ministrations of the guiding and reconciling functions were being performed [SEE EXHIBIT 7].

In regulating penance, the Council enjoined priests to "pour wine and oil into the wounds of the one injured after the manner of a skilful physician" (Canon 21). On the assumption that "bodily infirmity is sometimes caused by sin," the Council decreed and commanded "that when physicians of the body are called to the bedside of the sick, before all else they admonish them to call for the physician of souls, so that after spiritual health has been restored to them, the application of bodily medicine may be of greater benefit. . . ." (Canon 22). A disobedient physician was to "be cut off from the church till he has made suitable satisfaction for his transgression." The same Canon forbade "that a physician advise a patient to have recourse to sinful means for the recovery of bodily health," under pain of anathema.[17]

Eventually this standardization proved incapable of meeting the diverse needs of the rising middle class which the towns and the new money economy supported. Nevertheless, modern catholicism appropriately regards the era of medieval Christendom as the golden age of the Western Church, when acknowledgment and acceptance of the

---

[17] Fourth Lateran Council, Canons 21–22, in *Disciplinary Decrees of the General Councils, Text, Translation, and Commentary*, by H. J. Schroeder (St. Louis, Mo. and London: B. Herder Book Co., 1937), pp. 260, 263. By permission. The formal enumeration of seven official sacraments came at the Council of Florence in 1439, and was reaffirmed by the Council of Trent (1545–1563) against the Protestant insistence upon only two sacraments as dominically instituted. The seven had been accepted, however, throughout the twelfth century, having been acknowledged by Peter Lombard (1100–1160) and, of course, by Thomas Aquinas (c. 1225–1274). But Hugo of St. Victor (c. 1096–1141), Peter's older contemporary, listed thirty sacraments. See *The Oxford Dictionary of the Christian Church*, ed. F. L. Cross (London and New York: Oxford University Press, 1957), p. 1198.

healing power of divine grace, sacramentally mediated, were quite unanimous amongst European Christians.

## 8.  Reconciling in Renaissance and Reformation

Although in matters of Christian doctrine the sixteenth-century Reformation ushered in a new religious era, with respect to pastoral care the fourteenth, fifteenth, and sixteenth centuries comprise a period which appears to be of a single piece. Reconciling individual persons to a righteous God polarized all soul care during the Renaissance as well as the Reformation. Earlier in the epoch, reconciling took the form primarily of mediating to men, or of helping them mystically to achieve, divine forgiveness; in the sixteenth century, pastors and churches utilized also the reconciling mode of discipline.

Preoccupation with spiritual reconciliation—and, indeed, even complete union—with God, and therefore with mankind as God's beloved creature, is reflected throughout the two great literary monuments that symbolize at once the final achievement of the Middle Ages and the inauguration of an era of cultural rebirth: *The Divine Comedy*, by Dante Alighieri (1265–1321) of Florence, and *The Imitation of Christ*, by Thomas à Kempis (c. 1380–1471) of Zwolle. Each masterpiece in its own way conceived the culminating human endeavor as an arduous but wonderful achievement of entire integrity of body, soul, and mind with God and his universe. For Dante, the pilgrimage led through purgatory to paradise under the guidance alternately of reason, symbolized by Vergil, and of supernatural revelation, symbolized by Beatrice. Reasserting his practical interest in this pilgrimage of man, Dante in the final vision proclaims, "To my high fantasy here power failed; but now my desire and my will, like a wheel which evenly is moved, the Love was turning which moves the Sun and the other stars."[18] In a different manner *The Imitation of Christ*, summarizing and guiding the fervid devotion of the followers of Gerhard Groote, the Brethren of the Common Life, also focused on life here and now united with God; the true imitator of the Master cries to God:

> You are the goal for which all good men are striving; you are the highest peak of all that has life, the lowest deep that underlies all speech. Nothing is so great a comfort to your servants as to trust in you above all else.[19]

---

18 *The Divine Comedy of Dante Alighieri* (Paradiso, Canto XXXIII), tr. Charles Eliot Norton (3 vols., second edn., Boston and New York: Houghton, Mifflin and Company, 1893), III, 215.
19 From *The Imitation of Christ* by Thomas à Kempis, translated by Ronald Knox and Michael Oakley, Trs. © Evelyn Waugh and Michael Oakley, 1959, published by Sheed & Ward, Inc., New York, III.59.4, p. 179. By permission.

Luther's famous quest for certainty of personal salvation—*um ein gnädigen Gott zu kriegen*—had long been the religious quest of Renaissance man, and at his opening of the Reformation movement the art and craft of achieving and granting certainty of salvation was already highly developed. The great Christian mystics of the Renaissance era, especially in Germany and Spain, sought the same assurance of the soul's reconciliation with God as did the members of many lay and clerical monastic organizations of the era. Standardized sacramental ministrations had only partly embraced the new bourgeois spirit of the late Middle Ages, as this spirit sought a highly personal and varied religious expression. Earlier monastic prescriptions of spiritual ladders for achieving the *visio dei*, such as that developed by Bernard of Clairvaux, came to be employed by many secular clergy and middle-class laity alike. Thus the age's humanism posed a challenge to objectified sacramentalism even before Luther's theocentrism found a "merciful God" available to the believer who "took the second place" under God. For the young Luther, as for many another before him, individual, auricular confession became a central religious act demanding complete personal involvement and ultimate concern, if a man were to know himself to be forgiven and made righteous by God. Influential pastors were skilled spiritual masters able to impart to or elicit from individuals an assurance of their spiritual well-being. Luther's fundamental challenge to medieval catholicism was not that it wrongly concerned itself with divine-human reconciliation, but that it made this reconciliation too easy and too mechanical.

A rich variety of interpretations and expressions of the pastoral function of reconciling were produced by the Reformation movement both in protestantism and catholicism. Hardly a more skillful master of leading individuals to certain salvation ever lived than St. Ignatius Loyola, founder of the Society of Jesus [SEE EXHIBIT 14]. The Italian Gaspar Cardinal Contarini welcomed the new religious emphasis upon the justification of individual sinners before God. In the Rhineland Martin Bucer, and after him John Calvin, developed systems of ecclesiastical discipline which worked out in detail the ways in which reconciliation of the believer with God involved reconciliation with his fellow believers. In English-speaking Christianity, William Tyndale and other early Protestants understood reconciliation with God to launch lives into horizontal reconciliation; the procedure for both thrusts was found in the biblical covenant, understood as a contract between God and man, and between man and man.

The variety of expressions of the reconciling function that the Reformation evoked demanded that pastors understand and be involved with the common life of ordinary men and women. Generally speaking, protestantism achieved identification with the common life by first allowing and then encouraging clerical marriage, which meant that clergy undertook full social and economic responsibilities as householders. True to the medieval understanding of priests as persons empowered to dispense sacramental grace, catholicism could not take that step, but instead revised the education of the clergy and accepted as normative the Jesuits' social involvement in place of the traditional monastic withdrawal from society. Reconciling sinners to God and believers to their brethren preoccupied Renaissance and Reformation pastoral care so thoroughly that the functions of healing, sustaining, and guiding became, however important, subordinate.

9. Sustaining the Souls of Enlightenment Christians

By means of the Enlightenment, the western societies came during the seventeenth and eighteenth centuries to achieve explanations and understandings of life and the world that relied on no necessary reference to God or religion. Generally speaking, Christianity accommodated itself to the Enlightenment by concentrating upon the immortality of the soul as the chief interest of religion and upon the achievement of personal morality as the chief value of religion. Pastoral care during this era therefore focused on sustaining human souls through the perplexities, difficulties, and pitfalls of their earthly pilgrimage and, in a subordinate way, on guiding believers into paths of personal morality.

For English-speaking Christians, the great codifier and transmitter of pastoral care for the age of the Enlightenment was the Puritan divine, Richard Baxter (1615–1691), whose *Gildas Salvianus, or The Reformed Pastor* (1656) schooled generation after generation of helping practitioners in the cure of souls. Baxter tersely defined the shepherding of souls as consisting in two things:

1. In revealing to men that happiness, or chief good, which must be their ultimate end.
2. In acquainting them with the right means for the attainment of this end, and helping them to use them, and hindering them from the contrary.

In regard to the first, Baxter set the aim of "shewing men the certainty and excellency of the promised felicity, and the perfect blessedness in the life to come, compared with the vanities of this present life" so as to "turn the stream of their cogitations and affections, and bring them to a due contempt of this world, and set them on seeking the durable treasure." The second element of soul care demanded that "the wrong way must be disgraced, the evil of all sin must be manifested, and the danger that it hath brought us into, and the hurt it hath already done us, must be discovered" so that individuals might rely on God's promises and gifts alone.[20] While other writers stated their ideas in words that ac-

---

[20] Richard Baxter, *The Reformed Pastor*, ed. Hugh Martin (London: SCM Press Ltd., 1956; Richmond, Va.: John Knox Press, 1963), pp. 48–49. By permission.

corded with their church traditions, the reigning consensus made Enlightenment pastoral care primarily a matter of sustaining the immortal soul through the dangers of temporal existence, especially the dangers of immorality.

In different countries of the West, and in different religious traditions of the western churches, this ministry of sustaining and guiding took on different colorations and emphases. English-speaking Puritanism, finely represented by the writings of John Bunyan [SEE EXHIBIT 17], looked to the Bible as furnishing the Christian pilgrim with equipment necessary to overcome the dire impediments to progress through finite existence. Classical protestantism, in its Lutheran, Reformed, and Anglican varieties, stressed right belief and right living as implied by that belief. German Pietism, which found an eighteenth-century English expression in evangelical enthusiasm, sought to induce and nurture a "religion of the heart" whereby the soul might find refuge from attacks upon traditional Christian dogma [SEE EXHIBIT 18]. Meanwhile catholicism's cultus was elaborated by rites and ceremonies and visual aids that appealed highly to the senses and emotions as it strove to save the souls of the devout from seduction by secular interests. All these movements demanded that pastors become experts in personal, experimental religion, and together they developed types of "pastoral theology" or *pastoralia* as means toward that end.

Concomitantly the psychology of religion received new attention as a device by which to discover and describe the kinds of troubles through which believers needed to be sustained. Just as the pastoral function of guiding into moral living took new impetus from this sustaining interest, so pastors sought to analyze the means and processes by which conversions occurred and thus brought the function of reconciling into close relation with the primary task of sustaining. Significantly, this period saw the termination of Christian pastoral interest in witchcraft, for extraecclesiastical healing arts underwent such progress that physical and psychological explanations of and cures for ills and irrational behavior replaced the explanation of demon possession and the cures of exorcism or execution. Thus it was during the Enlightenment that pastoral healing lapsed into a desuetude from which it has as yet not fully recovered.

Enlightenment man, however he regarded Christianity, confidently regarded human nature as unchanging and as capable of a new flowering if only loosed from the fetters of tradition. As education cultivated the mind and as hygiene helped the body toward this flowering, so the pastoral ministry nurtured and sustained the soul for its high and eternal destiny. Supported by a conversionist ministry of reconciling and a moralistic concern for guiding, this sustaining function pursued the goal of personal religious virtuosity. Pastors as sustainers fell under demands to be virtuosos in matters religious and became, in fact, professional religionists. The unavoidable failure to fulfill completely that demand provided important movements emphasizing the lay pastorate, aptly illustrated by German pietistic societies and the Wesleyan classes. Similarly, in catholicism, the new movements of the Jansenists and Molinists arose to emphasize religious virtuosity and evoked sharp attacks from the dominant Jesuits.

While in the earliest Christian era sustaining had polarized pastoral care, owing to Christian hopelessness about the historical future, in the Enlightenment period sustaining became the dominant pastoral function for quite different reasons. Historical hopes and human aspirations for this life ran very high indeed, and in this context pastoral sustenance sought primarily to hold before believers their individual destinies beyond this life, however full this life might become.

## 10.   Pastoral Guidance in the Era of Religious Privacy

The cultural confidence that inspired man in the western nations between the French Revolution and the First World War had as its counterpart a broad tendency to regard religion and religious commitment as an inviolably private aspect of individual, personal life. In his famous *Reden* (1799), Friedrich Schleiermacher, the father of modern Protestant theology, declared, "According to the principles of the true church, the mission of a priest in the world is a private business, and the temple should also be a private chamber where he lifts up his voice to give utterance to religion."[21] Modern Western civilization insisted so adamantly on the privacy of religion that the rulers of several European countries forced the papacy in 1773 to abolish the Society of Jesus, which guarded and managed the public functions of the Roman Catholic Church; Jesuits existed as an underground movement until their re-establishment, as a more specifically religious society, in 1814.

The privacy of religion placed church membership on a voluntary basis and cultivated ecclesiastical pluralism. The function of guiding personal, private, pluralistic decisions of troubled persons pervaded pastoral concern and pastoral activity throughout the nineteenth century and at the same time built the foundation for a later preoccupation with psychology and the psychology of religion.

The opening of this era saw revolutions political, social, and intellectual, out of which modern nationalism, bourgeois morality, and technology were born. These movements undercut the identification of nations and peoples as traditionally and uniformly Christian, and they withdrew the state support on which ecclesiastical power had been built and preserved. Relegating religion to the realm of private opinion and

---

21 Friedrich D. E. Schleiermacher, *On Religion, Speeches to its Cultured Despisers*, tr. John Oman (New York: Harper & Brothers, Publishers, 1958), pp. 174–175. By permission.

church identification to the realm of personal choice placed Christianity on a new footing but by no means eliminated its influence. The great revivals of the nineteenth century, out of which sprang mammoth missionary endeavors by the Protestant churches, appealed to individual, private, decision to accept Jesus Christ as personal Lord and Savior. Christianity became a guardian of the bourgeois ethic of respectability, appealing primarily to personal morality and, in such phenomena as the Social Gospel, to the voluntary endeavor to build a just society. Family life as the arena in which private convictions might appropriately and intimately be shared, became a major focus of religious and pastoral concern.

Guidance of children into Christian living by means of the nurturing process of Christian education, no less than the guidance of adults into Christian living by means of revivalism, set individuals on a path in which righteous living was portrayed as possible and prudential. Pastoring thus focused on guidance as the main asset that Christianity might offer individuals in their careers from the cradle to the grave. Moral guidance rested on the underpinning of a kind of religious guidance that strove to lead individuals into a convincing and beneficial consciousness of the presence of God [SEE EXHIBITS 19 AND 20]. This subjective, personal, private denotation of religion produced a variety of religious experiences even wider than the pluralistic variety of religion itself. Religious experience became the subject of investigatory and classificatory efforts that produced a new psychology of religion, perhaps best expressed in the writings of the American philosopher-psychologist, William James [SEE EXHIBIT 21]. Theologically, pastors understood themselves as experts in the theory and practice of this very various religion.

Subsidiary pastoral functions, of course, continued but took their shape from this individualistically eductive guidance. The century produced significant faith-healing movements of such force as to form new religions, for example, Christian Science. Sustaining on this subjective basis became largely a ministry of spiritual comforting in the face of stubborn realities of the physical or material world. Private religion brooked no continuation of older forms of church disciplines, but discipline was seized upon anew as the basis for some rigoristic sectarian movements, for example, the Mormons. The reconciling ministry in its mode of forgiveness moved mainly in the direction of leading people to make decisions for Christ. Thus, healing, sustaining, and reconciling became subordinate to guidance, as guiding aimed at eliciting from the individual's own spiritual life and religious conviction the norms by which to make the great and small decisions of living.

PART 3

# THE FOUR
# PASTORAL
# FUNCTIONS

The ministry of pastoral care has been defined and the historical epochs during which that ministry was carried on through the ages have been delineated. The four pastoral functions of healing, sustaining, guiding, and reconciling have alternately and variously risen to prominence amidst the changing cultural, psychological, intellectual, and religious circumstances of men and women throughout the Christian Era. Although in any given historic epoch one function polarized the entire pastoral endeavor around itself, it has been seen that in each era all the four functions remained in operation. Keeping in mind the ever-changing pattern of their prominence in relation to one another, it becomes helpful now to view from historical perspective each of the four functions in turn. For, indeed, each function has undergone its own development, elaboration, and transmutation as it has found expression in terms of different psychologies, faced different cultural circumstances, embodied itself in different modes, and employed different means. Having briefly sketched a generic history of the Christian pastoral endeavor, we now examine the specific histories—or "profiles" or "biographies"—of the four pastoral functions.

In this section we intend only to hold each pastoral function under historical examination long enough to illuminate its characteristic operations, modes, and means, and we make no pretense to exhaustive historical treatment nor even to rigid chronological presentation. Healing has been a very complex function, touching upon a vast variety of arts and practices, such as exorcism, magic, witchcraft, medicine, psychiatry, and so forth. By contrast, sustaining is a largely self-contained and stable ministry. Pastoral guiding has had a very complex career and today is probably regarded as the most viable of all pastoral ministries. On the other hand, it is extremely rewarding to survey the history of reconciling, even though this function is exercised today mainly in the mode of forgiveness and in quite formalized means. Therefore, our discussions of the four functions will be uneven in length and will follow no preconceived pattern, but each function will be examined historically in an attempt to analyze its major modes and means, and to assess its potential contributions to our own times.

## 1. Healing

Healing is a pastoral function that aims to overcome some impairment by restoring a person to wholeness and by leading him to advance beyond his previous condition. The wholeness which pastoral healing seeks to achieve is, therefore, not simple restoration of circumstances that prevailed before impairment began. Rather, when mending or restoration takes place under Christian pastoral care, it is hoped that the troubled person will become integrated on a higher spiritual level than he has previously experienced. A man whose appendix is diseased to the extent that it needs to be removed can become healed by surgery that restores him to the normal condition that prevailed before the organ was removed. In the Christian pastoral understanding of healing, however, healing is more than mere restoration, for it includes a forward gain over the condition prevailing before illness. The man who has had his appendix removed may be challenged by the dangers of illness and surgery to find a new depth to his life by drawing upon Christian resources. Sickness always presents a crisis, always intrudes into the usual rhythms of our living, and sometimes in its severity brings us to a full stop. Every sick person who calls for help is by this call on the threshold of becoming aware of his generic human frailty. Things that previously seemed tremendously important, like status, money, and family, may suddenly be seen as of quite relative importance. The sick person may perceive that he is finally defenseless, a creature who is prone to disintegration and who will one day succumb, and therefore he may achieve a new sense of the fragility of life, like that of the psalmist:

Like as a father pitieth his children, so the Lord pitieth them that
fear him.
For he knoweth our frame; he remembereth that we are dust.
As for man, his days are as grass: as a flower of the field, so he
flourisheth.
For the wind passeth over it and it is gone; and the place thereof
shall know it no more.

(Psalm 103:13–16, Authorized Version)

On the other hand, experiencing the precariousness of his life may
move a man to give thanks for the freedom and health he does have,
and thus he may be changed by the crisis. Paul Tournier relates that

When my wife broke her leg two years ago, she said to me: "The
hospitals are always full; it is only right that for once it should be my
turn to go there." It is, then, life and health which turn out to be the
unmerited gifts, and the prolongation of life and the re-establishment of
health, for which medicine labours with all its strength, are seen to be
a blessing from the merciful God, a respite, a stay of execution. We may
ask why God grants us this respite.[22]

Healing as restoration and advance has always been an important
function of the ministry of the cure of souls. Its history is continuous
and rich in diversity and range. At various times the church has emphasized first one and then another aspect of the healing ministry, using a
variety of instrumentalities and methods.
  I. *Anointing.* In the early centuries of the church's life, anointing with oil or unction was a popular and meaningful method of healing.
Oil was blessed at a public service, or in the sick room, either by a bishop
or by some charismatic person who might be a bishop or priest or layman or even a laywoman. The oil was then administered either by the
clergy or laity, or the patient might anoint himself. Usually that part of
the body which was thought to be ill was anointed with the sign of the
cross. Other parts of the body were also anointed; some authors recommend three, others five, and some up to twenty places. Sometimes the
anointings were to be repeated as often as daily for a week.[23] In a number
of instances water, blessed along with the oil, was drunk. Both the
water and the oil were intended to drive away the fevers and the unclean
spirits which were believed to be responsible for the malady.[24] Anointing
of the senses, including the old tradition of anointing of loins and mouth,
may perhaps reflect some idea that demons were prone to attack the

---

22 Paul Tournier, *A Doctor's Casebook in the Light of the Bible,* tr. Edwin
Hudson (New York: Harper & Brothers, 1960), p. 173. By permission.
23 See Ludwig Eisenhofer and Joseph Lechner, *The Liturgy of the Roman Rite,*
tr. A. J. and E. F. Peeler (New York: Herder and Herder, 1961), p. 383.
24 See F. W. Puller, *The Anointing of the Sick in Scripture and Tradition*
(London: S.P.C.K., second edn., rev., 1910), p. 83.

person through the senses, or even, more crudely, that they entered the body through orifices and the anointing of these entrances by making the sign of the cross in holy oil would repulse the onslaught.

By the ninth century, however, the custom of anointing for healing was beginning to undergo some fundamental changes in Western Christianity. Unction was becoming extreme unction as a specific preparation of the soul for death. Bishop Theodulf of Orleans (d. 818 A.D.), one of the theological advisors to Emperor Charles the Great, sent his clergy directions for pastoral care, specifying that the oil which is blessed should be applied on fifteen different parts of the body. He wrote:

> When the sick man has been anointed in the way that has been set forth, let him be enjoined by the priest to say the Lord's Prayer and the Creed, and to commend his spirit into the hands of God, and to fortify himself with the sign of the cross, and to bid farewell to the living. Then let the priest communicate him. . . .[25]

In Theodulf's view we see a clear notion of unction as a last rite. This idea gained momentum and became dominant until quite recent times, when efforts have been made to revive unction as a healing ministration.

II. *Saints and Relics.* An exceedingly interesting aspect of the healing ministry of the church is healing through contact with relics, usually purporting to be a part of the body of a saint or something intimately connected with the life of Mary or Jesus. Bits of bone, hair, clothing, wood from the cross, and even milk said to be from the breasts of the Virgin, have been believed to be almost overpowering in their therapeutic value. A twelfth-century chronicler tells us that, in 887 A.D., the relics of St. Martin of Tours were brought from Auxerre, and when two cripples, who had been earning an easy livelihood begging, heard of it, they decided to get out of the territory as quickly as possible lest they be healed. Their worst fears were well founded, for the relics arrived in the city before they might leave, and both were cured in spite of themselves.[26] Belief in the healing power of relics was so widespread that wealthy and influential persons often kept relic collections in order to have the correct cure for each disease, since some were supposed to be more effective than others for certain ills. Martin Luther's prince, Frederick the Wise, Duke of Saxony, built such a collection of relics, although Luther sought to draw attention to other means of overcoming illness [SEE EXHIBIT 12].

Prayers to certain saints have been considered especially conducive to healing. The concern of a particular saint for victims of a certain disease was usually determined by the manner in which the saint died.

---

[25] Theodulf, *Capitulare*, cited by Puller, *op. cit.*, p. 194. By permission.
[26] Henry Charles Lea, *A History of the Inquisition of the Middle Ages* ( 3 vols., New York: Harper & Brothers, 1888), I, 47–48.

Saint Agatha, an early Christian martyr, was supposed to have had her breast cut off as she was being put to death, and therefore diseases of the female breast came under her charge as the patron saint of nursing women. Saint Apollonia was supposed to have had her teeth knocked out and her jaw broken; prayers were directed to her to relieve toothache. Diseases of the legs and feet were under the supervision of St. John. Measles became known as St. Lazarus' disease. No less than 130 saints can be named who were considered powerful over specific diseases. Drugs, balms, and ointments were sometimes used to reinforce healing by invocation of saints, and these carried the names of the appropriate patron saints. In modern pharmacopoeias, drugs bear such names as St. Bartholomew's fever liniment, St. Jacob's oil, and St. German's tea.[27]

Shrines were often built to commemorate certain saints or to house spiritually powerful relics. The shrine at the Cathedral of Cologne claimed to contain the skulls of the three "Wise Men of the East," and sick persons from all over Europe came there to be healed. In the same city, the church of St. Gereon contained the therapeutic relics of its patron. Not to be outdone, the monastery, erected to commemorate the supposed martyrdom of Ursula and her 11,000 virgins by the Huns at Cologne, had its interior walls covered with bones claimed to be those of the martyred women.[28] In modern times, the most famous healing shrines are those of Lourdes in France and of St. Anne de Beaupré in Canada. Today these shrines are probably visited by more people than attended the most famous ones during the Middle Ages.

III. *Charismatic Healers.* The Christian ministry of healing has often been exercised by especially charismatic persons. Some men and women with special healing powers have become historically renowned as healers. The church canonized Edward the Confessor in 1161 A.D. because of his piety and because he was able to perform healing miracles. Indeed, one special disease, scrofula, or tuberculosis of the glands of the neck, became known as "king's disease" because Edward was especially successful in treating it by the laying on of hands. His successors were supposed to have inherited his healing power in relation to this ill. Even after leading his realm to a breach with the papacy, Henry VIII of England (d. 1547) continued the practice of healing. He dispensed "cramp rings" to be used for preventing cramps and fits, and Queen Elizabeth I wore one of the blessed rings continually. Charles II of England (d. 1685) was an especially busy healer of scrofula and of other diseases, and even while he was exiled in the Netherlands, he was besieged by victims seeking cure. Queen Anne (d. 1714) was the last of

---

[27] Benjamin Lee Gordon, *Medieval and Renaissance Medicine* (New York: Philosophical Library, 1959), pp. 34–35. By permission.
[28] Howard W. Haggard, *Devils, Drugs, and Doctors* (New York: Harper & Row, Publishers, 1929), p. 301. By permission.

English royalty to practice healing.[29] St. Francis of Assisi (d. 1226) is revered for having performed healing miracles [SEE EXHIBIT 9]. After his conversion, George Fox (d. 1691), founder of the Quaker movement, became widely reputed for healing not only mental diseases but also bodily ills. His followers, wary of what the authorities might do if any hysterical belief in him as a miracle worker developed, toned down his healing successes. Regardless of attempts to minimize this charisma, it seems certain that Fox's ministry included a considerable number of healings, which were probably described in a lost work called "Book of Miracles."[30]

Pastoral healing at the hands of charismatic persons appeared as a special power of both clergy and laymen after the Reformation in both the Protestant and Catholic traditions. Many interesting records reflect this ongoing ministry, few of them more arrestingly than those regarding Pastor John Christopher Blumhardt (1805–1880), Lutheran pastor in the village of Möttlingen in the Black Forest, whose very homiletical powers had therapeutic effects. His biographer reported the following cure of an unbelieving workman afflicted by an apparently incurable disease of the skin; as a last, desperate resort, the man sought out the noted pastor.

> He came across the pastor, just as Blumhardt was putting on his robes before preaching in the church. The man's disease was one of those which had for long weighed upon Blumhardt's compassion, and he recognized the symptoms at once; for scarcely had the man begun to describe his sickness, when Blumhardt said, "My friend, you see I have very little time, and I can see how wretched you are; go into the church now, and be very attentive, and may the Saviour help you." The man could scarcely control his indignation and fury at this rebuff. He murmured to himself, "There's your merciful Blumhardt! there are your pious people! I'm to go to church, am I?" However, he resolved to go in, hoping the pastor might say something for his guidance in the sermon. Blumhardt preached on the text: "Ask, and it shall be given you." The man was quite unconscious how much Blumhardt's words impressed him; he still kept on murmuring to himself: "He does not talk of me or for me," and half in admiration, half in anger, he left the church and the town after the service, and began his walk home. "These pious people," "this compassion," reiterated themselves in his mind, though joined now with many of the words of the sermon. But soon these conflicting thoughts were mingled with a new sensation: he began to experience a peculiar feeling in his skin, which seemed to start and spread from certain spots; and the feeling waxed stronger and stronger with the thought, "Am I being healed?" Full of excitement, he

---

[29] Haggard, *op. cit.*, pp. 294–296.
[30] See Vernon Noble, *The Man In Leather Breeches* (New York: Philosophical Library, 1953), pp. 73–74.

hurried home, demanded a light, went alone into his bedroom, and
saw that the healing had begun. (Blumhardt says that the process took
a fortnight.) The man waited till he was quite sure of the result, and
then hurried to Elberfeld, to send word to Blumhardt, through some
friends of the latter, of the joyful news.[31]

Such accounts of faith-healing in our own day are neither unknown
nor rendered incredible by the fact that some of them raise suspicions
of charlatanry. Genuine healing powers of certain charismatic persons—
not excluding physicians—are widely recognized today despite their seeming imperviousness to scientific inquiry and description.[32]

IV. *Exorcism.* A dramatic aspect of pastoral healing has been
exorcism—the driving away of malevolent spirits by means of sacred
words and holy rites. Jesus himself performed exorcisms, according to
gospel accounts, and from the beginning his followers healed in like
manner. Early it was required of persons about to be baptized that they
should be purified and healed by having evil spirits driven out of their
bodies and souls. Bishop Cyril of Jerusalem in the fourth century exhorted all candidates for baptism to undergo exorcism, and one of the
very early Latin missals known to us contains an elaborate rite for the
exorcism of candidates. In the latter, the exorcist places his hands upon
the head of the prostrate catechumen and pronounces a long adjuration.
The God of Abraham, Isaac, Jacob, and Moses is invoked to send an
angel; the cursed devil is commanded to bow before divine judgment,
acknowledge God and Christ, and flee from the servants of God about
to be baptized; the sign of the cross on the candidate's forehead becomes the talisman which the demon will never dare to violate. This
rite of exorcism in connection with baptism remains at least vestigially
in many modern baptism rites in which parents and godparents vow, in
the name of the child, to renounce the devil, and the sign of the cross
is made on the forehead.[33]

The practice of exorcism at first was not confined to the clergy. Both
Tertullian and Origen claimed that the simplest and most unlearned of
the faithful might cast out demons by prayer and adjuration. In the
Eastern Church, the specific office of exorcist was never established, but

---

31 F. Zündel, *Pfarrer J. C. Blumhardt, Ein Lebensbild* (Zürich, 1880), pp. 437–
438, as cited in translation by Percy Dearmer, *Body and Soul; An Enquiry into
the Effect of Religion Upon Health. . .* (New York: E. P. Dutton & Company,
1909), pp. 397–398. By permission.
32 See Jerome D. Frank, *Persuasion and Healing; A Comparative Study in
Psychotherapy* (Baltimore: The Johns Hopkins Press, 1961).
33 Cyril of Jerusalem, Procatachesis 9, *NPNF:2.* VII, 3. The Latin exorcism
formula from the Gelasian Sacramentary is cited by L. Duchesne, *Christian
Worship; Its Origin and Evolution,* tr. M. L. McClure (fifth edn., London:
Society for Promoting Christian Knowledge, 1931), pp. 299–300. For such a
modern baptismal rite, see *The Book of Common Prayer* (American), pp. 276,
280.

persons who possessed the charismatic power of exorcism were ordained deacon or sub-deacon. By the time of Pope Cornelius (251–252), the Roman Church had developed the order of exorcist as one of four minor orders of clergy. As the practice of infant baptism superseded the initiation of adult converts into the church, the order of exorcist came gradually to be absorbed into the priesthood.

But the absorption of the exorcist's work into normal ministerial orders did not stop the need for exorcism or its practice. A particularly vivid account of such a healing is found in the diary of a Spanish abbess involved in an epidemic of demon possession in Madrid between 1628 and 1631. She wrote:

> When I began to find myself in this state I felt within me movements so extraordinary that I judged the cause could not be natural. I recited several orisons [prayers] asking God to deliver me from such terrible pain. Seeing that my state did not change, I several times begged the prior to exorcise me; as he was not willing to do so and sought to turn me from it, telling me that all I related was only the outcome of my imagination, I did all that in me lay to believe it, but the pain drove me to feel the contrary. At length on the day of Our Lady the prior took a stole, and after having offered up several prayers, asked God to reveal to me whether the demon was in my body by unmasking him, or else to take away these sufferings and this pain which I felt inwardly. Long after he had begun the exorcisms and while I was feeling happy to find myself free, for I no longer felt anything, I suddenly fell into a sort of swooning and delirium, doing and saying things of which the idea had never occurred to me in my life. . . . This continued in the same way during three months and I rarely felt myself in my normal and natural state. Nature had given me so tranquil a character that even in childhood I was quite unlike my age and loved neither the games, liveliness nor movement habitual to it. Accordingly it could not but be regarded as a supernatural thing that having reached the age of twenty-six years and become a nun and even an abbess, I committed follies of which I had never before been capable. . . .[34]

Strange as they may seem to moderns, examples as dramatic as the story of the Spanish abbess might be cited out of every epoch of Christian history to illustrate the church's continual interest and active involvement in healing bodily ills. Protestants have, by and large, taken a skeptical attitude toward possession, and wherever the Protestant ethos dominated, exorcism was rarely used. In England attempts at exorcising by a vagrant preacher in the early seventeenth century resulted in a Canon which, in effect, forbade exorcism by the clergy. Evangelical Protestants, as a whole, adopted Luther's attitude. While firmly believing in

---

[34] L. F. Calmeil, *De La Folie*, cited by T. K. Oesterreich, *Possession; Demoniacal and Other*, tr. D. Ibberson (London: Kegan Paul, Trench, Trubner and Co., Ltd., 1930), p. 41. By permission.

the reality and power of Satan, they recommended that prayer alone be used to cure diabolical attacks [SEE EXHIBIT 18].

In our own day, the office of exorcist is considered in the Roman Church to be one of several steps toward ordination to the priesthood, and it is usually bestowed sometime during seminary studies. Only a priest is authorized to use the exorcising powers, and in so doing he must carefully follow the prescriptions of the *Rituale Romanum* while at the same time he dutifully regards the laws of provincial and diocesan synods, which, for the most part, require the bishop's permission before exorcism is done.

V. *Magico-Medicine.* Early and medieval Christians believed in the demonic production of both mental and physical disease, and a variety of prayers, adjurations, ritualistic acts, and consecrated potions were used as remedies. With the earliest encounter between Christianity and the so-called barbarian peoples of Europe, Christian incantations, rituals, and holy objects came to be used to reinforce the healing power of herbal unguents and of medicines that seem to have no rational relation to diseases. In epilepsy, attributed apparently to demonic activity, water from the skull of a suicide was poured down the patient's throat so that the demon might taste the meaning of destruction and exit hastily. A major magico-medical work of Anglo-Saxon origin, *The Leechdom of Bald*, suggests that the choice treatment for a man struck by an adder is to wash a black snail in a dish of holy water and then drink the water.[35] About 1000 A.D. there was compiled from various sources another Anglo-Saxon magico-medical book, *Lacnunga*, many of whose recipes reveal a combination of half-forgotten Greek medicine, Anglo-Saxon folk-magic, and Christian healing practices. As a preventive against enchantment against elves, this book prescribes a faintly Christianized pagan remedy that involved writing scriptural words on the paten (or communion-plate), mixing therein herbs and consecrated wine, and water brought by a virgin; the inscription was to be washed off the plate with the liquid, which then was carried to the church and masses and psalms sung over it; in the name of the Trinity it was drunk. Another medicament recommended by *Lacnunga* was compounded by this very involved prescription:

> To make a good bone salve that is good for headache and for infirmity of all organs, shall serve: Rue, radish and "ampre", flag, fever-few, ashthroat, boarthroat, celandine, beet and betonicas, rib-wort, and red hove, helenium, alexanders roots, cluftonge and clote, "lithewort" and lambscress, hillwort, hazel, couch-grass, woodruff and a sprout of "wræt", springwort, spearwort, waybroad and wormwood, lupins and "æferths", hedge-clivers, and hop-plants, yarrows and cuckoo sorrels, henbanes and broad-leek. Take an equal amount of all these plants. Put

---

[35] Gordon, *op. cit.*, pp. 557 and 361ff.

in a mortar. Pound everything together and add clusters of ivy-berries thereto. And take ashbark and willow twigs and oak bark and "wir" bark and crabapple bark and sallow bark and woodbine leaves; all these shall be taken from the nether part and from the eastwide side of the trees. Let all these barks be scraped together and boiled in holy water until they are well softened. Add them then to the plants in the mortar. Pound everything together. Then take hart's grease and goat's grease and well matured mulberry negus, and bull's grease and boar's grease and ram's grease; let them all be melted together and poured into a round lump. Then let all the bones be heaped together that one may be able to collect; and let the bones be broken up with the back of an axe and seethed, and the fat skimmed and worked into a round lump. Then let old butter be taken and the plants and the barks boiled, all being put together. When it has once come to the boil let it set. Then scrape all the grease into the pan, as much salve as thou mayest desire to have and as thou mayest be able to reduce to a tar. Set over the fire; let cook, not boil too much, until the salve be done. Filter through cloth. Set again over the fire. Take then nine cloves of garlic that has been blessed; pound in wine, wring through cloth; scrape myrrh the plant into it and font-holy wax, and burning storax and white incense. Then pour into the salve, so much that it be the amount of 3 eggshells. Take then old soap and marrow of an old ox, and eagle's marrow. Add then the tars and mix then with a quick-beam [spoon] until the salve be brown. Sing then over it *Benedictus Dominus Deus meus* [*i.e.*, Psalm cxliv], and the other *Benedictus Dominus Deus Israel* [*i.e.*, Luke 1:68 and Psalm lxxii:18], and the *Magnificat*, and the *Credo in Unum* [*i.e.*, the "Nicene" Creed], and the prayer, *Matthew, Mark, Luke, John*. Be the sore where it may, let the salve be smeared on the head first.[36]

It was, however, after rather thorough absorption of the European peoples into the Catholic Church that the great day of Christian pastoral healing came into being by virtue of employing a marvelously articulated sacramental system for the relief of bodily ills [SEE EXHIBIT 11].

VI. *Pastoral Healing Today*. While healing has persisted as an important part of the church's repertory of helping concerns, some eras more than others produced specific systems of pastoral healing. During the Middle Ages, western catholicism looked to the sacraments to infuse divine grace that was physically curative as well as spiritually redeeming. In the Renaissance and the Enlightenment, these specifics underwent experimental examination, and since then they have been taken over by and developed into an exact and exacting healing science by the pro-

---

36 " 'Lacnunga' A Magico-Medical Commonplace Book," XXXI a., ed. by J. H. G. Grattan assisted by Charles Singer, in Grattan and Singer, *Anglo-Saxon Magic and Medicine* (Published for The Wellcome Historical Medical Museum by Geoffrey Cumberlege, London: Oxford University Press, 1952), pp. 111, 113. By permission.

fessions of medicine and pharmacy. Similarly, hospitals, once under monastic or diocesan management, are now administered and staffed by persons whose professional life is defined without necessary reference to the church.

In modern times there has appeared among pastors a renewed interest in spiritual healing, or faith-healing, by charismatic persons performing the healing ministry of the church. Some such healers have repudiated the worth of medical healing in their endeavor to recapture for the church a ministry now largely conducted outside the church. Yet modern medicine and psychiatry often have valued highly the work of pastors as an important adjunct to the healing enterprise. In spite of renewed interest today in pastoral healing by the laying on of hands, by unction, by prayer and exorcism, and by sacramental ministrations, it must be recognized that all this activity remains isolated from the central understandings of healing that prevail in Western civilization. On the other hand, in creative enterprises in which pastors have joined themselves to teams of physicians and psychiatrists in the healing function, they by and large have eschewed the great tradition of pastoral healing and have tended to explain their activity in terms developed by extra-pastoral healers.

Pastoral healing surely continues in our time, but the function has become contracted, isolated, or confused about itself in relation both to other applications of the healing art and to the Christian pastoral tradition of healing. It remains quite unclear whether or how this function of the cure of souls is to be expressed at a time when its historical forms may well be beyond the possibility of resuscitation. Of the four functions of pastoral care, healing seems at once most problematical in itself and most open to new and fresh expressions in combination with the functions of sustaining, guiding, and reconciling.

## 2.  Sustaining

Because sustaining was the central and reigning function of the cure of souls during the first epoch of the Christian experience, most of the writings that have come to be regarded as sacred Christian Scripture reflect, insofar as they bear upon the pastoral ministry, the overriding prominence of that function. In the initial era, Christians thought that the entire trend of history was downward and away from realizing human destiny under God—a destiny that would come cataclysmically by a divine act reversing in eternity history's trend. At the end of that first period, however, it came to be seen that historical circumstances constituted a mixture of movements, some trending toward fulfillment and some trending toward destruction. The sustaining ministry then naturally fastened upon and applied itself to circumstances thrusting away from a person's true destiny, but Christians nevertheless insisted that, even when these circumstances destroyed life, beyond destruction lay man's final fulfillment.

During these early centuries of the Christian tradition, pastoral sustaining took form in a fourfold task of helping persons troubled by an overwhelming sense of loss. The first task of *preservation* sought to maintain a troubled person's situation with as little loss as possible. Second, this function offered the *consolation* that actual losses could not nullify the person's opportunity to achieve his destiny under God. Third, *consolidation* of the remaining resources available to the sufferer built a platform from which to face up to a deprived life. Finally came *redemption*, by embracing the loss and by setting out to achieve whatever historical fulfillment might be wrested from life in the face of irretrievable deprivation.

While the fourfold task of sustaining arose out of a particular transmutation of Christian conviction about historical existence, it nevertheless equipped Christian pastors to ameliorate personal troubles that are, of course, ubiquitous. At one time or another, every man encounters some experience that drives him headlong away from what he takes to be human fulfillment. It can be almost anything—sudden and unprepared-for success, bereavement, certain types of social and economic demotion, an inheritance of new responsibilities, the loss or threat of loss of health, serious bodily impairment that brooks no recuperation, and so forth. Instead of mobilizing creatively to meet such events that challenge us, we may become confused, or overly aggressive, or hopeless, or take to a chemical solution like drugs, or back away disconsolate. Perhaps one does so for only a short time while he consolidates for a new advance, but sometimes such a retreat threatens to lapse into pathological withdrawal, which may involve more and more facets of life and elicit self-defeating and debilitating defensive maneuvers. At times we can easily understand going backward, but in other instances we cannot fathom the hidden elements in the dynamic which makes for persistent retreat. A businessman is given a long-hoped-for promotion, and within weeks he may be seen by colleagues and family to be in a most alarming state of personal disarray; something in this man confronted with that situation has unleashed forces he could not creatively cope with at the time.

Situations which would tend to trigger retreat for persons in one culture might not so affect persons with a different world view. For example, it is probable that John Calvin considered dying to be an occasion not for sustaining against retreat, but rather for reconciling the soul with God and man [SEE EXHIBIT 13]. Far from prompting fear or anxiety, dying was thought of as one's entry into his true home, and the dying person was seen by Calvin to be in the process of becoming spiritually stronger! Our own culture at the present time identifies bereavement as an event freighted with danger and considers bereaving an important occasion for a sustaining ministry even though it may elicit prominently the pastoral function of reconciling. A skilled pastor or friend can often help the mourner face his ambivalences toward the deceased, including his hostility and guilt, and thus reconcilation by confession and forgiveness may be a *sine qua non* of successful grieving.

Although the customary occasions for sustaining may evoke other pastoral functions, the fourfold task of sustaining becomes operative in any situation where the sense dominates that all of life is running downhill.

I. *Preservation.* Usually the first task is *preservation,* or holding the line against other threats [SEE EXHIBIT 10], or further loss, or excessive retreat. In bereavement there may appear an inability on the part of the bereaved to commence mourning. One may be so numbed by his loss that his retreat borders on pathological denial. Some pastoral helpers have found various ways to induce grieving so that retreat may be kept within normal limits.

A dramatic example of sustaining by holding the line is an incident recorded by a psychotherapist of his therapy with a deeply troubled girl. He says that, after a period of well-being, the patient telephoned and seemed badly disturbed because medical tests had indicated a possible uterine carcinoma. He wrote:

> When she arrived for therapy, I was shocked by her appearance. There were no external anxiety symptoms, but there was the pallor of death, and her face and eyes were those of a person making the last futile, wild struggle for life. Her body seemed frail and limp with defeat. Instead of going to my chair, I touched her head in a gesture of sympathy, whereupon she put her head against my stomach and clung to me, releasing the sobs that had not been able to come. When she spoke, it was of her fear and of this final, terrible defeat after the long, uphill struggle. I spoke to her of faith and courage, of the fact that she might not have cancer, and of the fact that medical science was often able to deal successfully with cancer.
>
> As I sat down, she moved to a position where she could clasp my hands and look directly into my eyes. As I saw the depth of her terror, I felt something that I had felt in my psychotic patients in a mental hospital. "Oh Dr. ——, I'm so scared," she said; and then, as I spoke to her, she became very calm and began repeating my words in a trance-like voice, "Yes, I *can* have faith," she said, and I realized that for her the only reality was in my voice and in our hands, and in our eyes. As I felt the completeness of her psychological surrender, I realized with a sudden, internal jolt that she had entered a psychotic state. For just a second of time I felt fear and self-doubt, and then I thought, "Of course I can meet it—I can't let B. down." Her eyes were still fixed on mine in that unwavering stare, and the upsurge of strength

I experienced went out to her, and then she relaxed and her eyelids flickered; and, as I watched her move and speak, I saw that she was not psychotic, and I felt that I had held her from the abyss of internal isolation on the edge of which she wavered.

She moved back to her chair, stretched out in it, and spoke the peace she now felt. I, too, felt a deep sense of peace and unity. She said that for the first time, she was relaxed. Then, searching the limits of the safety she had found, she asked whether faith in God could keep her from having cancer. Feeling that she needed realistic authority, I told her I believed that God works through natural law; that, if she had cancer, He would not change that; but that He would be with her through the ordeal, if it came to that.[37]

In this very dramatic instance of preservation, a desperate girl has called for her psychotherapist to embolden her flickering faith with strength and resources that were his, not hers. His means of preservation were in the last analysis ineffable, but in a turbulent moment the encounter has tapped half-buried and dormant sources of strength in both persons that would remain mute save in the face of ultimate questionings and seekings. A life that was plunging away from fulfillment has found a stopping point, and total retreat has been checked. Through the ages pastors have found many means of helping preserve distraught persons from destruction by an overwhelming sense of misery. These means—a touch, a glance, a word, a gesture—could never be enumerated or classified, but their usefulness remains apparent nevertheless. Preservation is the first task of sustaining.

II. *Consolation.* After *preservation*, in whatever degree that it may be necessary and by whatever means, then *consolation* is in order. Hopefully, a pastor will be as sensitive in the matter of timing for consolation as was John Chrysostom in his letter to a young widow [SEE EXHIBIT 5]; he tells her that he abstained from writing when her sorrow was at its height so that she could have her fill of mourning—for only then could she benefit from his consolations.

Seen in historic perspective, pastoral consolation serves to relieve one's sense of misery by bringing the sufferer into an understanding of his still belonging to the company of hopeful living. Cyprian comforted the about-to-be-martyred Christians in Thibaris with the message that they were known by God and that they belonged in their struggles to the saints both on earth and in heaven [SEE EXHIBIT 4]. From long before the Christian era comes this classic Hebrew religious utterance of consolation in the midst of ineluctable loss:

---

[37] Stanley W. Standal and Raymond J. Corsini (eds.), *Critical Incidents in Psychotherapy* (Englewood Cliffs, N.J.: Prentice-Hall, Inc., 1959), p. 66. By permission.

The Lord is my shepherd; I shall not want.

He maketh me to lie down in green pastures: he leadeth me beside the still waters.

He restoreth my soul: he leadeth me in the paths of righteousness for his name's sake.

Yea, though I walk through the valley of the shadow of death, I will fear no evil: for thou art with me; thy rod and thy staff they comfort me.

Thou preparest a table before me in the presence of mine enemies: thou anointest my head with oil; my cup runneth over.

Surely goodness and mercy shall follow me all the days of my life: and I will dwell in the house of the Lord for ever.

(Psalm 23, Authorized Version)

Nor has specifically Christian literature in the modern idiom diminished the power of religious comfort, encouragement, and strength in the face of trouble that can be overcome not in the external facts of life but only in the depth of the human soul; the familiar hymn consoles by its assurance that the sufferer is not alone:

Abide with me: fast falls the eventide;
The darkness deepens; Lord, with me abide:
When other helpers fail, and comforts flee,
Help of the helpless, O abide with me.

Swift to its close ebbs out life's little day,
Earth's joys grow dim, its glories pass away,
Change and decay in all around I see;
O thou who changest not, abide with me.

I need thy presence ev'ry passing hour;
What but thy grace can foil the tempter's power?
Who, like thyself, my guide and stay can be?
Through cloud and sunshine, Lord, abide with me.

I fear no foe, with thee at hand to bless;
Ills have no weight, and tears no bitterness.
Where is death's sting? where, grave, thy victory?
I triumph still, if thou abide with me.

Hold thou thy cross before my closing eyes;
Shine through the gloom and point me to the skies;
Heav'n's morning breaks, and earth's vain shadows flee:
In life, in death, O Lord, abide with me. Amen.[38]

---

[38] By Henry Francis Lyte, 1847; Lyte is said to have written the hymn in 1820 after visiting a dying friend who repeated the phrase, "Abide with me." See *The Hymnal 1940 Companion* by The Joint Commission on the Revision of the Hymnal of the Protestant Episcopal Church in the United States of America (New York: The Church Pension Fund, 1949), p. 289, where several versions of the hymn's origin are summarized. The text appears in most current

Consolation serves as the second task in pastoral sustaining by helping to relieve a disconsolate person from his sense of misery, even while acknowledging that the damaging or robbing experience that initiated disconsolation remains irreparable in and of itself. Our citation of a classical and a modern hymn of consolation must not suggest that consolation can be brought about only by recourse to memorable phrases. It may involve the physical gesture of helping to "keep one's chin up," or the imparting of a blessing, or merely the turn of the mood that comes about after a period of silent accompaniment. Consolation, however, is distinct from preservation. Preservation finds a stopping point for regressive movement; consolation relieves the sense of misery that began and increased during the regressive movement.

III. *Consolidation.* Relief from misery enables the sustaining ministry to proceed with a regrouping of remaining resources despite loss, a new mobilization which we call *consolidation.* In this act, suffering is put into perspective within the totality of living, and the deprived person gathers himself together again.

The chaplain of a hospital for rehabilitation of teen-aged drug addicts in a large American city reported the following conversation with an eighteen-year-old girl:

GIRL: Well, I lost my schooling and got pretty low. You know what I've been doing, Reverend.

CHAPLAIN: I know.

GIRL: What do I do now? I'm here. I took the cure. But where's up?

CHAPLAIN: You want to move ahead.

GIRL: I can't go back before all that. Good or bad—and most of it's been bad—I'm different. Like you say, I've got to go ahead somewhere . . . [pause] . . . but I don't know where.[39]

Or, a bereaved widow who moves in existential retreat before the loss of her husband gets control of herself, receives consolation, and then perceives, perchance, that she still has her children to live for.

In the act of consolation, the pastor's sustaining ministry helps the troubled person select out of a seeming totality of woe some foundation for reconstruction of life. The actual loss can be seen for what it is, a partial loss. Not all things in life are tumbling down, although it has seemed that way, and now the actual deprivation can be embraced. One can literally "face up to it" by embracing the loss and building again. Perhaps the regrouping is done on the basis of the hackneyed adage that "misery loves company." Whatever the means or device, this

---

collections of Protestant hymns—*inter alia, The Hymnal of the Protestant Episcopal Church in the United States of America 1940* (New York: The Church Pension Fund, 1940), no. 467.

[39] Private files of the authors.

third mode of the sustaining ministry yearns to set the loss within the total focus of life and thus to enable the deprived person to accept his deprived life as the only life left him to live.

IV. *Redemption.* Finally, the pastoral function of sustaining helps a deprived person, who has embraced his loss and regrouped his remaining resources, begin to build an ongoing life that once more pursues its fulfillment and destiny on a new basis. The loss is not restored—should that be possible we would have the ministry of healing, for healing operates in circumstances in which loss is retrievable or harm is reparable and the retrieving or repair offers opportunity for spiritual advance. While the sustaining ministry works also toward some spiritual advance, it hopes to recover a positive approach to life that cannot achieve restoration of the *status quo ante.* Perhaps the widow redeems her loss by incorporating her husband's virtues into her own life; perhaps the widower becomes somehow both mother and father to his orphaned children. The character of redemption of loss was well understood by Jeremy Taylor, who showed how to take advantage of incapacities such as illness and even death by embracing them as good [SEE EXHIBIT 16]. John Milton's famous sonnet expresses the way in which he redeemed the loss of his eyesight:

> When I consider how my light is spent,
>   E're half my days, in this dark world and wide,
>   And that one Talent which is death to hide,
>   Lodg'd with me useless, though my Soul more bent
> To serve therewith my Maker, and present
>   My true account, least he returning chide,
>   Doth God exact day-labour, light deny'd,
>   I fondly ask; But patience to prevent
> That murmur, soon replies, God doth not need
>   Either man's work or his own gifts, who best
>   Bear his milde yoak, they serve him best, his State
> Is Kingly. Thousands at his bidding speed
>   And post o're Land and Ocean without rest:
>   They also serve who only stand and waite.

V. *Sustaining in Christian History.* Historic development of the Christian ministry of sustaining has, in fact, wrought few changes in the operation of the four tasks for sustaining. Nevertheless, relative weighting of the possibility of human fulfillment within historic existence has placed these tasks in a changing relationship to one another and has altered the relationship of sustaining to the other three functions of the ministry of the cure of souls. We have seen how in the earliest epoch of Christian pastoral experience it was generally assumed that historic fulfillment was minimal, and therefore downward movements were expected as life's normal course and even welcomed as opportunities for reaching trans-historical fulfillment.

On the other hand, the era of Enlightenment evoked a prominent sustaining ministry under quite different conditions. It was then assumed that very much of human fulfillment might be found within the conditions of historic existence. Sustaining therefore sought to show how a quick recovery from loss might be made by moral living under Christian sanctions. Under the ruling virtues of deity, morality, and immortality, the sense of loss induced by devastating, untoward, or tragic human circumstances was minimized in a way that made recovery seem facile and almost automatic.

Moderns assume that historic existence furnishes almost unlimited possibilities for the fruition of human life, but at the same time they perceive better than their predecessors the enormous subtlety of the forces that can trigger retreat and make life seem to plunge downhill. Although situations which provide occasions for the ministry of sustaining change, and although in our time commonly assumed "profits" of living can become as devastating as commonly assumed "losses," sustaining continues to be a very prominent pastoral function. As new occasions for retreat appear, so do new modes of preservation, consolation, consolidation, and redemption. In the midst of these changes, the Christian struggle against forces that drive the human spirit away from fulfillment continues, as noted by Pierre Teilhard de Chardin, S.J., who wrote:

> No, if he is to practise to the full the perfection of his Christianity, the Christian must not falter in his duty to resist evil. On the contrary . . . he must fight sincerely and with all his strength, in union with the creative force of the world, to drive back evil—so that nothing in him or around him may be diminished. . . . [T]he believer is the convinced ally of all those who think that humanity will not succeed unless it strives with all its might to realize its potentialities.[40]

Through the hymnody of the church, through personal ministrations by clergy and lay Christians, and, not least, by an enormous mass of devotional literature, the sustaining ministry operates in our time much as it has in the past centuries. Its fourfold task continues to be a meaningful part of the Christian cure of souls and promises to be a creative ministry into and through our own time of confusion and transition.

## 3. Guiding

Guiding is that function of the ministry of the cure of souls which arrives at some wisdom concerning what one ought to do when he is faced with a difficult problem of choosing between various courses of

---

[40] Pierre Teilhard de Chardin, *The Divine Milieu* (New York: Harper & Brothers, Publishers, 1960), p. 64. By permission.

thought or action. Fundamentally, the guiding ministry assumes that useful wisdom, which edifies and illuminates the meaning and direction of a person's life, can be made available within the framework of the helping act. This wisdom may be thought of as having its origin from within the troubled person himself, from the experience of the counselor, from the common values regnant in their mutually shared culture, from a superior wisdom available to the counselor, or even from a body of truth or knowledge independent of both the counselor and counselee. In any case, the wisdom must be fashioned or shaped to the immediate circumstances of the troubled person in order that it may be appropriated and used in the context of the particular trouble at hand. Guiding as a pastoral function does not develop ethical principles for their own sake or for general application to the processes of living, but rather forges decision-guiding wisdom in the heat of specific troubles and strives to facilitate its use in particular situations. Its first interest is a troublesome choice ready at hand, and only second, if ever, does it pay attention to absolute morals.

I. *Advice-giving.* The modes of the ministry of guidance may be ranged along a continuum from advice-giving at one pole to an activity of listening and reflecting at the other pole. Advice-giving is a supportive and helpful ministry when the thing most needed is the superior point of view of the counselor, or the knowledge and wisdom outside both the helper and the one helped which the counselor is able to shape specifically for the counselee's use. This mode of guidance we call inductive, for it wishes to lead the perplexed person into a prior and authoritative set of values in terms of which he may reach his decision.

Advice-giving can take many forms. There is a form of counseling which proceeds from the general to the particular, or from the universal to the individual. This form normally demands a casuistry, consisting of a body of rules and principles for correct action from which may be selected those that apply logically and directly to the specific situation at hand. Christian literature includes many compendiums and handbooks of casuistry, written for the edification and instruction of pastors to guide their hearing of confessions, their teaching, and their general advice-giving in regard to moral action [SEE EXHIBITS 7 AND 19]. Jeremy Taylor's *Ductor Dubitantium*, published in 1660, was such a book, which cloaked in classical garb its cases and examples that they might not be readily recognized by readers. For example:

> Quintus Milvius, being in love with the wife of Muræna, and she with him,—Milvius resolves to kill his wife, Virginia, and run away with the wife of Muræna, or force her from him; he acquaints his freed-man, Priscus Calvus, with his purpose, but he, to divert his purpose of murder and adultery, persuades his patron, Milvius, rather to lie with Muræna's wife now, than to do such things of hazard, and evil voice, and dis-

honour: and his advice was charitable, and prevailed; for though the adultery was future, yet the intended murder was present, and the evil was lessened as much as it could, and no man prejudiced, but the life of one saved. But if he believes, that by this act Virginia will be so exasperated, that she will turn adulteress in revenge, or kill her husband; this is not to be advised. . . .[41]

Another form of advice-giving seeks to bring the penitent or troubled person into a situation which will be conducive to his welfare; this form is related to, but nevertheless distinct from, evangelism (understood as ecclesiastical enlistment), since it seeks to initiate the client into the wisdom or help he needs. *The Spiritual Exercises* of St. Ignatius Loyola is an excellent example of this form [SEE EXHIBIT 14]. Ignatius was anxious that the spiritual director should remain in the background, and never force or drive the person under his care, nor in any way impose the director's own views or predilections, nor even press the validity of a certain body of wisdom or truth. Rather, the director follows from behind, watching to see in what way God might be leading the retreatant, remaining alert to encourage him in his trials and to guard against rash promises and temptations; he is to "leave the Creator to act immediately with the creature, and the creature with its Creator and Lord."[42] The director is to help the penitent to know wisdom when he sees it and to shepherd him toward and into a disciplined Christian life. In other words, the director is able to discern the character of the spirit which is leading the retreatant on, and he is to advise and alert the retreatant as to whether he is beckoned forward by the spirit of God or by some other. Ignatius was not disposed to doubt that the invitations of the spirit of God are always into the protection and wisdom of the church, not always involving a religious vocation but certainly leading the devout layman to need the church's grace and truth. In any event, the picture of the director as following behind, shepherding the troubled person into that which he needs, resembles the practice of referring a needy person to a therapeutic setting which it is believed will benefit him.

II. *Devil-craft.* Historically the ministry of guidance, like other functions of soul care, has engaged in devil-craft as an important activity. It was Luther's conviction that no man ought to be alone against Satan, and that God instituted the church and the ministry of the Word in order that believers might join hands and help one another; thus would be thwarted Satan's ability to defeat and destroy any lone individual. Satan and his cohorts were thought to use the strategem of isolating the

---

[41] Jeremy Taylor, *Ductor Dubitantium*, V, 21, in *The Whole Works of The Right Rev. Jeremy Taylor, D.D.* (3 vols., London: Henry G. Bohn, 1867), III, 170.
[42] Ignatius Loyola, *The Spiritual Exercises*, Fifteenth Annotation [SEE EXHIBIT 14].

sinner and convincing him that no help was available from others or from Jesus Christ. Church discipline on this view assumed that the ranks needed to be strong, and it helped each believer to interlock his faith and strength with that of others in order to resist the assault that was ever poised over the church and over individual Christians.

Great store has been set on counselors who were good fighters against Satan and who knew his tactics and strategy. John Bunyan's autobiography, *Grace Abounding to the Chief of Sinners* [SEE EXHIBIT 17], tells how he withdrew from a certain counselor who knew nothing about devil-craft and was therefore of little use when Satan was employing relentless and effective war. Bunyan wrote:

> About this time I took an opportunity to break my mind to an ancient Christian, and told him all my case; I told him also, that I was afraid I had sinned the sin against the Holy Ghost; and he told me, he thought so too. Here, therefore, I had but cold comfort; but talking a little more with him, I found him, though a good man, a stranger to much combat with the devil. Wherefore I went to God again, as well as I could, for mercy still.
>
> Now also did the tempter begin to mock me in my misery, saying, "That seeing I had thus parted with the Lord Jesus and provoked him to displeasure, who would have stood between my soul and the flame of devouring fire, there was now but one way, and that was, to pray that God the Father would be a Mediator betwixt his Son and me. . . ."
>
> . . . Oh! I saw it was as easy to persuade him to make a new world, a new covenant, or a new Bible . . . as to pray for such a thing.[43]

Devil-craft as an aspect of pastoral guidance was held to be exceedingly important from the fourteenth through the seventeenth century in both the Catholic and Protestant traditions; it has been employed first by one and then by another of the pastoral functions of sustaining, guiding, healing, and reconciling. Everywhere it was agreed that Satan was a major adversary with whom the Christian would be locked in mortal spiritual combat for as long as he lived; however, various conditions and times dictated particular understandings and insights, and cast counseling as devil-craft within its own peculiar mold. On the whole, devil-craft belonged under the function of sustaining in the ministry and thought of John Bunyan. Bunyan saw his life beset on every side by the traps and snares of a wicked and evil world. His task basically was that of preserving his soul on its journey through this vale of woe to its heavenly reward. One needed to know how the devil operated in order to hold

---

43 John Bunyan, "Grace Abounding to the Chief of Sinners," *The Complete Works of John Bunyan*, ed. John P. Gulliver (Philadelphia: Bradley, Garretson & Co., 1872), p. 51.

the line against his assaults. But an important aspect of fighting the devil was to reject his temptations by following the Bible as the source of wisdom for use in decisions of great perplexity. We have seen devil-craft in healing as exorcism; it was an interesting aspect of reconciling, especially in the medieval penitentials; and it has been an obviously important aspect of guiding.

III. *Listening.* Toward the other end of the continuum from advice-giving to reflecting is the mode of guiding which emphasizes listening in one of three ways.

There is listening which aims toward clarification under the simple idea that, unless the counselor restrains his temptation to do most of the talking, he will never know what the counselee is trying to say. Dietrich Bonhoeffer has put the matter well:

> Many people are looking for an ear that will listen. They do not find it among Christians, because these Christians are talking where they should be listening. But he who can no longer listen to his brother will soon be no longer listening to God either; he will be doing nothing but prattle in the presence of God too. This is the beginning of the death of the spiritual life, and in the end there is nothing left but spiritual chatter and clerical condescension arrayed in pious words. One who cannot listen long and patiently will presently be talking beside the point and be never really speaking to others, albeit he be not conscious of it. Anyone who thinks that his time is too valuable to spend keeping quiet will eventually have no time for God and his brother, but only for himself and for his own follies.[44]

Listening has been deemed indispensable to the repertory of the counselor for another reason. Under conditions in which the inner state of the troubled person is the key to a resolution of his difficulty, it becomes necessary for the conselee to unburden himself by ventilating his inner pressures. A homily concerning the meaning of counseling, delivered by Origen of Alexandria (d. 254 A.D.), exhorted that talking out problems and difficulties was good for emotional health. Origen gave wise advice on choosing a good counselor.

> See, then, what holy scripture teaches us, that it is not right to bury sin in our hearts. . . . But if a man become his own accuser, in accusing himself and confessing he vomits out his sin, and dissipates the whole cause of his sickness. Only, look round carefully to find the proper person to whom to confess your sin. Prove your doctor first, the man to whom you must disclose the reason of your weakness, that he be one who knows how to sympathize with a sufferer, to weep

---

[44] Dietrich Bonhoeffer, *Life Together,* tr. John W. Doberstein (New York: Harper & Brothers, Publishers, 1954), pp. 97–98. By permission.

with a mourner, one who understands the word of sympathy, and then if he, a man who has thus shown himself a learned and merciful doctor, tells you to do anything, or gives you any advice, do it. . . .[45]

Finally, listening may aim to help the ministry of guidance by reflecting back to the troubled person the inner meaning of what he is saying, in order that he may hear clearly his own thoughts when they are hidden from him, or confused, or equivocal. This kind of guiding develops insights in the belief that self-understanding will provide one of the essential keys both to the solution of the counselee's difficulties and to his spiritual growth. A Cistercian monk, whose name we do not know, wrote sometime during the thirteenth century a beautiful and moving confession, a portion of which neatly illustrates the importance of self-understanding to decision-making.

> If I dared not look into my conscience I would remain in ignorance about myself, but now that I look within my soul, I am appalled by what I see. The deeper I look, the more terrible are the things I find. I have not ceased to sin, from the moment when my first sin was committed long ago; nor do I cease to sin now. I am so used to sinning that I can look on the evil I have done without sorrow or tears. That alone is like a sign of damnation. When one of the members of the body is without feeling, it is sometimes a sign that it is already moribund. One cannot cure an illness of which one is unconscious.[46]

The modern psychological emphasis on uncovering inner dissonances and repressions so that the counselee can work through with the therapist the dynamics of his inner chaos, has firm antecedents in the introspection of the monastic life and in the mysticism that arose out of the medieval Christian monasteries. Although our recent psychology diverges greatly from that of the Catholic mystics, there appears between the two a similar profound conviction that troubles—especially those surrounding important decision-making activity—abide in the human spirit.

IV. *The Importance of Decisions.* The history of the pastoral function of guiding shows constant effort to understand and describe human decisions and woes in their various detailed parts and yet *sub specie aeternitatis.* In the Catholic tradition, this was accomplished mainly by discussing troubles in the language of demonism or by utilizing

---

45 Origen, *In Psalm xxxvii,* Hom. ii.6, quoted by R. C. Mortimer, *The Origins of Private Penance in the Western Church* (Oxford: at the Clarendon Press, 1939), pp. 28–29. By permission.

46 From the *Meditatio Piisima,* tr. Geoffrey Webb and Adrian Walker in *The School of Self-knowledge, A Symposium from Mediaeval Sources* (London: A. R. Mowbray and Co., Limited, 1956), p. 35. By permission.

the understanding of the capital sins. In Protestant circles, where the system of capital sins was rejected as too mechanical and anachronistic, the church's guiding ministry still aimed at regarding human decisions as highly significant before God.

If a man were possessed or obsessed by demons, he could make exceedingly detailed descriptions of his condition in a way that allowed him to acknowledge that he was a participant in a salvation drama of cosmic proportions. By the time of John Cassian [SEE EXHIBIT 6], and with the subsequent modifications produced by Benedict of Nursia and Gregory the Great, a system of psychological understandings was articulated that was amazing in its detail and depth. Pride was seen as the root sin, with six others arranged around it and nourished by it. Later on, even more details of the system of capital sins were elaborated by considering each of the seven to be a breeding ground for many other sins. Speaking of the evils bred from pride, a late twelfth- or early thirteenth-century writing drawn up by an abbess in England protrayed pride as a lion and described in detail the manifold offspring of the beast that assailed devout women with their interlocking and involved temptations. She wrote:

> The Lion of Pride hath very many whelps: and I will name some of them. *Vana Gloria* [Vain Glory], is called the first: that is, whoso thinketh highly of any thing that she doth, and is well pleased if she is praised, and is displeased if she is not esteemed as highly as she would like. The second whelp is called *Indignatio* [Disdain]: that is, if one is scornful of anything that she seeth in another, or heareth, or if she despiseth chastisement or instruction from one lower. The third whelp is *Hypocrisis* [Hypocrisy]: that is one who maketh herself seem better than she is. The fourth is *Presumptio* [Presumption]: that is, she who undertaketh more than she can accomplish, or meddleth in things that do not fall to her. The fifth whelp is called Disobedience: that is, that child which doth not obey his parents; the underling, his prelate; the parishioner, his priest; the maid, her mistress; every inferior, his superior. The sixth whelp is *Loquacitas* [Loquacity]: she who feedeth this whelp, that is of much speaking, boasteth, and judgeth others; she lieth at times; she gabbeth, upbraideth, chideth, flattereth, stirreth laughter. The seventh whelp is Blasphemy: this whelp's nurse is she who sweareth great oaths, or curseth bitterly, or speaketh evil of God or of His saints, because of any thing that she suffereth, seeth, or heareth. The eighth whelp is Impatience: this whelp he feedeth who is not patient under all wrongs and in all evils. The ninth whelp is Contumacy: and this whelp feedeth one who is head-strong in any thing that she hath undertaken to do, be it good, be it evil, so that no wiser counsel can bring her out of her unrestrained action. Many others there are that come of wealth, and of prosperity, of high family, of handsome clothes, of wit, of beauty, of strength; of high living there waxeth pride, and of holy habits. Many more whelps than I have named the Lion

of Pride hath whelped, but of these, think and give heed very greatly, for I do but go over them lightly, and but name them.[47]

In art, through homilies, and by various teaching devices, the capital or cardinal sins were embedded in the understanding of western man for well over a thousand years, and they provided him with a way by which he could discuss himself in his relationship to others and to God in a single unified system. Any person could begin with his own besetting sin, and, by tracing its interrelationship to other sins, he would finally find himself at the core question of life—namely, his relation to God. The system of capital sins allowed one to speak of man's condition *coram deo* while at the same time describing minutely a man's troubles in relation to himself and to others.

Since the Reformation, and more pervasively since the Enlightenment, however, men and women have increasingly viewed personal problems and decisions in ways which do not reflect or derive from traditional Christian notions of life and action. Increasingly the proximate concerns of prudence rather than the ultimate concern of salvation have set the context for ethical decision. This circumstance has raised important questions of identity for the pastoral function of guiding. When men understand themselves in an intramundane context, traditional forms of pastoral guidance seem almost always irrelevant, often oppressive, and at best quaint [SEE EXHIBITS 19 AND 20]. Perplexity surrounds the question as to how pastoral guiding might maintain its historic rootage as part of Christian soul care and still creatively engage the personal motivations, decisions, and actions of modern man.

## 4.  Reconciling

"Reconciliation," as a term describing both the accomplishment of God in Christ and the service of all Christians (cf. II Cor. 5: 19ff.), has been so prominent in Christian lore that only with careful specification may it be used to designate the fourth great function of pastoral care. In its pastoral connotation, the "ministry of reconciliation" means helping alienated persons to establish or renew proper and fruitful relationships with God and neighbor. This function of the cure of souls stands alongside healing, sustaining, and guiding, but it is distinguishable from them both historically and analytically.

I. *Two Modes.*  Forgiveness and discipline are the two modes of reconciling, but they always appear in actual practice to be interdependent.

---

[47] "The Whelps of Pride," from *The Rule of Anchoresses* (*Ancrene Riwle*), ed. J. Morton (Camden Society, 1853), quoted by Roger Sherman Loomis and Rudolph Willard, *Medieval English Verse and Prose in Modernized Versions* (New York: Appleton-Century-Crofts, Inc., 1948), pp. 53–54. By permission.

On the one hand, reconciliation takes place through forgiveness, which can be a proclamation, or an announcement, or even a very simple gesture indicating that, in spite of the walls of pride and hurt which separate and alienate men, something has occurred to re-establish and reunite persons to each other and, indeed, to God. Confession and repentance may be considered necessary preconditions to forgiveness, or to the appropriation of forgiveness as a reality in the life of the alienated person. This mode will be discussed more fully below.

On the other hand, discipline as a mode of reconciling may include a fraternal word of correction, or a priestly admonition, or even sterner measures directed toward confession, repentance, and amendment of life. One of the clearest delineations of Christian pastoral discipline ever made is found in Calvin's *Institutes*:

> But because some persons, in their hatred of discipline, recoil from its very name, let them understand this: if no society, indeed, no house which has even a small family, can be kept in proper condition without discipline, it is much more necessary in the church, whose condition should be as ordered as possible. Accordingly, as the saving doctrine of Christ is the soul of the church, so does discipline serve as its sinews, through which the members of the body hold together, each in its own place. Therefore, all who desire to remove discipline or to hinder its restoration—whether they do this deliberately or out of ignorance—are surely contributing to the ultimate dissolution of the church. For what will happen if each is allowed to do what he pleases? Yet that would happen, if to the preaching of doctrine there were not added private admonitions, corrections, and other aids of the sort that sustain doctrine and do not let it remain idle. Therefore, discipline is like a bridle to restrain and tame those who rage against the doctrine of Christ; or like a spur to arouse those of little inclination; and also sometimes like a father's rod to chastise mildly and with the gentleness of Christ's Spirit those who have more seriously lapsed.[48]

In some of its other expressions, discipline appears to serve a protective purpose as well as that of goading or restraining. In this way the troubled Christian is helped to remain within the ranks of the faithful, and is thereby guarded against temptations and assaults of evil forces by admonitions and acts of support on the part of the church. Sometimes discipline has been seen as a protection not only against the devil but against the wrath of God. The so-called "Second Exhortation" in *The Book of Common Prayer* of the Episcopal Church in the United States puts this matter very succinctly. The rubric stipulates that, when the

---

[48] John Calvin, *Institutes of the Christian Religion* (IV.xii.1), ed. John T. McNeill, tr. Ford Lewis Battles ("The Library of Christian Classics," XXI, London: S. C. M. Press, Ltd.; Philadelphia: The Westminster Press, 1960), pp. 1229–1230. By permission.

minister gives warning for the celebration of the holy Communion, he may read this exhortation, or such part of it as he deems helpful. He exhorts, in part:

> And if ye shall perceive your offenses to be such as are not only against God, but also against your neighbours; then ye shall reconcile your-selves unto them; being ready to make restitution and satisfaction, ac-cording to the uttermost of your powers, for all injuries and wrongs done by you to any other; and being likewise ready to forgive others who have offended you, as ye would have forgiveness of your offenses at God's hand: for otherwise the receiving of the holy Communion doth nothing else but increase your condemnation. Therefore, if any of you be a blasphemer of God, an hinderer or slanderer of his Word, an adulterer, or be in malice, or envy, or in any other grievous crime; repent you of your sins, or else come not to that holy Table.[49]

Another type of discipline, expressed in canon law and church custom, provided a path by which troubled persons might make satisfac-tions and thus find their way back into fellowship with the church. This discipline became the condition and the means of pastoral reconciliation, yet it was designed for the alleviation of trouble. At times the church clearly marked the channels through which men and women who had bruised and abused one another could, under God, find their way to-gether again. The ancient Canons of the Council of Nicaea in A.D. 325 provided that those who had been excommunicated because of their lapse under the persecution of Licinius were to do penance of three years' "hearing," which meant that they were to stand in the narthex of the church during services and were not permitted to come into the main sanctuary. Afterwards they were to do seven years' "kneeling"; they could kneel during services within the nave amidst the standing congregation. Then there was a prescribed period as "co-standers," during which the penitent could join normally in the services with others, except that he could not receive the sacrament of the altar. Finally, full reconciliation was accomplished. While the provisions seem harsh to us today, they were in reality a fine ritual for reconciliation—commonly accepted pro-cedures by which the wayward and straying could belong again to the fellowship of the church.

II. *Forgiveness in Church History.* Reconciling as a function of the ministry of the cure of souls has had an interesting historical de-velopment. It is helpful to mark its changes in emphasis through the years, for its history gives a perspective on present dilemmas and also helps to clarify modern vocabulary and concepts.

As early as the second epoch of Christian pastoring, and especially in the writings of some of the classical fathers, such as Origen and

---

[49] *The Book of Common Prayer* (American), p. 87.

Tertullian, one discerns four main elements in pastoral reconciliation. First there was *preparation*, or spiritual counsel, which might be given by any Christian and was designed to help the believer decide whether or not he needed the potent medicine of public confession; if so, the counseling helped him prepare for the ordeal. Then followed the *confession* itself, called "exomologesis," or public confession before the entire congregation [SEE EXHIBIT 2]. Third, *penance* was done publicly and openly before pagans and Christians alike. During the time of the penance, the penitent was excommunicated from the central act of Christian worship, the Eucharist. After a suitable penance had been done, *reconciliation* to God and with the church was thought to have been accomplished and the bishop received the sinner back into communion with prayer and a blessing.

The early church considered public confession before the congregation as the norm, but the practice was eroded by the reluctance on the part of many of the faithful to resort to it. But before the advent of the penitentials, the center of interest and focus in the act of reconciliation was the *confession* itself. Tertullian thought confession had enormous therapeutic value. With the coming of the penitentials, however, and the consequent shift to private confession, the center of therapeutic power was seen in the doing of *penance* [SEE EXHIBIT 7]. The early medieval penitentials assumed that the church through its priesthood was wise and knowledgeable enough to diagnose and to assign the proper remedy for spiritual faults, but the substance of penitential medicine was itself profane as well as sacred. The penitentials prescribed all kinds of remedies for spiritual and worldly ills. These included prayers, recitations, postures, dietary restrictions, sexual abstinence, and so forth, and for very grave offenses, like murder, a penitent might be assigned a penance of living the remainder of his life in a monastery. Normally the sinner worked out his own salvation in the affairs of his daily life.

By the thirteenth century, however, there gained ascendancy the idea that the sacrament of penance itself exercised a reconciling power that was vested in the church and dispensed by its priesthood. When this happened, interest focused on the last element of forgiveness, which became known as the *absolution*. Absolution as a sacramental power was itself the remedy, and penance became no more the medicine to remedy sin but a satisfaction for sin by which the temporal penalties incurred by misdoings were shortened or avoided. The modern Roman Catholic understanding of confession has come to rest on the idea that it is done in order to obtain the absolution. Prümmer stated that *"The essential form* of the sacrament of Confession" is the verbal formula, "I then absolve you of your sins in the name of the Father, and of the Son, and of the Holy Ghost." This sacrament "duly received" by the penitent, he claimed, not only effects "the remission of all sin and eternal punishment" but "the infusion (or increase) of sanctifying grace, the virtues and the gifts of the Holy Ghost," and "the revival of all merits previously acquired in the state of grace."[50]

The Protestant Reformation attained a general consensus on two attitudes in regard to confession. It was not to be compulsory, and it was not necessarily made orally to an ordained minister. The Latin Catholic Church had ruled that each member of the faithful was to confess to his own priest at least once each year. This rule the Protestant Reformation rejected in favor of general confessions made by the congregation in the context of its regular worship.

Beyond this agreement, each reformer and his followers went his own way, emphasizing this or that aspect of confession and the dangers to be avoided. Joseph Hall, the Anglican Bishop of Norwich, wrote in 1628 a treatise called, "The Old Religion," in which he found it necessary to discuss the novelty of permitting absolution before penance. He wrote:

> But now, immediately upon the Confession made, the hand is laid upon the Penitent, and he is received to his right of communion; and, after his absolution, certain works of piety are enjoined him, for the chastisement of the flesh, and expurgation of the remainders of sin. . . .
>
> In common apprehension, this new order can be no other than preposterous . . . like Easter before Lent.[51]

Luther emphasized the helpfulness of confession in the reconciling of men to God and to one another, and he held to the conviction that confession was to be a mutual act in which the faithful were to "priest" each other in hearing confessions and in proclaiming the pardon won for believers in Jesus Christ. In 1520 he wrote:

> Of private confession . . . I am heartily in favor . . . for it is a cure without an equal for distressed consciences. For when we have laid bare our conscience to our brother and privately made known to him the evil that lurked within, we receive from our brother's lips the word of comfort spoken by God Himself; and, if we accept it in faith, we find peace in the mercy of God speaking to us through our brother.[52]

III. *Calvin and Church Discipline.* The continental Reformed tradition of the Rhineland and Low Countries took very seriously the

---

[50] Dominic M. Prümmer, *Handbook of Moral Theology*, tr. Gerald W. Shelton, ed. John Gavin Nolan (New York: P. J. Kenedy & Sons, 1957), pp. 294, 296. By permission.

[51] Joseph Hall, "The Old Religion," IX.4, *Works*, ed. Josiah Pratt (10 vols., London: Printed by C. Whittingham, 1808), IX, 277.

[52] Martin Luther, *The Babylonian Captivity of the Church*, tr. A. T. W. Steinhaeuser, *Works of Martin Luther* (6 vols., Philadelphia: Muhlenberg Press, 1943), II, 250. By permission.

ministry of reconciling as a function of the cure of souls. Calvin returned to Geneva in 1541 only after he had been convinced by the city fathers that they were serious in their determination to make it a godly and Christian city. Geneva was to be a model of Protestant Christendom in which Protestant ideals and understandings were to hold sway. There were to be four classes of ministers: pastors, teachers, deacons, and elders. The elders, who were to make "fraternal corrections," held a remarkable place in the organization of the church and in the administration of the city; in them Calvin provided for an order of lay spiritual directors. The elders were appointed by the city magistrates and were to be selected from the various districts of the city on the basis of their good character and spiritual wisdom. Their task was to watch over the lives of all the people and to guide and lovingly admonish the disorderly and erring.

Where it was necessary, stronger measures could be employed in a particularly difficult case by calling in the Genevan church Consistory for consultation and assistance. The Consistory included all the ministers and the other elders; it was the principal organ of church discipline, and over it Calvin or another minister presided. McNeill stated that "Weekly, on Thursday mornings, offenders noted by the watchful elders were haled by a police officer before the Consistory. They were often privately counseled and admonished in advance by Calvin or another minister." Then discussion before the entire Consistory would ensue and appropriate corrective measures would be taken for the good of the offender. "The records of the Consistory and of the councils exhibit extraordinary minuteness and variety in the offenses reported for correction. Non-attendance at church . . . hankering after medieval religious practices . . . drunkenness, gambling, profanity, family alienations, wife beating and adultery" show in the records. Like admonition, much of the correction sought to imitate the early Christian acts of penance. In many instances, the prescribed remedy effected a real correction of behavior and attitude and achieved reconciliation with God and fellow man.[53] The Geneva experiment was by far the most interesting and creative attempt in the Reformation to revive disciplinary reconciliation as a part of the cure of souls. In no other Christian tradition has this mode of reconciliation achieved such refinement as it did with the Calvinists.

Discipline as a mode of the pastoral function of reconciling nevertheless encountered many failures in Geneva, even during Calvin's tenure as chief administrator of the church there. Discipline became narrow and hardened until it degenerated into correction by legalism, while personal admonition tended toward accusation. In the first place, Calvin could not conceive of the church apart from an intimate connection with the civil authorities. Geneva was to be a little Christendom with

---

[53] John T. McNeill, *The History and Character of Calvinism* (New York: Oxford University Press, 1957), p. 165. By permission.

built-in lines of authority and responsibility between the church and government. Structurally there was little distinction between concerns for individual needs and concerns for the peace, order, and good morals of the city. The aim of individual growth tended to be subordinated to claims of institutional maintenance. Moreover, Genevan church life was harassed and threatened in a world full of turmoil and contention, and it was not able to tolerate the anxiety which accompanies any serious attempt to make room for human failure in the interest not only of humaneness but of healing and growth. Genevan Calvinists were always tempted to clamp down on situations when therapeutic interests called for patience and flexibility. Finally, Geneva tried to solve its disciplinary dilemmas by banishment, incarceration, and even burning.

The left wing of the Reformation, including the Congregationalists, Baptists, Quakers, and, later, the Methodists, laid stress on the mutual responsibility of the members of the church for each other's physical and spiritual welfare. Modern protestantism has often rightly been accused of excessive individualism; however, at various times in the course of history, all these left-wing groups have shown a lively and serious interest in open confession before either the entire congregation or various groups within the membership. The group, after hearing the confession, would then pool its wisdom and concern for the correction and restoration of the erring brother. The early Methodists were especially interested in this form of group therapy. Out of their "classes" and "societies" certain individuals were drawn together under "a more strictly remedial discipline." Into the "bands" were invited "people who especially 'needed to pour out their hearts' to one another. . . . Each member, beginning with the leader, was to confess his faults and temptations and the state of his soul, and to accept criticism. In order to be admitted to the group each had to declare his desire to be told all his faults, even if this should 'cut to the quick.' "[54]

It was left-wing protestantism which was able by and large to move beyond theoretical formulations of a priesthood of all believers to a reconciling ministry of pastoral care performed by the laity, as an integral part of the formal life of the congregation. The following excerpts are taken from the records of Mount Tabor Baptist Church in Kentucky:

Third Saturday in July 1803,

The Church met and after worship, proceeded to do business; 1st A report was brot against Sister Arnett, for drinking too much, and it appears she is guilty, we therefore, appoint Sisters Baugh, Philips, and Clack, to cite her to our next meeting. . . .

---

[54] John T. McNeill, *A History of the Cure of Souls* (New York: Harper and Row, Publishers, Incorporated, 1951), p. 279. By permission.

### Third Friday in August 1803

The Church met and after worship proceeded to business, 1st The committee appointed to labour with and cite sister Arnett to this meeting, Report they acted agreable to the order of the Church, and say she appear,d to be humble, and very sorry for what she had done, therefore the Church restore her to fellowship[.][55]

IV. *Modern Desuetude of Reconciling.* There are many indications that the function of reconciling as a creative and meaningful part of Christian pastoral care has fallen upon evil days. Perhaps more than the other three functions of the cure of souls, reconciling has suffered from misunderstanding and erosion.

In his provocative and helpful book, *Preface to Pastoral Theology*, Seward Hiltner argued that the ministry of reconciliation, which he called by the generic term "church discipline," abrogates the pastoral posture. He claimed that

> the original intention of Christian discipline was *equally* to bring back the offender and to preserve the church. . . . [W]ith the growth of the church as a social institution the emphasis swung heavily to discipline for the sake of the church—with the assumption that what was good for the church was bound to be good for the offender.

Finally, "When what was 'good for the church' acquired associations of power over people . . . ," then the function of discipline as soul care became secondary.[56] Because the motive of church purity always attended the function of reconciling, some important figures in the Protestant pastoral tradition did, indeed, consider the matter of scandal so seriously that they neglected to be equally concerned with the individual needs of people.

Richard Baxter, for example, in *The Reformed Pastor* was sensitive to the fact that a great deal of skill is required in matters of reconciling, yet his attitude toward the lax and the sinners seems harsh and intolerant. After some remarks about exerting skill in administering discipline, he advocated confronting most sinners in such a way as to shake their hearts to make them see the evil and bad effects of sin on themselves and on God. Baxter was convinced that to neglect discipline would corrupt Christianity in the eyes of the world and make worldlings believe "that

---

[55] "MSS. Volume of Mount Tabor Church, 1798–1870," in William Warren Sweet, *Religion on the American Frontier, The Baptists 1783–1830, A Collection of Source Material* (Chicago: University of Chicago Press, 1931), pp. 260–261. By permission.

[56] Seward Hiltner, *Preface to Pastoral Theology* (Nashville: Abingdon Press, 1958), p. 65; see also pp. 66–68. By permission.

Christ is no more for holiness than Satan, or that the Christian religion exacteth holiness no more than the false religions of the world."[57]

In the Catholic tradition, reconciling has tended to be thought of at times not so much as a means to keep the congregation unspotted, but rather as *quid pro quo* punishment. This tendency was especially noticeable when, by commutation of penance, penalties were compressed into briefer and more tolerable ones, and when by composition the terms of the penance were converted into money payments. "By the tenth century commutation and composition were widely accepted as normal elements in penance."[58]

Both the Protestant and Catholic developments here noted are, indeed, antithetical to reconciling as a legitimate mode of the cure of souls. In protestantism, reconciling in the mode of discipline has been discredited by excesses and failures of the Calvinistic system. The Catholic Inquisition, too, was an experiment in church discipline as a mode of pastoral reconciling which the Western world at large has looked upon with revulsion. Fashioned in the thirteenth century for detection and suppression of heresy, this movement enlisted inquisitors who approached sinners and heretics in the hope that they might be cured of their errors and returned to the fold of the faithful [SEE EXHIBIT 11]. Eventually it collapsed as a humane and fit instrument for reconciling, in large part owing to pastoral pride. Thinking themselves acting only for the salvation of the souls of the accused, inquisitors felt warranted in dispensing with rigorous legal codes for dealing with persons charged with heresy or error. Thus, torture and even death could be resorted to as appropriate stratagems by which to deal with the principalities of darkness that engulfed certain souls. Ironically, had the judge-confessors not thought of themselves as pastors but as officers of the law, and thus had they acted in strict accordance with civil rules of evidence and legal procedure, the Inquisition might have escaped the enormities into which it fell.[59]

Also, a most serious failure occurred in the mode of reconciling by forgiveness. As administrators of confession, penance, and absolution, the clergy have been restrained from professional practices that might have furthered their own growth in the art of hearing confessions and assigning penances. One of the tragedies in the history of the cure of souls has resulted from the strict secrecy imposed upon confessors, to the extent that neither supervision of the practice nor any discussion of concrete pastoral situations could develop. When in 1215 the Catholic Church

---

57 Richard Baxter, *The Reformed Pastor*, ed. Hugh Martin (London: SCM Press Ltd., 1956; Richmond, Va.: John Knox Press, 1963), p. 62.

58 McNeill, *A History of the Cure of Souls*, p. 124. By permission.

59 Henry Charles Lea, *A History of the Inquisition of the Middle Ages* (3 vols., New York: Harper & Brothers, 1888), I, 399ff.

required each of its faithful to say his confession at least once each year to his own parish priest, the tradition of absolute secrecy was in full force. Canon 21 of the Fourth Lateran Council, which made this practice binding throughout Western Christendom, stipulated that every believer who had reached the age of discretion must make a full annual confession of his sins to the local priest and must perform his penance dutifully. Failure to comply with this provision, and with its accompanying rule requiring at least annual Communion, resulted in banishment from the church and in prohibition of Christian burial. Only with the local parish priest's permission might a believer make his confession to an outside priest, who otherwise could not absolve him. Any priest who revealed by word or sign what had been confessed to him earned for himself the severest ecclesiastical penalties.[60]

Regardless of the particular circumstances that evoked these strictures, the ministry of pastoral forgiveness has paid heavily for the fact that they made it impossible for spiritual guides to learn their art from the records of specific cases of reconciling by forgiveness. The fact that the modern helping professions have been able to share and transmit wisdom gained in concrete experience has been a priceless possession. Only so—by learning from actual experiences of masters—can apprentices become journeymen. In these modern professions, the more difficult cases can have the benefit of pooled wisdom; especially talented practitioners can be certified and unqualified ones can be debarred—all because of a freedom from absolute secrecy that does not violate confidences. The result of the church's rigidity in this matter has been that, on the Catholic side, penance continues to be a formalized affair done in a rather perfunctory manner by the mass of the faithful, while, on the Protestant side, only a handful of charismatically gifted persons are able to be creative confessors.

In response to the church's dilemmas in regard to the reconciling ministry, a provocative voice has been raised recently by O. Hobart Mowrer, a research psychologist, who stands horrified at what he believes to be the church's captivity to Freudian understandings of human troubles, especially guilt. Mowrer believes that guilt is the major affliction of man today, and that in and behind the troubles which men experience with each other lie the profound realization and the reality that one has broken his responsibility and trust for his fellow human beings.[61]

In our own time, the weakness of reconciling as a function of pas-

---

[60] See Oscar D. Watkins, *A History of Penance* (London: Longmans, Green and Co., 1920), pp. 748–749.

[61] Mowrer has published several writings that express these views, especially the article, "Even There, Thy Hand," *The Chicago Theological Seminary Register*, LII:1 (January 1962), 1–17; see also Ross Snyder, "Toward What is Mowrer in Motion?" *ibid.*, pp. 17–21.

toral care is obvious. There is no place in the structure and rhythm of the life of modern congregations where a serious discussion concerning the state of one's soul is expected. At one time confession and penance in the Catholic tradition, and in the Protestant church the pastor's periodic inquiry about one's readiness for the Communion, served that purpose. The clergyman met his people for a kind of conversation that did not mistake itself for idle chit-chat or organization talk but concerned itself with the current issues of the world and one's place in it as a Christian. With the loss of this role, the clergyman must extemporize as he goes along. This is not an impossibility, but it requires special personal gifts. In this situation many clergymen feel deeply that much of the counseling they do puts them in the class of the amateur psychiatrist or social worker. Part of the reason for this anxiety may be the feeling that usual pastoral routines provide no contact with alienated people face to face in situations that define the minister as one who is alerted to and talented in a certain kind of spiritual conversation that can knit together broken bonds between God and man. This extemporizing virtually deprives the church of its ministry of pastoral reconciling at a time when alienation is at the root of much human woe and anxiety.

PART 4

# PASTORAL CARE
# PAST AND PRESENT

## 1. Summary

In the foregoing pages definitions have been adumbrated of pastoral care in its various functions and their modes, the major historical epochs of Christian pastoring have been delineated, and each of the four functions has been described in detail. These definitions, delineations, and descriptions arose from reflecting upon an enormous corpus of documents that record the manifold ways in which pastoring has taken place throughout nineteen centuries of Christian experience. A representative sample of pastoral records has been selected as exhibits, which comprise Part Five of this book. These exhibits, in fact, represent each of the eight major epochs of pastoral care, and they richly illustrate the four functions of pastoral care in their several modes. Notwithstanding, care has been taken not to force them into any fixed mold. They are presented chronologically, with just enough introductory comment to enable the less expert reader to study each excerpt in its own historical context. The authors invite the reader to draw his own conclusion, to disagree with or qualify their analyses, and, hopefully, to find himself incited to explore on his own the vast regions of recorded pastoral care. The main aim of this book is to introduce ideas, to incite interest, and to invite insights—not to reach definitive judgments. Nevertheless, it is appropriate to indicate several themes, correctives, and opportunities which the past of Christian pastoring presses upon those presently concerned with the helping professions. Whether or not the past teaches lessons that might regulate the future, it is palpable that the present may profit from a broad perspective upon the past.

A historic perspective upon pastoral care yields a few notable estimates of the present state of pastoring. The most obvious and primary of these is that, throughout the Christian pastoral experience down to recent times, ritual has played a substantially important role in the performance of the four major pastoral functions. Modern pastoral disregard for its ritual inheritance represents the sharpest discontinuity with the great tradition of pastoring. Whether this discontinuity frees or merely impoverishes modern pastors is a value judgment that every reader is entitled to make for himself. However, one of the lessons of history is that when pastoral ritual diminishes, pastoral authority proportionately wanes.

Second, two particular confusions permeate the modern pastoral profession. On the one hand, there has been a blurring and over-generalization of the entire pastoral ministry. When pastoral specificity is lost, ordained ministers tend to interpret their institutionally administrative, publicly sacerdotal, and homiletical and educational functions as synonymous with pastoral care. On the other hand, the loss of specific pastoral authority and the generalization of pastoral work have thrown pastors back upon the patterns, procedures, and functions of the various other helping professions. Pastors who in this age have imitated doctors, lawyers, psychiatrists, psychologists, counselors, and social workers, like pastors who imitated the current helping professions of other ages, frequently become merely incompetent amateurs or inexpert apprentices in arts properly belonging to others. Pastoral care as a helping profession assumes a posture that distinguishes it from the institutional, liturgical, homiletical, and educational functions of the ministerial profession, and this distinction is sharpened—not blurred—by the fact that the pastoral role derives its authority from the exercise of the public ministerial roles. As pastors lead their congregations in prayer and worship and exhortation, they renew and re-symbolize their ability to be representative persons bearing the wisdom, resources, and authority of Christian faith. No other helping profession in our society possesses a ready way to exhibit ritually its representation of a distinct tradition of helping.

Third, our survey of the history of pastoral care suggests that much modern agitation over the incursions of the regnant popular or academic psychology into the arena of the church's helping work is tilting at windmills. In every historic epoch, pastoring has utilized—and by utilizing has helped to advance and transform—the psychology or psychologies current in that epoch. Those who would object that modern pastoral use of contemporaneous psychology betrays the Christian tradition are, in fact, themselves the innovators. Nowhere in history has Christianity adumbrated solely from its own lore a distinct psychology, either theoretically or popularly understood. To appreciate traditional pastoring is to stand ready to adopt and adapt current psychological insights and applications without abdicating the distinctly pastoral role.

Finally, a study of the history of pastoral care strongly suggests that the function of reconciling is the most viable and the readiest of all pastoral ministrations in our age. Many indications point to reconciling as the polarizing function which is emerging in our transitional times. Sustaining is the function least jostled by the forces of transition, and its old modes and means continue to recommend themselves. Healing stands in great confusion because non-pastoral healing professions have learned both to encompass and to outstrip pastoral methods of healing. Probably modern pastors focus upon the guiding function more sharply than upon the other three, but they do so as amateurs imitative of other psychotherapeutical artists who accomplish their work in contexts that are liberated from traditional and antiquated Christian moral values. Meanwhile, modern studies of the mental health needs of Americans, together with modern assessments of the limitations of various non-pastoral helping professions, suggest that in the area of reconciling a strong felt need has arisen for pastoral ministrations, and, at the same time, that no effective substitute for such pastoring exists in the other helping professions. Much of the rich history of pastoral reconciling stands ready to be recaptured and applied to modern circumstances; thus, it seems to the present writers that the most opportune function today is that of reconciling.

In summary, we find four lessons in the history of pastoral care. Ritual is an indispensable pastoral procedure which renews pastoral authority. Pastoral care is distinct from other ministerial work and is distinct from the work of other helping professions. Pastoral care has always utilized current psychologies and produces no unique psychology of its own. Reconciling is the most opportune pastoral function today. While we are sensitive to the fact that other students may fairly reach other conclusions, we now conclude our essay by discussing briefly each of these four matters.

## 2. Ritual in Pastoral Care

Sooner or later in the process of history, each of the four functions of the cure of souls came to express itself in established and enduring ritual practices. Despite the pervasive modern desire to rationalize aspects of life which previous generations ritualized, the ritualization of every feature of pastoral helping is probably the most striking lesson to be learned from a historical view of this profession. Most of the attached exhibits show ways in which pastoral ritual expressed itself. From quite early times and on, rituals for anointing with oil and for exorcising evil spirits gave ceremonial articulation to the pastoral ministry of healing. Rituals for sustaining are richly exemplified in the "art of dying" literature that was prolific during the later Middle Ages and the Renaissance [SEE EXHIBIT 10]. Guiding expressed itself ceremonially in planned spiritual retreats [SEE EXHIBIT 14] and in forms for auricular confession [SEE EXHIBIT 19]. Reconciling was communicated and enacted by exomologesis [SEE EXHIBIT 2], and a particularly fine later example is found in the liturgy for public repentance developed by John Knox [SEE EXHIBIT 15].

Pastoral care is exercised by representative Christian persons whose authority is normally established by the ritual of ordination, and in some communions this authority is liturgically renewed whenever a clergyman enters a pastoral relationship with a new congregation. Moreover, the ordained pastor—the norm if not the monopolist of the representative Christian person—repeatedly renews and sustains his pastoral authority through his involvement in numerous ritualistic acts that publicize him as a ceremonial person.

Down to the day before yesterday, this ritual way of proceeding has spontaneously and naturally expressed itself in the means by which pastors have dealt with troubled persons. That is, the ritually established authority of the pastor's public ministries carried over to his private ministry throughout the great tradition. Probably more than anything else, this ritual establishment, renewal, and exercise of the pastor's role as a representative Christian person, bearing the resources, wisdom, and authority of the Christian faith, have set pastoral care apart from the work of other helping persons. Neither in the past nor in the present has any other helping profession been so firmly or so repeatedly grounded in the liturgical action of a community of persons sharing a common vision of life. Just as the pastor's authority is founded and nurtured in ritual, so the fulness of his helping power has been—and can be—brought to bear ritualistically.

In fact, no human group, secular or religious, can function or endure without ritual, and the ceremonial feature of pastoral care touches and evokes something both primitive and pervasive in human life. By ritual a group becomes conscious of itself and of what it believes. Through emblem and symbol, ritual dramatizes what a group presupposes and cherishes, what it celebrates, and to what it aspires. Ritual gives living immediacy to a group's *raison d'être*. Christian ceremonies of healing, such as unction, enact the conviction that the author and donor of health of soul and body is God, in whom the sick Christian finds hope of healing. Christian sustaining nurtures the dying believer in his travail by means of dramatized belief in life after death and rewards in heaven for the faithful. Ceremonial reconciliation, whether in the mode of discipline or of forgiveness, elaborates actually the reknitting of alienated, broken relationships with God and with fellow man.

Moreover, ritual produces and expresses consensus, no more in the peace-making dance ceremony of the Andaman Islanders[62] than in the demonstrative action described by Tertullian in the process of reconciliation by public confession [SEE EXHIBIT 2]. An interesting example of the power of ritual to make and display consensus is found in Knox's order for public repentance [SEE EXHIBIT 15], where individual dissent is rendered odious; this liturgy admonishes the congregation in these words:

> Now only rests, that you remit and forget all offenses which you have conceived heretofore by the sin and fall of this our brother; accept and embrace him as a member of Christ's body; let none take upon him-[self] to reproach or accuse him for any offenses that before this hour he has committed. And that he may have the better assurance of your good will and reconciliation, prostrate yourselves before God and render him thanks for the conversion and repentance of this our brother.

Foolhardy indeed would be that member of the congregation who took upon himself to hold a grudge against the penitent after these stern words and earnest actions; the penitent reconciled by this ritual not only *felt* restored to God and man—indeed, he *was* restored.

One of the values of pastoral ritual arises from its power to channel action by establishing patterns for predictable behavior. As a prescribed way of acting in disturbing situations such as those that call for pastoral care, ritual provides a map making explicit the "right" or expected and reliable action at the very moment when it is most difficult to invent appropriate ways of behaving. The ever-unprecedented situation of dying provides occasion so troubling that, lacking some map for action, persons may flounder or fall into isolation or immobility; in past ages, Christian rituals for dying provided ways by which one might participate familiarly with his neighbors and family in his own demise. There have been well-established, ritual, "right" ways to die, and also "right" ways for mourners to act before and interact with the dying man. He and his intimates might respond to each other helpfully through an interpersonal litany that assists the dying man to perform acceptably his last and most crucial act. Without such ritual behavior, the dread situation tends to paralyze both the dying man and those who yearn both to sustain him and to learn how to die themselves.

Ritual or "right" ways of coping with acute and unprecedented situations are demanded by the very nature of crises. Crises are special

---

[62] See A. R. Radcliffe-Brown, "The Nature and Functions of Ceremonials," in *Theories of Society*, ed. by T. Parsons *et al.* (2 vols., Glencoe, Ill.: The Free Press, 1961), II, 1193.

situations in which previously learned responses are no longer effective and operative. We die but once. Major illnesses may be our lot but a few times. Only the professional mourner learns by practice to be a good mourner. Rituals for such crises provide patterns that, in spite of the danger of formalism, allow participation and communication by unpracticed people, and they tend to ameliorate helplessness and guilt at a time when personal inventiveness for communication may be most depleted and unreliable.

This high evaluation of ritual in pastoral care by no means leaves out of account the possibility of ritual failures. Formalism is a deterioration of once richly significant ceremonial into mere routine. Symbols can become mere shells and ritualistic acts can become empty, irrelevant forms. Much auricular confession in our time is, as few, even of its advocates, would deny, perfunctory and mechanical, and thus for many a meaningless gesture. Rituals like that of exorcism have been evacuated of once profound meaning and are rarely performed today, while others, like unction, have been transformed into uses nearly opposite to their original purposes. Quite beyond and less obvious than formalism is the more general failure of ceremonial paucity. Pastoral care today suffers less from ritual perfunctoriness than from ritual paucity. The individualism and spiritual inwardness that characterized the era of pastoral care immediately preceding our period of transition mustered little enthusiasm for ceremonial acts and broadly suspected the group solidarity out of which ritual arises. This attitude has eroded ritual resources in significant areas of the ministry of soul care. Our age is one in which society ritualizes in divorce proceedings the rupture of marital relationships, but the pastoral ministry of reconciliation stands bereft of rituals for reconciliation of marital relationships suffering disruption. Broader areas of human alienation cry out for the means by which to dramatize the end of enmity, however temporary the suspension of alienation may be.

Few would doubt that one of the most effective modern ritual actions for helping troubled persons is seen in the operations of Alcoholics Anonymous, whose meetings consist of ritualized means of sustaining and reconciling and are masterful blends of stereotyped action and free expression. In this respect "A. A." stands in sharp and embarrassing judgment on the church's timidity and confusion over therapeutic ritual.

Even where it is agreed that ritualistic action during times of personal calamity would be therapeutic, the type of ritual which would be appropriate remains a matter of continuing debate. What is to be done— literally, *what is to be done*—in times of acute bereavement? From a point of view frequently advocated by physicians, rest and quiet are needed and are achieved often by sedatives. Contrariwise, some mental health theorists insist that this sedation of the bereaved interferes with or delays normal and necessary grief work. The development of meaningful pastoral ritual depends upon a growing consensus between the different helping practitioners who engage a given troubled client—the doctor, the lawyer, the counselor, the psychiatrist, the social worker, and the pastor. How and where can this consensus arise in the modern mélange of specialization, divergent traditions, conflicting vocabularies, and in the uncertain state of present knowledge about mental health problems? When in certain eras churchly understandings, insights, and procedures dominated, it was simple to know what one ought to do and when, in connection with a host of personal problems. Today such is not the case. The rapid pace of research, the burgeoning of the mental health professions, and the stubbornness of modern philosophical quandaries make difficult any agreement as to what symptoms have positive value for human growth and what are malignant; when and where rebellion is therapeutic and when and where it is deleterious; what anxiety and fear mean in connection with maturity and regression, and so forth. In our culture at the present time, these and many related questions await consensual answers, and it is extremely difficult to determine what might be "right" ritualistic action even in situations, like bereavement, where "right" ritual would be desirable.[63]

What does this failure in consensus signify for pastoral care today, especially in connection with ritual? Is ours a time of transition, a prelude to a new day of unity of understandings, an overture to the discovery of new and creative pastoral rituals? Who will be the chief mental health ritualists of the future—physicians, marriage counselors, social workers, psychiatrists, or pastors? Will pastors be able to discover rituals of soul care appropriate and viable for this day, rituals that will speak from deep within Christian witness and at the same time share in the understandings of other practitioners in the healing arts? These questions are not rhetorical. They lead not to firm answers, but to the suggestion of opportunities for continuing discussion and exploration. That ritual acts are powerful means of pastoral healing, guiding, sustaining, and reconciling troubled persons there can be no doubt. Pastoral care may either rediscover from its great tradition the appropriateness of ritual to its ministrations, or it may forfeit ritual to the other helping professions.

## 3.  Pastoral Care in Transition

The predicaments, fashions, and experimentations of Christian pastoral care in our century all indicate that ours is a transitional period, characterized by confusion as to the nature, purpose, and functions of

---

[63] See Orrin E. Klapp, *Ritual and Cult* ("Annals of American Sociology," Washington, D.C.: Public Affairs Press, 1956), esp. pp. 33–35; and Robert N. Wilson, "Disaster and Mental Health," in *Man and Society in Disaster*, ed. G. W. Baker and D. W. Chapman (New York: Basic Books, Inc., 1962).

pastoral care, and by willingness to experiment with new methods, modes, and techniques.

One force that thrusts modern pastoral care into its predicament is the serious rethinking of human trouble and therapy that preoccupies and stimulates our generation. Modern man senses keenly the ambiguities of his existence and plumbs the profundities out of which these ambiguities spring. Moderns marvel at the inexhaustible inventiveness and ingenuity that people display in involving themselves in troubles and predicaments, and, as a corollary, we stand in awe of the helping professions and healing arts that seem able to make many of these hurts endurable or escapable. We look back to such seminal nineteenth-century thinkers as Kierkegaard, Nietzsche, Freud, and Dostoyevsky with appreciation for their recognition that human problems bubble up irresistibly from the deeps of human existence, that life itself is a ferment of hurts. But even yesterday's prophets have not fully foretold our today. Surely pastoral care will reflect the confusions and yearnings that accompany such transitions.

Yet as perceptions, identifications, and descriptions of man come to be focused ever more sharply upon personal troubles themselves, the very concreteness with which the helping professions approach their work raises the demand for more—and more expert—helping persons. In the general field of mental health, for example, much past and most present thinking searches for diagnoses and remedies for persons beset by mental unhealth, and professional helpers are tragically scarce. Newer insights into the mental health movement as designed to aid in releasing creative human potentialities would, of course, demand a vast multiplication of a working force highly trained and expert. The same short-handedness plagues virtually every helping profession, and similar reorientations increase the demand for trained workers. In these circumstances, pastoral care as a helping profession need never fear that it will be left high and dry with no significant assistance that it can render.

The hard task that lies ahead for pastoral care is not so much to find need for its services, but rather to come to understand itself as having quite definite services to render. From this task it has been distracted by much fashionable current literature that portrays pastoral care as the funnel through which flows the totality of the life and work of the Christian church. We have defined and described pastoral functions in an effort to distinguish them clearly from the church's liturgical, homiletical, educational, institutional, evangelistic, and community responsibilities. For we believe that, important as are these other endeavors, they are, in fact, distinct from the work of pastoral care. Moreover, we have tried to make a clear demarcation between the pastor as a professional helping person and his colleagues in other helping professions such as medicine, law, psychiatry, social rehabilitation, and counseling. These others the pastor cannot be, and insofar as he simply imitates their postures, he abdicates his own. Pastoral care's task is to find itself as *one* specific posture employing certain special functions, and then to discover in its work with individual human beings in real-life situations how its resources actually help troubled persons.

Another force driving pastoral care to confusions is the general religious uncertainty of our day. The wisdom, the resources, and the authority of Christian religion are shifting sands in the sea of modernity. Christian faith as practiced and understood and lived out by our grandparents, we must admit, speaks a language largely out of tune with the speech of today. We must be willing to face the probability that inherited Christian faith knows few of the questions and few of the answers by which to understand and help modern individuals in trouble. For example, Christian faith has built much of its wisdom, resources, and authority on the notion that a sharp and self-evident line between life and death may be taken for granted. Now, advances in sciences allied to the practice of medicine and surgery distinguish between biological death and clinical death and see both of these as relative, not fixed, entities. Traditional Christian faith has drawn sharp lines between good and bad, lines that are blurred for anybody who takes seriously Dostoyevsky's insight into the dialectical relationship between personal good and personal evil which makes mockery of an older morality, to say nothing of moralism. Moreover, modern man's full-fledged acceptance of responsibility for the destiny of mankind, and perhaps even for the future of life on this planet, can have little use for the traditional Christian distinctions between temporal and eternal realms of being and activity. Moderns sense so keenly the difficulties of accomplishing man-to-man reconciliation that the traditional Christian emphasis upon man's reconciliation to a personal being called God pales into relative irrelevance or falls toward the end of the agenda of human concerns. However much these developments may be deplored by apologetical and dogmatic theology, they constitute the real-life situation of most modern men and women, including not only troubled persons but also the pastors who would help them.

Therefore, while healing, guiding, sustaining, and reconciling troubled individuals still command the concern and energy of representative Christian persons, profound doubts have arisen to question whether the wisdom, resources, and authority of Christian faith determine a proper posture from which to help troubled people. Humbled by these developments and dubieties, our generation tends to investigate the pastoral posture itself, and in their confusion and openness pastors tend to apprentice themselves to journeymen in the helping arts of medicine, psychiatry, social work, education, penology, counseling, and so forth. In many respects, this has been an exciting and fructifying restlessness. However, it is our recommendation that, just as these other helping arts must in our time undergo rethinking and reorientation in relation to their own traditions, so must pastoral care as a distinct helping art. At least, a first tentative step in that direction would be to re-appreciate and re-appropriate the grand tradition of Christian pastoring. Thus, we deplore most of all the growing sense of discontinuity, the tendency to assume the irrelevancy of the past, which these developments engender. We plead that an historical perspective be allowed to enrich the current dialogue between pastoral care and the other helping professions and arts.

## 4.   Pastoral Care and Pastoral Psychologies

Throughout its history, Christian pastoral care has borrowed from the societies in which it lived and has adapted to its pastoral use various theories of the human soul. In only one epoch, in the West from the time of Charlemagne until the beginnings of the Renaissance, did the church dominate intellectual and scholarly endeavor sufficiently to generate the philosophical understandings of mind and soul which shaped pastoral practice. In most of the historical epochs of pastoring, non-churchly agencies have devised the theoretical psychologies that pastors employed in their work.

Academic or theoretical thought about the nature of man has been but one of two equally important sources of pastoral psychology. Pastors' encounters with concrete vicissitudes have enabled pastoral psychology to adopt popular ideas of human troubles. These unsophisticated notions of the origin, dynamic, and cure of human woe always have paralleled, sometimes have lagged behind, and frequently have contradicted the regnant academic psychologies. In our own times, for example, psychological understandings developed by Sigmund Freud still command attention, although they are far from evoking consensus, among academicians. Practitioners of the pastoral arts seldom encounter human problems expressed in terms of Freud's own theories. Rather, they meet a popular vocabulary of the soul that is influenced by Freud's thought in a vague, unsophisticated way. Any comments upon the history of pastoral psychology as it relates to pastoral care must constantly keep in mind both popular and academic psychology as sources. For popular notions of demon possession, of pagan magic, of witchcraft, of visions and miracles and incantations, have from time to time exercised as distinct an influence upon pastoral practice as have the theories of the mind and soul articulated by successively dominant schools of psychological thought.

At the risk of oversimplification it is possible briefly to summarize the major academic psychologies that have provided the intellectual framework for the articulation of pastoral psychology. In the primitive period, Christian pastoring adopted first Judaic then gnostic understandings of the human soul as fettered by its incasement in historic time and materiality; then it was thought that only by struggling against such "principalities and powers" as ruled over this world might the spirit be freed to deal constructively with its woes. As the Christian movement came to terms with Hellenistic culture, first as a dissident minority and then as a new principle of social unity, the academic psychology of the Stoics became the intellectual framework for pastoral psychology, and by Chrysostom's time Stoicism furnished specific patterns of pastoring [SEE EXHIBIT 5].

The formulator of the theoretical psychology that ruled western Europe throughout the period of its Christianization was Augustine of Hippo (354–430), who understood the human soul in terms of Neo-Platonic voluntarism. Augustine's formulations were transformed by the intellectualism of thinkers who were impressed by the rediscovery of Aristotle in the twelfth and thirteenth centuries, and for a time Augustinian and Thomistic psychologies vied with one another for supremacy in the schools. Both these psychological theories were challenged and finally overthrown by Renaissance thought, which sought to know the operation and manifestation of the soul rather than its essential nature. Juan Luis Vives (1492–1540), the Spanish humanist, expressed tersely the viewpoint of "The First Psychiatric Revolution" when he relegated the question of the soul's essence to the theologians and dialecticians, claiming that the more important subject was the soul's dynamic function and characteristic.[64] Conceiving the soul's operations as a proper field of empirical study brought an eventual end to demonology and gave rise to the "faculty psychology" that distinguished and elaborated the psychological functions of sense, imagination, passions, and reason. Modern psychological theories have proliferated into various and sometimes contradictory schools, but all have shared the assumptions advanced by such philosophers as Kant, Hegel, Feuerbach, and Nietzsche to the effect that the notion of the soul's immortality is itself a psychological phenomenon not to be taken as metaphysical truth. Much Christian thinking since the Enlightenment has stubbornly resisted this modern psychological thought, not primarily because it is inimical to Christian pastoral care, but because it attacks the traditional alliance between Christian doctrine (especially touching the soul's immortality) and the older faculty psychology.

Our exhibits indicate profusely that in every previous epoch, Christian pastors have welcomed and utilized theoretical insights from the regnant academic psychologies of the prevailing culture. With equal clarity they show that popular psychological notions and terminologies provide the garb in which men's troubles present themselves. These

---

[64] See Gregory Zilboorg and George W. Henry, *A History of Medical Psychology* (New York: W. W. Norton & Company, Inc., 1941), esp. pp. 112, 190–191; these authors trace to Vives "The First Psychiatric Revolution" in ch. 7.

popular notions thus influence pastors, and, in turn, also the pastoral theorists, to adumbrate remedial systems viable for the shape and content of the troubles brought to the church's door. Out of the Augustinian-Neo-Platonic-voluntaristic psychology, coupled with Stoic ideas, the church once fashioned an elaborate and comprehensive pastoral psychology based on cardinal sins and chief virtues. This system conceived the struggle of the human soul as, at root, a contest between temptations to pride and elicitations of humility, and dominated the intellectual formulations of the church's pastoral care for almost a millennium [SEE EXHIBITS 6 AND 8]. During the first half of that millennium, the rude peoples of western Europe interpreted their troubles to pastors as demon possession, which the church sought to relieve by curative sacramental ministrations. During that period but especially toward the end of it, the popular psychology had molded pastoral theory and practice to a significant degree by elaborating the notion of demon possession into an intricate system of devils, witches, spirits, and angels [SEE EXHIBIT 11].

Since the Enlightenment, pastoral (and theological) psychology has found itself confronted by academic, and increasingly by popular, psychologies that did not see themselves as specifically related to Christian understandings. Some forms of depth psychology, both in their theoretical and common-sense versions, contain polemical references to the once widely accepted theory that the immortal soul and its relations to God and to man were matters into which religion had the deepest insight and over which religion held ultimate control.[65]

From time to time, old compromises have been challenged by new psychological theory and the church has reacted by tenaciously defending old adjustments. In both its Catholic and Protestant forms, modern Christian doctrine has clung stubbornly to alliances it made with faculty psychology early in the Enlightenment, even while modern pastors found themselves attracted to a congeries of theoretical psychologies and confronted by a plethora of popular notions of depth psychology all of which ill accorded with these pastors' doctrinal convictions.

Sometimes pastoral psychologists have advocated new but overly simple compacts between the pastoral endeavor and particular schools of psychology. To give but one classic example, Kenneth E. Kirk (1886–1954) built an entire pastoral theory and plan of action around the psychological system of William McDougall (1871–1938), but Kirk had hardly published his recommendations before university psychology began to reject McDougall's system.[66] It is notable that Kirk evaded ques-

---

[65] See C. G. Jung, *Modern Man in Search of a Soul* (New York: Harcourt, Brace and Company, 1933), especially the preface by Cary F. Baynes.
[66] See Kenneth E. Kirk, *Some Principles of Moral Theology and Their Application* (London: Longmans, Green and Co., 1920), *passim*. Kirk relied primarily upon McDougall's *Social Psychology* (1908), citing also his *Physiological Psy-*

tions of the popular psychological notions that shape specific pastoral problems by assuming that the traditional Christian vocabulary of moral theology, built on the conception of cardinal sins and virtues, would adequately articulate contemporary hurts. This instance, perhaps extreme but certainly not singular, serves to suggest that hasty adoptions of particular psychological systems may result in pastoral psychologies of quite temporary usefulness.

One of the features, noted above, indicating that ours is a transitional time in pastoral care, is the widespread openness of pastoral practitioners and pastoral psychologists to insights arising from a welter of new investigations into the nature and dynamic of human troubles. This openness has not escaped criticism from those who advocate that traditional Christian doctrine should regulate pastoral care. The lesson to be learned in this connection from the history of pastoral care is simply that openness to new psychological theories and notions in fact represents and continues a powerful trend found in every epoch of pastoring. The great tradition of pastoral care stands constantly ready to receive its ideas and its vocabulary both from psychological theoreticians and from popular language about the soul. The normative feature of pastoral care in historic perspective is neither a uniquely Christian psychology nor a particular language in which human trouble must be described, but it is the constancy of the pastoral posture and of the four pastoral functions of healing, sustaining, guiding, and reconciling.

If wisdom for a transitional period in pastoral care is to be gleaned from the great pastoral tradition, that wisdom might be summarized in a few maxims: (1) Beware of easy alliances with specific systems of academic psychology, for their days are usually short. (2) Remain open to the insights of various and even conflicting psychological theories, for man's capacity for trouble is complex, intricate, and inventive. (3) Receive readily the popular vocabulary that describes human troubles, usually in earthy and concrete fashion, for the pastoral task is to help troubled persons and not merely to teach them a new terminology for their troubles. (4) Finally, revere the historic functions of pastoral care with their traditional modes and means, realizing that, while the relative importance of these functions changes from one time and place to another, all four functions have endured many revolutions in psychology, both academic and popular.

## 5.   Emergence of a New Era?

This summary of the present state of pastoral care as seen from a historical perspective cannot end without noting certain indications

---

*chology* (1905) and *Psychology* (1912). Kirk was ingenious at reconciling Mc-Dougall's earlier psychological theories of conscience with those of Thomistic theology.

that a new epoch of pastoral activity is about to emerge from our present time of transition. Evidence of an emerging era dominated by reconciling can be found, but this evidence supports no clear and unequivocal prognostication. There appears a picture made up of blurred outlines, outlines that may be painted over by subsequent shifts and movements in the helping professions. Such as they are, these outlines embolden us to dare set down what we see as indications for the immediate future of pastoring under Christian auspices. Sustaining seems the most widely practiced of the pastoral functions. Guiding seems at present to engender a fascination disproportionate to its promise for the future. Reconciling seems to gain a prominence that might allow it to polarize the other functions. Healing seems capable of recrudescence under the sponsorship of reconciling. The tentativeness of these predictions is proportionate to their brevity.

The sustaining function of the cure of souls in our day continues to be a crucially important helping ministry, sufficiently versatile to be adapted to circumstances of urban-industrial living. Everywhere today busy pastors are called upon to sustain troubled persons in, through, and beyond a plethora of hurts that brook no direct restoration. In terms of time and emotional energy, perhaps of all the pastoral functions sustaining demands most from ordained clergymen. Several reasons can be adduced to explain the continuing viability of this function. The mobility of persons in modern societies has torn the fabric of neighborly relations that recently helped people withstand devastating disruptions of living. Tightly knit communities once furnished friends and neighbors who could stand by in moments of shock, whereas in a society on wheels the task of providing such sustenance to urban and suburban people falls heavily upon the clergy. Unlike members of other helping professions, the competent pastor appears regularly in the homes of his people as a trusted professional person whose values and commitments are known. In many respects, the local congregation and its clergyman's pastoral concern have become a modern institutional embodiment of neighborly sustaining that is carried out specifically by the pastor.[67]

Despite the present-day practical importance of sustaining, guiding as a pastoral function seems to command highest attention in our time. A rich and varied literature on pastoral counseling is available to clergy during their professional preparation and practice. Opportunities for clinical training in hospitals and counseling centers stimulate critical reflection about, and provide competent supervision over, pastoral counseling. During recent years, counseling has been the chief locus of concern for pastoral theology and pastoral psychology. Even while sustaining

---

[67] Some staggering indications of the prominence of clergy as professional helpers were reported by Gerald Gurin, Joseph Veroff, and Shiela Feld, *Americans View Their Mental Health* ("Joint Commission on Mental Health Monograph Series," 4, New York: Basic Books, Inc., 1960), ch. X.

may have demanded more of the pastor's time and energy than other functions, counseling has become the gate through which new intellectual formulations of pastoring have entered and claimed attention. In part this emphasis upon counseling has arisen from religion's twin needs to digest the theoretical formulations that arise from psychiatry and psychology, and to utilize this theory in pastoral helping. Broadly speaking, the dominant mode of recent helping activity has been what we have called individually eductive guiding, and undoubtedly the most provocative research and writing about the helping professions have concentrated upon counseling. The vast majority of training opportunities for clergy, meanwhile, have been under auspices of institutions whose central concern was counseling as the chief model of the helping art.

The very fact that pastoral guiding has become fascinating insofar as it became subsidiary to the other helping arts seems to indicate that the current interest in pastoral counseling, however valuable in other ways, holds little promise as a pole around which the entire pastoral ministry may be magnetized. We see more creative opportunities in another direction; namely, the ministry of reconciling. This function, closely allied with but dominating the function of healing, appears on the verge of an important revival. In spite of the fact that reconciling, in both modes of forgiveness and discipline, has suffered recent neglect, it remains in heavy demand. We foresee in the resuscitation of the reconciling function, synthesized with that of healing, the best hope for a transformed pastoral care that is at once continuous with the history of pastoring, integrated with the churches' theological formulations, open to new psychological insights, and able to meet creatively the aspirations and needs of modern men and women.

The reconciling function enjoys an extraordinarily rich heritage in the church and remains a manner of helping for which there is, as yet, no prominent non-pastoral substitute. The burden of guilt under which moderns live—guilt engendered by alienation from fellow man that interprets itself as also alienation from God—is a form of human trouble with which the pastoral ministry has had longer and deeper familiarity than has any other helping profession.[68] Partly by virtue of insisting that broken human relationships involve a breach in man's ultimate relationship with his Creator, pastoral care takes the human need for reconciliation with a seriousness unsurpassed by that of other healing arts. Urban mobility and the consequent shifting of patterns of family life have exacerbated parents' guilt over their children, and, later on, children's guilt over the problem of responsibility for aging parents. Lacking the protection of well-patterned and stable expectations, modern marriage throws husbands and wives into situations where more and more arise questions and burdens and inadequacies in their responsibilities to one

---

[68] See David Belgum, *Guilt: Where Religion And Psychology Meet* (Englewood Cliffs, N.J.: Prentice-Hall, Inc., 1963).

another.[69] Thus, the related matters of guilt, responsibility, relationship, alienation, and reconcilation comprise a genus of modern human trouble for which the reconciling ministry is peculiarly well suited.

Reconciling persons who suffer from ruptured relationships is an aim woven into the very fabric of the church's liturgy and theology as well as its pastoral care. It is natural that the clergyman among representatives of the helping arts is most expected to be peacemaker and reconciler. That the clergy are so very frequently turned to by persons with marital difficulties involving relationships with spouses and by persons with other problems of human relationships occasions no surprise.[70] To him alienated persons confess their yearnings and ambivalences and even hatreds in sure knowledge that their attitudes will be both judged and forgiven, and in the hope that their relationships will be reconciled. His ritual functions of baptizing, of declaring God's forgiveness of sin, of solemnizing matrimony, and so forth, both announce and renew his authority as a person peculiarly concerned with establishing and restoring relationships of profound significance between man and man and between man and God.

Pastoral reconciling finds a natural connection today with pastoral healing, because, in the Christian vision of life, restored relationships not only achieve a *status quo ante* but represent a spiritual advance over relationships that have never suffered breaches. This characteristic of Christian pastoral reconciling suits the mood of modern man for personal growth and his expectation that the whole of one's life in relationship to others will be characterized by the increasing release of one's creative powers.

Reconciling, therefore, seems to be the pastoral function presently most open to experimentation, new discussion, and revived application. Should this function loom, as might be expected, increasingly important in the years to come, that circumstance would entail raising basic questions about the church's discipline and its interest in forgiveness—the two modes in which pastoral reconciling has historically been expressed. From the vantage point of a renewed emphasis upon reconciling, the practitioner of the pastoral art may enter more fully into conversations with representatives of the other healing arts, not only as a listener but as an artist able to make significant contributions from accumulated wisdom gained through two millennia of hearing confessions, pronouncing forgiveness, and exercising discipline in an effort to bring to reconciliation countless numbers of men and women in every area of the Western world. Such a renewed emphasis upon reconciling could precipitate the ministry of the cure of souls into a new realization of its therapeutic power for our time.

---

[69] See, among many books dealing with pastoral opportunities in marriage problems, J. Kenneth Morris, *Premarital Counseling* (Englewood Cliffs, N.J.: Prentice-Hall, Inc., 1960), and Dean Johnson, *Marriage Counseling: Theory and Practice* (Englewood Cliffs, N.J.: Prentice-Hall, Inc., 1961.)

[70] See Gurin, Veroff, and Feld, *op. cit.*, p. 325.

PART 5

EXHIBITS

# Exhibit One

## ENDURING
## THE END
## OF THE WORLD
### II CLEMENT

## Introduction

Although no writing preserved to us records the specific and detailed pastoral care that the earliest Christians practiced, a number of extant documents —gospels, epistles, "acts," homilies, revelations, both within and without the canonical list of Scriptures —provide an oblique view into early pastoral concerns and activities. One of these is a lengthy sermon, perhaps from second-century Corinth, a document traditionally known as the "Second Epistle of Clement." This sermon quite bluntly proposes that all actions assisting troubled persons should be decided upon in the light of an imminent end of the world, a circumstance that exhorts utter purity of life.

Despite its traditional title, neither is II Clement a letter nor is it from the hand of the late first-century bishop of Rome, Clement. Actually, very little is known about the sermon's provenance. Scholars have ascribed it to Rome, Corinth, and Alexandria, and have dated it as early as 96 A.D. and as late as 325 A.D. One piece of external evidence indicates that the sermon was read—to the salutary benefit of all— to Corinthian congregations on various occasions during the last third of the second century.

Regardless of questions of authorship, place, and date, II Clement provides a fine protrayal of early Christians' yearning for the end of time and of their emphasis upon purity of life as preparatory for the last judgment. From the document we learn that, even in the beginning, pastoral care was molded by the outlook upon the world—the *Weltanschauung*—of Christian people in their own time and place. Here we see a clear emphasis upon the pastoral function of sustaining that posited itself on the imminent end of the world. The writer called for repentance while there is still time, for very soon time would run out. In order to hasten amendment of life in one another, Christians should join earnestly in mutual admonition and in supporting one another to keep all safe from the temptations and evils that swiftly drew this world to a cataclysmic close under the power of God. Life's normal processes, indeed, were to be suspended and all resources mobilized for the day of judgment. Questions of human justice and interest in tedious processes of healing were pushed into the background; it mattered little that a believer suffer now, for "a time of blessedness awaits him; he shall live again with the fathers above, and rejoice to an eternity wherein is no sorrow."

The following excerpts from II Clement epitomize pastoral care under that sense of the shortness of time which characterized the New Testament and other primitive Christian writings.

# ENDURING THE END OF THE WORLD

From: *The Second Epistle of Clement* (c. 150?), author unknown.

## IV

Let us, then, not merely call him Lord, for this will not save us. For he says, "Not everyone that saith to me Lord, Lord, shall be saved, but he that doeth righteousness." So then, brethren, let us confess him in our deeds, by loving one another, by not committing adultery, nor speaking one against another, nor being jealous, but by being self-controlled, merciful, good; and we ought to sympathise with each other, and not to be lovers of money. By these deeds we confess him, and not by the opposite kind. And we must not fear men rather than God. For this reason, if you do these things, the Lord said, "If ye be gathered together with me in my bosom, and do not my commandments, I will cast you out, and will say to you, Depart from me, I know not whence ye are, ye workers of iniquity."

## V

Wherefore, brethren, let us forsake our sojourning in this world, and do the will of him who called us, and let us not fear to go forth from this world, for the Lord said, "Ye shall be as lambs in the midst of wolves," and Peter answered and said to him, "If then the wolves tear the lambs?" Jesus said to Peter, "Let the lambs have no fear of the wolves after their death; and do ye have no fear of those that slay you, and can do nothing more to you, but fear him who after your death hath power over body and soul, to cast them into the flames of hell." And be well assured, brethren, that our sojourning in this world in the flesh is a little thing and lasts a short time, but the promise of Christ is great and wonderful, and brings us rest, in the kingdom which is to come and in everlasting life. What then shall we do to attain these things save lead a holy and righteous life, and regard the things of this world as not our own, and not desire them? For by desiring to obtain these things we fall from the way of righteousness.

## VI

And the Lord says:—"No servant can serve two masters." If we desire to serve both God and Mammon it is unprofitable to us, "For what is the advantage if a man gain the whole world but lose his soul?" Now the world that is, and the world to come are two enemies. This world speaks of adultery, and corruption, and love of money, and deceit, but that world bids these things farewell. We cannot then be the friends of both; but we must bid farewell to this world, to consort with that which is to come. We reckon that it is better to hate the things which are here, for they are little, and short-lived, and corruptible, but to love the things which are there, the good things which are incorruptible. For if we do the will of Christ we shall gain rest; but if not, nothing shall rescue us from eternal punishment, if we neglect his commandments. And the Scripture also says in Ezekiel that, "if Noah and Job and Daniel arise, they shall not rescue their children in the captivity." But if even such righteous men as these cannot save their children by their own righteousness, with what confidence shall we enter into the palace of God, if we keep not our baptism pure and undefiled? Or who shall be our advocate if we be not found to have pious and righteous works?

\* \* \* \* \*

## VIII

Let us repent then while we are on the earth. For we are clay in the hand of the workman; for just as the potter, if he make a vessel, and it be bent or broken in his hand, models it afresh, but if he has come so far as to put it into the fiery oven, he can do nothing to mend it any more; so also let us, so long as we are in this world, repent with all our heart of the wicked deeds which we have done in the flesh, that we may be saved by the Lord, while we have a time for repentance. For after we have departed from this world, we can no longer make confession, or repent any more in that place. So then, brethren, if we do the will of the Father, if we keep the flesh pure, and if we observe the commandments of the Lord, we shall obtain eternal life. For the Lord says in the Gospel, "If ye did not guard that which is small, who shall give you that which is great? For I tell you that he who is faithful in that which is least, is faithful also in that which is much." He means, then, this:—Keep the flesh pure, and the seal of baptism undefiled, that we may obtain eternal life.

*   *   *   *   *

## X

Wherefore, my brethren, let us do the will of the father who called us, that we may live, and let us rather follow after virtue, but give up vice as the forerunnner of our sins, and let us flee from ungodliness lest evil overtake us. For, if we are zealous to do good, peace will follow after us. For this cause it is not possible for a man to find it, when they bring in human fears, and prefer the pleasures of the present to the promises of the future. For they do not know how great torment the pleasures of the present entail, and what is the joy of the promised future. And if they did these things by themselves it could be endured, but, as it is, they are continuing in teaching evil to innocent souls, and do not know that they will incur a double judgment, both themselves and their hearers.

*   *   *   *   *

## XII

Let us then wait for the kingdom of God, from hour to hour, in love and righteousness, seeing that we know not the day of the appearing of God. For when the Lord himself was asked by someone when his kingdom would come, he said: "When the two shall be one, and the outside as the inside, and the male with the female neither male nor female." Now "the two are one" when we speak with one another in truth, and there is but one soul in two bodies without dissimulation. And by "the outside as the inside" he means this, that the inside is the soul, and the outside is the body. Therefore, just as your body is visible, so let your soul be apparent in your good works. And by "the male with the female neither male nor female" he means this, that when a brother sees a sister he should have no thought of her as female, nor she of him as male. When you do this, he says, the kingdom of my Father will come.

\* \* \* \* \*

## XVI

Seeing therefore, brethren, that we have received no small opportunity for repentance; let us, now that we have time, turn to the God who calls us, while we still have one who awaits us. For if we bid farewell to these enjoyments, and conquer our soul, by giving up its wicked lusts, we shall share in the mercy of Jesus. But you know that "the day" of judgment is already "approaching as a burning oven, and some of the heavens shall melt," and the whole earth shall be as lead melting in the fire, and then shall be made manifest the secret and open deeds of men. Almsgiving is therefore good even as penitence for sin; fasting is better than prayer, but the giving of alms is better than both; and love "covers a multitude of sins," but prayer from a good conscience rescues from death. Blessed is every man who is found full of these things; for almsgiving lightens sin.

## XVII

Let us then repent with our whole heart, that none of us perish by the way. For if we have commandments to do this also, to tear men away from idols and to instruct them, how much more is it our duty to save from perishing a soul that already knows God? Let us then help one another, and bring back those that are weak in goodness, that we may all be saved, and convert and exhort one another. And let us not merely seem to believe and pay attention now, while we are being exhorted by the Elders, but also when we have gone home let us remember the commandments of the Lord, and let us not be dragged aside by worldly lusts, but let us try to come here more frequently, and to make progress in the commands of the Lord; that we may "all have the same mind" and be gathered together unto life. For the Lord said: "I come to gather together all the nations, tribes, and languages." Now by this he means the day of his appearing, when he will come and ransom each of us according to his works. And the unbelievers "shall see his glory" and might, and they shall be amazed when they see the sovereignty of the world given to Jesus and shall say: Woe unto us, that it was thou, and we knew it not, and did not believe, and were not obedient to the Elders, when they told us of our salvation. "And their worm shall not die and their fire shall not be quenched, and they shall be a spectacle to all flesh." He means that day of judgment, when they shall see those who were ungodly among us and perverted the commandments of Jesus Christ. But the righteous who have done good, and have endured torture, and have hated the indulgences of the soul, when they see how those who have done amiss, and denied Jesus by word or deed, are punished with terrible torture in unquenchable fire, shall give "glory to their God," saying, There shall be hope for him who has served God with all his heart.

## XVIII

Let us then also belong to them who give thanks, who have served God, and not to the ungodly who are judged. For I myself too am altogether sinful, and I have not yet escaped temptation, but I am still in the midst of the devices of the devil, yet I am striving to follow after righteousness, that I may have the strength at least to draw near to it, in fear of the judgment to come.

## XIX

Therefore, brothers and sisters, following the God of truth, I am reading you an exhortation to pay attention to that which is written, that you may both save yourselves and him who is the reader among you. For as a reward I beg of you that you repent with all your heart, and give to yourselves salvation and life. For if we do this we shall set a mark for all the younger, who wish to work in the cause of piety and the goodness of God. And let us not be displeased or be vexed in our foolishness when any one admonishes us, and turns us from unrighteousness to righteousness. For sometimes when we do evil we do not know it because of the double-mindedness and unbelief which is in our breasts, and we are "darkened in our understanding" by vain desires. Let us then do righteousness, that we may be saved at the end. Blessed are they who obey these instructions: though they suffer for a short time in this world, they shall gather the immortal fruit of the resurrection. Let not, then, the pious grieve if he endure sorrow at this present time; a time of blessedness awaits him; he shall live again with the fathers above, and rejoice to an eternity wherein is no sorrow.

## XX

But neither let it grieve your mind that we see the unrighteous enjoying wealth, and the servants of God oppressed. Let us then have faith, brothers and sisters: we are contending in the contest of the living God, and we are being trained by the life which now is, that we may gain the crown in that which is to come. None of the righteous has attained a reward quickly, but waits for it; for if God should pay the recompense of the righteous speedily, we should immediately be training ourselves in commerce and not in godliness; for we should seem to be righteous when we were pursuing not piety but gain. For this reason divine judgment punishes a spirit which is not righteous and loads it with chains.

To the only invisible God, the father of truth, who sent forth to us the Saviour and prince of immortality, through whom he also made manifest to us truth and the life of heaven, to him be the glory for ever and ever. Amen.

The Second Epistle of Clement to the Corinthians.

Reprinted by permission of the publishers from The Loeb Classical Library, translated by Kirsopp Lake, THE APOSTOLIC FATHERS, I, Cambridge, Mass.: Harvard University Press, 1912; pp. 133–139, 141, 143–145, 147–149, 155–163 (numbering of verses omitted).

# Exhibit Two

## EXOMOLOGESIS
### TERTULLIAN OF CARTHAGE

### Introduction

The earliest Latin writer on Christianity known to us is Quintus Septimius Florens Tertullian (c. 160–c. 220), whose career as a theologian was spent in his native Carthage in North Africa. A gift for phrase-making, a highly trained legal mind, and interests that ranged over all phases of Christianity enabled Tertullian to lay down the lines of a practical, ethical, churchly emphasis that dominated Western Christianity. Also he described in great detail the practice of Christians in his own time. About A.D. 203 he composed a long treatise *On Repentance*. Some four years later, his rigoristic views led him to side with the Montanists, who stressed spiritualism and asceticism. Yet his doctrinal writings, especially on Christology and the Trinity, make him a Latin patristic theologian ranking second only to Augustine.

Tertullian's trenchant teachings on penance and the pastoral administration of penance prompted Cyprian of Carthage to regard him as the chief theological authority on this subject during the Decian persecution at the middle of the third century. From Tertullian we receive a picture of the practice of public confession of sin and performance of penance in the presence of the entire congregation, and an explicit teaching that the penance must be commensurate to the sin. Both his portrayal and his teaching exerted influence on the pastoral care of disturbed consciences for centuries after his death.

In I Cor. 5:9ff., Paul indicated that a brother in the faith found guilty of certain gross sins was to be excommunicated. II Cor. 2:5ff. told that the erring brother was to be comforted and forgiven. Here, in brief, is a picture of the practice of the early church. The offensive brother was rebuked publicly within the congregation and excommunicated—that is, he was denied participation in the Eucharist and shunned by Christian people until his amendment; or else, the guilty brother was chided or counseled privately to confess his sins publicly before all the Christian brethren—a procedure called by Tertullian "exomologesis." The sinner in the latter situation was suspended for a time from participation in Eucharist; sooner or later he was re-admitted to full participation with a blessing from the bishop.

In the following reading from *On Repentance*, Tertullian vividly described exomologesis and adduced theological and psychological justifications for it. The penitent was to regard exomologesis as partly and sometimes wholly a payment for sin, payment which attenuated or reduced the punishment otherwise due after death. Confession thus became a kind of medicine of humiliation, possessing power to make better men and better Christians, and as such demonstrating God's mercy. Tertullian warned people in the congregation against self-righteousness and the penitent against being overly ashamed, because, after all, Christian people belonged to each other both in God's grace and in their sin. Finally, Tertullian confessed his own identification with the sinner. "I am a sinner," he declared, "branded with every mark of infamy and born for nothing else but penance."

In his work *On Purity*, written during his Montanist days, Tertullian raised a problem that was debated vigorously pro and con by the later fathers of the church. Granting the system of penance for sins committed after baptism, was there a class of sins for which there might be no reconciliation with and forgiveness by the church? With Origen of Alexandria, Tertullian refused to extend reconciliation and forgiveness to the sins of idolatry, unchastity, and homicide. His reasons for this attitude were twofold. If the church readmitted persons guilty of these gross sins, how might the church claim to be the holy people of God? Second, in these most serious cases, authority to effect forgiveness and reconciliation belonged only to the Lord. If the church claimed such authority, taught Tertullian, it unlawfully assumed power over the fruit of penance, that is, forgiveness. The idolater, adulterer, or murderer might only live in exemplary shame until death, depending wholly on the merciful grace of God.

Tertullian's extensive writings, of which the following paragraphs are but a tiny sample, show how pastoral care turned toward the function of reconciliation in the face of problems posed by the persecutions, and away from the function of sustaining that had been prominent when earlier Christians still expected the world to end imminently.

# EXOMOLOGESIS

From: *On Penitence* (c. 203), by Tertullian.

A point I now insist upon is this, that the penance which has been revealed to us by the grace of God, which is required of us and which brings us back to favor with the Lord, must never, once we have known and embraced it, be violated thereafter by a return to sin. In this case, no plea of ignorance excuses you; for you have known the Lord, you have accepted His law and then, after doing penance for your sins, you give yourself over to sin again. Therefore the more you are detached from ignorance, the more you are attached to wilful disobedience; for if you were sorry for your sins because you began to fear the Lord, why did you choose to cancel that which fear inspired, if not for the reason that you have ceased to fear? In truth, it is nothing but wilful disobedience which destroys the fear of God.

\*   \*   \*   \*   \*

But that stubborn enemy of ours [*i.e.*, the devil] never gives his wickedness a rest. Rather he is then most furious when he sees that a man is completely free; then he is most on fire when he is quenched. He must needs grieve and groan that, when pardon is granted for sins, so many works of death in man are mastered, so many titles of his former dominion are erased. He grieves that that sinner, the servant of Christ, is to judge him and his angels. Therefore he watches, he attacks, he lays siege, in the hope that by some means or other he may be able to strike at his eyes with concupiscence of the flesh or entangle his soul in worldly delights or destroy his faith through a fear of the civil authorities or bring him to deviate from the right way by perverted doctrines. Never is he at a loss for stumbling blocks or temptations.

\*   \*   \*   \*   \*

No one is so devoted [*i.e.*, as God]. Therefore He will take you back as His son, even though you will have wasted what He gave you. Even though you come back stripped of all things, He will receive you—precisely because you have come back. He will be happier over your return than over another's self-control, but only if you repent from the bottom of your heart, only if you contrast your hunger with the repletion of your father's servants, only if you abandon the filthy herd of swine, only if you seek out your Father, even though He be offended, and say to Him: *Father, I have sinned and I am no longer worthy to be called Thine.* Confession lightens an offense as much as concealment aggravates it, for confession is counseled by satisfaction and concealment by impenitence.

Since this second and last penitence is so serious a matter, it must be tested in a way which is proportionately laborious. Therefore it must not be performed solely within one's conscience but it must also be shown forth in some external act. This external act, rather expressively designated by the Greek word for it in common use, is the exomologesis. Herein we confess our sin to the Lord, not as though He were ignorant of it, but because satisfaction receives its proper determination through confession, confession gives birth to penitence and by penitence God is appeased.

Exomologesis, then, is a discipline which leads a man to prostrate and humble himself. It prescribes a way of life which, even in the matter of food and clothing, appeals to pity. It bids him to lie in sackcloth and ashes, to cover his body with filthy rags, to plunge his soul into sorrow, to exchange sin for suffering. Moreover, it demands that you know only such food and drink as is plain; this means it is taken for the sake of your soul, not your belly. It requires that you habitually nourish prayer by fasting, that you sigh and weep and groan day and night to the Lord your God, that you prostrate yourself at the feet of the priests and kneel before the beloved of God, making all the brethren commissioned ambassadors of your prayer for pardon.

Exomologesis does all this in order to render penitence acceptable and in order to honor God through fear of punishment, so that in passing sentence upon the sinner it may itself be a substitute for the wrath of God and, by temporal punishment, I will not say prevent eternal torments but rather cancel them. Therefore, in humbling a man it exalts him. When it defiles him, he is cleansed. In accusing, it excuses. In condemning, it absolves. In proportion as you have had no mercy on yourself, believe me, in just this same measure God will have mercy upon you.

Most men, however, shun this duty as involving the public exposure of themselves, or they put it off from day to day, thinking more about their shame, it seems to me, than about their salvation. They are like men who have contracted some disease in the private parts of the body, who conceal this from the knowledge of the physicians and thus preserve their modesty but lose their lives. It is, I suppose, unbearable to shame that it should offer satisfaction to the Lord after He has been offended, and that it should enter once more into the possession of that salvation which has been wasted.

Oh you are a brave fellow, surely, in your shyness—wearing a bold front for sin, a bashful one for pardon! As for me, I have no room for shame when I profit at its expense and when shame itself exhorts a man, as it were, and says to him: "Regard me not! For thy sake it is better that I be lost." If ever the danger to shame is serious, this is certainly the case when it stands in the presence of insult and mockery, when one man is exalted through another's ruin, when one ascends over another who is laid low. But among brethren and fellow-servants, where there is one hope, fear, joy, sorrow and suffering, because there is one Spirit from one Lord and Father, why do you think these men are any different from yourself? Why do you flee, as from scoffers, those who share your misfortunes? The body can not rejoice at the suffering of a single one of its members; the whole body must needs suffer along with it and help in its cure.

Where there are two together, there is the Church—and the Church is Christ. When, therefore, you stretch forth your hands to the knees of the brethren, you are in touch with Christ and you win the favor of Christ by your supplications. In like manner, when they shed tears for you, it is Christ who suffers, Christ who supplicates the Father. And what the Son requests is always easily obtained. Great is the profit, I'm sure, which the concealment of a sin promises to modesty! For it is plain, is it not, that if we withdraw something from the knowledge of men, we shall also hide it from God? Is this the relative importance which we attach to human respect and God's knowledge? Is it better to be condemned in secret than to be absolved in public?

"Oh but it is a painful thing to undertake exomologesis in this way!" I should prefer to say that one suffers pain because one has sinned. Or, rather, when penance is to be performed, there is no longer any question of suffering, since it is become a means of salvation. It is painful to be cut and to be cauterized and to be tortured by some medicinal caustic. Nevertheless, remedies which are unpleasant justify the pain they give by the cure they effect, and they render present suffering agreeable because of the advantage which is to come in the future.

Let us suppose that besides the shame which is their principal concern they are also afraid of the bodily mortification involved, which requires that, unwashed and filthy, they live without joy, in rough sackcloth and frightful ashes, their faces wasted with fasting. Well, is it fitting that we beg pardon for sin in scarlet and purple? Come, then, bring a pin to part the hair and powder to polish the teeth and scissors to trim the nails and, if any meretricious beauty, any artificial bloom may be had, hasten and apply it to the lips or cheeks! Yes, and seek out baths of greater luxury, sequestered in garden spots or by the sea. Multiply expenses, search for the rich, gross flesh of fatted fowls, refine old wine and, if anyone should ask you why you make good cheer, then say to him: "I have sinned against the Lord. I am in danger of perishing forever. Therefore am I now weakened and wasted and tormented, so that I may win for myself the pardon of God whom I have injured by my sin!"

Men who seek public office are neither ashamed nor reluctant to put up with discomforts of body and soul alike in striving for what they want, yes and not only with discomforts but even with humiliating affronts of every kind. What rough garments do they not affect! What homes do they not besiege with visits, late at night and early in the morning! They bow low whenever they meet a person of consequence. They frequent no carousals. They gather at no drinking bouts. Rather, they are exiles from the enjoyment of indulgence and festivity—and all for the fleeting pleasure of a single year! Shall we, with eternity at stake, hesitate to bear what they who seek axes and rods are able to endure? Shall we fail to offer to the Lord, when He is offended, that renunication of food and fine apparel to which the gentiles condemn themselves, when no one at all has been offended? These are they of whom the Scripture makes mention: *Woe to those who bind their sins together, as though with a long rope.*

If you shrink from exomologesis, then meditate in your heart on hell which exomologesis will extinguish for you. Picture to yourself, first of all, how great this punishment is so that you will not hesitate to use the means which you have to escape it. What shall we think of that great vault of eternal fire when some of its tiny vents shoot out such bursts of flame that nearby cities are either all destroyed or, from day to day, expect this same destruction? The most majestic mountains burst asunder giving birth to their engendered fire and—a fact which proves to us the eternity of damnation—although they do burst asunder, although they are consumed, yet never are they extinct. Meanwhile, who will not see in these tortured mountains exemplary illustrations of the damnation with which we are threatened? Who will not agree that sparks such as these are, as it were, projectiles and admonitory missiles from some immense and immeasurable fire?

Therefore, since you know that in exomologesis you have a second safeguard against hell which backs up that first line of defense, the Lord's Baptism, why do you abandon the means of salvation which is yours? Why are you slow to take hold of something which will restore you to health? Even dumb, irrational animals recognize, in due season, remedies supplied to them by God. When a stag is transfixed by an arrow, it knows that it must eat dittany in order to expel the arrowhead with its barbs projecting backwards from the wound. If a swallow blinds her young, she has learned to restore their sight with her own peculiar herb, the celandine.

Will the sinner knowingly spurn exomologesis, which has been instituted by God for his restoration? that exomologesis which restored the king of Babylon to his royal throne? Long did he offer to the Lord a sacrifice of penance, performing his exomologesis for seven squalid years, his nails growing wild like the talons of an eagle, his hair unkempt like the shaggy mane of a lion. Oh the blessedness of this harsh treatment! One whom men shunned with horror, God received! The ruler of Egypt, on the contrary, pursuing the people of God, whom he had persecuted for a long time and long kept back from their Lord, fell upon them in battle and, after all the warnings of the plagues, he perished in the parted sea, passable to none but the chosen people, when the waves rolled back upon him. For he had rejected penitence and its instrument, exomologesis.

Why should I say more about these two planks, so to speak, of safety for mankind? Why more concern for the emplovment of my pen than for the obligations of my own conscience? Since I am a sinner, branded with every mark of infamy and born for nothing else but penance, I cannot easily keep silence about something which Adam himself, the author of the human race and also of sin against the Lord, does not pass over in silence, once he is restored, through exomologesis, to his own particular paradise.

*       *       *       *       *

From: *On Purity* (c. 217–222), by Tertullian.

We agree that the cases where penance is required are sins. These we divide according to two issues: some will be remissible, others irremissible. Accordingly, no one doubts that some deserve correction, others condemnation. Either pardon or punishment balances the account of every sin, pardon after correction, punishment after condemnation. With reference to this distinction we have already premised certain scriptural antitheses, some retaining, others forgiving sins. But John will also teach us: *If anyone know that his brother sins a sin which is not unto death, he shall pray and life will be given him because he sins not unto death.* This will be remissible. *There is a sin unto death; not for this do I say that anyone should pray.* This will be irremissible. Accordingly, where there is room for prayer there also is room for remission. Where there is no room for prayer there, likewise, neither is there room for remission.

According to this distinction of sins the form of penance is also determined. One will be such as is able to win pardon, that is to say, in the case of a sin which is remissible. The other will be such as is by no means able to win it, that is to say, in the case of a sin which is irremissible. And now it remains to consider, in particular, the position of adultery and fornication, and to determine in which class of sins they must be placed.

But first I shall dispose of an objection which is raised by the opposition respecting that form of penance which we assert categorically is without pardon. "If there is a kind of penance," they say, "which is without pardon, then you should not perform it at all, for nothing should be done which is fruitless. And penance will be performed without fruit if it be without pardon. But now every kind of penance ought to be performed; therefore every kind will win pardon, lest it be without fruit. For if it should be without fruit, it ought not to be performed. But it is performed without fruit, if it is to be without pardon."

Quite consistently do they raise this objection since they have unlawfully assumed power over the fruit—forgiveness, I mean—of this penance also. Penance will indeed be without fruit as far as they are concerned who receive peace from men; as far as we are concerned, however, who bear in mind that the Lord alone forgives sins, and I mean, of course, mortal sins, it will not be without fruit. For when it is placed in the Lord's keeping and, thereafter, lies prostrate before Him, it will, on this very account, effect forgiveness all the more surely, since it asks it of God alone, since it does not suppose that peace granted by men satisfies for its offenses, since it would rather suffer shame before the Church than be in communion with it.

And so it stands before her doors, warning others by its exemplary shame. It calls to its assistance the tears of the brethren and returns home richer for their compassion than it would be for their company. And if it reaps not here the harvest of peace, it sows the seed of it with the Lord. It does not lose its fruit but rather makes provision for it. It will not fail of its reward, if it fail not in its duty. And so penance of this kind is not done in vain, nor is a discipline such as this harsh. Both do honor to God. The former will more easily obtain what it asks, since it does not delude itself with fancies; the latter will be all the more helpful in that it is not guilty of presumption.

*Tertullian, Treatises on Penance,* tr. and anno. William P. Le Saint, S.J., S.T.D. (Westminster, Md.: The Newman Press, 1959; London: Longmans, Green and Co., 1959), pp. 21–22, 28–29, 31–37, 59–61. By permission.

# Exhibit Three

## INSTRUCTIONS FOR RECONCILIATION

### DIDASCALIA APOSTOLORUM

## Introduction

Since few contemporaneous descriptions of the inner life of Christian congregations during the first three centuries have been preserved to us, special interest attaches to one such writing, known as *Didascalia Apostolorum*. Like many second- and third-century Christian books, this one claimed authority as representing the doctrine of Jesus' closest followers; originating in Northern Syria in the first half of the third century, the book's Syriac title translates as "The Catholic Teaching of the Twelve Apostles and holy Disciples of our Redeemer." It contains much miscellaneous information about Syrian church life. The author, probably himself a physician, rails against Christians who thought it proper to observe Jewish ceremonial laws, describes various liturgical practices, advises how Christians should comport themselves during persecutions, treats of the just distribution of the alms of believers, and touches upon many aspects of church administration.

A major portion of *Didascalia Apostolorum* is a treatise on the office and pastoral functions of the bishop (an office which, interestingly enough, is distinguished from that of deacons rather than from that of presbyters). The writer stood adamantly against the rigoristic doctrine forbidding forgiveness to Christians who committed the grievous sins of idolatry, adultery, and murder, and he demanded that, if God's mercy be interpreted in its true breadth, bishops should administer penance and absolution for these worst sins. Leniency was pleaded on grounds of Scripture by the device of interpreting allegorically various Old Testament passages.

The portion of *Didascalia Apostolorum* given here in translation sets forth four analogies by which to understand the character and duty of the chief minister of pastoral care. The bishop is to be a *judge* as God is a judge; he is to be a *parent* as chickens and birds are parental over their eggs and their young; he is to be a *shepherd* who partakes of the suffering of the flock he tends; he is to be a *physician* who heals and cauterizes the wounds of his patients. Thus the pastoral office, even as early as the third century, was seen as consisting of the four functions of guiding, sustaining, reconciling, and healing. The far-reaching influence of this early analysis of pastoral care can be measured by reference to modern writings on the subject; one prominent Roman Catholic treatise points out that the confessor must be "a *judge* to hear the culprit's confession," must "act the part of the Shepherd," and "must be a *physician*" and "a *Father.*"[71]

Of course, the Syrian did not organize his material neatly around these four functions, but nevertheless he called upon bishops to fulfill these ideal aspects of their office. In dealing explicitly with the administration of forgiveness to persons guilty of grave sin, he also indicated that, in his time and place, pastoral care had come to be polarized around the function of reconciling alienated persons to the church, to God, and to one another—an emphasis that stands in marked contrast to the primitive church's preoccupation with sustaining troubled people until the imminent end of the world.

From the following excerpts have been excised some long citations of Scripture, especially Old Testament passages, but enough such citations remain to show the author's preference for allegorical interpretation.

---

71 Caspar E. Schieler, *Theory and Practice of the Confessional*, ed. H. J. Heuser, introduction by Most Rev. S. G. Messmer (second edn., New York: Benziger Brothers, 1905), pp. v–vi.

# INSTRUCTIONS FOR RECONCILIATION

From: *Didascalia* (c. 225), by an unknown Syrian.

Therefore judge severely, O Bishop, like Almighty God, and receive those who repent with compassion like God; and reprove, and beseech and teach, for even the Lord God has promised with oaths pardon to those who have sinned, as Ezekiel the prophet has said, "And thou, son of man, say to them of the house of Israel; Thus ye say, our transgressions and our sins are upon us, and in them we pine away; how should we then live? Say unto them, As I live, saith the Lord God, I do not wish the death of the sinner, but that the wicked should repent of his evil way and live; repent therefore and turn from your evil deeds, and ye shall not die, ye house of Israel." Here therefore he gives hope to those who have sinned when they repent, that they may have forgiveness in their repentance; and their hope may not be cut off, and that they may not remain in their sins, nor add to these; but that they may repent and weep for their sins, and be converted with all their heart; and those who have not sinned may remain without sins; lest these also should have need of weeping and sighings and forgiveness. How knowest thou, O man that hath sinned, how many may be the days of thy life in this world that thou mayest repent, for thou knowest not thy departure from this world; lest thou shouldest die in thy sins and have no repentance, as it is said in David, "In Sheol who confesseth to Thee?" Therefore every one who hath pity on himself and remaineth without sins, may remain without danger; so that the righteousness which was done by him of old may be kept for him. Thou therefore, O Bishop, judge thus, first severely, and afterwards receive with mercy and clemency [him who] has promised to repent, reprove him and make him sorry and persuade him, because of the word that was said in David thus, "Thou wilt not give up the soul of him that confesseth to Thee." Again, in Jeremiah He saith thus, about the repentance of those that sin, "He that falleth, shall he not rise; or he that turneth away [shall he] not turn back? Why hath My people turned away with a shameless turning; they are held fast in their thoughts, and do not wish to repent and be converted." Because of this therefore receive him who repenteth, not doubting in the least, and be not prevented by those who have no mercy, those who say, We must not be defiled by those. For the Lord God hath said, "The fathers shall not die for the children, nor the children for the fathers." And again in Ezekiel he saith thus, "The word of the Lord came unto me, saying, Son of man, when a land sinneth against Me, and doeth wickedness before Me, I will stretch out My hand against it, and I will destroy from it the staff of bread, and I will send famine upon it, and I will destroy from it man and beast. Though these three men were in it, Noah, and Daniel, and Job, they should deliver their souls by their righteousness, saith the Lord God." The Scripture therefore plainly sheweth that if the righteous be found with the wicked, he will not perish with him, but every man shall live by his righteousness, and if he be prevented, he is prevented by his own sins. In Wisdom again He saith, "Every man is bound with the cord of his sins." Every one of the laity therefore shall give an account of his own sin and no man will be hurt because of the foreign sins of others. Not even Judas did cause us any loss by praying with us, but he alone perished. Noah also in the Ark and two of his sons who were saved, were blessed; but Ham, the other, was not blessed; but his seed was cursed, because he mocked at his father, for going out to the beasts. We do not require you therefore to confirm those who delight in death, hate their brethren, and love quarrels, for which reason they are ready to kill; but help those who are very sick, and are in danger and sin, and deliver them from death, not according to the hardness of their heart and their word and their thoughts. For it is not required of thee, O Bishop, that being the head thou shouldst listen to the tail, that is to say, to the layman, to the quarrelsome man who delights in the destruction of another; but look thou only at the command of the Lord God, and for this reason, that they may not expect to perish, nor be defiled with the sins of others. . . .

It is required of you, O Bishops, according to the Scriptures, that ye judge those who sin with pity and mercy. For him that walketh on the brink of a river and falleth, if thou leave him in the river, thou pushest and throwest him down and committest murder; or when a man has fallen by the side of a river's brink, and nearly perishes, stretch out thy hand to him quickly and draw him up that he perish not: thus therefore do, that thy people may learn and be wise, and also that he that sinneth, may not perish utterly, but that thou mayest look to him that hath sinned, be angry with him, and command them to put him out. And when he is put out, be ye not angry with him, and contend with him, but let them keep him outside of the Church, and then let them go in and make supplication for him, for even our Saviour made supplication to His Father for those that had sinned, as it is written in the Gospel, "My Father, they know not what they do, nor what they speak, yet, if it be possible, forgive them." Then thou, O Bishop, command him to come in, and thyself ask him if he repents. If he be worthy to be received into the Church, appoint him days of fasting according to his fault, two, or three, or five, or seven weeks, and thus allow him to go, saying to him all that is proper for admonition and doctrine. Reprove him, and tell him to be humble-minded, and to pray and make supplication in the days of fasting, that he be found worthy of the forgiveness of sins, as it is written in Genesis, "Thou hast sinned, cease. Let thy repentance be with thee, and thou shalt have power over it." Look also at Miriam the sister of Moses, when she had spoken against Moses, and afterwards she repented, and was thought worthy of forgiveness, it was said by the Lord, "If her father had but spit in her face, would she not have been ashamed and separated for seven days without the camp, and then she would have come in?" Thus also it is required of you to act towards those who promise to repent of their sins. Put them out of the Church as it is proper for their faults, and afterwards receive them as a merciful Father. If then the Bishop himself cause scandal, how can he rise and search for the sin of any one, or reprove for it, and command sentence by his hands? . . .

Therefore, O Bishop, teach, and reprove, and loosen by pardon, and know that thy place is that of God Almighty, and thou hast received power to forgive sins, for it is said to you Bishops, "All that ye shall bind on earth shall be bound in Heaven; and all that ye shall loose shall be loosed." As therefore thou hast power to loose, know thyself and thy conduct and thy works, that in this life they may be . . . [worthy] of thy place, but there is no man among the sons of men who is without sins, for it is written, "There is no man that is pure from the uncleanness of sin, no, not one, even if he have lived only one day in this world." Because of this the conversation and the conduct of the works of the righteous, and of the first Fathers were written, that it might be known that in each one of them was found just a little sin, that it might be known that the Lord God alone is sinless, as David said, "That thou mightest be justified in thy sayings and be clear in thy judgments." For the uncleanness of the righteous is to ourselves a comfort and a consolation and a good hope, that we, though we have also sinned a little, have an expectation of getting pardon. There is therefore no man without sin. But thou, according to thy strength, be diligent that thou be not overtaken in aught, and be careful about every one, lest any man should be offended, and should perish because of thee; because the layman is careful of his own soul alone, but thou carriest the weight of every man, and it is a very great burden that thou bearest; "for he to whom the Lord hath given much, from him much will be required." Forasmuch, therefore, as thou bearest the burdens of all men, be watchful. For it is written that the Lord said to Moses, "Thou and Aaron shall bear the sins of the priesthood." For thus, as thou shalt give a sufficient answer for many, so thou shalt care for every one; that thou mayest keep those that are whole, and admonish those that sin, and correct and reprove and punish and lighten them by means of repentance and pardon; and when a sinner repents and weeps, receive him; and when the people have prayed for him, lay [thy hands] upon him, and allow him thenceforth to be in the Church. Those who sleep and are negligent restore and rouse and confirm, and pray for them and heal them, for thou knowest where is the reward to thee if thou hast done thus; so if thou neglectest it, a great danger will come upon thee. . . . Thou shalt leave the ninety and nine on the mountain, and go to seek her that was lost; and when thou findest her carry her upon thy shoulders, rejoicing, because thou hast found her that was lost; bring her and mingle her with the flock. Thus obey thou also, O Bishop; visit the one that is lost, and seek the one that has wandered, and restore the one that is far away, because thou hast power to forgive the sins of him that has fallen . . . for thou fillest the place of the Christ. Because of this also our Saviour said to him that had sinned, "Thy sins are forgiven thee; thy faith hath made thee whole; go in peace." Peace then is the Church of quiet and rest; she in whom He established those whom He loosed from their sins whole and without spot, having a good hope, and being diligent in the cultivation of works and afflictions. As a wise and sympathetic physician He cures all men, and mostly those who have wandered in their sins, for "the whole have no need of a physician, but they that are sick." Thou also, O Bishop, art made the physician of His Church, therefore do not restrain the medicine that thou mayest heal those that are sick in their sins, but cure them by every means and make them whole and establish them safe in the Church; that thou be not taken by this word which the Lord spake, "Ye have ruled them with violence and levity." Lead not therefore with violence; be not vehement, nor judge sharply, nor be merciless, nor deride the people who are under thy hand, nor hide from them the word of repentance, for that would be to have ruled them with violence and levity. But if ye oversee my people harshly and punish them with violence, and drive them and expel them, and do not receive them that have sinned, but harshly and mercilessly hide repentance from them, thou wilt even be a helper in their conversion to evil, and in scattering the flocks to be food for the beasts of the field, that is to say, to the wicked men of this world, but not to men in truth, but to the beasts, to the heathen, to the heretics; for him who goes out of the Church they follow immediately, like evil beasts, to swallow him for food; because of thine own harshness, he then that goeth out of the Church, either goeth and entereth in unto the heathen, or plunges into heresies; he will be entirely a stranger, and be removed from the Church, and from the hope of God, and thou wilt be guilty of his ruin, because thou wert ready to put out and to cast away those who sin; and when they repented and returned, thou didst not wish to receive them. Behold, thou art fallen under the condemnation of this word which said, "Your feet hasten to evil, and are swift to shed blood; affliction and misery are in their paths, and the way of peace have they not known." The Way of Peace is our Saviour, as He said, "Forgive the sins of those who sin, that your sins also may be forgiven; give and it shall be given unto you," which is, "Give the pardon of sins, that you also may receive pardon." He also teaches us that we should be constant in prayers at all times, and that we should say, "Forgive us our debts and our sins, as we also forgive our debtors." For if thou forgivest not those that sin, how canst thou receive forgiveness? Behold, will not thy mouth accuse thee, and thou wilt convict thyself of having said, "I forgive" when thou hast not forgiven, but hast verily murdered; for he who puts any one out of the Church without mercy, what else does he do but murder bitterly, and shed blood without pity? For if a righteous man is unjustly killed by any one by means of the sword, he is received to rest with God; but he who puts any one out of the Church and receives him not again, kills verily evilly and bitterly for eternity; and God gives to be food to cruel fire for ever, him who puts out of the Church, and does not look at the mercy of God, and does not remember His goodness to the penitent, and does not bear the likeness of the Christ, nor pay attention to any people who repent of the multitude of their failings that they may receive pardon from him. . . .

*       *       *       *       *

Hear therefore, ye Bishops, and hear, ye laymen, that as the Lord hath said, I will judge between ram and ram, and between sheep and sheep, that is to say, between Bishop and Bishop, and between layman and layman; for if the layman love the layman, let the layman also love the Bishop and honour him, and reverence him as father and lord and god after God Almighty, for it is said to the Bishop by means of the Apostles, that "all who hear you hear Me, and all that injure you injure Me, and Him that sent Me." Again, let the Bishop love the laymen as children, and nourish and inflame them with the zeal of his love, like eggs, that chickens may come from them; hatch them like chickens and nourish them as with the nourishment of winged fowls. O Bishop! teach and admonish every one. Those who are deserving of reproof reprove, and make them sorry, as for conversion and not for destruction. Admonish as for repentance, and correct them, so that thou mayest make their ways straight and smooth for them, and make stable their mode of life. Keep what is in health, that is to say, keep carefully him who is steadfast in the faith, and feed all the people in peace. That which is weak strengthen, that is to say, him who is tempted, strengthen by means of admonition. That which is sick heal, that is to say, him who is sick with doubt of the faith heal by means of doctrine. That which is broken bind up, that is to say, him who is beaten or struck or broken by his sins or halting in the way of righteousness, bind him up, that is to say, cure him by means of intercession and admonition; raise him from his fall and encourage him; shew him also that there is hope for him. Bind him up and heal him; admit him also to the Church. That which has wandered persuade, that is to say, him that is abandoned in sins, and excommunicated as for reproof, leave not without, but teach and admonish and convert, and receive him into thy flock, that is to say, him who by the multitude of his falls has cut off his hope, and has let his soul go to perdition; do not allow him to perish utterly, lest by means of temptation or much negligence he sleep, and through the heaviness of his slumber he forget his life, and be removed and turned from the flock, that is to say, from the Church, and he come to perdition; for since he has got out of the fold and is removed from the flock, a wolf will eat him as he wanders, and he will perish utterly. But do thou visit him, admonish and teach and convert him, command him and encourage him to awaken; tell him that there is hope, and cut this off from their minds, that they may not say nor think that which was said of old, that "Our iniquities and sins are upon us, and by them we are corrupted; how then can we live?" It is not required of us that we should say or think these things, or suppose that their hope is cut off on account of the multitude of their sins, but that they should know that the mercies of God are many, that He hath promised with oaths and good counsel, pardon to those who have sinned. If then a man sin, and know not the Scriptures, and be not persuaded of the long-suffering and pity of God, and knoweth not the boundaries of pardon and repentance, he perisheth by this, that he knoweth not. Therefore thou, O Bishop, as a shepherd, a partaker in suffering, who are full of love and tenderness, be assiduous in visiting thy flock. Count the flock. Seek that which has wandered, as said the Lord God Jesus the Christ, our Teacher and our Good Shepherd.

\* \* \* \* \*

If then there be false brethren [who], on account of envy or the jealousy of enemies, and of Satan, who works by them, bring a false accusation against one of the brethren, or even a true one, those shall know that every one who investigates about these things, in order to accuse or blaspheme about any one, he is the son of anger, and where anger is, God is not; for anger is of Satan, who by means of these false brethren never allows peace to be in the Church. Therefore when ye know them, those that are so far wanting in sense, first of all believe them not, and secondly, Bishops and Deacons, beware of them, how ye say ought of the things that ye have heard from them to any of the brethren. Consider about him against whom they bring an accusation, investigate wisely, compare his actions, and if he be found to merit reproof, according to the doctrine of our Lord which He hath spoken in the Gospel, reprove him between thee and him; if he repent, and be converted, save him. And if he will not be convinced, reprove him before two or three, and fulfil that which was said, that at the mouth of two or three witnesses every word shall be established; for therefore, brethren, it is required for witness, that it stand upon the mouth of two or three witnesses, because the Father, and the Son, and the Holy Ghost testify about the works of men; for where there is admonition of doctrine, there is also discipline and conversion of those who have wandered. Therefore at the mouth of two or three witnesses every word shall be established.

And if he obey not, reprove him before all the Church; if he do not hear even the Church, let him be counted unto thee as a heathen and as a publican. Because the Lord hath said unto you, O Bishops, that henceforth ye receive not that man into the Church as Christians and be not partakers with him; for not even the heathen or the wicked publicans dost thou receive into the Church, nor make thyself partaker with them, unless they first repent, promising so that they may believe, and never henceforth again do evil deeds; for therefore our Lord and Saviour gave room for repentance to those who have sinned; for even I Matthew, who am one of the twelve Apostles, who speak to you by this Didascalia, I was a publican of old, and because I believed, grace came upon me, and I repented from my former works, and I was thought worthy to become an Apostle and a preacher of the Word of God. Again also John the Baptist, that he might seek, preached in the Gospel to publicans, not to cut off their hope, but taught them how they should act in future. When they asked him for a reply he said to them, "Do not exact more than what is commanded and appointed for you." And also Zacchæus in repentance the Lord received, making a request of him. We do not refuse salvation even to the heathen if they repent and renounce and remove from themselves their error. Therefore let him be accounted to you as a heathen and as a publican, he who is convicted of evil works and of falsehood; and afterwards if he promise to repent as the heathen, when they wish and promise to repent and say, "We believe," we receive them into the congregation that they may hear the Word, but we do not communicate with them until they receive the seal and are confirmed. Thus also we do not communicate with these until they shew the fruits of repentance; for they can certainly come in, if they wish to hear the Word, that they may not perish utterly, but in prayer they take no part, but go outside; because that even they, when they see that they do not take part in the Church, restrain themselves, and repent of their former deeds, and become eager to be received into the Church in prayer. They also who see them and hear that they have gone out like publicans may fear, and take heed to themselves that they sin not, lest it happen thus to them also, and they go out of the Church, being reproved for sin or for falsehood. Do not utterly prevent them then from entering the Church, and hearing the discourse of the Bishop; for even our Lord and Saviour did not completely reject and cast out the publicans and sinners, but even ate with them. Because of this also the Pharisees murmured against Him, saying, "He eateth and drinketh with publicans and sinners." Then our Saviour answered and said against their thoughts and murmurings, "They that are whole have no need of a physician, but they that are sick." Therefore have intercourse with those who have been reproved for their sins, and are in a bad state, and attach them to you, and take care of their [interests], and talk ye with them and console them, keep hold of them, and cause them to be converted; and afterwards when every one of them has repented, and has shewn the fruits of repentance, thereafter receive him in prayer as [ye do] to the heathen. As therefore thou baptizest a heathen, and thereafter receivest him, so on that man also lay the hand, every one praying for him; thereafter bring him in and let him partake with the Church. Let that laying on of the hand be to him instead of baptism; for if by the laying on of the hand and by baptism they receive the communication of the Holy Ghost . . . therefore as a sympathetic physician sharing in suffering, heal all those who have sinned, and distribute with all wisdom, offer healing for the help of their lives; and be not ready to cut off the members of the Church, but make use of the Word of Remedies, also of admonitions of preparation and of the plasters of supplication; for if an ulcer goes deep, and diminishes his flesh, by means of curative medicines nourish it, and reduce it. If there be in it foulness, by a sharp medicine, that is to say by the word of reproof, purify it; and if more flesh should spring up, by a harsh medicine, that is to say, by the communication of judgment shave it off and reduce it. If there be in it gangrene, burn it with a cautery, that is to say, with the incision of a long fast, cut off the putridness of the ulcer. If the ulcer grow and get the better of the cauteries, decide about that which is corrupt, then after much consultation with other physicians cut off that member which is corrupt that it destroy not all the body. Be not ready to amputate speedily, and do not rush in a hurry and run to the saw of many teeth, but first use scalpels, and cut the ulcer, that the cause of the evil which is hidden inside it may be seen openly and be known, that the whole body may be kept from being affected. But if thou see a person who does not wish to repent, but has completely cut off hope of himself, then with grief and sorrow cut him off and cast him out of the Church. For if thou findest that that accusation of calumny is false, and ye pastors with the Deacons have received the falsehood as truth, because of the accepting of persons, or because of offerings which ye have received; and ye change judgments, because ye wish to do the will of the Evil one, and him who is accused, being guiltless of this accusation, ye put out and cast him from the Church, ye will give an account in the day of the Lord; for it is written, "Thou shalt not respect persons in judgment," and again the Scripture hath said, that a "bribe blindeth the eyes of seers, and perverteth righteous words." And again it hath said, "Deliver the oppressed, judge the orphans, justify the widows"; and judge righteous judgment in the gates. Take heed then that ye be not respecters of persons and be condemned by the word of the Lord, who hath spoken thus, "Woe unto those that make bitter sweet, and sweet bitter; and call light darkness, and darkness what is bright, and justify the wicked for his reward, and pass over the righteousness of the righteous." But be watchful, that ye condemn not any one iniquitously, and help the wicked, because that in condemning others ye are condemning yourselves; as the Lord hath said, that "with what judgment ye judge ye shall be judged, and as ye condemn, ye shall be condemned." Therefore remember and apply to yourselves this word, "Forgive, and it shall be forgiven you; condemn not, and ye shall not be condemned." If then, your judgment, O Bishops, be without respect of persons, look at him who is the accuser of his brother, if he be a false brother, if for the sake of envy or jealousy or calumny he have brought disturbance on the Church of God, and he should kill him who is calumniated by him, being put out of the Church and delivered to the destruction of fire; thou therefore judge him severely, because he has brought an evil thing against his brother, as it were from his own imagination; if he had not found that it goes before to his hearing; he would have killed his brother in the fire; for it is written, that "every one who sheddeth man's blood, his blood shall be shed for the blood which he hath shed." When that one then is found out to be thus, put him out of the Church with a great reprimand as a murderer; and after a time, if he promise to repent, admonish him, and lay a hard discipline upon him; and thereafter put on [your] hand and receive him into the Church; and take heed and observe him that is such, lest again it happen against some one else. And if you see him after he has entered the Church, that again he quarrels and wishes to accuse others also, and chatters and fabricates, and casts blame upon many falsely: put him out, that he may never again disturb and trouble the Church; for he that is such, even if he be within, because he is not suitable to the Church, is of no advantage to her.

---

*The Didascalia Apostolorum in English,* tr. from the Syriac by Margaret Dunlop Gibson (Horae Semiticae No. II, London: Cambridge University Press, 1903), pp. 28–29, 32–33, 34–36, 41–42, 54–57. By permission.

# Exhibit Four

## ON FACING MARTYRDOM

### CYPRIAN

## Introduction

After several decades of peace and toleration of Christians, a widespread persecution suddenly was ordered throughout the Roman Empire by the Emperor Decius in the year 250. Although cut short by the Emperor's death the following year, this persecution posed for the first time a single, drastic, empire-wide crisis for all congregations of Christians. Thousands of believers compromised themselves either by paying homage to the genius of the Emperor, by bribing others to make the required sacrifice in their stead, or by purchasing forged certificates of their conformity with the state religion. During the persecution, pastors worked to stiffen the religious loyalty of the faithful, and for years afterward they dealt with the difficult problem of disciplining lapsed Christians who sought readmission to the church.

The churchman who most ardently advocated acceptance of the prescribed penalties for refusing to sacrifice, and who pleaded for a uniform policy for dealing with the lapsed, was Cyprian, bishop of Carthage from 248 until his death as a martyr ten years later. Building upon the rigorism that he learned from his Carthaginian predecessor Tertullian, Cyprian taught that, since the church was one in

113

doctrine, it must be one in discipline, and that bishops as guardians of the single doctrine must be the dispensers of a single discipline. In a number of short treatises and stern letters, Cyprian spelled out the implications of his view of the unity of the church, the absolute authority of bishops, and the necessity of standing steadfastly for the faith in the face of persecution. Thus Cyprian originated ancient catholicism's emphasis upon the unity of the church and the absolute authority of its bishops. Broadly speaking, his view of the duties of Christians facing persecution and of pastors in the wake of persecution prevailed until persecutions ceased early in the fourth century. Important as his writings were to a developing Catholic ecclesiology, Cyprian's tracts and epistles also combined profound pastoral concern with rigid insistence upon church discipline administered by the church's authoritative officers.

In several writings on the problems of the lapsed, Cyprian taught that only bishops might set the conditions under which Christians of faltering faith should be readmitted to the church —which he took to be readmission into communion with the bishop. Another writing that represents his contribution to pastoral care is a long letter to the Christians at Thibaris, a nearby town in Proconsular Africa.

Written at the height of the Decian persecution, the letter sought to prepare people for an hour of dire trouble by exhorting them to die rather than compromise their Christian conviction. Cyprian mitigates their loneliness by invoking a host of believers who have persevered in the faith. Their impending fate he makes into a summons by their Lord to witness. He links them with a long line of heroes who have died for God's sake. He assures them that their path of pain and death is well trodden by fellow believers. He surrounds them with the supporting attention and the bracing prayers of all Christians living and dead. He likens their martyrdom to Christ's crucifixion and makes it the grand finale of faithful living. He holds out the promise of sublime reward in that the martyrs would rejoice in heaven with Abraham, Isaac, Jacob, all the patriarchs, and prophets and apostles. All this Cyprian casts in the form of a mighty exhortation—a language in the pastoral repertory of rhetoric appropriate to set a seemingly hopeless crisis in the context of ultimate meaning and concern, thus making the crisis bearable even with buoyancy.

Cyprian's letter is reproduced here in its entirety, including his copious quotations from Scripture.

# ON FACING
# MARTYRDOM

From: *Letter to the People of Thibaris* (c. 250),
by Cyprian.

Cyprian to the people abiding at Thibaris, greeting. I had indeed thought, beloved brethren, and prayerfully desired—if the state of things and the condition of the times permitted, in conformity with what you frequently desired—myself to come to you; and being present with you, then to strengthen the brotherhood with such moderate powers of exhortation as I possess. But since I am detained by such urgent affairs, that I have not the power to travel far from this place, and to be long absent from the people over whom by divine mercy I am placed, I have written in the meantime this letter, to be to you in my stead. For as, by the condescension of the Lord instructing me, I am very often instigated and warned, I ought to bring unto your conscience also the anxiety of my warning. For you ought to know and to believe, and hold it for certain, that the day of affliction has begun to hang over our heads, and the end of the world and the time of Antichrist to draw near, so that we must all stand prepared for the battle; nor consider anything but the glory of life eternal, and the crown of the confession of the Lord; and not regard those things which are coming as being such as were those which have passed away. A severer and a fiercer fight is now threatening, for which the soldiers of Christ ought to prepare themselves with uncorrupted faith and robust courage, considering that they drink the cup of Christ's blood daily, for the reason that they themselves also may be able to shed their blood for Christ. For this is to wish to be found with Christ, to imitate that which Christ both taught and did, according to the Apostle John, who said, "He that saith he abideth in Christ, ought himself also so to walk even as He walked." Moreover, the blessed Apostle Paul exhorts and teaches, saying, "We are God's children; but if children, then heirs of God, and joint-heirs with Christ; if so be that we suffer with Him, that we may also be glorified together."

Which things must all now be considered by us, that no one may desire anything from the world that is now dying, but may follow Christ, who both lives for ever, and quickens His servants, who are established in the faith of His name. For there comes the time, beloved brethren, which our Lord long ago foretold and taught us was approaching, saying, "The time cometh, that whosoever killeth you will think that he doeth God service. And these things they will do unto you, because they have not known the Father nor me. But these things have I told you, that when the time shall come, ye may remember that I told you of them." Nor let any one wonder that we are harassed with constant persecutions, and continually tried with increasing afflictions, when the Lord before predicted that these things would happen in the last times, and has instructed us for the warfare by the teaching and exhortation of His words. Peter also, His apostle, has taught that persecutions occur for the sake of our being proved, and that we also should, by the example of righteous men who have gone before us, be joined to the love of God by death and sufferings. For he wrote in his epistle, and said, "Beloved, think it not strange concerning the fiery trial which is to try you, nor do ye fall away, as if some new thing happened unto you; but as often as ye partake in Christ's sufferings, rejoice in all things, that when His glory shall be revealed, ye may be glad also with exceeding joy. If ye be reproached in the name of Christ, happy are ye; for the name of the majesty and power of the Lord resteth on you, which indeed on their part is blasphemed, but on our part is glorified." Now the apostles taught us those things which they themselves also learnt from the Lord's precepts and the heavenly commands, the Lord Himself thus strengthening us, and saying, "There is no man that hath left house, or land, or parents, or brethren, or sisters, or wife, or children, for the kingdom of God's sake, who shall not receive sevenfold more in this present time, and in the world to come life everlasting." And again He says, "Blessed are ye when men shall hate you, and shall separate you from their company, and shall cast you out, and shall reproach your name as evil for the Son of man's sake. Rejoice ye in that day, and leap for joy; for, behold, your reward is great in heaven."

The Lord desired that we should rejoice and leap for joy in persecutions, because, when persecutions occur, then are given the crowns of faith, then the soldiers of God are proved, then the heavens are opened to martyrs. For we have not in such a way given our name to warfare that we ought only to think about peace, and draw back from and refuse war, when in this very warfare the Lord walked first—the Teacher of humility, and endurance, and suffering—so that what He taught to be done, He first of all did, and what He exhorts to suffer, He Himself first suffered for us. Let it be before your eyes, beloved brethren, that He who alone received all judgment from the Father, and who will come to judge, has already declared the decree of His judgment and of His future recognition, foretelling and testifying that He will confess those before His Father who confess Him, and will deny those who deny Him. If we could escape death, we might reasonably fear to die. But since, on the other hand, it is necessary that a mortal man should die, we should embrace the occasion that comes by divine promise and condescension, and accomplish the ending provided by death with the reward of immortality; nor fear to be slain, since we are sure when we are slain to be crowned.

Nor let any one, beloved brethren, when he beholds our people driven away and scattered by the fear of persecution, be disturbed at not seeing the brotherhood gathered together, nor hearing the bishops discoursing. All are not able to be there together, who may not kill, but who must be killed. Wherever, in those days, each one of the brethren shall be separated from the flock for a time, by the necessity of the season, in body, not in spirit, let him not be moved at the terror of that flight; nor, if he withdraw and be concealed, let him be alarmed at the solitude of the desert place. He is not alone, whose companion in flight Christ is; he is not alone who, keeping God's temple wheresoever he is, is not without God. And if a robber should fall upon you, a fugitive in the solitude or in the mountains; if a wild beast should attack you; if hunger, or thirst, or cold should distress you, or the tempest and the storm should overwhelm you hastening in a rapid voyage over the seas, Christ everywhere looks upon His soldier fighting; and for the sake of persecution, for the honour of His name, gives a reward to him when he dies, as He has promised that He will give in the resurrection. Nor is the glory of martyrdom less that he has not perished publicly and before many, since the cause of perishing is to perish for Christ. That Witness who proves martyrs, and crowns them, suffices for a testimony of his martyrdom.

Let us, beloved brethren, imitate righteous Abel, who initiated martyrdoms, he first being slain for righteousness' sake. Let us imitate Abraham, the friend of God, who did not delay to offer his son as a victim with his own hands, obeying God with a faith of devotion. Let us imitate the three children Ananias, Azarias, and Misael, who, neither frightened by their youthful age nor broken down by captivity, Judea being conquered and Jerusalem taken, overcame the king by the power of faith in his own kingdom; who, when bidden to worship the image which Nebuchadnezzar the king had made, stood forth stronger both than the king's threats and the flames, calling out and attesting their faith by these words: "O king Nebuchadnezzar, we are not careful to answer thee in this matter. For the God whom we serve is able to deliver us from the burning fiery furnace; and He will deliver us out of thine hands, O king. But if not, be it known unto thee, that we do not serve thy gods, nor worship the golden image which thou hast set up." They believed that they might escape according to their faith, but they added, "and if not," that the king might know that they could also die for the God they worshipped. For this is the strength of courage and of faith, to believe and to know that God can deliver from present death, and yet not to fear death nor to give way, that faith may be the more mightily proved. The uncorrupted and unconquered might of the Holy Spirit broke forth by their mouth, so that the words which the Lord in His Gospel spoke are seen to be true: "But when they shall seize you, take no thought what ye shall speak; for it shall be given you in that hour what ye shall speak. For it is not ye that speak, but the Spirit of your Father which speaketh in you." He said that what we are able to speak and to answer is given to us in that hour from heaven, and supplied; and that it is not then we who speak, but the Spirit of God our Father, who, as He does not depart nor is separated from those who confess Him, Himself both speaks and is crowned in us. So Daniel, too, when he was required to worship the idol Bel, which the people and the king then worshipped, in asserting the honour of his God, broke forth with full faith and freedom, saying, "I worship nothing but the Lord my God, who created the heaven and the earth."

What shall we say of the cruel tortures of the blessed martyrs in the Maccabees, and the multiform sufferings of the seven brethren, and the mother comforting her children in their agonies, and herself dying also with her children? Do not they witness the proofs of great courage and faith, and exhort us by their sufferings to the triumphs of martyrdom? What of the prophets whom the Holy Spirit quickened to the foreknowledge of future events? What of the apostles whom the Lord chose? Since these righteous men were slain for righteousness' sake, have they not taught us also to die? The nativity of Christ witnessed at once the martyrdom of infants, so that they who were two years old and under were slain for His name's sake. An age not yet fitted for the battle appeared fit for the crown. That it might be manifest that they who are slain for Christ's sake are innocent, innocent infancy was put to death for His name's sake. It is shown that none is free from the peril of persecution, when even these accomplished martyrdoms. But how grave is the case of a Christian man, if he, a servant, is unwilling to suffer, when his Master first suffered; and that we should be unwilling to suffer for our own sins, when He who had no sin of His own suffered for us! The Son of God suffered that He might make us sons of God, and the son of man will not suffer that he may continue to be a son of God! If we suffer from the world's hatred, Christ first endured the world's hatred. If we suffer reproaches in this world, if exile, if tortures, the Maker and Lord of the world experienced harder things than these, and He also warns us, saying, "If the world hate you, remember that it hated me before you. If ye were of the world, the world would love its own: but because ye are not of the world, but I have chosen you out of the world, therefore the world hateth you. Remember the word that I said unto you, The servant is not greater than his lord. If they have persecuted me, they will also persecute you." Whatever our Lord and God taught, He also did, that the disciple might not be excused if he learns and does not.

Nor let any one of you, beloved brethren, be so terrified by the fear of future persecution, or the coming of the threatening Antichrist, as not to be found armed for all things by the evangelical exhortations and precepts, and by the heavenly warnings. Antichrist is coming, but above him comes Christ also. The enemy goeth about and rageth, but immediately the Lord follows to avenge our sufferings and our wounds. The adversary is enraged and threatens, but there is One who can deliver us from his hands. He is to be feared whose anger no one can escape, as He Himself forewarns, and says: "Fear not them which kill the body, but are not able to kill the soul; but rather fear Him which is able to destroy both body and soul in hell." And again: "He that loveth his life, shall lose it; and he that hateth his life in this world, shall keep it unto life eternal." And in the Apocalypse He instructs and forewarns, saying, "If any man worship the beast and his image, and receive his mark in his forehead or in his hand, the same also shall drink of the wine of the wrath of God, mixed in the cup of His indignation, and he shall be tormented with fire and brimstone in the presence of the holy angels, and in the presence of the Lamb; and the smoke of their torments shall ascend up for ever and ever; and they shall have no rest day nor night, who worship the beast and his image."

For the secular contest men are trained and prepared, and reckon it a great glory of their honour if it should happen to them to be crowned in the sight of the people, and in the presence of the emperor. Behold a lofty and great contest, glorious also with the reward of a heavenly crown, inasmuch as God looks upon us as we struggle, and, extending His view over those whom He had condescended to make His sons, He enjoys the spectacle of our contest. God looks upon us in the warfare, and fighting in the encounter of faith; His angels look on us, and Christ looks on us. How great is the dignity, and how great the happiness of the glory, to engage in the presence of God, and to be crowned, with Christ for a judge! Let us be armed, beloved brethren, with our whole strength, and let us be prepared for the struggle with an uncorrupted mind, with a sound faith, with a devoted courage. Let the camp of God go forth to the battle-field which is appointed to us. Let the sound ones be armed, lest he that is sound should lose the advantage of having lately stood; let the lapsed also be armed, that even the lapsed may regain what he has lost: let honour provoke the whole; let sorrow provoke the lapsed to the battle. The Apostle Paul teaches us to be armed and prepared, saying, "We wrestle not against flesh and blood, but against powers, and the princes of this world and of this darkness, against spirits of wickedness in high places. Wherefore put on the whole armour, that ye may be able to withstand in the most evil day, that when ye have done all ye may stand; having your loins girt about with truth, and having put on the breastplate of righteousness; and your feet shod with the preparation of the Gospel of peace; taking the shield of faith, wherewith ye shall be able to quench all the fiery darts of the wicked one; and the helmet of salvation, and the sword of the Spirit, which is the word of God."

Let us take these arms, let us fortify ourselves with these spiritual and heavenly safeguards, that in the most evil day we may be able to withstand, and to resist the threats of the devil: let us put on the breast-plate of righteousness, that our breast may be fortified and safe against the darts of the enemy: let our feet be shod with evangelical teaching, and armed, so that when the serpent shall begin to be trodden and crushed by us, he may not be able to bite and trip us up: let us bravely bear the shield of faith, by the protection of which, whatever the enemy darts at us may be extinguished: let us take also for protection of our head the helmet of salvation, that our ears may be guarded from hearing the deadly edicts; that our eyes may be fortified, that they may not see the odious images; that our brow may be fortified, so as to keep safe the sign of God; that our mouth may be fortified, that the conquering tongue may confess Christ its Lord: let us also arm the right hand with the sword of the Spirit, that it may bravely reject the deadly sacrifices; that, mindful of the Eucharist, the hand which has received the Lord's body may embrace the Lord Himself, hereafter to receive from the Lord the reward of heavenly crowns.

Oh, what and how great will that day be at its coming, beloved brethren, when the Lord shall begin to count up His people, and to recognise the deservings of each one by the inspection of His divine knowledge, to send the guilty to Gehenna, and to set on fire our persecutors with the perpetual burning of a penal fire, but to pay to us the reward of our faith and devotion! What will be the glory and how great the joy to be admitted to see God, to be honoured to receive with Christ, thy Lord God, the joy of eternal salvation and light—to greet Abraham, and Isaac, and Jacob, and all the patriarchs, and prophets, and apostles, and martyrs—to rejoice with the righteous and the friends of God in the kingdom of heaven, with the pleasure of immortality given to us—to receive there what neither eye hath seen, nor ear heard, neither hath entered into the heart of man! For the apostle announces that we shall receive greater things than anything that we here either do or suffer, saying, "The sufferings of this present time are not worthy to be compared with the glory to come hereafter which shall be revealed in us." When that revelation shall come, when that glory of God shall shine upon us, we shall be as happy and joyful, honoured with the condescension of God, as they will remain guilty and wretched, who, either as deserters from God or rebels against Him, have done the will of the devil, so that it is necessary for them to be tormented with the devil himself in unquenchable fire.

Let these things, beloved brethren, take hold of our hearts; let this be the preparation of our arms, this our daily and nightly meditation, to have before our eyes and ever to revolve in our thoughts and feelings the punishments of the wicked and the rewards and the deservings of the righteous: what the Lord threatens by way of punishment against those that deny Him; what, on the other hand, He promises by way of glory to those that confess Him. If, while we think and meditate on these things, there should come to us a day of persecution, the soldier of Christ instructed in His precepts and warnings is not fearful for the battle, but is prepared for the crown. I bid you, dearest brethren, ever heartily farewell.

Cyprian, Epistle LV, To the People of Thibaris, Exhorting to Martyrdom, tr. by Ernest Wallis, *The Ante-Nicene Fathers*, ed. Alexander Roberts and James Donaldson (Buffalo: Christian Literature Company, 1886), vol. V, pp. 347–350.

# Exhibit Five

## GESTALT OF GRIEF

### JOHN CHRYSOSTOM

## Introduction

The nickname of John Chrysostom (c. 347–407)—meaning "golden-mouthed"—enshrines the memory of his extraordinary ability as a preacher, but the man earned also a just fame as exegete, liturgist, moralist, and pastor. Educated in rhetoric and theology in the city of Antioch, his preference for the monastic life was overridden by a call to lead a moral reform in the church in Antioch and, later, in Constantinople, where he spent a stormy career as bishop. Roundly despised as he was by persons in high places whose morals he censured, Chrysostom was also deeply revered by multitudes of devout Christians who shared his concern for personal holiness.

Especially among the latter, Chrysostom adroitly exercised his rich pastoral gifts in such a way that his caring for troubled people was not cribbed by his strict morality. Although remembered primarily for eloquent sermons and for a definitive treatise on the priesthood, Chrysostom's correspondence with ordinary Christians facing common problems of life is exemplified by the well-known letter to a young widow. This writing comes from an early period in his life, perhaps even before the time of his ordination as deacon, but it shows him sensitive to problems posed by inescapable human predicaments.

Christian faith molded the form of Chrysostom's pastoral concern, but its content he took over entire from Stoicism. Whole clusters of psychological understandings and pastoral techniques that appear in this letter find their source in the Tusculan Disputations of Cicero (106–43 B.C.). The orator wrote:

These therefore are the duties of comforters: to do away with distress root and branch, or allay it, or diminish it as far as possible, or stop its progress and not allow it to extend further, or to divert it elsewhere. . . .

But it is necessary in dealing with diseases of the soul, just as much as in dealing with bodily diseases, to choose the proper time. . . .

The first remedial step therefore in giving comfort will be to show that either there is no evil or very little; the second will be to discuss the common lot of life and any special feature that needs discussion in the lot of the individual mourner; the third will be to show that it is utter folly to be uselessly overcome by sorrow when one realizes that there is no possible advantage.[72]

Four hundred years later, Chrysostom comforted a young widow by appealing to reason and moderation after the first blows of bereavement had passed; he proved that a seemingly evil loss was actually a beneficent gain; he helped the widow see her own individual advantages over the circumstance of women whose men were slain in war, for she was at her husband's side when he died.

So Chrysostom, like pastors in every epoch, used the psychology of his time as a source of practical wisdom about how to proceed in a delicate pastoral situation. He appealed to understandings that the widow herself undoubtedly shared. Her grief he assuaged essentially by confronting her with her own condition as a human being, and by urging her toward a response that she knew to be right and good. Therefore, the distinctively Christian character of the letter lies not in its approach, nor in its methodology of counseling, nor even in its conception of bereavement and the healing of grief, but rather in Chrysostom's conviction that personal events befalling the widow would convey God's mercies and that God had prepared for her a destiny in heaven to be attained by a chaste and obedient life as a widow.

---

[72] Marcus Tullius Cicero, *Tusculan Disputations*, III.xxxi.76; xxxii.77, tr. J. E. King, The Loeb Classical Library (Cambridge, Mass.: Harvard University Press, 1927), pp. 315, 317. By permission.

# GESTALT
# OF GRIEF

From: *Letter to a Young Widow* (c. 380),
by John Chrysostom.

That you have sustained a severe blow, and that the weapon directed
from above has been planted in a vital part all will readily admit, and
none even of the most rigid moralists will deny it; but since they who
are stricken with sorrow ought not to spend their whole time in mourning and tears, but to make good provision also for the healing of their
wounds, lest, if they be neglected their tears should aggravate the wound,
and the fire of their sorrow become inflamed, it is a good thing to listen
to words of consolation, and restraining for a brief season at least the
fountain of thy tears to surrender thyself to those who endeavour to
console thee. On this account I abstained from troubling you when
your sorrow was at its height, and the thunderbolt had only just fallen
upon you; but having waited an interval and permitted you to take your
fill of mourning, now that you are able to look out a little through the
mist, and to open your ears to those who attempt to comfort you, I
also would second the words of your handmaids by some contributions
of my own. For whilst the tempest is still severe, and a full gale of sorrow is blowing, he who exhorts another to desist from grief would only
provoke him to increased lamentations and having incurred his hatred
would add fuel to the flame by such speeches besides being regarded
himself as an unkind and foolish person. But when the troubled water
has begun to subside, and God has allayed the fury of the waves, then
we may freely spread the sails of our discourse. For in a moderate storm
skill may perhaps play its part; but when the onslaught of the wind is
irresistible experience is of no avail. For these reasons I have hitherto held
my peace, and even now have only just ventured to break silence because
I have heard from thy uncle that one may begin to take courage, as
some of your more esteemed handmaids are now venturing to discourse
at length upon these matters, women also outside your own household,
who are your kinsfolk, or are otherwise qualified for this office. Now if
you allow them to talk to you I have the greatest hope and confidence
that you will not disdain my words but do your best to give them a
calm and quiet hearing. Under any circumstances indeed the female sex
is the more apt to be sensitive to suffering; but when in addition there
is youth, and untimely widowhood, and inexperience in business, and a
great crowd of cares, while the whole life previously has been nurtured
in the midst of luxury, and cheerfulness and wealth, the evil is increased

many fold, and if she who is subjected to it does not obtain help from on high even an accidental thought will be able to unhinge her. Now I hold this to be the foremost and greatest evidence of God's care concerning thee; for that thou hast not been overwhelmed by grief, nor driven out of thy natural condition of mind when such great troubles suddenly concurred to afflict thee was not due to any human assistance but to the almighty hand the understanding of which there is no measure, the wisdom which is past finding out, the "Father of mercies and the God of all comfort." "For He Himself" it is said "hath smitten us, and He will heal us; He will strike, and He will dress the wound and make us whole."

For as long as that blessed husband of thine was with thee, thou didst enjoy honour, and care and zealous attention; in fact you enjoyed such as you might expect to enjoy from a husband; but since God took him to Himself He has supplied his place to thee. And this is not my saying but that of the blessed prophet David for he says "He will take up the fatherless and the widow," and elsewhere he calls Him "father of the fatherless and judge of the widow;" thus in many passages thou wilt see that He earnestly considereth the cause of this class of mankind.

But lest the continual repetition of this name of widow should upset thy soul, and disconcert thy reason, having been inflicted on thee in the very flower of thy age, I wish first of all to discourse on this point, and to prove to you that this name of widow is not a title of calamity but of honour, aye the greatest honour. For do not quote the erroneous opinion of the world as a testimony, but the admonition of the blessed Paul, or rather of Christ. For in his utterances Christ was speaking through him as he himself said "If ye seek a proof of Christ, who is speaking in me?" What then does he say? "Let not a widow be enrolled under threescore years of age" and again "but the younger widows refuse" intending by both these sayings to indicate to us the importance of the matter. And when he is making regulations about bishops he nowhere prescribes a standard of age, but in this case he is very particular on the point, and, pray, why so? not because widowhood is greater than priesthood, but because widows have greater labour to undergo than priests, being encompassed on many sides by a variety of business public and private. For as an unfortified city lies exposed to all who wish to plunder it, so a young woman living in widowhood has many who form designs upon her on every side not only those who aim at getting her money but also those who are bent upon corrupting her modesty. And besides these we shall find that she is subjected to other conditions also likely to occasion her fall. For the contempt of servants[,] their negligence of business, the loss of that respect which was formerly paid, the sight of contemporaries in prosperity, and often the hankering after luxury, induce women to engage in a second marriage. Some there are who do not choose to unite themselves to men by the law of marriage, but do so secretly and clandestinely. And they act thus in order to enjoy the praise of widowhood; thus it is a state which seems to be not reproached, but admired and deemed worthy of honour among men, not only amongst us who believe, but even amongst unbelievers also. For once when I was still a young man I know that the sophist who taught me (and he exceeded all men in his reverence for the gods) expressed admiration for my mother before a large company. For enquiring, as was his wont, of those who sat beside him who I was, and some one having said that I was the son of a woman who was a widow, he asked of me the age of my mother and the duration of her widowhood, and when I told him that she was forty years of age of which twenty had elapsed since she lost my father he was astonished and uttered a loud exclamation, and turning to those present "Heavens!" cried he "what women there are amongst the Christians." So great is the admiration and praise enjoyed by widowhood not only amongst ourselves, but also amongst those who are outside the Church. And being aware of all this the blessed Paul said "Let not a widow be enrolled under threescore years of age." And even after this great qualification of age he does not permit her to be ranked in this sacred society but mentions some additional requisites "well reported of for good works, if she have brought up children[,] if she have lodged strangers[,] if she have washed the saints['] feet[,] if she have relieved the afflicted, if she have diligently followed every good work." Heavens! what testing and scrutiny! how much virtue does he demand from the widow, and how precisely does he define it! which he would not have done, had he not intended to entrust to her a position of honour and dignity. And "the younger widows" he says "refuse["]; and then he adds the reason; "for when they have waxed wanton against Christ they will marry." By this expression he gives us to understand that they who have lost their husbands are wedded to Christ in their stead. Observe how he asserts this by way of indicating the mild and easy nature of this union; I refer to the passage "when they have waxed wanton against Christ they will marry," as if He were some gentle husband who did not exercise authority over them, but suffered them to live in freedom. Neither did Paul confine his discourse on the subject to these remarks, but also in another place again he has manifested great anxiety about it where he says "Now she who liveth in pleasure is dead while she liveth; but she who is a widow indeed and desolate hath set her hope in God, and continueth in prayers and supplications day and night." And writing to the Corinthians he says "But she is more blessed if she abide thus.["] You see what great praise is bestowed upon widowhood, and this in the New Testament, when the beauty of virginity also was clearly brought to light. Nevertheless even the lustre of this state could not obscure the glories of widowhood, which shines on brightly all the same, keeping its own value. When then we make mention of widowhood from time to time, do not be cast down, nor consider the matter a reproach; for if this be a matter of reproach, far more so is virginity. But this is not the case; no! God forbid. For inasmuch as we all admire and welcome women who live continently whilst their husbands are yet alive must we not be delighted with those who manifest the same good feeling concerning their husbands when they have departed this life, and praise them accordingly? As I was saying then, as long as you lived with the blessed Therasius you enjoyed honour and consideration such as is natural for a wife to receive from a husband; but now in his place you have God who is the Lord of all, who hath of old been thy protector and will be so now still more and with yet greater earnestness; and as I have already said He hath displayed no slight token of his providential care by having preserved thee whole and unharmed in the midst of such a furnace of anxiety and sorrow, and not suffering thee to undergo anything undesirable. Now if He has not permitted any shipwreck to take place in the midst of so much rough water, much more will He preserve thy soul in calm weather and lighten the burden of thy widowhood, and the consequences of it which seem to be so terrible.

Now if it is not the name of widow which distresses you, but the loss of such a husband I grant you that all the world over amongst men engaged in secular affairs there have been few like him, so affectionate, so gentle, so humble, so sincere, so understanding, so devout. And certainly if he had altogether perished, and utterly ceased to be, it would be right to be distressed, and sorrowful; but if he has only sailed into the tranquil haven, and taken his journey to Him who is really his king, one ought not to mourn but to rejoice on these accounts. For this death is not death, but only a kind of emigration and translation from the worse to the better, from earth to heaven, from men to angels, and archangels, and Him who is the Lord of angels and archangels. For here on earth whilst he was serving the emperor there were dangers to be expected and many plots arising from men who bore ill-will, for in proportion as his reputation increased did the designs also of enemies abound; but now that he has departed to the other world none of these things can be suspected. Wherefore in proportion as you grieve that God has taken away one who was so good and worthy you ought to rejoice that he has departed in much safety and honour, and being released from the trouble which besets this present season of danger, is in great peace and tranquillity. For is it not out of place to acknowledge that heaven is far better than earth, and yet to mourn those who are translated from this world to the other? For if that blessed husband of thine had been one of those who lived a shameful life contrary to what God approved it would have been right to bewail and lament for him not only when he had departed, but whilst he was still living; but inasmuch as he was one of those who are the friends of God we should take pleasure in him not only whilst living, but also when he has been laid to rest. And that we ought to act thus thou hast surely heard the words of the blessed Paul "to depart and to be with Christ which is far better." But perhaps you long to hear your husband's words, and enjoy the affection which you bestowed upon him, and you yearn for his society, and the glory which you had on his account, and the splendour, and honour, and security, and all these things being gone distress and darken your life. Well! the affection which you bestowed on him you can keep now just as you formerly did.

For such is the power of love, it embraces, and unites, and fastens together not only those who are present, and near, and visible but also those who are far distant; and neither length of time, nor separation in space, nor anything else of that kind can break up and sunder in pieces the affection of the soul. But if you wish to behold him face to face (for this I know is what you specially long for) keep thy bed in his honour sacred from the touch of any other man, and do thy best to manifest a life like his, and then assuredly thou shalt depart one day to join the same company with him, not to dwell with him for five years as thou didst here, nor for 20, or 100, nor for a thousand or twice that number but for infinite and endless ages. For it is not any physical relation, but a correspondence in the way of living which qualifies for the inheritance of those regions of rest. For if it was identity of moral constitution which brought Lazarus although a stranger to Abraham into the same heavenly bosom with him, and qualifies many from east and west to sit down with him, the place of rest will receive thee also with the good Therasius, if thou wilt exhibit the same manner of life as his, and then thou shalt receive him back again no longer in that corporeal beauty which he had when he departed, but in lustre of another kind, and splendour outshining the rays of the sun. For this body, even if it reaches a very high standard of beauty is nevertheless perishable; but the bodies of those who have been well pleasing to God, will be invested with such glory as these eyes cannot even look upon. And God has furnished us with certain tokens, and obscure indications of these things both in the Old and in the New Dispensation. For in the former the face of Moses shone with such glory as to be intolerable to the eyes of the Israelites, and in the New the face of Christ shone far more brilliantly than his. For tell me if any one had promised to make your husband king of all the earth, and then had commanded you to withdraw for twenty years on his account, and had promised after that to restore him to you with the diadem and the purple, and to place you again in the same rank with him, would you not have meekly endured the separation with due self-control? Would you not have been well pleased with the gift, and deemed it a thing worth praying for? Well then submit to this now, not for the sake of a kingdom on earth, but of a kingdom in Heaven; not to receive him back clad in a vesture of gold but robed in immortality and glory such as is fitting for them to have who dwell in Heaven. And if you find the trial very unbearable owing to its long duration, it may be that he will visit you by means of visions and converse with you as he was wont to do, and show you the face for which you yearn: let this be thy consolation taking the place of letters, though indeed it is far more definite than letters. For in the latter case there are but lines traced with the pen to look upon, but in the former you see the form of his visage, and his gentle smile, his figure and his movements, you hear his speech and recognize the voice which you loved so well.

But since you mourn also over the loss of security which you formerly enjoyed on his account, and perhaps also for the sake of those great hopes of distinction which were dawning (for I used to hear that he would speedily arrive at the dignity of præfect, and this, I fancy, it is which more especially upsets and distresses thy soul) consider I pray the case of those who have been in a higher official position than his, and yet have brought their life to a very pitiable end. Let me recall them to your memory: you probably know Theodore of Sicily [d. 371] by reputation: for he was one of the most distinguished men; he surpassed all in bodily stature and beauty as well as in the confidence which he enjoyed with the Emperor, and he had more power than any member of the royal household, but he did not bear this prosperity meekly, and having entered into a plot against the Emperor he was taken prisoner and miserably beheaded; and his wife who was not a whit inferior to thy noble self in education and birth and all other respects was suddenly stripped of all her possessions, deprived even of her freedom also, and enrolled amongst the household slaves, and compelled to lead a life more pitiable than any bondmaid, having this advantage only over the rest that owing to the extreme severity of her calamity she moved to tears all who beheld her. And it is said also that Artemisia who was the wife of a man of high reputation, since he also aimed at usurping the throne, was reduced to this same condition of poverty, and also to blindness; for the depth of her despondency, and the abundance of her tears destroyed her sight; and now she has need of persons to lead her by the hand, and to conduct her to the doors of others that she may obtain the necessary supply of food. And I might mention many other families which have been brought down in this way did I not know thee to be too pious and prudent in disposition to wish to find consolation for thy own calamity out of the misfortunes of others. And the only reason why I mentioned those instances to which I referred just now was that you might learn that human things are nothingness but that truly as the prophet says "all the glory of man is as the flower of grass." For in proportion to men's elevation and splendour is the ruin wrought for them, not only in the case of those who are under rule, but also of the rulers themselves. For it would be impossible to find any private family which has been immersed in such great calamities as the ills in which the imperial house has been steeped. For untimely loss of parents, and of husbands, and violent forms of death, more outrageous and painful than those which occur in tragedies, especially beset this kind of government.

Now passing over ancient times, of those who have reigned in our own generation, nine in all, only two have ended their life by a natural death; and of the others one was slain by a usurper, one in battle, one by a conspiracy of his household guards, one by the very man who elected him, and invested him with the purple, and of their wives some, as it is reported, perished by poison, others died of mere sorrow; while of those who still survive one, who has an orphan son, is trembling with alarm lest any of those who are in power dreading what may happen in the future should destroy him; another has reluctantly yielded to much entreaty to return from the exile into which she had been driven by him who held the chief power. And of the wives of the present rulers the one who has recovered a little from her former calamities has much sorrow mingled with her joy because the possessor of power is still young and inexperienced and has many designing men on all sides of him; and the other is ready to die of fear, and spends her time more miserably than criminals condemned to death because her husband ever since he assumed the crown up to the present day has been constantly engaged in warfare and fighting, and is more exhausted by the shame and the reproaches which assail him on all sides than by actual calamities. For that which has never taken place has now come to pass, the barbarians leaving their own country have overrun an infinite space of our territory, and that many times over, and having set fire to the land, and captured the towns they are not minded to return home again, but after the manner of men who are keeping holiday rather than making war, they laugh us all to scorn; and it is said that one of their kings declared that he was amazed at the impudence of our soldiers, who although slaughtered more easily than sheep still expect to conquer, and are not willing to quit their own country; for he said that he himself was satiated with the work of cutting them to pieces. Imagine what the feelings of the Emperor and his wife must be on hearing these words!

And since I have made mention of this war, a great crowd of widows has occurred to me, who in past times derived very great lustre from the honour enjoyed by their husbands, but now are all arrayed in a dark mourning robe and spend their whole time in lamentation. For they had not the advantage which was enjoyed by thy dear self. For thou, my excellent friend, didst see that goodly husband of thine lying on his bed, and didst hear his last words, and receive his instructions as to what should be done about the affairs of the family, and learn how by the provisions of his will they were guarded against every kind of encroachment on the part of rapacious and designing men. And not only this, but also when he was yet lying dead thou didst often fling thyself upon the body, and kiss his eyes, and embrace him, and wail over him, and thou didst see him conducted to burial with much honour, and didst everything necessary for his obsequies, as was fitting, and from frequent visits to his grave thou hast no slight consolation of thy sorrow. But these women have been deprived of all these things, having all sent out their husbands to war in the hope of receiving them back again, instead of which it has been their lot to receive the bitter tidings of their death. Neither has any one come back to them with the bodies of their slain, or bringing anything save a message describing the manner of their death. And some there are who have not even been vouchsafed this record, or been enabled to learn how their husbands fell, as they were buried beneath a heap of slain in the thick of battle.

And what wonder if most of the generals perished thus, when even the Emperor himself having been blockaded in a certain village with a few soldiers did not dare to go out and oppose the assailants, but remained inside and when the enemy had set fire to the building was burnt to death together with all that were therein, not men only, but horses, beams and walls, so that the whole was turned into a heap of ashes? And this was the tale which they who departed to war with the Emperor brought back to his wife in place of the Emperor himself. For the splendours of the world differ in no-wise whatever from the things which happen on the stage, and the beauty of spring flowers. For in the first place they flee away before they have been manifested; and then, even if they have strength to last a little while, they speedily become ready to decay. For what is more worthless than the honour and glory which is paid by the multitude? what fruit has it? what kind of profit? what serviceable end does it meet? And would that this only was the evil! but in fact besides failing to get anything good from the possession, he who owns this most cruel mistress is continually forced to bear much which is painful and injurious; for mistress she is of those who own her, and in proportion as she is flattered by her slaves does she exalt herself against them, and ties them down by increasingly harsh commands; but she would never be able to revenge herself on those who despise and neglect her; so much fiercer is she than any tyrant and wild beast. For tyrants and wild animals are often mollified by humouring, but her fury is greatest when we are most complaisant to her, and if she finds any one who will listen to her, and yield to her in everything there is no kind of command from which in future she can be induced to abstain. Moreover she has also another ally whom one would not do wrong to call her daughter. For after she herself has grown to maturity and fairly taken root amongst us, she then produces arrogance, a thing which is no less able than herself to drive the soul of those who possess it into headlong ruin.

Tell me then dost thou lament this that God hath reserved thee from such a cruel bondage, and that He has barred every avenue against these pestilential diseases? For whilst thy husband was living they ceased not continually assaulting the thoughts of thy heart, but since his death they have no starting point whence they can lay hold of thy understanding. This then is a discipline which ought to be practised in future—to abstain from lamenting the withdrawal of these evils, and from hankering after the bitter tyranny which they exercise. For where they blow a heavy blast they upset all things from the foundation and shatter them to pieces; and just as many prostitutes, although by nature ill favoured and ugly, do yet by means of enamels and pigments excite the feelings of the youthful whilst they are still tender, and when they have got them under their control treat them more insolently than any slave; so also do these passions, vainglory and arrogance, defile the souls of men more than any other kind of pollution.

On this account also wealth has seemed to the majority of men to be a good thing; at least when it is stripped of this passion of vainglory it will no longer seem desirable. At any rate those who have been permitted to obtain in the midst of their poverty popular glory have no longer preferred wealth, but rather have despised much gold when it was bestowed upon them. And you have no need to learn from me who these men were, for you know them better than I do, Epaminondas, Socrates, Aristeides, Diogenes, Krates who turned his own land into a sheep walk. The others indeed, inasmuch as it was not possible for them to get rich, saw glory brought to them in the midst of their poverty, and straightway devoted themselves to it, but this man threw away even what he possessed; so infatuated were they in the pursuit of this cruel monster. Let us not then weep because God has rescued us from this shameful thraldom which is an object of derision and of much reproach; for there is nothing splendid in it save the name it bears, and in reality it places those who possess it in a position which belies its appellation, and there is no one who does not laugh to scorn the man who does anything with a view to glory. For it is only he who has not an eye to this who will be enabled to win respect and glory; but he who sets a great value on popular glory, and does and endures everything for the sake of obtaining it is the very man who will fail to attain it, and be subjected to all the exact opposites of glory, ridicule, and accusation, scoffing, enmity and hatred. And this is wont to happen not only among men, but also among you women, and indeed more especially in your case. For the woman who is unaffected in mien, and gait, and dress, and seeks no honour from any one is admired by all women, and they are ecstatic in their praise and call her blessed, and invoke all manner of good things upon her; but a vainglorious woman they behold with aversion and detestation, and avoid her like some wild beast and load her with infinite execrations and abuse. And not only do we escape these evils by refusing to accept popular glory, but we shall gain the highest advantages in addition to those which have been already mentioned, being **trained** gradually to loosen our hold of earth and move in the direction of heaven, and despise all worldly things. For he who feels no need of the honour which comes from men, will perform with security whatever good things he does, and neither in the troubles, nor in the prosperities of this life will he be very seriously affected; for neither can the former depress him, and cast him down, nor can the latter elate and puff him up, but in precarious and troubled circumstances he himself remains exempt from change of any kind. And this I expect will speedily be the case with your own soul, and having once for all torn yourself away from all worldly interests you will display amongst us a heavenly manner of life, and in a little while will laugh to scorn the glory which you now lament, and despise its hollow and vain mask. But if you long for the security which you formerly enjoyed owing to your husband, and the protection of your property, and immunity from the designs of any of those persons who trample upon the misfortunes of others "Cast thy care upon the Lord and He will nourish thee." "For look," it is said, "to past generations and see, who ever placed his hope on the Lord and was put to shame, or who ever called upon Him, and was neglected, or who ever remained constant to His commandments and was forsaken?" For He who has alleviated this intolerable calamity, and placed you even now in a state of tranquillity will also avert impending evils; for that you will never receive another blow more severe than this you would yourself admit. Having then so bravely borne present troubles, and this when you were inexperienced, you will far more easily endure future events should any of the things contrary to our wishes, which God forbid, occur. Therefore seek Heaven, and all things which conduce to life in the other world, and none of the things here will be able to harm thee, not even the world-ruler of darkness himself, if only we do not injure ourselves. For if any one deprives us of our substance, or hews our body in pieces, none of these things concern us, if our soul abides in its integrity.

Now, once for all, if you wish your property to abide with you in security and yet further to increase I will show thee the plan, and the place where none of those who have designs upon it will be allowed to enter. What then is the place? It is Heaven. Send away thy possessions to that good husband of thine and neither thief, nor schemer, nor any other destructive thing will be able to pounce upon them. If you deposit these goods in the other world, you will find much profit arising from them. For all things which we plant in Heaven yield a large and abundant crop, such as might naturally be expected from things which have their roots in Heaven. And if you do this, see what blessings you will enjoy, in the first place eternal life and the things promised to those who love God, "which eye hath not seen, nor ear heard, neither have they entered into the heart of man," and in the second place perpetual intercourse with thy good husband; and you will relieve yourself from the cares and fears, and dangers, and designs, and enmity and hatred which beset you here.

For as long as you are surrounded with this property there will probably be some to make attempts upon it; but if you transfer it to Heaven, you will lead a life of security and safety, and much tranquillity, enjoying independence combined with godliness. For it is very irrational, when one wishes to buy land, and is seeking for productive ground, if, Heaven being proposed to him instead of earth, and the possibility presented of obtaining an estate there he abides still on earth, and puts up with the toils that are connected with it; for it often disappoints our hopes.

But since thy soul is grievously upset and vexed on account of the expectation often entertained that thy husband would attain the rank of prefect, and the thought that he was untimely snatched away from that dignity[,] consider first of all this fact, that even if this hope was a very well grounded one[,] nevertheless it was only a human hope, which often falls to the ground; and we see many things of this kind happening in life, those which were confidently expected having remained unfulfilled, whereas those which never even entered the mind have frequently come to pass, and this we constantly see occurring everywhere in cases of governments and kingdoms, and inheritances, and marriages. Wherefore even if the opportunity were very near at hand, yet as the proverb says "between the cup and the lip there is many a slip" and the Scripture saith "from the morning until the evening the time is changed."

So also a king who is here to-day is dead to-morrow; and again this same wise man illustrating the reversal of men's hopes says "many tyrants have sat down upon the ground, and one that was never thought of has worn the crown." And it was not absolutely certain that if he lived he would arrive at this dignity; for that which belongs to the future is uncertain, and causes us to have various suspicions. For on what grounds was it evident that had he lived he would have attained that dignity and that things would not have turned out the other way, and that he would have lost the office he actually held either from falling a victim to disease, or from being exposed to the envy and ill will of those who wished to excel him in prosperity, or from suffering some other grievous misfortune. But let us suppose, if you please, that it was perfectly evident that in any case had he survived he would have obtained this high distinction; then in proportion to the magnitude of the dignity would have been the increased dangers, and anxieties, and intrigues which he must have encountered. Or put these even on one side, and let us suppose him to traverse that sea of difficulties safely, and in much tranquillity; then tell me what is the goal? not that which he has now reached; no, not that, but something different, probably unpleasant and undesirable. In the first place his sight of heaven, and heavenly things would have been delayed, which is no small loss to those who have put their trust in things to come; and in the next place, even had he lived a very pure life yet the length of his life and the exigencies of his high office would have prevented his departing in such a pure condition as has now been the case.

In fact it is uncertain whether he might not have undergone many changes and given way to indolence before he breathed his last. For now we are confident that by the grace of God he has taken his flight to the region of rest, because he had not committed himself to any of those deeds which exclude from the kingdom of Heaven; but in that case after long contact with public business, he might probably have contracted great defilement. For it is an exceedingly rare thing for one who is moving in the midst of such great evils to hold a straight course, but to go astray, both wittingly and against his will, is a natural thing, and one which constantly occurs. But, as it is, we have been relieved from this apprehension, and we are firmly persuaded that in the great day he will appear in much radiance, shining forth near the King, and going with the angels in advance of Christ and clad with the robe of unutterable glory, and standing by the side of the King as he gives judgment, and acting as one of His chief ministers. Wherefore desisting from mourning and lamentation do thou hold on to the same way of life as his, yea even let it be more exact, that having speedily attained an equal standard of virtue with him, you may inhabit the same abode and be united to him again through the everlasting ages, not in this union of marriage but another far better. For this is only a bodily kind of intercourse, but then there will be a union of soul with soul more perfect, and of a far more delightful and far nobler kind.

John Chrysostom, "Letter to a Young Widow," tr. W. R. W. Stephens, *Nicene and Post-Nicene Fathers*, ed. Philip Schaff (New York: Christian Literature Company, 1889), First Series, vol. IX, pp. 121–128.

# Exhibit Six

## THE DYNAMICS OF SIN
### *JOHN CASSIAN*

## Introduction

As Germanic peoples in the early fifth century began
to overrun the western provinces of the Roman Empire, certain church leaders took it upon themselves
to gather together vast stores of information about
classical and Eastern Church life and to codify these
traditions for adoption by the Western or Latin-
speaking Church. If the most famous of these figures
were Jerome (c. 342–420) and Augustine (354–430),
by no means the least influential was their less well-
known contemporary John Cassian (c. 360–435).
Cassian spent his earlier years in travel, studying the
life and practice of Christian monks in Palestine,
Asia Minor, and Egypt, in preparation for the important work of introducing monasticism into the
Latin church. About 415 he established two monastic
communities near Marseilles, where he lived and
wrote detailed descriptions of the eastern monks' life
and thought. In his book called the *Conferences*, he
reported his interviews with the great leaders of eastern monasteries, and in the *Institutes* he set forth
explicit rules for monastic living—rules that a century
later were modified by Benedict of Nursia (480–550)
into the primary charter of Latin monasticism. Toward the end of his life, Cassian's attention was

drawn by the Council of Ephesus (431) to christological problems, about which he wrote a treatise, *On the Incarnation of the Lord.*

The *Conferences* and *Institutes* of Cassian set out a detailed psychology and symptomatology of sin in a fashion that laid the foundations for the entire edifice of Latin Catholic moral theology that has lasted even into modern times. Cassian conceived of eight "principal faults" as the fundamental nosology of the human spirit: gluttony, fornication, avarice, anger, dejection, accidie (sloth, torpor), vainglory, and pride. The origin of his list of spiritual diseases is obscure; perhaps it had a pagan background or was a partly Christianized, gnostic version of a pagan understanding of spiritual diseases.[73] If so, its non-Christian connotations were forgotten or suppressed as these faults became part of the ethos of Christian hermit-monks in the Egyptian desert where Cassian visited. At any rate, Cassian popularized the scheme and its underlying psychology in the West, where his monastic rules were specifically designed to cure these very spiritual maladies. It became the basis of the understanding of sin and pastoral care in the Celtic Church, and thence, via the penitentials, was popularized in western Europe amongst lay people, even as the same scheme received prominent attention in the Benedictine monasteries. By adapting Cassian's faults, Gregory the Great (c. 540–604) specified what became the traditional Seven Deadly Sins: pride, covetousness, lust, envy, gluttony, anger, and sloth (for accidie Gregory named *tristitia*, sorrowfulness, melancholy).

Already in Cassian's "Conference of Abbot Serapion," these principal faults had been developed into a sophisticated nosology that anticipated their development into a fully articulated psychology. Gregory combined pride and vainglory into a single and the chief sin, which he placed at the head of the list; pride became the root of all sins, and through this root all the others were directly related to the spirit's rebellion against God.

But Cassian in his own right, while not carrying the development to its fullest elaboration, achieved remarkable insights. For example, he perceived that each person had his own special besetting sin, and he saw that the evil spirits did not attack every man in precisely the same way. He argued that therapy must identify the besetting sin so that it might be cured and the spirit might then avoid the sins that developed from that particular

---

[73] See Morton W. Bloomfield, *The Seven Deadly Sins* (East Lansing: Michigan State College Press, 1952), esp. p. 66.

malady. This relation between evils was Cassian's other profound
insight, for he tells us that at least six of the sins are linked together in a chain in such a way that to succumb to one made an
opening for another. Thus, gluttony would surely give rise to
fornication, and fornication to covetousness, and so forth.

The following selections, which set out Cassian's understanding of the eight principal faults, come from his report on
his interview with one Abbot Serapion, a director of a group of
monks in Egypt; Serapion's precise identity is uncertain.

# THE DYNAMICS
# OF SIN

From: *The Conferences* (c. 420), by John Cassian.

## Conference of Abbot Serapion
## on the eight principal faults

### Chapter I

In that assembly of Ancients and Elders was a man named Serapion,
especially endowed with the grace of discretion, whose Conference I
think it is worth while to set down in writing. For when we entreated him
to discourse of the way to overcome our faults, so that their origin and
cause might be made clearer to us, he thus began.

### Chapter II

There are eight principal faults which attack mankind; viz., first
gastrimargia, which means gluttony, secondly fornication, thirdly phi-
largyria, i.e., avarice or the love of money, fourthly anger, fifthly dejection,
sixthly acedia [var., accidie], i.e., listlessness or low spirits, seventhly
cenodoxia, i.e., boasting or vain glory, and eighthly pride.

### Chapter III

Of these faults then there are two classes. For they are either natural
to us as gluttony, or arise outside of nature as covetousness. But their
manner of acting on us is fourfold. For some cannot be consummated

without an act on the part of the flesh, as gluttony and fornication, while some can be completed without any bodily act, as pride and vainglory. Some find the reasons for their being excited outside us, as covetousness and anger; others are aroused by internal feelings, as accidie and dejection.

## Chapter IV

And to make this clearer not only by a short discussion to the best of my ability, but by Scripture proof as well, gluttony and fornication, though they exist in us naturally (for sometimes they spring up without any incitement from the mind, and simply at the motion and allurement of the flesh) yet if they are to be consummated, must find an external object, and thus take effect only through bodily acts. For "every man is tempted of his own lust. Then lust when it has conceived beareth sin, and sin when it is consummated begets death." For the first Adam could not have fallen a victim to gluttony unless he had had material food at hand, and had used it wrongly, nor could the second Adam be tempted without the enticement of some object, when it was said to Him: "If Thou art the Son of God, command that these stones be made bread." And it is clear to everybody that fornication also is only completed by a bodily act, as God says of this spirit to the blessed Job: "And his force is in his loins, and his strength in the navel of his belly." And so these two faults in particular, which are carried into effect by the aid of the flesh, especially require bodily abstinence as well as spiritual care of the soul; since the determination of the mind is not in itself enough to resist their attacks (as is sometimes the case with anger or gloominess or the other passions, which an effort of the mind alone can overcome without any mortification of the flesh); but bodily chastisement must be used as well, and be carried out by means of fasting and vigils and acts of contrition; and to this must be added change of scene, because since these sins are the results of faults of both mind and body, so they can only be overcome by the united efforts of both. And although the blessed Apostle says generally that all faults are carnal, since he enumerates enmities and anger and heresies among other works of the flesh, yet in order to cure them and to discover their nature more exactly we make a twofold division of them: for we call some of them carnal, and some spiritual. And those we call carnal, which specially have to do with pampering the appetites of the flesh, and with which it is so charmed and satisfied, that sometimes it excites the mind when at rest and even drags it against its will to consent to its desire. Of which the blessed Apostle says: "In which also we all walked in time past in the desires of our flesh, fulfilling the will of the flesh and of our thoughts, and were by nature children of wrath even as the rest." But we call those spiritual which spring only from the impulse of the mind and not merely contribute no pleasure to the flesh, but actually bring on it a weakness that is harmful to it, and only feed a diseased mind with the food of a most miserable pleasure. And therefore these need a single medicine for the heart: but those which are carnal can only be cured, as we said, by a double remedy. Whence it is extremely useful for those who aspire to purity, to begin by withdrawing from themselves the material which feeds these carnal passions, through which opportunity for or recollection of these same desires can arise in a soul that is still affected by the evil. For a complicated disease needs a complicated remedy. For from the body the object and material which would allure it must be withdrawn, for fear lest the lust should endeavour to break out into act; and before the mind we should no less carefully place diligent meditation on Scripture and watchful anxiety and the withdrawal into solitude, lest it should give birth to desire even in thought. But as regards other faults intercourse with our fellows is no obstacle, or rather it is of the greatest possible use, to those who truly desire to get rid of them, because in mixing with others they more often meet with rebuke, and while they are more frequently provoked the existence of the faults is made evident, and so they are cured with speedy remedies.

*        *        *        *        *

## Chapter VII

And to go on in the order which we proposed, with our account of the way in which the other passions act (our analysis of which was obliged to be interrupted by this account of gluttony and of the Lord's temptation) vain-glory and pride can be consummated even without the slightest assistance from the body. For in what way do those passions need any action of the flesh, which bring ample destruction on the soul they take captive simply by its assent and wish to gain praise and glory from men? Or what act on the part of the body was there in that pride of old in the case of the above mentioned Lucifer; as he only conceived it in his heart and mind, as the prophet tells us: "Who saidst in thine heart: I will ascend into heaven, I will set my throne above the stars of God. I will ascend above the heights of the clouds, I will be like the most High." And just as he had no one to stir him up to this pride, so his thoughts alone were the authors of the sin when complete and of his eternal fall; especially as no exercise of the dominion at which he aimed followed.

## Chapter VIII

Covetousness and anger, although they are not of the same character (for the former is something outside our nature, while the latter seems to have as it were its seed plot within us) yet they spring up in the same way, as in most instances they find the reasons for their being stirred in something outside of us. For often men who are still rather weak complain that they have fallen into these sins through irritation and the instigation of others, and are plunged headlong into the passions of anger and covetousness by the provocation of other people. But that covetousness is something outside our nature, we can clearly see from this; viz., that it is proved not to have its first starting point inside us, nor does it originate in what contributes to keeping body and soul together, and to the existence of life. For it is plain that nothing belongs to the actual needs and necessities of our common life except our daily meat and drink: but everything else, with whatever zeal and care we preserve it, is shown to be something distinct from the wants of man by the needs of life itself. And so this temptation, as being something outside our nature, only attacks those monks who are but lukewarm and built on a bad foundation, whereas those which are natural to us do not cease from troubling even the best of monks and those who dwell in solitude. And so far is this shown to be true, that we find that there are some nations who are altogether free from this passion of covetousness, because they have never by use and custom received into themselves this fault and infirmity. And we believe that the old world before the flood was for long ages ignorant of the madness of this desire. And in the case of each one of us who makes his renunciation of the world a thorough one, we know that it is extirpated without any difficulty, if, that is, a man gives up all his property, and seeks the monastic discipline in such a way as not to allow himself to keep a single farthing. And we can find thousands of men to bear witness to this, who in a single moment have given up all their property, and have so thoroughly eradicated this passion as not to be in the slightest degree troubled by it afterwards, though all their life long they have to fight against gluttony, and cannot be safe from it without striving with the utmost watchfulness of heart and bodily abstinence.

## Chapter IX

Dejection and accidie generally arise without any external provocation, like those others of which we have been speaking: for we are well aware that they often harass solitaries, and those who have settled them-

selves in the desert without any intercourse with other men, and this
in the most distressing way. And the truth of this any one who has lived
in the desert and made trial of the conflicts of the inner man, can easily
prove by experience.


## Chapter X

Of these eight faults then, although they are different in their
origin and in their way of affecting us, yet the six former; viz., gluttony,
fornication, covetousness, anger, dejection, accidie, have a sort of connexion with each other, and are, so to speak, linked together in a chain,
so that any excess of the one forms a starting point for the next. For from
superfluity of gluttony fornication is sure to spring, and from fornication covetousness, from covetousness anger, from anger, dejection, and
from dejection, accidie. And so we must fight against them in the same
way, and with the same methods: and having overcome one, we ought
always to enter the lists against the next. For a tall and spreading tree
of a noxious kind will the more easily be made to wither if the roots
on which it depends have first been laid bare or cut; and a pond of water
which is dangerous will be dried up at once if the spring and flowing
channel which produce it are carefully stopped up. Wherefore in order
to overcome accidie, you must first get the better of dejection: in order
to get rid of dejection, anger must first be expelled: in order to quell
anger, covetousness must be trampled under foot: in order to root out
covetousness, fornication must be checked: and in order to destroy
fornication, you must chastise the sin of gluttony. But the two remaining faults; viz., vainglory and pride, are connected together in a somewhat similar way as the others of which we have spoken, so that the
growth of the one makes a starting point for the other (for superfluity
of vainglory produces an incentive to pride); but they are altogether
different from the six former faults, and are not joined in the same
category with them, since not only is there no opportunity given for them
to spring up from these, but they are actually aroused in an entirely
different way and manner. For when these others have been eradicated
these latter flourish the more vigorously, and from the death of the others
they shoot forth and grow up all the stronger: and therefore we are attacked by these two faults in quite a different way. For we fall into each
one of those six faults at the moment when we have been overcome by
the ones that went before them; but into these two we are in danger of
falling when we have proved victorious, and above all after some splendid
triumph. In the cases then of all faults just as they spring up from the
growth of those that go before them, so are they eradicated by getting

rid of the earlier ones. And in this way in order that pride may be driven out vainglory must be stifled, and so if we always overcome the earlier ones, the later ones will be checked; and through the extermination of those that lead the way, the rest of our passions will die down without difficulty. And though these eight faults of which we have spoken are connected and joined together in the way which we have shown, yet they may be more exactly divided into four groups and sub-divisions. For to gluttony fornication is linked by a special tie: to covetousness anger, to dejection accidie, and to vainglory pride is closely allied.

## Chapter XI

And now, to speak about each kind of fault separately: of gluttony there are three sorts: (1) that which drives a monk to eat before the proper and stated times; (2) that which cares about filling the belly and gorging it with all kinds of food, and (3) that which is on the lookout for dainties and delicacies. And these three sorts give a monk no little trouble, unless he tries to free himself from all of them with the same care and scrupulousness. For just as one should never venture to break one's fast before the right time so we must utterly avoid all greediness in eating, and the choice and dainty preparation of our food: for from these three causes different but extremely dangerous conditions of the soul arise. For from the first there springs up dislike of the monastery, and thence there grows up disgust and intolerance of the life there, and this is sure to be soon followed by withdrawal and speedy departure from it. By the second there are kindled the fiery darts of luxury and lasciviousness. The third also weaves the entangling meshes of covetousness for the nets of its prisoners, and ever hinders monks from following the perfect self-abnegation of Christ. And when there are traces of this passion in us we can recognize them by this; viz., if we are kept to dine by one of the brethren we are not content to eat our food with the relish which he has prepared and offers to us, but take the unpardonable liberty of asking to have something else poured over it or added to it, a thing which we should never do for three reasons: (1) because the monastic mind ought always to be accustomed to practise endurance and abstinence, and like the Apostle, to learn to be content in whatever state he is. For one who is upset by taking an unsavoury morsel once and in a way, and who cannot even for a short time overcome the delicacy of his appetite will never succeed in curbing the secret and more important desires of the body; (2) because it sometimes happens that at the time our host is out of that particular thing which we ask for, and we make him feel ashamed of the wants and bareness of his table, by exposing his poverty which he would rather was only known to God; (3) because sometimes other people do not care about the relish which we ask for, and so it turns out that we are annoying most of them while intent on satisfying the desires of our own palate. And on this account we must by all means avoid such a liberty. Of fornication there are three sorts: (1) that which is accomplished by sexual intercourse; (2) that which takes place without touching a woman, for which we read that Onan the son of the patriarch Judah was smitten by the Lord [see Genesis 38:4–10]; and which is termed by Scripture uncleanness: of which the Apostle says: "But I say to the unmarried and to widows, that it is good for them if they abide even as I. But if they do not contain let them marry: for it is better to marry than to burn;" (3) that which is conceived in heart and mind, of which the Lord says in the gospel: "Whosoever looketh on a woman to lust after her hath already committed adultery with her in his heart." And these three kinds the blessed Apostle tells us must be stamped out in one and the same way. "Mortify," says he, "your members which are upon the earth, fornication, uncleanness, lust, etc." And again of two of them he says to the Ephesians: "Let fornication and uncleanness be not so much as named among you:" and once more: "But know this that no fornicator or unclean person, or covetous person who is an idolater hath inheritance in the kingdom of Christ and of God." And just as these three must be avoided by us with equal care, so they one and all shut us out and exclude us equally from the kingdom of Christ. Of covetousness there are three kinds: (1) That which hinders renunciants from allowing themselves to be stripped of their goods and property; (2) that which draws us to resume with excessive eagerness the possession of those things which we have given away and distributed to the poor; (3) that which leads a man to covet and procure what he never previously possessed. Of anger there are three kinds: one which rages within, which is called in Greek *thumos*; another which breaks out in word and deed and action, which they term *orgē*: of which the Apostle speaks, saying "But now do ye lay aside all anger and indignation;" the third, which is not like those in boiling over and being done with in an hour, but which lasts for days and long periods, which is called *mēnis*. And all these three must be condemned by us with equal horror. Of dejection there are two kinds: one, that which springs up when anger has died down, or is the result of some loss we have incurred or of some purpose which has been hindered and interfered with; the other, that which comes from unreasonable anxiety of mind or from despair. Of accidie there are two kinds: one of which sends those affected by it to sleep; while the other makes them forsake their cell and flee away. Of vainglory, although it takes various forms and shapes, and is divided into different classes, yet there are two main kinds: (1) when we are puffed up about carnal things and things visible, and (2) when we are inflamed with the desire of vain praise for things spiritual and unseen.

## Chapter XII

But in one matter vainglory is found to be a useful thing for beginners. I mean by those who are still troubled by carnal sins, as for instance, if, when they are troubled by the spirit of fornication, they formed an idea of the dignity of the priesthood, or of reputation among all men, by which they may be thought saints and immaculate: and so with these considerations they repell the unclean suggestions of lust, as deeming them base and at least unworthy of their rank and reputation; and so by means of a smaller evil they overcome a greater one. For it is better for a man to be troubled by the sin of vainglory than for him to fall into the desire for fornication, from which he either cannot recover at all or only with great difficulty after he has fallen. And this thought is admirably expressed by one of the prophets speaking in the person of God, and saying: "For My name's sake I will remove My wrath afar off: and with My praise I will bridle thee lest thou shouldest perish," i.e., while you are enchained by the praises of vainglory, you cannot possibly rush on into the depths of hell, or plunge irrevocably into the commission of deadly sins. Nor need we wonder that this passion has the power of checking anyone from rushing into the sin of fornication, since it has been again and again proved by many examples that when once a man has been affected by its poison and plague, it makes him utterly indefatigable, so that he scarcely feels a fast of even two or three days. And we have often known some who are living in this desert, confessing that when their home was in the monasteries of Syria they could without difficulty go for five days without food, while now they are so overcome with hunger even by the third hour, that they can scarcely keep on their daily fast to the ninth hour. And on this subject there is a very neat answer of Abbot Macarius [c. 300–c. 390] to one who asked him why he was troubled with hunger as early as the third hour in the desert, when in the monastery he had often scorned food for a whole week, without feeling hungry. "Because," said he, "here there is nobody to see your fast, and feed and support you with his praise of you: but there you grew fat on the notice of others and the food of vainglory." And of the way in which, as we said, the sin of fornication is prevented by an attack of vainglory, there is an excellent and significant figure in the book of Kings, where, when the children of Israel had been taken captive by Necho, King of Egypt, Nebuchadnezzar, King of Assyria, came up and brought them back from the borders of Egypt to their own country, not indeed meaning to restore them to their former liberty and their native land, but meaning to carry them off to his own land and to transport them to a still more distant country than the land of Egypt in which they had been prisoners. And this illustration exactly applies to the case

before us. For though there is less harm in yielding to the sin of vainglory than to fornication, yet it is more difficult to escape from the
dominion of vainglory. For somehow or other the prisoner who is
carried off to a greater distance, will have more difficulty in returning to
his native land and the freedom of his fathers, and the prophet's rebuke
will be deservedly aimed at him: "Wherefore art thou grown old in a
strange country?" since a man is rightly said to have grown old in a
strange country, if he has not broken up the ground of his faults. Of
pride there are two kinds: (1) carnal, and (2) spiritual, which is the
worse. For it especially attacks those who are seen to have made progress
in some good qualities.

## Chapter XIII

Although then these eight faults trouble all sorts of men, yet they
do not attack them all in the same way. For in one man the spirit of
fornication holds the chief place: wrath rides rough shod over another:
over another vainglory claims dominion: in another pride holds the
field: and though it is clear that we are all attacked by all of them, yet
the difficulties come to each of us in very different ways and manners.

## Chapter XIV

Wherefore we must enter the lists against these faults in such a way
that every one should discover his besetting sin, and direct his main
attack against it, directing all his care and watchfulness of mind to
guard against its assault, directing against it daily the weapons of fasting,
and at all times hurling against it the constant darts of sighs and groanings from the heart, and employing against it the labours of vigils and
the meditation of the heart, and further pouring forth to God constant
tears and prayers and continually and expressly praying to be delivered
from its attack. For it is impossible for a man to win a triumph over any
kind of passion, unless he has first clearly understood that he cannot
possibly gain the victory in the struggle with it by his own strength and
efforts, although in order that he may be rendered pure he must night
and day persist in the utmost care and watchfulness. And even when he
feels that he has got rid of this fault, he should still search the inmost
recesses of his heart with the same purpose, and single out the worst
fault which he can see among those still there, and bring all the forces
of the Spirit to bear against it in particular, and so by always overcoming the stronger passions, he will gain a quick and easy victory over
the rest, because by a course of triumphs the soul is made more vigorous,
and the fact that the next conflict is with weaker passion insures him a

readier success in the struggle: as is generally the case with those who are wont to face all kinds of wild beasts in the presence of the kings of this world, out of consideration for the rewards. . . . Such men, I say, direct their first assault against whatever beasts they see to be the strongest and fiercest, and when they have despatched these, then they can more easily lay low the remaining ones, which are not so terrible and powerful. So too, by always overcoming the stronger passions, as weaker ones take their place, a perfect victory will be secured for us without any risk. Nor need we imagine that if any one grapples with *one* fault in particular, and seems too careless about guarding against the attacks of others, he will be easily wounded by a sudden assault, for this cannot possibly happen. For where a man is anxious to cleanse his heart, and has steeled his heart's purpose against the attack of any one fault, it is impossible for him not to have a general dread of all other faults as well, and take similar care of them. For if a man renders himself unworthy of the prize of purity by contaminating himself with other faults, how can he possibly succeed in gaining the victory over that one passion from which he is longing to be freed? But when the main purpose of our heart has singled out one passion as the special object of its attack, we shall pray about it more earnestly, and with special anxiety and fervour shall entreat that we may be more especially on our guard against it and so succeed in gaining a speedy victory. For the giver of the law himself teaches us that we ought to follow this plan in our conflicts and not to trust in our own power; as he says: "Thou shalt not fear them because the Lord thy God is in the midst of thee, a God mighty and terrible: He will consume these nations in thy sight by little and little and by degrees. Thou wilt not be able to destroy them altogether: lest perhaps the beasts of the earth should increase upon thee. But the Lord thy God shall deliver them in thy sight; and shall slay them until they be utterly destroyed."

"The Works of John Cassian," tr. by Edgar C. S. Gibson, *Nicene and Post-Nicene Fathers*, ed. Philip Schaff (Buffalo: Christian Literature Company, 1889), Second Series, vol. XI, pp. 339–340, 342–346.

# Exhibit Seven

## PRESCRIPTIONS
## FOR SINS
### HALITGAR

## Introduction

In early ninth-century France, each locality seems
to have had its own favorite handbook for the
administration of penance by which errant Christians
made amends for their sins as a condition of restoration to good standing in the church. This diversity
of penitential practice (which often required public
confession) disturbed Ebbo, archbishop of Reims
during the reign of Louis the Pious, one of Charlemagne's sons. Ebbo commissioned one of his suf-
fragans, Halitgar, bishop of Cambrai in the north
of France from 817 until 831, to compile a standard
penitential from the writings of the Church Fathers
and the official Canons of the church. The new handbook was to be used by all the clergy under Ebbo's
jurisdiction and was to make penitential practice
uniform.

Halitgar's was a difficult task, for the type of
church discipline enjoined by the popular Celtic
penitentials was unknown to the Fathers and the
Canons. From Gregory the Great, Prosper of Aquitaine, and other traditional writings, Halitgar compiled a manual of five books, and from various
penitentials he drew together a sixth book called
*Poenitentiale Romanum*. Although the current style

of invoking the authority of Rome for important writings excuses Halitgar from the charge of mendacity, this sixth book was closely akin to current Celtic penitentials and can hardly be of Roman provenance. Apparently, however, his work achieved the desired standardization of penitential practice and was widely accepted as bearing Roman authority. The manual was completed about 830 A.D.

Halitgar's penitential specified that confession, penance, and reconciliation were to be done privately rather than publicly, and it made the priest rather than the bishop the chief officer for administering penance. Fasting became a reduction in the amount of food or a temporary omission of food, rather than involving, as it had in many previous penitentials, prescriptions against certain foods like meat, butter, wine, or beer. However, the usual practice of commuting penance into money payment was allowed, and this payment was to be set in proportion to the penitent's wealth. Recitation of psalms and prayers, and the employment of certain postures and gestures, were regarded as especially therapeutic; the penitent might be required to say the Lord's Prayer with hands extended upward or with body bent and arms held outward—devices known to previous penitentials in which many combinations of genuflections and bowings with psalmody and prayer are found.

One of Halitgar's more severe penances was flagellation, which had been thought of as appropriate for persons prone to sins of the flesh like gluttony and lust, but Halitgar imposed it upon the priest who stammered during his chanting of the prayer after the elevation of the chalice. Absolutions in this penitential, as in those upon which it was based, were simple prayers of reconciliation which appealed to the pardoning mercy of God; only in the twelfth century had the sacramental character of penance so developed as to call for declaratory formulae absolving sins.

Halitgar's penitential of course occupies a prominent place in the development of penance. Also, it is fascinating for its specification of the kinds of behavior that were regarded as sinful. Sharp distinctions were drawn, as for example in the sixty-seventh prescription, between simple kissing, lascivious kissing, and kissing "with pollution or embrace," and the last brought a penance twice as heavy as the first. Altogether, the writing shows vividly the minute care with which Christian pastors sought to regulate the behavior of the zestful peoples of Europe's "dark ages."

# PRESCRIPTIONS
# FOR SINS

From: *The So-Called Roman Penitential* (c. 830),
by Halitgar.

### [HALITGAR'S PREFACE]

Here begins the sixth [book]. We have also added to this work
of our selection another, a Roman penitential, which we have taken from
a book repository of the Roman Church, although we do not know by
whom it was produced. We have determined that it should be joined
to the foregoing decisions of the canons for this reason, that if perchance those decisions presented seem to anyone superfluous, or if he
is entirely unable to find there what he requires respecting the offenses
of individuals, he may perhaps find explained, in this final summary, at
least the misdeeds of all.

### PROLOGUE

## How Bishops or Presbyters Ought to Receive Penitents

As often as Christians come to penance, we assign fasts; and we
ourselves ought to unite with them in fasting for one or two weeks, or as
long as we are able; that there be not said to us that which was said
to the priests of the Jews by our Lord and Savior: "Woe unto you scribes,
who oppress men, and lay upon their shoulders heavy loads, but ye yourselves do not touch these burdens with one of your fingers." For no one
can raise up one who is falling beneath a weight unless he bends himself
that he may reach out to him his hand; and no physician can treat the
wounds of the sick, unless he comes in contact with their foulness. So
also no priest or pontiff can treat the wounds of sinners or take away
the sins from their souls, except by intense solicitude and the prayer of
tears. Therefore it is needful for us, beloved brethren, to be solicitous
on behalf of sinners, since we are "members one of another" and "if one
member suffers anything, all the members suffer with it." And therefore,
if we see anyone fallen in sin, let us also make haste to call him to penance by our teaching. And as often as thou givest advice to a sinner,
give him likewise at once a penance and tell him to what extent he ought
to fast and expiate his sins; lest perchance thou forget how much it be-

hooves him to fast for his sins and it become necessary to thee to inquire of him regarding his sins a second time. But the man will perhaps hesitate to confess his sins a second time, and be judged yet more severely. For not all clerics who come upon this document ought to appropriate it to themselves or to read it; only those to whom it is needful, that is, the presbyters. For just as they who are not bishops and presbyters (those on whom the keys of the kingdom of heaven have been bestowed) ought not to offer the sacrifice so also others ought not to take to themselves these decisions. But if the need arises, and there is no presbyter at hand, a deacon may admit the penitent to holy communion. Therefore as we said above, the bishops or presbyters ought to humble themselves and pray with moaning and tears of sadness, not only for their own faults, but also for those of all Christians, so that they may be able to say with the Blessed Paul: "Who is weak and I am not weak; who is scandalized and I am not on fire." When therefore, anyone comes to a priest to confess his sins, the priest shall advise him to wait a little, while he enters into his chamber to pray. But if he has not a chamber, still the priest shall say in his heart this prayer:

Let Us Pray

> Lord God Almighty, be Thou propitious unto me a sinner, that I may be able worthily to give thanks unto Thee, who through Thy mercy hast made me, though unworthy, a minister, by the sacerdotal office, and appointed me, though slight and lowly, an intermediary to pray and intercede before our Lord Jesus Christ for sinners and for those returning to penance. And therefore our Governor and Lord, who will have all men to be saved and to come to the knowledge of the truth, who desirest not the death of the sinner but that he should be converted and live, accept my prayer, which I pour forth before the face of Thy Clemency, for Thy menservants and maidservants who have come to penance. Through our Lord Jesus Christ.

Moreover, he who on coming to penance sees the priest sad and weeping for his evil deeds, being himself the more moved by the fear of God, will be the more grieved and abhor his sins. And any man who is approaching for penance, if thou seest him in a state of ardent and constant penitence, receive him forthwith. Him who is able to keep a fast which is imposed upon him, do not forbid, but allow him to do it. For they are rather to be praised who make haste quickly to discharge the obligation due, since fasting is an obligation. And so give commandment to those who do penance, since if one fasts and completes what is commanded him by the priest, he will be cleansed from his sins. But if he turns back a second time to his former habit or sin, he is like a dog that returns to his own vomit. Therefore, every penitent ought not only to perform the fast that is commanded him by the priest but also, after he has completed those things that were commanded him, he ought, as long as he is commanded, to fast either on Wednesdays or on Fridays. If he does those things which the priest has enjoined upon him, his sins shall be remitted; if, however, he afterward fasts of his own volition, he shall obtain to himself mercy and the kingdom of heaven. Therefore, he who fasts a whole week for his sins shall eat on Saturday and on the Lord's day and drink whatever is agreeable to him. Nevertheless, let him guard himself against excess and drunkenness, since luxury is born of drunkenness. Therefore the Blessed Paul forbids it, saying: "Be not drunk with wine, wherein is luxury"; not that there is luxury in wine, but in drunkenness.

Here ends the Prologue.


## [DIRECTIONS TO CONFESSORS]

If anyone perchance is not able to fast and has the means to redeem himself, if he is rich, for seven weeks [penance] he shall give twenty solidi [*i.e.*, shillings]. But if he has not sufficient means, he shall give ten solidi. But if he is very poor, he shall give three solidi. Now let no one be startled because we have commanded to give twenty solidi or a smaller amount; since if he is rich it is easier for him to give twenty solidi than for a poor man to give three solidi. But let everyone give attention to the cause to which he is under obligation to give, whether it is to be spent for the redemption of captives, or upon the sacred altar, or for poor Christians. And know this, my brethren, that when men or women slaves come to you seeking penance, you are not to be hard on them nor to compel them to fast as much as the rich, since men or women slaves are not in their own power; therefore lay upon them a moderate penance.

Here begins the form for the administration of Penance.

In the first place the priest says, Psalm XXXVII, "Rebuke me not O Lord in thy indignation." And after this he says, "Let us pray," and Psalm CII, "Bless the Lord O my soul" as far as "shall be renewed." And again he says: "Let us pray," and Psalm L, "Have mercy," as far as "Blot out my iniquities," [*sic*] After these he says, Psalm LXIII, "O God, by thy name," and he says, "Let us pray," and says, Psalm LI, "Why dost thou glory," as far as "the just shall see and fear." And he says, "Let us pray:"

> O God of whose favor none is without need, remember, O Lord, this Thy servant who is laid bare in the weakness of a transient and earthly body. We seek that Thou give pardon to the confessant, spare the suppliant, and that we who according to our own merit are to blame may be saved by thy compassion through our Lord Jesus Christ.

## Another Prayer

O God, beneath Whose eyes every heart trembles and all consciences are afraid, be favorable to the complaints of all and heal the wounds of everyone, that just as none of us is free from guilt, so none may be a stranger to pardon, through our Lord Jesus Christ.

## A Prayer

O God of infinite mercy and immeasurable truth, deal graciously with our iniquities and heal all the languors of our souls, that laying hold of the remission which springs from Thy compassion, we may ever rejoice in Thy blessing. Through our Lord Jesus Christ.

## A Prayer

I beseech, O Lord, the majesty of Thy kindness and mercy that Thou wilt deign to accord pardon to this Thy servant as he confesses his sins and evil deeds, and remit the guilt of his past offenses—Thou who did'st carry back the lost sheep upon Thy shoulders and did'st hearken with approval to the prayers of the publican when he confessed. Wilt Thou also, O Lord, deal graciously with this Thy servant; be Thou favorable to his prayers, that he may abide in the grace of confession, that his weeping and supplication may quickly obtain Thy enduring mercy, and, readmitted to the holy altars and sacraments, may he again be made a partaker in the hope of eternal life and heavenly glory. Through our Lord Jesus Christ.

## Prayer of the Imposition of Hands

Holy Lord, Father Omnipotent, Eternal God, Who through Thy son Jesus Christ our Lord hast deigned to heal our wounds, Thee we Thy lowly priests as suppliants ask and entreat that Thou wilt deign to incline the ear of Thy mercy and remit every offense and forgive all the sins of this Thy servant and give unto him pardon in exchange for his afflictions, joy for sorrow, life for death. He has fallen from the celestial height, and trusting in Thy mercy, may he be found worthy to persevere by Thy rewards unto good peace and unto the heavenly places unto life eternal. Through our Lord Jesus Christ.

Here begins the Reconciliation of the Penitent on Holy Thursday. First he says Psalm L with the antiphon "Cor mundum."

## A Prayer

Most gracious God, the Author of the human race and its most merciful Corrector, Who even in the reconciliation of the fallen willest that I, who first of all need Thy mercy, should serve in the workings of

Thy grace through the priestly ministry, as the merit of the suppliant vanisheth may the mercy of the Redeemer become the more marvelous. Through our Lord Jesus Christ.

### Another Prayer

Almighty, everlasting God, in Thy compassion relieve this Thy confessing servant of his sins, that the accusation of conscience may hurt him no more unto punishment than the grace of Thy love [may admit him] to pardon. Through our Lord Jesus Christ.

### Another Prayer

Almighty and merciful God, Who hast set the pardon of sins in prompt confession, succor the fallen, have mercy upon those who have confessed, that what is bound by the chain of things accursed, the greatness of Thy love may release.

### A Prayer over the Sick

O God, Who gavest to Thy servant Hezekiah an extension of life of fifteen years, so also may Thy greatness raise up Thy servant from the bed of sickness unto health. Through our Lord Jesus Christ.

## [PRESCRIPTIONS OF PENANCE]

## Of Homicide

1. If any bishop or other ordained person commits homicide. If any cleric commits homicide, he shall do penance for ten years, three of these on bread and water.

2. If [the offender is] a layman, he shall do penance for three years, one of these on bread and water; a subdeacon, six years; a deacon, seven; a presbyter, ten; a bishop, twelve.

3. If anyone consents to an act of homicide that is to be committed, he shall do penance for seven years, three of these on bread and water.

4. If any layman intentionally commits homicide he shall do penance for seven years, three of these on bread and water.

5. If anyone overlays an infant, he shall do penance for three years, one of these on bread and water. A cleric also shall observe the same rule.

## Of Fornication

6. If anyone commits fornication as [did] the Sodomites, he shall do penance for ten years, three of these on bread and water.

7. If any cleric commits adultery, that is, if he begets a child with

the wife or the betrothed of another, he shall do penance for seven years; however, if he does not beget a child and the act does not come to the notice of men, if he is a cleric he shall do penance for three years, one of these on bread and water; if a deacon or a monk, he shall do penance for seven years, three of these on bread and water; a bishop, twelve years, five on bread and water.

8. If after his conversion or advancement any cleric of superior rank who has a wife has relations with her again, let him know that he has committed adultery; therefore, that he shall do penance as stated above.

9. If anyone commits fornication with a nun or one who is vowed to God, let him be aware that he has committed adultery. He shall do penance in accordance with the foregoing decision, each according to his order.

10. If anyone commits fornication by himself or with a beast of burden or with any quadruped, he shall do penance for three years; if [he has] clerical rank or a monastic vow, he shall do penance for seven years.

11. If any cleric lusts after a woman and is not able to commit the act because the woman will not comply, he shall do penance for half a year on bread and water and for a whole year abstain from wine and meat.

12. If after he has vowed himself to God any cleric returns to a secular habit, as a dog to his vomit, or takes a wife, he shall do penance for six years, three of these on bread and water, and thereafter not be joined in marriage. But if he refuses, a holy synod or the Apostolic See shall separate them from the communion of the Catholics. Likewise also, if a woman commits a like crime after she has vowed herself to God, she shall be subject to an equal penalty.

13. If any layman commits fornication as the Sodomites did, he shall do penance for seven years.

14. If anyone begets a child of the wife of another, that is, commits adultery and violates his neighbor's bed, he shall do penance for three years and abstain from juicy foods and from his own wife, giving in addition to the husband the price of his wife's violated honor.

15. If anyone wishes to commit adultery and cannot, that is, is not accepted, he shall do penance for forty days.

16. If anyone commits fornication with women, that is, with widows and girls, if with a widow, he shall do penance for a year; if with a girl, he shall do penance for two years.

17. If any unstained youth is joined to a virgin, if the parents are willing, she shall become his wife; nevertheless they shall do penance for one year and [then] become man and wife.

18. If anyone commits fornication with a beast he shall do penance for one year. If he has not a wife, he shall do penance for half a year.

19. If anyone violates a virgin or a widow, he shall do penance for three years.

20. If any man who is betrothed defiles the sister of his betrothed, and clings to her as if she were his own, yet marries the former, that is, his betrothed, but she who has suffered defilement commits suicide—all who have consented to the deed shall be sentenced to ten years on bread and water, according to the provisions of the canons.

21. If anyone of the women who have committed fornication slays those who are born or attempts to commit abortion, the original regulation forbids communion to the end of life. What is actually laid down they may mitigate somewhat in practice. We determine that they shall do penance for a period of ten years, according to rank, as the regulations state.

## Of Perjury

22. If any cleric commits perjury, he shall do penance for seven years, three of these on bread and water.

23. A layman, three years; a subdeacon, six; a deacon, seven; a presbyter, ten; a bishop, twelve.

24. If compelled by any necessity, anyone unknowingly commits perjury, he shall do penance for three years, one year on bread and water, and shall render a life for himself, that is, he shall release a man or woman slave from servitude and give alms liberally.

25. If anyone commits perjury through cupidity, he shall sell all his goods and give to the poor and be shaven and enter a monastery, and there he shall serve faithfully until death.

## Of Theft

26. If any cleric is guilty of a capital theft, that is, if he steals an animal or breaks into a house, or robs a somewhat well-protected place, he shall do penance for seven years.

27. A layman shall do penance for five years; a subdeacon, for six; a deacon, for seven; a presbyter, for ten; a bishop, for twelve.

28. If anyone in minor orders commits theft once or twice, he shall make restitution to his neighbor and do penance for a year on bread and water; and if he is not able to make restitution he shall do penance for three years.

29. If anyone violates a tomb, he shall do penance for seven years, three years on bread and water.

30. If any layman commits theft he shall restore to his neighbor what he has stolen [and] do penance for the three forty-day periods on bread and water; if he is not able to make restitution, he shall do pen-

ance for one year, and the three forty-day periods on bread and water, and [he shall give] alms to the poor from the product of his labor, and at the decision of the priest he shall be joined to the altar.

## Of Magic

31. If one by his magic causes the death of anyone, he shall do penance for seven years, three years on bread and water.

32. If anyone acts as a magician for the sake of love but does not cause anybody's death, if he is a layman he shall do penance for half a year; if a cleric, he shall do penance for a year on bread and water; if a deacon, for three years, one year on bread and water; if a priest, for five years, two years on bread and water. But if by this means anyone deceives a woman with respect to the birth of a child, each one shall add to the above six forty-day periods, lest he be accused of homicide.

33. If anyone is a conjurer-up of storms he shall do penance for seven years, three years on bread and water.

## Of Sacrilege

34. If anyone commits sacrilege—(that is, those who are called augurs, who pay respect to omens), if he has taken auguries or [does it] by any evil device, he shall do penance for three years on bread and water.

35. If anyone is a soothsayer (those whom they call diviners) and makes divinations of any kind, since this is a demonic thing he shall do penance for five years, three years on bread and water.

36. If on the Kalends of January, anyone does as many do, calling it "in a stag," or goes about in [the guise of] a calf, he shall do penance for three years.

37. If anyone has the oracles which against reason they call "Sortes Sanctorum," or any other "sortes," or with evil device draws lots from anything else, or practices divination he shall do penance for three years, one year on bread and water.

38. If anyone makes, or releases from, a vow beside trees or springs or by a lattice, or anywhere except in a church, he shall do penance for three years on bread and water, since this is sacrilege or a demonic thing. Whoever eats or drinks in such a place, shall do penance for one year on bread and water.

39. If anyone is a wizard, that is, if he takes away the mind of a man by the invocation of demons, he shall do penance for five years, one year on bread and water.

40. If anyone makes amulets, which is a detestable thing, he shall do penance for three years, one year on bread and water.

41. It is ordered that persons who both eat of a feast in the abominable places of the pagans and carry food back [to their homes] and eat it subject themselves to a penance of two years, and so undertake what they must carry out; and [it is ordered] to try the spirit after each oblation and to examine the life of everyone.

42. If anyone eats or drinks beside a [pagan] sacred place, if it is through ignorance, he shall thereupon promise that he will never repeat it, and he shall do penance for forty days on bread and water. But if he does this through contempt, that is, after the priest has warned him that it is sacrilege, he has communicated at the table of demons; if he did this only through the vice of gluttony, he shall do penance for the three forty-day periods on bread and water. If he did this really for the worship of demons and in honor of an image, he shall do penance for three years.

43. If anyone has sacrificed under compulsion [in demon worship] a second or third time, he shall be in subjection for three years, and for two years he shall partake of the communion without the oblation; in the third year he shall be received to full [communion].

44. If anyone eats blood or a dead body or what has been offered to idols and was not under necessity of doing this, he shall fast for twelve weeks.

## Of Various Topics

45. If anyone intentionally cuts off any of his own members, he shall do penance for three years, one year on bread and water.

46. If anyone intentionally brings about abortion, he shall do penance for three years, one year on bread and water.

47. If anyone exacts usury from anybody, he shall do penance for three years, one year on bread and water.

48. If by power or by any device anyone in evil fashion breaks into or carries off another's goods, he shall do penance as in the above provision and give liberal alms.

49. If by any device anyone brings a slave or any man into captivity or conveys him away, he shall do penance as stated above.

50. If anyone intentionally burns the courtyard or house of anybody, he shall do penance as stated above.

51. If anyone strikes another through anger and sheds blood or incapacitates him, he shall first pay him compensation and secure a physician. If he is a layman [he shall do penance] for forty days; a cleric, two forty-day periods; a deacon, six months; a presbyter, one year.

52. If anyone engages in hunting, if he is a cleric he shall do penance for one year; a deacon shall do penance for two years; a presbyter, for three years.

53. If anyone belonging to the ministry of holy Church is dishonest in respect to any task or neglects it, he shall do penance for seven years, three years on bread and water.

54. If anyone sins with animals after he is thirty years of age, he shall undergo [a penance of] fifteen years and shall [then] deserve the communion. But let the nature of his life be inquired into, whether it deserves somewhat more lenient treatment. If he continually persists in sinning, he shall have a longer penance. But if those who are of the above-mentioned age and have wives commit this offense, they shall undergo [a penance of] twenty-five years in such a way that after five years they shall deserve the communion with the oblation. But if some who have wives and are more than fifty years old commit this sin, they shall deserve the viaticum [only] at the end of life.

## Of Drunkenness

55. One who is drunk then with wine or beer violates the contrary command of the Savior and his Apostles; but if he has a vow of holiness, he shall expiate his guilt for forty days on bread and water; a layman, indeed, shall do penance for seven days.

56. A bishop who commits fornication shall be degraded and do penance for sixteen years.

57. A presbyter or a deacon who commits natural fornication, if he has been elevated before taking the monastic vow, shall do penance for three years, shall ask pardon every hour, and shall perform a special fast every week except during the days between Easter and Pentecost.

## Of Petty Cases

58. If by accident anyone in neglect lets the host drop and leaves it for wild beasts and it is devoured by some animal, he shall do penance for forty days. But if not [by accident], he shall do penance for one year.

59. If he communicates it in ignorance to those excommunicated from the Church, he shall do penance for forty days.

60. If through negligence the host falls to the ground, there shall be a special fast.

61. We ought to offer [the sacrament] for good rulers; on no account for evil rulers.

62. Presbyters are, indeed, not forbidden to offer for their bishops.

63. He who provides guidance to the barbarians shall do penance for three years.

64. They who despoil monasteries, falsely saying that they are re-

deeming captives, shall do penance for three years and shall give to the poor all the things which they have taken off.

65. He who eats the flesh of animals whose [manner of] death he does not know, shall do penance for the third part of a year.

66. We set forth the statutes of our fathers before us: boys conversing by themselves and violating the regulations of the seniors shall be corrected with three special fasts.

67. Those who kiss simply, seven special fasts. Lascivious kissing without pollution, eight special fasts. But with pollution or embrace, they shall be corrected with fifteen special fasts.

## Of Disorders Connected with the Sacrifice

68. If anyone does not well guard the host, and if a mouse eats it, he shall do penance for forty days. But he who loses his chrismal or the host alone in any place whatever so that it cannot be found, shall do penance for the three forty-day periods or for a year.

69. Anyone who spills the chalice upon the altar when the linens are being removed, shall do penance for seven days.

70. If the host falls into the straw, [the person responsible] shall do penance for seven days.

71. He who vomits the host after loading his stomach to excess shall do penance for forty days; if he casts it into the fire, twenty days.

72. A deacon who forgets to offer the oblation, and fails to provide linen until they offer it, shall do penance in like manner.

73. If those little animals are found in flour or in any dry food or in honey or in milk, that which is about their bodies is to be thrown out.

74. He who treats the host with carelessness so that it is consumed by worms and comes to nothing shall do penance for the three forty-day periods. If it was found entire with a worm in it, it shall be burnt, and then its ashes [shall be] concealed under the altar, and he who has been neglectful shall do penance for forty days.

75. If the host falls to the ground from the hand of the officiant, and if any of it is found, every bit of what is found shall be burnt in the place in which it fell, and its ashes [shall be] concealed beneath the altar, and the priest shall do penance for half a year. And if it is found, it shall be purified as above, and he shall do penance for forty days. If it only slipped to the altar, he shall perform a special fast.

76. If through negligence anything drips from the chalice to the ground, it shall be licked up with the tongue, the board shall be scraped, and [the scrapings] shall be burnt with fire; and he shall do penance for forty days. If the chalice drips on the altar, the minister shall suck it up, and the linen which came in contact with the drop shall be washed [three?] times, and he shall do penance for three days.

77. If the priest stammers over the Sunday prayer which is called "the perilous," once, forty psalms; a second time, one hundred strokes.

78. If one has taken his father's or brother's widow, such a person cannot be judged unless they have previously been separated from each other.

## Of Homicide

79. If anyone slays a man in a public expedition without cause, he shall do penance for twenty-one weeks; but if he slays anyone accidentally in defense of himself or his parents or his household, he shall not be under accusation. If he wishes to fast, it is for him to decide, since he did the thing under compulsion.

80. If he commits homicide in time of peace and not in a tumult, by force, or because of enmity in order to take [the victim's] property, he shall do penance for twenty-eight weeks and restore to his wife or children the property of him whom he has slain.

## Of Sick Penitents

81. But if anyone comes to penance, and if sickness ensues, and if he is not able to fulfill that which has been commanded him by the priest, he shall be received to holy communion, and if it is God's will to restore him to health, he shall fast afterwards.

82. If anyone fails to do penance and perchance falls into sickness and seeks to take communion, he shall not be forbidden; but give him the holy communion and command him that if it please God in his mercy and if he escapes from this sickness, he shall thereafter confess everything and then do penance.

## Of Those Who Die Excommunicate

83. But if anyone who had already confessed has died excommunicate and death seized him without warning, whether in the road or in his house, if there is a relative of his let the relative offer something on his behalf at the holy altar, or for the redemption of captives, or for the commemoration of his soul.

## Of Incestuous Persons

84. If anyone takes in marriage his wife's daughter, he cannot be judged unless they have first been separated. After they are separated, thou shalt sentence each of them for fourteen weeks, and they shall

never come together again. But if they want to marry, either the man or the woman, they are free to do so, but he shall not marry her whom he sent away.

85. In the case of one who takes in marriage a close relative or his step-mother or the widow of his uncle, and of one who takes his father's wife or his wife's sister—the decision is grave: [such an offender] shall be canonically condemned.

## Of Things Offered to Idols

86. If while he is an infant anyone through ignorance tastes of those thing which were offered to idols or of a dead body or of anything abominable, let that person fast for three weeks.

87. On account of fornication, moreover, many men do not know the number of the women with whom they have committed fornication: these shall fast for fifty weeks.

88. But if he ate without knowing it what was offered to idols or a dead thing, pardon shall be given him, since he did this unaware; nevertheless, he shall fast three weeks.

## Of Theft Committed through Necessity

89. If through necessity anyone steals articles of food or a garment or a beast on account of hunger or nakedness, pardon shall be given him. He shall fast for four weeks. If he makes restitution, thou shalt not compel him to fast.

90. If anyone steals a horse or an ox or an ass or a cow or supplies of food or sheep which feed his whole household, he shall fast as stated above.

## Of Adultery

91. If any woman misleads her mother's husband, she cannot be judged until she gives him up. When they are separated she shall fast fourteen weeks.

92. If anyone who has a lawful wife puts her away and marries another, she whom he marries is not his. He shall not eat or drink, nor shall he be at all in conversation with her whom he has wrongly taken or with her parents. Moreover, if the parents consent to it, they shall be excommunicated.

If a woman seduces the husband of another woman, she shall be excommunicated from the Christians.

93. If anyone of the Christians sees a Christian walking about, or one of his own relatives wandering, and sells him, he is not worthy to have a resting place among Christians, until he redeems him. But if he is not able to find the place where he is, he shall give the price which he received for him and shall redeem another from servitude and fast for twenty-eight weeks.

## Of the Penance for Those Thrice Married

94. If any man's wife is dead, he has the right to take another; likewise, also, in the case of a woman. If he takes a third wife, he shall fast for three weeks; if he takes a fourth or a fifth, he shall fast for twenty-one weeks.

## Of Him Who Lacerates Himself

95. If anyone cuts off his hair or lacerates his face with a sword or with his nails after the death of a parent, he shall fast for four weeks, and after he has fasted he shall then take communion.

96. If any pregnant woman wishes to fast, she has the right to do so.

97. A quack, man or woman, slayers of children, when they come to the end of life, if they seek penance with mourning and the shedding of tears,—if he desists, receive him: he shall fast for thirty weeks.

## Of Things Strangled

98. If any dog or fox or hawk dies for any cause, whether he is killed by a cudgel or by a stone or by an arrow which has no iron, these are all "things strangled." They are not to be eaten, and he who eats of them shall fast for six weeks.

99. If anyone strikes with an arrow a stag or another animal, and if it is found after three days, and if perchance a wolf, a bear, a dog, or a fox has tasted of it, no one shall eat it; and he who does eat of it shall fast for four weeks.

100. If a hen dies in a well, the well is to be emptied. If one drinks knowingly of it, he shall fast for a week.

101. If any mouse or hen or anything falls into wine or water, no one shall drink of this. If it falls into oil or honey, the oil shall be used in a lamp; the honey, in medicine or in something else needful.

102. If a fish has died in the fishpond, it shall not be eaten; he who eats of it shall fast for four days.

103. If a pig or a hen has eaten of the body of a man, it shall not

be eaten nor be used for breeding purposes, but it shall be killed and given to the dogs. If a wolf tears an animal, and if it dies, no one shall eat it. And if it lives and a man afterward kills it, it may be eaten.

## Of Polluted Animals

104. If a man has sinned with a goat or with a sheep or with any animal, no one shall eat its flesh or milk, but it shall be killed and given to the dogs.

105. If anyone wishes to give alms for his soul of wealth which was the product of booty, if he has already done penance, he has the right to give it. Here endeth.

---

"The So-Called Roman Penitential of Halitgar," *Medieval Hand-Books of Penance*, tr. and ed. by John T. McNeill and Helena M. Gamer (New York: Columbia University Press, 1938), pp. 297–314. By permission.

# Exhibit Eight

## PASSIONATE
## EMPATHY
### BERNARD OF CLAIRVAUX

### Introduction

In the year 1113, thirty Burgundian noblemen walked into the town of Cîteaux in France to enter the monastic house recently founded there on a rigorous rule in protest against the wealth and softness of the dominant Cluniac monks. Their enlister and their leader was twenty-two-year-old Bernard, son of a leading family of Fontaines-les-Dijon. Three years later the same Bernard established the second abbey of the Cistercian order in a dark and unpleasant valley of Burgundy that came to be known as Clair-vaux—"valley of light." From that time until his death in 1153, Bernard became the most winsome and perhaps the most influential man in Western Christendom. He promoted the extraordinary growth of the Cistercian order, healed schisms in the papacy, directed the life and affairs of his former pupil Pope Eugenius III, determined doctrinal controversies, broke the intellectual influence of the ingenious Abelard at Paris, conceived and taught a method of mystical piety, preached the Second Crusade, called princes and popes to task, and founded the military order of Knights Templar. Such affairs he directed not from thirst for personal power, but from passion that the church should be both pure and potent.

The most dramatic records of Bernard's varied and vigorous activities are many extant letters to a multitude of people on many subjects. One of the best-known of this correspondence is the letter to Robert of Châtillon, traditionally known as his nephew but actually a much younger first cousin. Robert had been pledged by his parents to the famous and affluent Abbey of Cluny, but on his own initiative entered the Cistercian order and while still quite young came under the obedience of Abbot Bernard at Clairvaux. Disturbed both by the rigors of the Cistercian rule and by his betrayal of his parents' promise, Robert fled to Cluny and there was received as a monk. In an utterly characteristic way, Bernard called on every power of his person to persuade Robert back to Clairvaux. This letter, at once tender and stern, shows Bernard's talents as a director of consciences —talents he employed eagerly with princes and commoners, with popes and novices. Even when there are excised from the letter long sections concerning rivalries and controversies between Cluniac and Cistercian monks, the letter reveals Bernard's capacity for placing himself fully in Robert's shoes, achieving such involvement that all that remained of Bernard in the transfer is a better conscience than Robert's. Yet at the same time the elder cousin contained himself and was able to heap upon his own person a mountain of blame that subtly drew Robert in the desired direction. Amidst all this Bernard argued minute details of the case, for the excised paragraphs distinguished between degrees of promises that parents might make regarding their children's entry into monasteries, and contended that Robert's parents' act did not bind him.

This letter, even though a very early writing of Bernard, exemplifies the guidance-by-utter-involvement that characterized the man's long career as a spiritual director. Seeking only to retire from the world, he was drawn intimately into affairs great and small. His remove allowed him at once to place himself under the circumstances of his correspondents, and to wield confident moral authority over those circumstances.

It is said that while the holy man dictated this letter to Robert, outdoors, rain came; Bernard would not be interrupted in the task laid upon him by God, and the letter miraculously remained dry while all things around it were made wet.

Bernard died in 1153 and was canonized in 1174.

## PASSIONATE
## EMPATHY

From: *To his nephew Robert* (c. 1119),
by Bernard.

Long enough, perhaps too long, have I waited, dearest Robert, for the Lord that he might deign to touch your soul and mine through yours, moving you to salutary regrets for your error and me to joy for your deliverance. But seeing myself still disappointed of my hope, I can no longer hide my sorrow, restrain my anxiety, or dissemble my grief. And so, against all the laws of justice, I who have been wounded am forced to recall him who wounded me; who have been spurned, him who spurned me; who have been smitten, him who struck the blow. In short I must cast myself at the feet of him who should cast himself at mine. Sorrow is not careful to count the cost: is not ashamed; does not nicely weigh the pros and cons; is not fearful for its dignity; respects no rules; it cares only that it has what it would be without, or lacks what it would have. "But," you will say, "I have hurt no one, spurned no one. Rather have I, spurned and repeatedly hurt, sought only to fly my oppressor. Who can I have hurt, if I have only avoided being hurt? Is it not wiser to yield to the persecutor than to resist him? To avoid him who strikes than to strike back?" Quite so; I agree. I am not writing to dispute with you, but to remove the grounds for dispute. To fly persecution implies no fault in him who flees but in him who persecutes. I do not deny this. I shall overlook the past. I shall not ask why or how the present state of affairs came about. I shall forget old injuries. To act otherwise were better calculated to open than to heal wounds. I am concerned with what lies closer to my heart. Unhappy man that I am who have not you by me, who cannot see you, who am obliged to live without you for whom to die would be to live, and to live without whom is no better than death! So I do not ask why you left me, I only grieve that you do not return; I do not blame your going away, I only blame your not coming back. Only come and there will be peace; return and there will be satisfaction. Return, I say, return, and I shall sing in my heart, "My brother who was dead has come to life again; was lost and is found."

No doubt it may have been my fault that you left. I was too severe with a sensitive youth, I was too hard on a tender stripling. Hence your grumbles against me (as I remember) while you were here; hence your ceaseless complaints about me even now that I am absent. The fault of this will not be laid at your door. I might, perhaps, excuse myself by saying that only in this way could the passions of youth have been curbed and that, at first, a strict way of life must be hard on a raw youth. I could quote Scripture to support me saying, "Smite thy son with a rod and thou shalt deliver his soul from hell," and "It is where he loves that the Lord bestows correction," and "The wounds of a friend are better than the deceitful kisses of an enemy." It may have been my fault that you left, as I have said. We will not let arguments about who is to blame delay correction of what is blameworthy. But it will surely begin to be your fault as well if you do not spare me now that I am sorry, if you do not forgive me now that I acknowledge myself to blame because, although I have been unwise in my treatment of you, I was certainly not malicious. And if you in future distrust my wisdom, you must know that I am not the same man I was, because I do not think you are what you used to be. Having changed yourself, you will find me changed too. You may now embrace me without hesitation as a companion whom you used to fear as a master. And so if you left through my fault, as you believe and I do not deny, or through your own fault, as many believe but I do not affirm, or, as I think more probable, through the fault of both of us, from now on you alone will be to blame if you do not return. If you would be free of all blame in the matter you must return. If you acknowledge your share of the blame, I forgive you. But you too must forgive me what I acknowledge as my share. Else if you acknowledge your share and at the same time dissemble it you will be too lenient with yourself, or if you refuse to forgive me even when I declare myself ready to make satisfaction, you will be too hard on me.

If you still refuse to come back you must seek another pretext to quiet your conscience because there will no longer be anything to fear from me. You need not fear that in future you will have any reason to fear me because even while you are not with me I have cast myself with my whole heart at your feet, moved thereto with all my affection. I humble myself before you, I assure you of my love: can you still be afraid? Be bold and come where humility beckons you and love draws you. Forearmed by my assurances, approach without fear. Now that I am become gentle, return to me from whom you fled when fierce. My severity frightened you away; let my tenderness draw you back. See, my son, how I long to lead you now not any more in the spirit of slavery to govern you in fear, but in the spirit of adoption whereby we cry "Abba, Father"; you who have been the cause of so much grief to me, I shall lead not with threats but with encouragements, not by menacing but by entreating. Perhaps anyone else would try another method. And indeed who would not rather insist on your guilt and inspire you with fear; face you with your vow and propose judgement. Who else would not scold your disobedience and be angry at your desertion, that you should have left the coarse habit for soft raiment, a fare of roots for delicacies, in fine poverty for riches. But I know your heart. I know that you can be lead [sic] more easily by love than driven by fear. And what need is there to goad you again who have not kicked against the goad, why make you more fearful who are already timid enough, abase you more who are by nature bashful, you who are schooled by your own reason, whose own conscience is a rod, and whose natural shyness is a discipline. And if it seems wonderful to anyone that a shy and timid boy should dare to desert both his vow and his monastery against the will of his brethren, the authority of his superior, the injunctions of the rule, let him wonder also that the sanctity of David was defrauded, the wisdom of Solomon deceived, the strength of Samson destroyed. What wonder if the Evil One should have been able to deceive a youth in a place of horror and a great wilderness who could deceive the first man when he was in the paradise of Eden. And this youth was not deceived by physical beauty like the old men of Babylon, nor by money like Giezi [var., Gehazi], nor by ambition like Julian the Apostate [Roman emperor, 361–363], but he was duped by sanctity, misled by religion, allured by the authority of age. Do you ask how?

First there came a certain Grand Prior sent by the chief of all the priors himself. Outwardly he came in sheep's clothing, but within he was a ravening wolf. Alas! The shepherds were deceived by his semblance to a sheep and admitted him alone into the fold. The smallest sheep in the fold did not fly from this wolf, he too was deceived and thought he was a sheep. What happened then? This wolf in sheep's clothing fascinated, allured, and flattered. He preached a new Gospel. He commended feasting and condemned fasting. He called voluntary poverty wretched and poured scorn upon fasts, vigils, silence, and manual labour. On the other hand he called sloth contemplation, gluttony, talkativeness, curiosity and all intemperance he commended as discretion. "When," he asked, "was God pleased with our sufferings; where do the Scriptures say that we should kill ourselves; what sort of religion is it to dig the soil, clear forests, and cart muck?" Does not Truth itself say, "It is mercy that wins favour with me and not sacrifice"; and "I do not wish for the death of a sinner but rather that he should turn from his ways and live"; and "Blessed are the merciful for they shall obtain mercy"? Why did God make food if we may not eat it? Why did he give us bodies if we may not look after them? In fact "Whose friend is he, that is his own enemy, and leaves his own cheer untasted?" "What healthy and sane man has ever hated his own flesh?"

By such sophistries the too credulous boy was talked round, led astray and led off by his deceiver. He was brought to Cluny and trimmed, shaved, and washed. He was taken out of his rough, threadbare, and soiled habit, and clothed with a neat and new one. Then with what honour, triumph, and respect was he received into the community! He was favoured beyond his contemporaries; a sinner in the desires of his heart, he was praised as if he were a conquering hero returned from battle. He was set up on high and, although a mere youth, was allocated to a position above many who were his seniors. He was befriended, flattered, and congratulated by the whole fraternity. Everyone made merry over him as though they were victors dividing the booty. O good Jesu, what a lot of trouble was taken for the ruin of one poor little soul! Who would be so hardhearted as not to soften at the sight of it! Whose soul, be it never so detached, would not be troubled by it! And who in the midst of all this would care to consult his conscience? And how could anyone amidst such vanities recognize the truth and achieve humility?

*     *     *     *     *

You foolish boy! Who has bewitched you to break the vows which adorned your lips? Will you not be justified or condemned out of your own mouth? Why then are you so anxious about the vow your parents made and yet so regardless of your own? It is out of your own mouth and not out of the mouth of your parents that you will be judged. Of your own vow, not of theirs, will you be called to render an account. Why does anyone try to bamboozle you with an Apostolic absolution, you whose own conscience is bound by a divine sentence, "No one putting their hand to the plough and looking back is fit for the kingdom of God"? Would they persuade you that you have not looked back who say to you, "Well done!" My son, if sinners shall entice you, consent not to them. Believe not every spirit. Be at peace with many, but let one in a thousand be your counsellor. Gird yourself, cast off your seducers, shut your ears to flatterers, search your own heart, for you know yourself best. Listen to your conscience, examine your intentions, consider the facts. Let your conscience tell you why you left your monastery, your brethren, your own place, and myself who am related to you by blood, but even more closely by spirit. If you left so as to lead a harder, higher, and more perfect life, fear not, you have not looked back, rather you can glory with the Apostle, saying, "Forgetting what I have left behind, intent on what lies ahead, I press on with the goal in view." But if it be otherwise, be not high minded but fearful because (you must pardon my saying this) whatever you permit yourself in food, unnecessary clothes, idle words, vain and curious travel in excess of what you promised when you were with us, is without any doubt to look back, to equivocate, to apostatize.

And I have said this, my son, not to put you to shame, but to help you as a loving father because if you have many masters in Christ, yet you have few fathers. For, if you will allow me to say so, I begot you in Religion by word and by example. I nourished you with milk when, while yet a child, it was all you could take. And I would have given you bread if you had waited until you grew up. But alas! how soon and how early were you weaned. Now I fear that all I had cherished with kindness, strengthened with encouragement, confirmed with prayers, is even now fading and wasting away. Sadly I weep, not for my lost labour, but for the unhappy state of my lost child. Do you prefer that another should rejoice in you who has not laboured for you? My case is the same as that of the harlot Solomon judged, whose child was stealthily taken by another who had overlain and killed her own. You too were taken from my side, cut from me. My heart cannot forget you, half of it went with you, and what remains cannot but suffer.

But our friends who have tried to do this thing, whose sword has pierced my side, whose teeth are spears and arrows and whose tongue is a sharp sword, for what advantage of yours have they done it, for what necessity? If I have in any way offended them (and I am not conscious of having done so) they have certainly paid me back in full. I would not wonder if I have received more than my share of retaliation, if indeed they have suffered anything like what I suffer now from them. It is not a bone of my bones, flesh of my flesh that they have taken, but it is the joy out of my heart, the fruit of my spirit, the crown of my hopes, and (so it seems to me) the half of my soul. Why have they done this thing? Perhaps they were sorry for you? Perhaps they feared that because I was like a blind man leading the blind, we would both fall into the ditch. So they took you under their leadership. Hard necessity! Grievous charity! So careful of your good that it must strike at mine. Is it not possible that you should be saved except at my cost? Ah! would that these men might save you apart from me. Would that if I die you, at least, may live! But how can this be? Does salvation rest rather in soft raiment and high living than in frugal fare and moderate clothing? If warm and comfortable furs, if fine and precious cloth, if long sleeves and ample hoods, if dainty coverlets and soft woollen shirts make a saint, why do I delay and not follow you at once? But these things are comforts for the weak, not the arms of fighting men. They who wear soft raiment are in kings' houses. Wine and white bread, honey-wine and pittances, benefit the body not the soul. The soul is not fattened out of frying pans! Many monks in Egypt served God for a long time without fish. Pepper, ginger, cummin, sage, and all the thousand other spices may please the palate, but they inflame lust. And would you make my safety depend on such things? Will you spend your youth safely among them? Salt with hunger is seasoning enough for a man living soberly and wisely. If we eat before we are hungry, then we must concoct mixtures with more and more I know not what far-fetched flavours to arouse our greed and stimulate our flagging appetites.

But what, you say, is to be done if one cannot live otherwise? Good. I know you are not strong, that you would now find it difficult to support a harder way of life. But what if you can act so as to make yourself able to do so? I will tell you how it could be done. Arouse yourself, gird your loins, put aside idleness, grasp the nettle, and do some hard work. If you act thus you will soon find that you only need to eat what will satisfy your hunger, not what will make your mouth water. Hard exercise will restore the flavour to food that idleness has taken away. Much that you would refuse to eat when you had nothing to do, you will be glad of after hard work. Idleness makes one dainty, hard work makes one hungry. It is wonderful how work can make food taste sweet which idleness finds insipid. Vegetables, beans, roots, and bread and water may be poor fare for one living at his ease, but hard work soon makes them taste delicious. You have become unaccustomed to our clothes and now you dread them as too cold in winter and too hot in summer. But have you not read, "They that fear the frost, the snow shall fall upon them"? You fear our vigils, fasts, and manual labour, but they seem nothing to anyone who considers the flames of hell. The thought of the outer darkness will soon reconcile anyone to wild solitudes. Silence does not displease when it is considered how we shall have to give an account of every idle word. With the picture before our eyes of that weeping and gnashing of teeth the difference between a rush mat and a feather bed seems small enough. If we spend well all the night enjoined by the Rule in psalmody, it will be a hard bed on which we cannot sleep. If we labour with our hands as much during the day as we are professed to do, rough indeed will be the fare we cannot eat.

Arise, soldier of Christ, I say arise! Shake off the dust and return to the battle. You will fight more valiantly after your flight, and you will conquer more gloriously. There are many soldiers of Christ who have begun valiantly, stood their ground well, and finished by conquering, but few who have returned to the battle after they had fled, thrown themselves once more into the thick of the danger from which they had escaped, and put to flight the foe from whom they had run. A thing is the more precious for being rare, so I rejoice that you can be one of those who are the more glorious for being so scarce. But if you are still fearful, I ask you why you should be afraid where there is no cause for fear, instead of where you have every reason to tremble. Do you think that because you have forsaken the front line the enemy has forsaken you? Far from it. He will follow you in flight more readily than he would fight you when striking back. He attacks you more willingly from behind than he would strive with you face to face. Can you sleep unarmed without anxiety in the morning hours when it was at that time that Christ rose from the dead? Do you not know that unarmed you are both more fearful and less to be feared? A multitude of armed men surround the house, and can you still sleep? Already they are scaling the ramparts, swarming over the barriers, pouring in at the rear. Would you be safer alone or with others? Naked in bed or armed in camp? Get up, arm yourself, and fly to your fellow soldiers whom you have forsaken by running away. Let the fear that drove you away also bring you back. Is it the weight and discomfort of arms that you shun, feeble soldier? Believe me when an enemy is at hand and darts begin flying a shield seems none too heavy, and a helmet and corselet are not noticed. Everything seems hard at first to someone coming suddenly from darkness into light, from leisure to labour. But when you have got away from your former habits you will soon get used to the labour. Practice soon makes perfect. What seemed difficult at first presently becomes quite easy. Even the bravest soldiers are apt to tremble when they first hear the bugle summon to battle, but after they have closed with the enemy hope of victory and fear of defeat soon inspires courage. Surrounded by a company of single-hearted brethren, what have you to fear? What have you to fear at whose side angels stand and whom Christ leads into battle encouraging his friends with the words, "Fear not, I have overcome the world." If Christ is with us, who is against us? You can fight with confidence where you are sure of victory. With Christ and for Christ victory is certain. Not wounds, nor falls, nor bruises, nor (were it possible) can a thousand deaths rob us of victory, if only we do not forsake the fight. Only by desertion can we be defeated. We can lose the victory by flight but not by death. Happy are you if you die in battle for after death you will be crowned. But woe to you if by forsaking the battle, you forfeit at once both the victory and the crown. May Christ save you from this, dear son, for at the last judgment you will incur a greater penalty on account of this letter of mine if, when you have read it, you do not take its lesson to heart.

Bernard of Clairvaux, *St. Bernard of Clairvaux Seen through his Selected Letters,* tr. Bruno Scott James (Chicago: Henry Regnery Company, 1953), pp. 8–12, 15–19. By permission.

# Exhibit Nine

## A HEALING
## MIRACLE
### FRANCIS OF ASSISI

### Introduction

As European Christian culture flourished during the high Middle Ages, people commonly considered all spiritual realities to take on physical form, and all physical realities to be the result of spiritual forces. So deeply did the earthly and heavenly realms seem to interpenetrate one another that our modern notion of "spiritual healing" was unthinkable; every restoration of nature came about by supernatural power, and all true spirituality resulted in the healing of natural disorders. Every holy object wrought its special cure, and pervasively holy persons could cure many maladies.

No person during this age was regarded more widely as a spiritual man, and therefore as a healer, than the saintly son of the cloth merchant Pietro Bernadone of Assisi in Italy, a son born in 1181/2 and named Francis. As a young man, Francis renounced worldly interests and inheritances to serve God, man, and nature by a life imitative of his conception of the lives of Jesus' apostles—a life of abject poverty in company with other poor and holy men. These ascetic associates, who called themselves the "poor men of Assisi," laid foundations for the mighty Franciscan Order (Friars Minor) of missionaries, social workers, hospitallers, teachers, and preachers in every late medieval European city and throughout the known world.

Even before he died, Francis became the object of hagiography, for his followers saw him as a uniquely holy man, and within two years of his death in 1226 he was pronounced an official saint of the church. Members of his order cherished and transmitted narratives of his thaumaturgy. One such disciple, Friar Ugolino di Monti Santa Maria, wrote down a series of seventy-five of the saint's acts. Later stories were added, and the compendium became "The Little Flowers of St. Francis"—the "Fioretti" (c. 1322). Francis and his miracles became the model of pastoral concern and healing ministry.

Francis' healing power displays itself wonderfully in the story of the healing of the leper. By utter obedience and faith the saint overcame the sick man's hostility, immunized himself against contamination, and purified not only the leper's foul body but also his immortal soul. This wonder-working power resided precisely in the saint's ability to abandon himself without reserve to the alleviation of the other's suffering, and this holiness had a salutary effect beyond anything that Francis imagined.

By the thirteenth century, the Christian ministry of healing had become focused in two areas. The older tradition of applying holy unguents was well specialized, and anointing with blessed oil (unction) was being reserved for persons *in extremis*. Partly in protest against this formal sacramentalism there emerged a charisma of healing concentrated in certain holy individuals, notably monks; thus, infirmaries for monks, and later hospitals for the public, were constructed near monasteries. Eventually, of course, the holy medicaments were discovered to have "natural" curative powers, and these were administered by charismatic professional men—and the long tradition of modern medicine was born. But before that development there appeared the great healers, of whom Francis was among the greatest. His astonishing powers are seen in the following brief excerpt from *The Little Flowers.*

# A HEALING
# MIRACLE

From: *The Little Flowers of St. Francis of Assisi* (c. 1322),
anonymous.

How St. Francis healed miraculously a leper
both in his body and in his soul,
and what the soul said to him on going up to heaven

The true disciple of Christ, St. Francis, as long as he lived in this miserable life, endeavoured with all his might to follow the example of Christ the perfect Master; whence it happened often, through the operation of grace, that he healed the soul at the same time as the body, as we read that Jesus Christ did; and not only he willingly served the lepers himself, but he willed that all the brothers of his Order, both when they were travelling about the world and when they were halting on their way, should serve the lepers for the love of Christ, who was for our sakes willing to be treated as a leper. It happened once, that in a convent near the one in which St. Francis then resided there was a hospital for leprosy and other infirmities, served by the brothers; and one of the patients was a leper so impatient, so insupportable, and so insolent, that many believed of a certainty (and so it was) that he was possessed of the devil, for he ill-treated with blows and words all those who served him; and, what was worse, he blasphemed so dreadfully our blessed Lord and His most holy Mother the blessed Virgin Mary, that none was found who could or would serve him. The brothers, in order to gain merit, endeavoured to accept with patience the injuries and violences committed against themselves, but their consciences would not allow them to submit to those addressed to Christ and to his Mother; and they determined to abandon this leper, but would not do so until they had signified their intention, according to the rule, to St. Francis. Having done so, St. Francis visited himself this perverse leper, and said to him, "May God give thee peace, my beloved brother!" and the leper answered, "What peace can I look for from God, who has taken from me peace and every other blessing, and made me a putrid and disgusting object?" And St. Francis answered, "My son, be patient; for the infirmities of the body are given by God in this world for the salvation of the soul in the next; there is great merit in them when they are patiently endured." The sick man answered: "How can I bear patiently the pain which afflicts me night and day? And not only am I greatly afflicted by my infirmity, but the monks thou hast sent to serve me make it even worse, for they do not serve me as they ought." Then St. Francis, knowing through divine revelation that the leper was possessed by the malignant spirit, began to pray, and prayed most earnestly for him. Having finished, he returned to the leper and said to him: "My son, I myself will serve thee, as thou art not satisfied with the others." "Willingly," answered the leper; "but what canst thou do more than they have done?" "Whatsoever thou wishest I will do for thee," answered St. Francis. "I will that thou wash me all over; for I am so disgusting that I cannot bear myself." Then St. Francis heated some water, in which he put a great many odoriferous herbs; he then undressed him, and began to wash him with his own hands, whilst another brother threw the water upon him, and, by a divine miracle, wherever St. Francis touched him with his holy hands the leprosy disappeared, and his flesh was perfectly healed; and as his body began to be healed, so likewise his soul was healed also. And the leper, seeing the leprosy beginning to disappear, felt a great sorrow and repentance for his sins, and began to weep bitterly. While his body was being purified externally of the leprosy through the cleansing of the water, so the soul internally was purified from sin by the washing of tears and repentance. Feeling himself completely healed both in his body and in his soul, he humbly confessed his sins, crying out in a loud voice, with many tears, "Unhappy me! I am worthy of hell for the wickedness of my conduct to the brothers, and for the impatience and blasphemy I have uttered against the Lord;" and for fifteen days he never ceased to weep bitterly for his sins, imploring the Lord to have mercy on him, and made a general confession to a priest. St. Francis, perceiving this evident miracle which the Lord had enabled him to work, returned thanks to God, and set out for a distant country; for out of humility he wished to avoid all glory, and in all his actions he sought only the glory of God, and not his own. It pleased God that the leper, who had been healed both in his body and in his soul, after having done penance for fifteen days, should fall ill of another infirmity; and having received the sacraments of the Church, he died most holily. His soul on its way to heaven appeared in the air to St. Francis, who was praying in a forest, and said to him, "Dost thou know me?" "Who art thou?" asked the saint. "I am the leper whom our Blessed Lord healed through thy merits, and to-day I am going to life eternal, for which I return thanks to God and to thee. Blessed be thy soul and thy body, blessed be thy holy words and works, for through thee many souls are saved in the world; and know that there is not a single day in which the angels and other saints do not return thanks to God for the holy fruits of thy preaching and that of thy Order in various parts of the world. Be comforted, then, and thank the Lord, and may His blessing rest on thee." Having said these words, he went up to heaven, and St. Francis was much consoled.

----

*The Little Flowers of St. Francis of Assisi*, tr. Henry Edward Manning (second edn., London: Burns & Oates Ltd., 1887), pp. 61–64.

# Exhibit Ten

## HOW TO DIE
### THE CRAFT OF DYING

## Introduction

As the European Middle Ages drew to their close during the fourteenth and fifteenth centuries, the idea of death peculiarly preoccupied men and women of every estate. In literature, painting, sculpture, song, and drama, Death—represented first by dead men and then as a personified entity—took on a horrible aspect as it stalked the earth claiming one by one all living things as its victims.[74] Each man's religious duty was to remember that he would soon die, that his mortal body's destiny was miserable decay, and that his soul's eternal career in bliss or in pain was set at the moment of dying.

Of course, Christian pastoral care in every age has reckoned with death as a serious personal crisis. Late medieval preoccupation with death produced its unique forms of this care in a vast literature recommending to common folk as well as nobles the art of dying well. This literature, conspicuously unpriestly in character, instructed friends and acquaintances to help the dying person, and gave the moribund man himself precise prescriptions to follow through his

---

[74] See J. Huizinga, *The Waning of the Middle Ages* (London: Edward Arnold & Co., and New York: St. Martin's Press, 1924), ch. XI.

crisis. Dying was conceived as an arduous and dangerous process through which Satan stood alert for an opportunity to attack and seduce the Christian soul. Some of this literature took the form of rude booklets of outline woodcuts whose panels pictured Death's devices and Satan's wiles and drew the reader's attention to these themes by providing frames to be colored—a sort of combination "comic book" and "coloring book." Some pictures showed a dying man lying in bed surrounded by friends and relatives praying for his soul, while under the bed demons with horns and claws awaited their chance to snatch the man from his faith and virtue into hell. It was deemed extremely important that the dying man remain firm in the articles of the faith. His ability to die willingly and joyfully was thought to earn its immediate reward from God, and despair was to be avoided at all costs. Eleventh-hour repentance for secret or long-forgotten sins was especially therapeutic. All was done so that, while destructive Death would surely get the body, the soul might find its escape to heaven.

A particularly fine example of this *Ars moriendi* literature is the treatise here excerpted, a work called *The Craft of Dying.* Its literary origin has not been determined with precision, but many evidences support the surmise that the work originated amongst Dominican monks in the region of Constance about the time of the Council of Constance (1414–1418), and that a work called *De arte moriendi* by the French theologian Jean la Charlier de Gerson (1363–1429) was a prominent source.[75] Before 1500 this work had been translated into English, and several versions of the tract appeared between 1490 and 1510 from the famous presses of William Caxton, Wynkyn de Worde, and Richard Pynson.

Here is exhibited one of the most sophisticated and most widely used guidebooks to the journey of death. Its eminent practicality makes it almost a "do-it-yourself" book of pastoral care for a dying man and his intimates. Religious themes, acts, gestures, objects, and words naturally played an indispensable role in warding off Satan while Death was encountered; but if it was impossible to obtain the services of an officially commissioned pastor, the pastoral work of steering the soul through the shoals of dying might be accomplished by the devout man assisted by devout associates. These excerpts analyze the special temptations that were thought to assail dying persons, prescribe

---

[75] Questions of authorship have been explored by Sister Mary Catherine O'Connor, *The Art of Dying Well: The Development of the Ars moriendi* (New York: Columbia University Press, 1942), pp. 11–60.

the means for examining his conscience, and recommend acts
devotion and prayer that were taken to avail in this awesor
crisis.

# HOW TO DI

From: *Ars Moriendi* (c. 1450?), author unknov

## HERE BEGINNETH THE BOOK OF THE CRAFT OF DYIN

Forasmuch as the passage of death, of the wretchedness of the ex
of this world, for uncunning [*i.e.*, ignorance] of dying—not only to lev
men [*i.e.*, laymen] but also to religious and devout persons—seeme
wonderfully hard and perilous, and also right fearful and horrible; the
fore in this present matter and treatise, that is of the Craft of Dying,
drawn and contained a short manner of exhortation, for teaching a
comforting of them that be in point of death. This manner of exhort
tion ought subtly to be considered, noted, and understood in the sig
of man's soul; for doubtless it is and may be profitable generally, to a
true Christian men, to learn and have craft and knowledge to die we

\*   \*   \*   \*   \*

## CHAPTER I
## THE FIRST CHAPTER IS OF COMMENDATION OF DEAT
## AND OF CUNNING [I.E., KNOWING HOW] TO DIE WELL

\*   \*   \*   \*   \*

## CHAPTER II
## THE SECOND CHAPTER IS OF MEN'S TEMPTATIONS
## THAT DIE

Know all men doubtless, that men that die, in their last sickne
and end, have greatest and most grievous temptations, and such as the
never had before in all their life. And of these temptations five be mo
principal.

I. The First is of the faith, forasmuch as faith is fundament of a
men's soul's-heal [*i.e.*, health]; . . . And forasmuch as there is such an
so great strength in the faith that withouten it there may no man b
saved.

Therefore the devil with all his might is busy to avert fully a man from the faith in his last end; or, if he may not, that he laboureth busily to make his doubt therein, or somewhat draw him out of the way or deceive him with some manner of superstitious and false errors or heresies. But every good Christian man is bound namely [*i.e.*, especially] habitually, though he may not actually and intellectually apprehend them, to believe, and full faith and credence give, not only to the principal articles of the faith, but also to all holy writ in all manner [of] things; and fully to obey the statutes of the church of Rome, and stably to abide and die in them. For as soon as he beginneth to err or doubt in any of them all, as soon he goeth out of the way of life, and his soul's heal. But wit [*i.e.*, know] thou well without doubt, that in this temptation, and in all other that follow after, the devil may not noy [*i.e.*, harm] thee, nor prevail against no [*i.e.*, any] man, in no wise, as long as he hath use of his free will, and of reason well disposed, but if [*i.e.*, unless] he will wilfully consent unto his temptation.

And therefore no very Christian [*i.e.*, true and good Catholic] man ought (not) to dread any of his illusions, or his false threatenings [var., persuasions], or his feigned fearings. . . . But manly, therefore, and stiffly and steadfastly abide and persevere; and die in the very [*i.e.*, true] faith and unity and obedience of our mother Holy Church.

And it is right profitable and good, as it is used in some religious [*i.e.*, monastic orders], when a man is in agony of dying, with an high voice oft times to say the Creed before him, that he that is sick may be mortified in stableness of the faith; and fiends that may not suffer to hear it may be voided and driven away from him. Also to stableness of very faith should strengthen a sick man principally the stable faith of our holy Fathers, Abraham, Isaac, and Jacob. Also the perseverant abiding faith of Job, of Raab the woman, and Achor, and such other. And also the faith of the Apostles, and other martyrs, confessors, and virgins innumerable. For by faith all they that have been of old time before us—and all they be now and shall be hereafter—they all please, and have [pleased] and shall please God by faith. For as it is aforesaid: Withouten faith it is impossible to please God.

Also double profit should induce every sick man to be stable in faith. One is: For faith may do all things; . . . Another is: For faith getteth a man all things. . . .

II. The Second Temptation is Desperation; the which is against [the] hope and confidence that every man should have unto God. For when a sick man is sore tormented and vexed, with sorrow and sickness of his body, then the devil is most busy to superadd sorrow to sorrow, with all [the] ways that he may, objecting his sins against him for to induce him into despair.

\*     \*     \*     \*     \*

Also the devil bringeth again into a man's mind that is in point of death specially those sins that he hath done, and was not shriven of, to draw him thereby into despair. But therefore should no man despair in no wise. For though any one man or woman had done as many thefts, or manslaughters, or as many other sins as be drops of water in the sea, and gravel stones in the strand, though he had never done penance for them afore, nor never had been shriven of them before—neither then might have time, for sickness or lack of speech, or shortness of time, to be shriven of them—yet should he never despair; for in such a case very contrition of heart within, with will to be shriven if time sufficed, is sufficient and accepted by God for to save him everlastingly: . . . .

. . . Therefore no man should despair, though it were so that it were possible that he alone had done all manner of sins that might be done in the world. For by despair a man getteth nought else but that God is much more offended thereby; and all his other sins be more grievous [var., augmented] in God's sight, and everlasting pain thereby increased infinitely to him that so despaireth.

Therefore against despair, for to induce him that is sick and laboureth in his dying to very trust and confidence that he should principally have to God at that time, the disposition of Christ in the cross should greatly draw him. Of the which *Saint Bernard* saith thus: What man is he that should not be ravished and drawn to hope, and have full confidence in God, and he take heed diligently of the disposition of Christ's body in the cross. Take heed and see: His head is inclined to salve thee; His mouth to kiss thee; His arms spread to be-clip [*i.e.*, embrace] thee; His hands thrilled [*i.e.*, pierced] to give thee; His side opened to love thee; His body along strait to give all Himself to thee.

Therefore no man should despair of forgiveness, but fully have hope and confidence in God; for the virtue of hope is greatly commendable, and of great merit before God. . . .

Furthermore, that no sinful man should in no wise despair—have he sinned never so greatly, nor never so sore, nor never so oft, nor never so long continued therein—we have open ensample in Peter that denied Christ; in Paul that pursued Holy Church; in Matthew and Zaccheus, the publicans; in Mary Maudeleyn [*i.e.*, Magdalene], the sinful woman, [in the woman] that was taken in avoutry [*i.e.*, adultery]; in the thief that hung on the cross beside Christ; in Mary Egyptian; and in innumerable other grievous and great sinners.

III. The Third Temptation is Impatience; the which is against charity, by the which we be bound to love God above all things. For they that be in sickness, in their death bed suffer passingly [*i.e.*, surpassingly] great pain and sorrow and woe; and namely they that die not by nature and course of age—that happeth right seldom, as open experience teacheth men—but die often through an accidental sickness; as a fever, a postune [*i.e.*, tumour], and such other grievous and painful and long sickness. The which many men, and namely those that be undisposed [*i.e.*, unprepared] to die and die against their will and lack very charity, maketh so impatient and grutching [*i.e.*, grudging], that other while [*i.e.*, at times], through woe and impatience, they become wood [*i.e.*, mad] and witless, as it hath been seen in many men. And so by that it is open and certain that they that die in that wise fail and lack very charity. . . . Therefore that man that will die well, it is needful that he grutch not in no [*i.e.*, any] manner of sickness that falleth to him before his death, or in his dying—be it never so painful or grievous—long time [or short time] dying; . . . . Then every man should be patient. . . . For by patience man's soul is surely had and kept, so by impatience and murmuration [*i.e.*, grudging] it is lost and damned. . . .

There shall no man have the kingdom of heaven that grutcheth and is impatient; and there may no man grutch that hath it. But as the great Clerk *Albert* saith, speaking of very contrition: If a very contrite man offereth himself gladly to all manner [of] afflictions of sickness and punishing of his sins, that he may thereby satisfy God worthily for his offences, much more then every sick man should suffer patiently and gladly his own sickness alone, that is lighter without comparison than many sicknesses that other men suffer; namely that sickness before a man's death is as a purgatory to him, when it is suffered as it ought; that is to understand, if it be suffered patiently, gladly, and with a free and kind will of heart. . . .

This temptation of impatience fighteth against charity, and without charity may no men be saved. . . . Then should all sicknesses of the body by reason be suffered patiently, without murmuration and difficulty. . . .

IV. The Fourth Temptation is Complacence, or pleasance of a man that he hath in himself; that is spiritual pride, with the which the devil tempteth and beguileth most religious, and devout and perfect men. For when the devil seeth that he may not bring a man out of faith, nor may not induce him into despair, neither to impatience, then he assaileth him by complacence of himself, putting such manner [of] temptations in his heart: O how stable art thou in the faith! how strong in hope! how sad in patience! O how many good deeds hast thou done! and such other thoughts . . . for a man may have so much delectation in such manner of complacence of himself that a man should be damned everlastingly therefore [*sic*].

. . . And therefore he that shall die must beware when he feeleth himself tempted with pride, that then he [low and] meek himself thinking on his sins: and that he wot [*i.e.*, know] never whether he be worthy everlasting love or hate, that is to say, salvation or damnation. Nevertheless, lest he despair, he must lift up his heart to God by hope, thinking and revolving [var., remembering] stably that the mercy of God is above all His works, and that God is true in all His words, and that He is truth and righteousness that never beguileth, neither is beguiled. . . . Every man should follow *Saint Antony* to whom the devil said: Antony, thou hast overcome me; for when I would have thee up by pride, thou keptest thyself a-down by meekness; and when I would draw thee down by desperation, thou keptest thyself up by hope. Thus should every man do, sick and whole, and then is the devil overcome.

V. The Fifth [Temptation] that tempteth and grieveth most carnal men and secular men, that be in overmuch occupation, and business outward about temporal things; that is their wives, their children, their carnal friends, and their worldly riches, and other things that they have loved inordinately before. For he that will die well and surely must utterly and fully put away out of his mind all temporal and outward things, and plenerly [i.e., fully] commit himself all to God. . . . And therefore it is right profitable, and full necessary in such a point of need, that a man conform his will to God's will in all things, as every man ought, both sick and whole. But it is seldom seen that any secular or carnal man—or religious either—will dispose himself to death; or furthermore, that is worse, will hear anything of the matter of death; [though indeed he be labouring fast to his endward, hoping that he shall escape the death and] that is the most perilous thing, and most inconvenient that may be in Christian man, as saith the worthy clerk [Peter] *Cantor Pariensis* [d. 1197]. . . .

But it is to be noted well that the devil in all these temptations abovesaid may compel no man, nor in no manner of wise prevail against him for to consent to him—as long as a man hath the use of reason with him—but if he will wilfully consent unto him; that every good Christian man, and also every sinful man—be he never so great a sinner—ought to beware of above all things. For the Apostle saith: God, he saith, is true, and will not suffer you to be tempted more than ye may bear; but He will give you such support in your temptations that ye may bear them.

*    *    *    *    *

## CHAPTER III
### THE THIRD CHAPTER CONTAINETH THE INTER-ROGATIONS THAT SHOULD BE ASKED OF THEM THAT BE IN THEIR DEATH BED, WHILE THEY MAY SPEAK AND UNDERSTAND

Now follow the interrogations of them that draw to the death, while they have reason with them and their speech. For this cause if any man is not fully disposed to die, he may the better be informed and comforted [thereto]. . . .

First ask him this:

Brother, art thou glad that thou shalt die in the faith of Christ? The sick man answereth: Yea.

Knowest thou well that thou hast not done as thou shouldst have done? He answereth: Yea.

Repentest thee thereof? He answereth: Yea.

Hast thou full will to amend thee, if thou mightest have full space of life? He answereth: Yea.

Believest thou fully that Our Lord Jesu Christ, God's Son, died for thee? He sayeth: Yea.

Thankest thou Him thereof with all thine heart? He answereth: Yea.

Believest thou verily that thou mayest not be saved but by Christ's [death and His] passion? He answereth: Yea.

Then thank Him thereof ever, while thy soul is in thy Body, and put all thy trust in His passion and in His death only, having trust in none other thing. To this death commit thee fully. [Var., with His death cover thee fully.] In His death wrap all thyself fully; and if it come to thy mind, or by thine enemy it be put into thy mind, that God will deem [*i.e.*, condemn] thee, say thus:

Lord, I put the death of Our Lord Jesu Christ between me and mine evil deeds, between me and the judgment; otherwise will I not strive with Thee.

If He say: Thou hast deserved damnation; say thou again: The death of our Lord Jesu Christ I put between me and mine evil merits, and the merits of His worthy passion I offer for merits I should have had, and alas I have not. Say also: Lord, put the death of my Lord Jesu Christ between me and Thy righteousness.

Then let him say this thrice, . . . Into thine hands, Lord, I commit my soul. And let the convent say the same. And if he may not speak, let the covent [*i.e.*, convent]—or they that stand about—say thus: . . . Into Thine hands, Lord, we commend his soul. And thus he dieth surely; and he shall not die everlastingly.

But though these interrogations abovesaid be competent and sufficient to religious and devout persons, nevertheless all Christian men, both secular and religious, . . . in their last end should be examined, enquired, and informed, more certainly and clearly, of the state and the health of their souls.

I. And First thus: Believest thou fully all the principal articles of the faith; and also all Holy Scripture in all things, after the exposition of the holy and true doctors of Holy Church; and forsakest all heresies and errors and opinions damned by the Church; and art glad also that thou shalt die in the faith of Christ, and in the unity and obedience of Holy Church?

The sick man answering: Yea.

II. The Second Interrogation shall be this: Knowledgest thou that often times, and in many manner wises, and grievously, thou hast offended thy Lord God that made thee of nought? . . .

He answereth: Yea.

III. The Third Interrogation shall be this: Art thou sorry in heart of all manner of sins that thou hast done against the high Majesty, and the Love of God, and the Goodness of God; and of all the goodness that thou hast not done, and mightest have done; and of all graces that thou hast slothed [i.e., neglected]—not only for dread of death, or any other pain, but rather [i.e., sooner] more for love of God and His righteousness —and for thou hast displeased His great goodness and kindness; and for the due order of charity, by the which we be bound to love God above all things; and of all these things thou askest the forgiveness of God? Desirest thou also in thine heart to have very knowing of all thine offences and forgets that thou hast done against God, and to have special repentance of them all?

He answereth: Yea.

IV. The Fourth Interrogation shall be this: Purposeth thou verily, and art in full will, to amend thee if thou mightest live longer; and never to sin more, deadly, wittingly, and with thy will: and rather than thou wouldest offend God deadly any more, to leave and lose wilfully all earthly things, were they never so lief [i.e., dear] to thee, and also the life of thy body thereto? And furthermore thou prayest God that He give thee grace to continue in this purpose?

He answereth: Yea.

V. The Fifth Interrogation shall be this: Forgivest thou fully in thine heart all manner [of] men that ever have done thee any manner [of] harm or grievance unto this time, either in word or in deed, for the love and worship of Our Lord Jesu Christ, of Whom thou hopest of forgiveness thyself; and askest also thyself to have forgiveness of all [them thou hast offended in any] manner wise?

He answereth: Yea.

VI. The Sixth Interrogation shall be this: Wilt thou that all manner [of] things that thou hast in any manner wise misgotten, be fully restored again,—so much as thou mayst, and art bound, after the value of thy goods; and rather leave and forsake all the goods of the world, if thou mayst not in none other wise?

He answereth: Yea.

VII. The Seventh Interrogation shall be this: Believest thou fully that Christ died for thee, and that thou mayst never be saved but by the mercy of Christ's passion; and thankest thou God thereof with all thine heart, as much as thou mayst?

He answereth: Yea.

Whoso may verily, of very good conscience and truth, withouten any feigning, answer yea to the foresaid seven interrogations, he hath an evident argument enough of health of his soul, that, and he died so, he shall be of the number of them that shall be saved.

Whosoever is not asked of another of these seven interrogations when he is in such peril of death—for there be right few that have the cunning [*i.e.,* knowledge] of this craft of dying—he must remember himself in his soul, and ask himself, and subtly feel and consider, whether he be so disposed as it is above said, or no. For without that a man be disposed in such wise finally, he may not doubtless [*i.e.,* without doubt, certainly] be saved everlastingly.

And what man that is disposed as is abovesaid, let him commend and commit himself, all in fear, fully to the passion of Christ; and continually—as much as he may, and as his sickness will suffer him—think on the passion of Christ; for thereby all the devil's temptations and guiles be most overcome and voided.

## CHAPTER IV
### THE FOURTH CHAPTER CONTAINETH AN INSTRUCTION: WITH CERTAIN OBSECRATIONS [I.E., SUPPLICATIONS] TO THEM THAT SHALL DIE

\* \* \* \* \*

## CHAPTER V
### THE FIFTH CHAPTER CONTAINETH AN INSTRUCTION UNTO THEM THAT SHALL DIE

But it is greatly to be noted, and to be taken heed of, that right seldom (that) any man—yea among religious and devout men—dispose themselves to death betimes as they ought. For every man weeneth himself to live long, and troweth [*i.e.,* accepts] not that he shall die in short time; and doubtless that cometh of the devil's subtle temptation. And often times it is seen openly that many men, through such idle hope and trust, have for-slothed themselves [*i.e.,* lost themselves through sloth], and have died intestate, or unavised [*i.e.,* unadvised], or undisposed [*i.e.,* unprepared], suddenly. And therefore every man that hath love and dread of God, and a zeal of . . . man's soul, let him busily induce and warn every of his even christians that is sick, or in any peril of body or of soul, that principally and first, over all other things, and withouten delays and long tarryings, he diligently provide and ordain for the spiritual remedy and medicine of his soul.

\* \* \* \* \*

And if the sick man hath lost his speech, and yet he hath full knowledge of the interrogations that be made to him, or the prayers that be rehearsed before him, then only with some outer sign, or with consent of heart, let him answer thereto. Nevertheless it is greatly to be charged and hasted [*i.e.*, urged] that the interrogations be made to him or [*i.e.*, before] he lose his speech; for if his answers be not likely, and seemeth not in all sides to be sufficient to full heal and perpetual remedy of his soul, then must he put thereto remedy and counsel in the best manner that it may be done.

Then there shall be told unto him plainly the peril that he should fall in, though he should and would be greatly a-feared thereof. It is better and more rightful that he be compunctious and repentant, with wholesome fear and dread, and so be saved, than that he be damned with flattering and false dissimulation; for it is too inconvenient [*i.e.*, inconsistent] and contrary to Christian religion, and too devil-like, that the peril of death and of soul—for any vain dread of a man, lest he were anything distroubled thereby—shall be hid from any Christian man or woman that should die. . . .

Also present to the sick the image of the crucifix; the which should evermore be about sick men, or else the image of our Lady, or of some other saint the which he loved or worshipped in his heal. Also let there be holy water about the sick; and spring [*i.e.*, sprinkle] often times upon him, and the others that be about him, that fiends may be voided from him.

If all things abovesaid may not be done, for hastiness [*i.e.*, suddenness] and shortness of time, then put forth prayers; and namely such as be directed to our Saviour, specially Our Lord Jesu Christ. When man is in point of death, and hasteth fast to his end, then should no carnal friends, nor wife, nor children, nor riches, nor no temporal goods, be reduced [*i.e.*, brought back] unto his mind, neither be communed of before him; only as much as spiritual health and profit of the sick man asketh and requireth.

*    *    *    *    *

## CHAPTER VI
### THE SIXTH CHAPTER CONTAINETH PRAYERS THAT SHOULD BE SAID UPON THEM THAT BE A-DYING OF SOME MAN THAT IS ABOUT THEM

Last of all it is to be known that the prayers that follow may be conveniently said upon a sick man that laboureth to his end. And if it is a religious person, then when the covent is gathered together with smiting of the table, as the manner is, then shall be said first the litany, with the psalms and orisons that be used therewith. Afterward, if he live yet, let some man that is about him say the orisons that follow hereafter, as the time and opportunity will suffer. And they may be often rehearsed again to excite the devotion of the sick man—if he have reason and understanding with him.

But nevertheless this ought not to be done of necessity, as though he might not be saved but if [*i.e.*, unless] it were done; but for the profit and devotion of the sick that laboureth to his endward it may, and it is well done, that it be done so. But among seculars that be sick let these prayers be said; as the devotion and disposition, and the profit of them and others that be about them ask and require, and as the time will suffice.

But alas there be full few, not only among seculars but also in diverse religious that have the cunning of this craft, and will be nigh and assist to them that be in point of death and departing out of this world; asking them, and exhorting and informing and praying for them, as it is abovesaid—namely when they that be in dying would not, or hope not, to die yet, and so the sick men's souls stand in great peril.

\*     \*     \*     \*     \*

## ORATIO

GO CHRISTIAN SOUL out of this world, in the Name of the Almighty Father that made thee of nought; in the Name of Jesu Christ, His Son, that suffered His passion for thee; and in the Name of the Holy Ghost, that was infounded [*i.e.*, shed] into thee. Holy angels, Thrones and Dominations, Princehoods, Protestates and Virtues, Cherubim and Seraphim, meet with thee. Patriarchs and prophets, apostles and evangelists, martyrs, confessors, monks and hermits, maidens and widows, children and innocents, help thee. The prayers of all priests and deacons, and all the degrees of Holy Church, help thee; that in peace be thy place, and thy dwelling in heavenly Jerusalem everlastingly; by the mediation of Our Lord Jesu Christ, that is Mediator between God and man. Amen.

*The Book of the Craft of Dying and other Early English Tracts Concerning Death. . .* , ed. by Frances M. M. Comper (London: Longmans, Green and Co., 1917), pp. 3, 5, 9–12, 13–16, 17–21, 22–27, 32, 35–37, 39–40, 47. By permission.

# Exhibit Eleven

## SACRAMENTAL
## MEDICINE

*KRAMER AND SPRENGER*

### Introduction

A famous medievalist has written that "the darkest horror produced by the medieval spirit on the wane" was "the delusion of witchcraft"; already by the end of the fifteenth century this delusion had been "fully developed into a fatally consistent system of theological zeal and judicial severity."[76] Not until the eighteenth century did European civilization exorcise the delusion of witchcraft; for some six centuries Christian pastoring concentrated enormous effort upon identifying witches and exorcising their victims.

Witchcraft, the exercise of superhuman powers, has had a long connection with Christianity, being mentioned in the Old and New Testaments and believed in by many of the Church Fathers. As a popular superstition in early medieval Europe, it received a new emphasis in the twelfth century after Western Christendom's contact with the Orient in the Crusades. During this time, witchcraft was primarily thought of as sorcery. As an illegal activity, divination and healings by means of witch-power were denounced in pulpit and confessional, but the

---

[76] J. Huizinga, *The Waning of the Middle Ages* (London: Edward Arnold & Co., and New York: St. Martin's Press, 1924), p. 181. By permission.

more stringent penalties, including death, could be inflicted only when serious concrete injuries were involved. In the late thirteenth century, however, ecclesiastical law began to see in sorcery a threat to the faith in the form of heresy. In 1258, Pope Alexander IV allowed the Inquisition to proceed against sorcerers whose acts conflicted with the articles of faith. Bit by bit the Inquisition succeeded in including sorcery under its jurisdiction and in portraying it as the most terrible of all crimes—a heretical denial of God's power by making a pact with Satan.

From the late thirteenth through the fifteenth century, popes commissioned inquisitors to deal with witchcraft, and mass persecutions of witches took place in the decades prior to the Reformation. In 1484 Pope Innocent VIII issued a bull aimed at eradicating witches. He appointed two Dominican teachers, Heinrich Kramer (Henricus Institoris), an Alsatian, and James Sprenger, dean of the theological faculty at Cologne, to investigate and prosecute witches throughout North Germany. Each man had previous experience as an inquisitor, having traveled widely in Europe hunting witches, and Kramer had already compiled a treatise on witchcraft. Together they composed a book that still stands as a classic document on the subject, *Malleus Maleficarum* ("The Hammer of Witches"), first published in 1486 or 1487. Soon this work became a standard diagnostic, judicial, and pastoral handbook on how to recognize and punish witches and how to exorcise the demons that possessed bewitched persons. They included in their work a vast range of historical data regarding witches and demons, and combined this information with that gained through their own broad experience.

Witches were thought to be persons who had compacted with devils in return for certain powers, including the power to command demons, and were believed to have vowed to venerate Satan and to surrender body and soul to him. Should a witch confess, either under torture or threat, the witch was usually remanded to the civil authorities for the severest penalties— usually, burning. For the pious, however, who were ever in danger from assault by evil spirits, the *Malleus Maleficarum* sought, among other aims, to teach how they might ward off demons.

The book discussed in some detail the machinations of incubus and succubus devils. An incubus demon was thought to be an angel who fell from grace on account of his lust for women, while the corresponding succubus appeared in the form of a woman and specialized in seducing men. Succubi collected semen from men in whom they induced orgasms, being careful to select fine specimens; then cunningly turning themselves into incubi, they used this material to impregnate chosen women with whom they copulated. The issue of this procedure was a person who would almost certainly become in due course the most evil of witches. On the basis of this belief, preventive measures against incubi and succubi were important, not only because of danger of pollution to the faithful by these evil sexual practices, but also as a way by which the witch population might be kept to a minimum.

From the fifteenth through the seventeenth century, while the whole of Europe was at once fascinated and horrified by witchcraft and demon possession, many works dealing with the subject were being published; in scope and detail this production in the field of the cure of souls was rivaled only by the multitudinous early-medieval penitential handbooks. One authority has listed more than 35 major treatises on witchcraft written and published from the time of Johannes Nider's *Formicarius* in 1475 to the Spanish work *Opus de Magica Superstitione*, by Pedro Ciruelo in 1539. Many of these books had a large number of editions—the *Malleus* went through 13 printings before 1520, and 16 more by the end of the seventeenth century.[77]

In all these books, however, the problem of diagnosing witches and demon possession was centrally important and very troublesome. The matter of identifying witches seemed to be settled for a while, at least, by the use of torture. The *Malleus* in Part III discussed complicated procedures whereby terror, exhortation, and pain were used to exact from the accused an admission of guilt and the naming of accomplices. On the other hand, diagnosis of demon possession was never settled satisfactorily.

One early seventeenth-century manual, *Compendium Maleficarum*, by an Italian friar named Francesco-Maria Guazzo, drew on 322 previous authorities on demonology to establish diagnostic symptoms, such as contortions, tearing of garments, lacerating the body, changes of voice, an extended or swollen tongue, panting, palpitation, vomiting, hiccoughs, distended bowels, flatulence, localized pains, and so forth. He further recommended that in difficult cases an accurate diagnosis might be obtained if a priest would place his hand and his stole on the possessed's head and recite certain formulae, whereupon the

---

[77] H. C. Lea, *Materials Toward A History of Witchcraft*, ed. A. C. Howland and G. L. Burr (3 vols., New York: Thomas Yoseloff, 1957), I, 260–416. By permission.

demons inside the sufferer would make the sick man shudder and shake and would cause sharp pains wherever they were lodged.[78] Another treatise, published in Antwerp in 1648, tells that the demons sometimes entered the possessed in the shape of a mouse or other small animal, causing a variety of symptoms, including the turning of skin color to yellow or ashen, a pinched look about the eyes, extraordinary emaciation, constriction of the members of the body, a lump in the anus, needle pricks felt around the heart, and convulsive seizures.[79] Another publication appearing in 1644 at Rouen classified symptoms by 11 indications, including such things as thinking oneself possessed, living outside the rules of society, being persistently ill, falling into heavy sleep, making sounds like an animal, and being tired of living.[80]

The material here excerpted from the *Malleus Maleficarum*, itself an exceedingly long and detailed work, consists of only three chapters of the second question of the second part. The first of these chapters prescribes remedies against incubi and succubi, chapter two sets forth remedies for persons bewitched by the limitation of the generative power, and chapter six sets out in detail the procedures for pastoral exorcism. It is to be noted that these sprinklings, prayers, litanies, and other ritualistic acts resemble the Service of Exorcism found in the *Rituale Romanum* of our own day, when exorcism of evil powers continues as a means of pastoral healing even where belief in witches has been dispelled.

# SACRAMENTAL MEDICINE

From: *Malleus Maleficarum* (1486),
by Heinrich Kramer and James Sprenger.

## CHAPTER I
## THE REMEDIES PRESCRIBED BY HOLY CHURCH
## AGAINST INCUBUS AND SUCCUBUS DEVILS

In the foregoing chapters on the First Question we have treated of the methods of bewitching men, animals and the fruits of the earth, and especially of the behaviour of witches in their own persons; how

---

[78] Paraphrasing R. H. Robbins, *The Encyclopedia of Witchcraft and Demonology* (New York: Crown Publishers, Inc., 1959), p. 396. By permission.
[79] Lea, *op. cit.*, III, 1064. By permission.
[80] Paraphrasing Robbins, *op. cit.*, p. 395. By permission.

they seduce young girls in order to increase their evil numbers; what is their method of profession and of offering homage; how they offer to devils their own children and the children of others; and how they are transported from place to place. Now I say that there is no remedy for such practices, unless witches be entirely eradicated by the judges, or at least punished as an example to all who may wish to imitate them; but we are not immediately treating of this point, which will be dealt with in the last Part of this work, where we set forth the twenty ways of proceeding against and sentencing witches.

For the present we are concerned only with the remedies against the injuries which they inflict; and first how men who are bewitched can be cured; secondly, beasts, and thirdly, how the fruits of the earth may be secured from blight or phylloxera [*i.e.*, vine-pest].

With regard to the bewitchment of human beings by means of Incubus and Succubus devils, it is to be noted that this can happen in three ways. First, as in the case of witches themselves, when women voluntarily prostitute themselves to Incubus devils. Secondly, when men have connexion with Succubus devils; yet it does not appear that men thus devilishly fornicate with the same full degree of culpability; for men, being by nature intellectually stronger than women, are more apt to abhor such practices. Thirdly, it may happen that men or women are by witchcraft entangled with Incubi or Succubi against their will. This chiefly happens in the case of certain virgins who are molested by In-cubus devils wholly against their will; and it would seem that such are bewitched by witches who, just as they very often cause other infirmities, cause devils to molest such virgins in the form of Incubi for the purpose of seducing them into joining their vile company. Let us give an example.

There is in the town of Coblenz a poor man who is bewitched in this way. In the presence of his wife he is in the habit of acting after the manner of men with women, that is to say, of practising coition, as it were, and he continues to do this repeatedly, nor have the cries and urgent appeals of his wife any effect in making him desist. And after he has fornicated thus two or three times, he bawls out, "We are going to start all over again"; when actually there is no person visible to mortal sight lying with him. And after an incredible number of such bouts, the poor man at last sinks to the floor utterly exhausted. When he has re-covered his strength a little and is asked how this has happened to him, and whether he has had any woman with him, he answers that he saw nothing, but that his mind is in some way possessed so that he can by no means refrain from such priapism. And indeed he harbours a great suspicion that a certain woman bewitched him in this way, because he had offended her, and she had cursed him with threatening words, telling him what she would like to happen to him.

But there are no laws or ministers of justice which can proceed to the avenging of so great a crime with no other warrant than a vague charge or a grave suspicion; for it is held that no one ought to be condemned unless he has been convicted by his own confession, or by the evidence of three trustworthy witnesses; since the mere fact of the crime coupled with even the gravest suspicions against some person is not sufficient to warrant the punishment of that person. But this matter will be dealt with later.

As for instances where young maidens are molested by Incubus devils in this way, it would take too long to mention even those that have been known to happen in our own time, for there are very many well-attested stories of such bewitchments. But the great difficulty of finding a remedy for such afflictions can be illustrated from a story told by Thomas of Brabant [*i.e.*, of Cantimpré, 1201–1272] in his *Book on Bees*.

I saw, he writes, and heard the confession of a virgin in a religious habit, who said at first that she had never been a consenting party to fornication, but at the same time gave me to understand that she had been known in this way. This I could not believe, but narrowly charged and exhorted her, with the most solemn adjurations, to speak the truth on peril of her very soul. At last, weeping bitterly, she acknowledged that she had been corrupted rather in mind than in body; and that though she had afterwards grieved almost to death, and had daily confessed with tears, yet by no device or study or art could she be delivered from an Incubus devil, nor yet by the sign of the Cross, nor by Holy Water, which are specially ordained for the expulsion of devils, nor even by the Sacrament of the Body of Our Lord, which even the Angels fear. But at last after many years of prayer and fasting she was delivered.

It may be believed (saving a better judgement) that, after she repented and confessed her sin, the Incubus devil should be regarded rather in the light of a punishment for sin than as a sin in itself.

A devout nun, named Christina, in the Low Country of the Duchy of Brabant, told me the following concerning this same woman. On the vigil of one Pentecost the woman came to her complaining that she dared not take the Sacrament because of the importunate molestation of a devil. Christina, pitying her, said: "Go, and rest assured that you will receive the Body of Our Lord to-morrow; for I will take your punishment upon myself." So she went away joyfully, and after praying that night slept in peace, and rose up in the morning and communicated in all tranquillity of soul. But Christina, not thinking of the punishment she had taken upon herself, went to her rest in the evening, and as she lay in bed heard, as it were, a violent attack being made upon her; and, seizing whatever it was by the throat, tried to throw it off. She lay down again, but was again molested, and rose up in terror; and this happened many times, whilst all the straw of her bed was turned over and thrown about everywhere, so at length she perceived that she was being persecuted by the malice of a devil. Thereupon she left her pallet, and passed a sleepless night; and when she wished to pray, she was so tormented by the devil that she said she had never suffered so much before. In the morning, therefore, saying to the other woman, "I renounce your punishment, and I am hardly alive to renounce it," she escaped from the violence of that wicked tempter. From this it can be seen how difficult it is to cure this sort of evil, whether or not it is due to witchcraft.

However, there are still some means by which these devils may be driven away, of which Nider [1380–1438] writes in his *Formicarius*. He says that there are five ways by which girls or men can be delivered: first, by Sacramental Confession; second, by the Sacred Sign of the Cross, or by the recital of the Angelic Salutation; third, by the use of exorcisms; fourth, by moving to another place; and fifth, by means of excommunication prudently employed by holy men. It is evident from what has been said that the first two methods did not avail the nun; but they are not on that account to be neglected, for that which cures one person does not necessarily cure another, and conversely. And it is a recorded fact that Incubus devils have often been driven away by the Lord's Prayer, or by the sprinkling of Holy Water, and also especially by the Angelic Salutation.

For S. Caesarius [c. 1180–1240] tells in his *Dialogue* that, after a certain priest had hanged himself, his concubine entered a convent, where she was carnally solicited by an Incubus. She drove him away by crossing herself and using Holy Water, yet he immediately returned. But when she recited the Angelic Salutation, he vanished like an arrow shot from a bow; still he came back, although he did not dare to come near her, because of that AVE MARIA.

S. Caesarius also refers to the remedy of Sacramental Confession. For he says that the aforesaid concubine was entirely abandoned by the Incubus after she was clean confessed. He tells also of a man in Leyden who was plagued by a Succubus, and was entirely delivered after Sacramental Confession.

He adds yet another example, of an enclosed nun, a contemplative, whom an Incubus would not leave in spite of prayers and confession and other religious exercises. For he persisted in forcing his way to her bed. But when, acting on the advice of a certain religious man, she uttered the word Benedicite, the devil at once left her.

Of the fourth method, that of moving to another place, he says that a certain priest's daughter had been defiled by an Incubus and driven frantic with grief; but when she went far away across the Rhine, she was left in peace by the Incubus. Her father, however, because he had sent her away, was so afflicted by the devil that he died within three days.

He also mentions a woman who was often molested by an Incubus in her own bed, and asked a devout friend of hers to come and sleep with her. She did so, and was troubled all night with the utmost uneasiness and disquiet, and then the first woman was left in peace. William of [Auvergne, c. 1180–1249, archbishop of] Paris notes also that Incubi seem chiefly to molest women and girls with beautiful hair; either because they devote themselves too much to the care and adornment of their hair, or because they are wont to try to excite men by means of their hair, or because they are boastfully vain about it, or because God in His goodness permits this so that women may be afraid to entice men by the very means by which the devils wish them to entice men.

The fifth method, that of excommunication, which is perhaps the same as exorcism, is exemplified in a history of S. Bernard [1090–1153]. In Aquitaine a woman had for six years been molested by an Incubus with incredible carnal abuse and lechery; and she heard the Incubus threaten her that she must not go near the holy man, who was coming that way, saying: "It will avail you nothing: for when he has gone away, I, who have till now been your lover, will become the cruellest of tyrants to you." None the less she went to S. Bernard, and he said to her: "Take my staff and set it in your bed, and may the devil do what he can." When she had done this, the devil did not dare to enter the woman's room, but threatened her terribly from outside, saying that he would persecute her when S. Bernard had gone away. When S. Bernard heard this from the woman, he called the people together, bidding them carry lighted candles in their hands, and, with the whole assembly which was gathered, excommunicated the devil, forbidding him evermore to approach that woman or any other. And so she was delivered from that punishment.

Here it is to be noted that the power of the Keys granted to S. Peter and his successors, which resounds on the earth, is really a power of healing granted to the Church on behalf of travellers who are subject to the jurisdiction of the Papal power; therefore it seems wonderful that even the Powers of the air can be warded off by this virtue. But it must be remembered that persons who are molested by devils are under the jurisdiction of the Pope and his Keys; and therefore it is not surprising if such Powers are indirectly kept at bay by the virtue of the Keys, just as by the same virtue the souls in purgatory can indirectly be delivered from the pains of the fire; inasmuch as this Power availeth upon the earth, ay, and to the relief of souls that are under the earth.

But it is not seemly to discuss the Power of the Keys granted to the Head of the Church as Christ's Vicar; since it is known that, for the use of the Church, Christ granted to the Church and His Vicar as much power as it is possible for God to grant to mere man.

And it is piously to be believed that, when infirmities inflicted by witches through the power of devils, together with the witches and devils

themselves, are excommunicated, those who were afflicted will no longer
be tormented; and that they will be delivered all the sooner by the use of
other lawful exorcisms in addition.

There is a common report current in the districts of the river Etsch,
as also in other places, that by the permission of God a swarm of locusts
came and devoured all the vines, green leaves and crops; and that they
were suddenly put to flight and dispersed by means of this kind of excommunication and cursing. Now if any wish that this should be ascribed
to some holy man, and not to the virtue of the Keys, let it be so, in the
name of the Lord; but of one thing we are certain, that both the power
to perform miracles and the power of the Keys necessarily presuppose a
condition of grace in him who performs that act of grace, since both
these powers proceed from grace granted to men who are in a state of
grace.

Again, it is to be noted that, if none of the aforesaid remedies are of
any avail, then recourse must be had to the usual exorcisms, of which we
shall treat later. And if even these are not sufficient to banish the iniquity
of the devil, then that affliction must be considered to be an expiatory
punishment for sin, which should be borne in all meekness, as are other
ills of this sort which oppress us that they may, as it were, drive us to seek
God.

But it must also be remarked that sometimes persons only think that
they are molested by an Incubus when they are not so actually; and this
is more apt to be the case with women than with men, for they are more
timid and liable to imagine extraordinary things.

In this connexion William of Paris is often quoted. He says: Many
phantastical apparitions occur to persons suffering from a melancholy
disease, especially to women, as is shown by their dreams and visions.
And the reason for this, as physicians know, is that women's souls are by
nature far more easily and lightly impressionable than men's souls. And
he adds: I know that I have seen a woman who thought that a devil
copulated with her from inside, and said she was physically conscious of
such incredible things.

At times also women think they have been made pregnant by an
Incubus, and their bellies grow to an enormous size; but when the time
of parturition comes, their swelling is relieved by no more than the expulsion of a great quantity of wind. For by taking ants' eggs in drink, or
the seeds of spurge or of the black pine, an incredible amount of wind
and flatulence is generated in the human stomach. And it is very easy
for the devil to cause these and even greater disorders in the stomach.
This has been set down in order that too easy credence should not be
given to women, but only to those whom experience has shown to be
trustworthy, and to those who, by sleeping in their beds or near by them,
know for a fact that such things as we have spoken of are true.

## CHAPTER II
## REMEDIES PRESCRIBED FOR THOSE WHO ARE
## BEWITCHED BY THE LIMITATION OF THE
## GENERATIVE POWER

Although far more women are witches than men, as was shown in the First Part of the work, yet men are more often bewitched than women. And the reason for this lies in the fact that God allows the devil more power over the venereal act, by which the original sin is handed down, than over other human actions. In the same way He allows more witchcraft to be performed by means of serpents, which are more subject to incantations than other animals, because that was the first instrument of the devil. And the venereal act can be more readily and easily bewitched in a man than in a woman, as has been clearly shown. For there are five ways in which the devil can impede the act of generation, and they are more easily operated against men.

As far as possible we shall set out remedies which can be applied in each separate kind of obstruction; and let him who is bewitched in this faculty take note to which class of obstruction his belongs. For there are five classes, according to Peter a Palude [d. 1342] in his Fourth Book, dist. 34, of the trial of this sort of bewitchment.

For the devil, being a spirit, has by his very nature power, with God's permission, over a bodily creature, especially to promote or to prevent local motion. So by this power they can prevent the bodies of men and women from approaching each other; and this either directly or indirectly. Directly, when they remove one to a distance from another, and do not allow him to approach the other. Indirectly, when they cause some obstruction, or when they interpose themselves in an assumed body. So it happened to that young Pagan who had married an idol, but none the less contracted a marriage with a girl; but because of this he was unable to copulate with her, as has been shown above.

Secondly, the devil can inflame a man towards one woman and render him impotent towards another; and this he can secretly cause by the application of certain herbs or other matters of which he well knows the virtue for this purpose.

Thirdly, he can disturb the apperception of a man or a woman, so that he makes one appear hideous to the other; for, as has been shown, he can influence the imagination.

Fourthly, he can suppress the vigour of that member which is necessary for procreation; just as he can deprive any organ of the power of local motion.

Fifthly, he can prevent the flow of the semen to the members in which is the motive power, by as it were closing the seminal duct so that it does not descend to the genital vessels, or does not ascend again from them, or cannot come forth, or is spent vainly.

But if a man should say: I do not know by which of these different methods I have been bewitched; all I know is that I cannot do anything with my wife: he should be answered in this way. If he is active and able with regard to other women, but not with his wife, then he is bewitched in the second way; for he can be certified as to the first way, that he is being deluded by Succubus or Incubus devils. Moreover, if he does not find his wife repellent, and yet cannot know her, but can know other women, then again it is the second way; but if he finds her repellent and cannot copulate with her, then it is the second and the third way. If he does not find her repellent and wishes to have connexion with her, but has no power in his member, then it is the fourth way. But if he has power in his member, yet cannot emit his semen, then it is the fifth way. The method of curing these will be shown where we consider whether those who live in grace and those who do not are equally liable to be bewitched in these manners; and we answer that they are not, with the exception of the fourth manner, and even then very rarely. For such an affliction can happen to a man living in grace and righteousness; but the reader must understand that in this case we speak of the conjugal act between married people; for in any other case they are all liable to bewitchment; for every venereal act outside wedlock is a mortal sin, and is only committed by those who are not in a state of grace.

We have, indeed, the authority of the whole of Scriptural teaching that God allows the devil to afflict sinners more than the just. For although that most just man, Job, was stricken, yet he was not so particularly or directly in respect of the procreant function. And it may be said that, when a married couple are afflicted in this way, either both the parties or one of them is not living in a state of grace; and this opinion is substantiated in the Scriptures both by authority and by reason. For the Angel said to Tobias: The devil receives power against those who are given over to lust: and he proved it in the slaying of the seven husbands of the virgin Sara.

Cassian [c. 360–435], in his *Collation of the Fathers*, quotes S. Antony [251?–356] as saying that the devil can in no way enter our mind or body unless he has first deprived it of all holy thoughts and made it empty and bare of spiritual contemplation. These words should not be applied to an evil affliction over the whole of the body, for when Job was so afflicted he was not denuded of Divine grace; but they have particular reference to a particular infirmity inflicted upon the body for some sin. And the infirmity we are considering can only be due to the sin of incontinence. For, as we have said, God allows the devil more power over that act than over other human acts, because of its natural nastiness, and because by it the first sin was handed down to posterity.

Therefore when people joined in matrimony have for some sin been deprived of Divine help, God allows them to be bewitched chiefly in their procreant functions.

But if it is asked of what sort are those sins, it can be said, according to S. Jerome [c. 342–420], that even in a state of matrimony it is possible to commit the sin of incontinence in various ways. See the text: He who loves his wife to excess is an adulterer. And they who love in this way are more liable to be bewitched after the manner we have said.

The remedies of the Church, then, are twofold: one applicable in the public court, the other in the tribunal of the confessional. As for the first, when it has been publicly found that the impotence is due to witchcraft, then it must be distinguished whether it is temporary or permanent. If it is only temporary, it does not annul the marriage. And it is assumed to be temporary if, within the space of three years, by using every possible expedient of the Sacraments of the Church and other remedies, a cure can be caused. But if, after that time, they cannot be cured by any remedy, then it is assumed to be permanent.

Now the disability either precedes both the contract and the consummation of marriage; and in this case it impedes the contract: or it follows the contract but precedes the consummation; and in this case it annuls the contract. For men are very often bewitched in this way because they have cast off their former mistresses, who, hoping that they were to be married and being disappointed, so bewitch the men that they cannot copulate with another woman. And in such a case, according to the opinion of many, the marriage already contracted is annulled, unless, like Our Blessed Lady and S. Joseph, they are willing to live together in holy continence. This opinion is supported by the Canon where it says (23, q. 1) that a marriage is confirmed by the carnal act. And a little later it says that impotence before such confirmation dissolves the ties of marriage.

Or else the disability follows the consummation of a marriage, and then it does not dissolve the bonds of matrimony. Much more to this effect is noted by the Doctors, where in various writings they treat of the obstruction due to witchcraft; but since it is not precisely relevant to the present inquiry, it is here omitted.

But some may find it difficult to understand how this function can be obstructed in respect of one woman but not of another. S. Bonaventura [1221–1274] answers that this may be because some witch has persuaded the devil to effect this only with respect to one woman, or because God will not allow the obstruction to apply save to some particular woman. The judgement of God in this matter is a mystery, as in the case of the wife of Tobias. But how the devil procures this disability is plainly shown by what has already been said. And S. Bonaventura says that he obstructs the procreant function, not intrinsically by harming the organ, but extrinsically by impeding its use; and it is an artificial, not a natural impediment; and so he can cause it to apply to one woman and not to another. Or else he takes away all desire for one or another woman; and this he does by his own power, or else by means of some herb or stone or some occult creature. And in this he is in substantial agreement with Peter a Palude.

The ecclesiastical remedy in the tribunal of God is set forth in the Canon where it says: If with the permission of the just and secret judgement of God, through the arts of sorceresses and witches and the preparation of the devil, men are bewitched in their procreant function, they are to be urged to make clean confession to God and His priest of all their sins with a contrite heart and a humble spirit; and to make satisfaction to God with many tears and large offerings and prayers and fasting.

From these words it is clear that such afflictions are only on account of sin, and occur only to those who do not live in a state of grace. It proceeds to tell how the ministers of the Church can effect a cure by means of exorcisms and the other protections and cures provided by the Church. In this way, with the help of God, Abraham cured by his prayers Abimelech and his house.

In conclusion we may say that there are five remedies which may lawfully be applied to those who are bewitched in this way: namely, a pilgrimage to some holy and venerable shrine; true confession of their sins with contrition; the plentiful use of the sign of the Cross and devout prayer; lawful exorcism by solemn words, the nature of which will be explained later; and lastly, a remedy can be effected by prudently approaching the witch, as was shown in the case of the Count who for three years was unable to cohabit carnally with a virgin whom he had married.

*   *   *   *   *

CHAPTER VI<br>
PRESCRIBED REMEDIES; TO WIT, THE LAWFUL<br>
EXORCISMS OF THE CHURCH, FOR ALL SORTS OF<br>
INFIRMITIES AND ILLS DUE TO WITCHCRAFT; AND THE<br>
METHOD OF EXORCISING THOSE WHO ARE BEWITCHED

It has already been stated that witches can afflict men with every kind of physical infirmity; therefore it can be taken as a general rule that the various verbal or practical remedies which can be applied in the case of those infirmities which we have just been discussing are equally applicable to all other infirmities, such as epilepsy or leprosy, for example. And as lawful exorcisms are reckoned among the verbal remedies and have been most often considered by us, they may be taken as a general type of such remedies; and there are three matters to be considered regarding them.

First, we must judge whether a person who has not been ordained as an exorcist, such as a layman or a secular cleric, may lawfully exorcise devils and their works. Bound up with this question are three others: namely; first, what constitutes the legality of this practice; secondly, the seven conditions which must be observed when one wishes to make private use of charms and benedictions; and thirdly, in what way the disease is to be exorcised and the devil conjured.

Secondly, we must consider what is to be done when no healing grace results from the exorcism.

Thirdly, we must consider practical and not verbal remedies; together with the solution of certain arguments.

For the first, we have the opinion of S. Thomas [c. 1225–1274] in Book IV, dist. 23. He says: When a man is ordained as an exorcist, or into any of the other minor Orders, he has conferred upon him the power of exorcism in his official capacity; and this power may even lawfully be used by those who belong to no Order, but such do not exercise it in their official capacity. Similarly the Mass can be said in an unconsecrated house, although the very purpose of consecrating a church is that the Mass may be said there; but this is more on account of the grace which is in the righteous than of the grace of the Sacrament.

From these words we may conclude that, although it is good that in the liberation of a bewitched person recourse should be had to an exorcist having authority to exorcise such bewitchments, yet at times other devout persons may, either with or without any exorcism, cast out this sort of diseases.

For we hear of a certain poor and very devout virgin, one of whose friends had been grievously bewitched in his foot, so that it was clear to the physicians that he could be cured by no medicines. But it happened that the virgin went to visit the sick man, and he at once begged her to apply some benediction to his foot. She consented, and did no more than silently say the Lord's Prayer and the Apostles' Creed, at the same time making use of the sign of the life-giving Cross. The sick man then felt himself at once cured, and, that he might have a remedy for the future, asked the virgin what charms she had used. But she answered: You are of little faith and do not hold to the holy and lawful practices of the Church, and you often apply forbidden charms and remedies for your infirmities; therefore are you rarely healthy in your body, because you are always sick in your soul. But if you would put your trust in prayer and in the efficacy of lawful symbols, you will often be very easily cured. For I did nothing but repeat the Lord's Prayer and the Apostles' Creed, and you are now cured.

This example gives rise to the question, whether there is not any

efficacy in other benedictions and charms, and even conjurations by way
of exorcism; for they seem to be condemned in this story. We answer
that the virgin condemned only unlawful charms and unlawful conjurations and exorcisms.

To understand these last we must consider how they originated, and
how they came to be abused. For they were in their origin entirely sacred;
but just as by the means of devils and wicked men all things can be
defiled, so also were these sacred words. For it is said in the last chapter
of S. Mark, of the Apostles and holy men: In My Name shall they cast
out devils; and they visited the sick, and prayed over them with sacred
words; and in after times priests devoutly used similar rites; and therefore
there are to be found to-day in ancient Churches devout prayers and holy
exorcisms which men can use or undergo, when they are applied by pious
men as they used to be, without any superstition; even as there are now
to be found learned men and Doctors of holy Theology who visit the
sick and use such words for the healing not only of demoniacs, but of
other diseases as well.

But, alas! superstitious men have, on the pattern of these, found for
themselves many vain and unlawful remedies which they employ in these
days for sick men and animals; and the clergy have become too slothful
to use any more the lawful words when they visit the sick. On this
account Gulielmus Durandus [1230–1296], the commentator on S. Raymond [of Penafort, c. 1175–1275], says that such lawful exorcisms may
be used by a religious and discreet priest, or by a layman, or even by a
woman of good life and proved discretion; by the offering of lawful
prayers over the sick: not over fruits or animals, but over the sick. For
the Gospel says: They shall place their hands upon the sick, etc. And
such persons are not to be prevented from practising in this way; unless
perhaps it is feared that, following their example, other indiscreet and
superstitious persons should make improper use of incantations. It is
these superstitious diviners whom that virgin we have mentioned condemned, when she said that they who consulted with such had weak, that
is to say bad, faith.

Now for the elucidation of this matter it is asked how it is possible
to know whether the words of such charms and benedictions are lawful
or superstitious, and how they ought to be used; and whether the devil
can be conjured and diseases exorcised.

In the first place, that is said to be lawful in the Christian religion
which is not superstitious; and that is said to be superstitious which is
over and above the prescribed form of religion. See *Colossians* ii: Which
things indeed have a show of wisdom in superstition: on which the gloss
says: Superstition is undisciplined religion, that is, religion observed with
defective methods in evil circumstances.

Anything, also, is superstition which human tradition without higher
authority has caused to usurp the name of religion; such as the interpola-

tion of hymns at Holy Mass, the alteration of the Preface for Requiems, the abbreviation of the Creed which is to be sung at Mass, the reliance upon an organ rather than upon the choir for the music, neglect to have a Server on the Altar, and such practices. But to return to our point, when a work is done by virtue of the Christian religion, as when someone wishes to heal the sick by means of prayer and benediction and sacred words (which is the matter we are considering), such a person must observe seven conditions by which such benedictions are rendered lawful. And even if he uses adjurations, through the virtue of the Divine Name, and by the virtue of the works of Christ, His Birth, Passion and Precious Death, by which the devil was conquered and cast out; such benedictions and charms and exorcisms shall be called lawful, and they who practise them are exorcists or lawful enchanters. See S. Isidore [c. 560–636], *Etym.* VIII, Enchanters are they whose art and skill lies in the use of words.

*     *     *     *     *

To return, then, to the actual point. When it is asked whether the disease is to be exorcised and the devil adjured, and which of these should be done first; it is answered that not the disease, but the sick and bewitched man himself is exorcised: just as in the case of a child, it is not the infection of the *fomes* which is exorcised, but the child itself. Also, just as the child is first exorcised, and then the devil is adjured to depart; so also is the bewitched person first exorcised, and afterwards the devil and his works are bidden to depart. Again, just as salt and water are exorcised, so are all things which can be used by the sick man, so that it is expedient to exorcise and bless chiefly his food and drink. In the case of baptism the following ceremony of exorcism is observed: the exsufflation towards the West and the renunciation of the devil; secondly, the raising of the hands with a solemn confession of the faith of the Christian religion; thirdly, prayer, benediction, and the laying on of hands; fourthly, the stripping and anointing with Holy Oil; and after baptism, the communion and the putting on of the chrisom. But all this is not necessary in the exorcism of one who is bewitched; but that he should first have made a good confession, and if possible he is to hold a lighted candle, and receive the Holy Communion; and instead of putting on a chrisom, he is to remain bound naked to a Holy Candle of the length of Christ's body or of the Cross. And then may be said the following:

I exorcise thee, Peter, or thee, Barbara, being weak but reborn in Holy Baptism, by the living God, by the true God, by God Who redeemed thee with His Precious Blood, that thou mayest be exorcised, that all the illusions and wickedness of the devil's deceits may depart and flee from thee together with every unclean spirit, adjured by Him

Who will come to judge both the quick and the dead, and who will purge the earth with fire. Amen.

Let us pray.

O God of mercy and pity, Who according to Thy tender loving-kindness chastenest those whom Thou dost cherish, and dost gently compel those whom Thou receivest to turn their hearts, we invoke Thee, O Lord, that Thou wilt vouchsafe to bestow Thy grace upon Thy servant who suffereth from a weakness in the limbs of his body, that whatever is corrupt by earthly frailty, whatever is made violate by the deceit of the devil, may find redemption in the unity of the body of the Church. Have mercy, O Lord, on his groaning, have mercy upon his tears; and as he putteth his trust only in Thy mercy, receive him in the sacrament of Thy reconciliation, through Jesus Christ Our Lord. Amen.

Therefore, accursed devil, hear thy doom, and give honour to the true and living God, give honour to the Lord Jesus Christ, that thou depart with thy words from this servant whom our Lord Jesus Christ hath redeemed with His Precious Blood.

Then let him exorcise him a second and yet a third time, with the prayers as above.

Let us pray.

God, Who dost ever mercifully govern all things that Thou hast made, incline Thine ear to our prayers, and look in mercy upon Thy servant labouring under the sickness of the body; visit him, and grant him Thy salvation and the healing virtue of Thy heavenly grace, through Christ our Lord. Amen.

Therefore, accursed devil, etc.

The prayer for the third exorcism.

O God, the only protection of human frailty, show forth the mighty power of Thy strong aid upon our sick brother (or sister), that being holpen by Thy mercy he (she) may be worthy to enter Thy Holy Church in safety, through Christ our Lord. Amen.

And let the exorcist continually sprinkle him with Holy Water. And note that this method is recommended, not because it must be rigidly observed, or that other exorcisms are not of greater efficacy, but that there should be some regular system of exorcism and adjuration. For in the old histories and books of the Church there are sometimes found more devout and powerful exorcisms; but since before all things the reverence of God is necessary, let each proceed in this matter as he finds it best.

In conclusion, and for the sake of clearness, we may recommend this form of exorcism for a person who is bewitched. Let him first make a good confession (according to the often-quoted Canon: If by sortilege, etc.). Then let a diligent search be made in all corners and in the beds and mattresses and under the threshold of the door, in case some instrument of witchcraft may be found. The bodies of animals bewitched to death are at once to be burned. And it is expedient that all bedclothes and garments should be renewed, and even that he should change his house and dwelling. But in case nothing is found, then he who is to be exorcised should if possible go into the church in the morning, especially on the Holier Days, such as the Feasts of Our Lady, or on some Vigil; and the better if the priest also has confessed and is in a state of grace, for then the stronger will he be. And let him who is to be exorcised hold in his hand a Holy Candle as well as he can, either sitting or kneeling; and let those who are present offer up devout prayers for his deliverance. And let him begin the Litany at "Our help is in the Name of the Lord," and let one be appointed to make the responses: let him sprinkle him with Holy Water, and place a stole round his neck, and recite the Psalm "Haste thee, O God, to deliver me"; and let him continue the Litany for the Sick, saying at the Invocation of the Saints, "Pray for him and be favourable; deliver him, O Lord," continuing thus to the end. But where the prayers are to be said, then in the place of the prayers let him begin the exorcism, and continue in the way we have declared, or in any other better way, as seems good to him. And this sort of exorcism may be continued at least three times a week, that so through many intercessions the grace of health may be obtained.

Finally, he must receive the Sacrament of the Eucharist; although some think that this should be done before the exorcism. And at his confession the confessor must inquire whether he is under any bond of excommunication, and if he is, whether he has rashly omitted to obtain absolution from his Judge; for then, although he may at his discretion absolve him, yet when he has regained his health, he must seek absolution also from the Judge who excommunicated him.

It should further be noted that, when the exorcist is not ordained to the Order of Exorcist, then he may proceed with prayers; and if he can read the Scriptures, let him read the beginnings of the four Gospels of the Evangelists, and the Gospel beginning, "There was an Angel sent"; and the Passion of our Lord; all of which have great power to expel the works of the devil. Also let the Gospel of S. John, "In the beginning was the Word," be written and hung round the sick man's neck, and so let the grace of healing be looked for from God.

But if anyone asks what is the difference between the aspersion of Holy Water and exorcism, since both are ordained against the plagues of the devil, the answer is supplied by S. Thomas, who says: The devil attacks us from without and from within. Therefore Holy Water is ordained against his attacks from without; but exorcism against those from within. For this reason those for whom exorcism is necessary are called *Energoumenoi*, from *En*, meaning In, and *Ergon*, meaning Work, since they labour within themselves. But in exorcising a bewitched person both methods are to be used, because he is tormented both within and without.

*Malleus Maleficarum*, tr. and with an Introduction, Bibliography and Notes by the Rev. Montague Summers (London: The Pushkin Press, 1948), pp. 164–173, 179–180, 183–184. By permission.

# Exhibit Twelve

## CONSOLING
## AN ANXIOUS MAN

*MARTIN LUTHER*

### Introduction

When the Reformation began in Germany, popular
piety appealed in spiritual distress for comfort from
14 special saints who, according to legend, had appeared to a shepherd in a vision of the Christ-child.
Prayers to these 14 were particularly efficacious to
relieve dire difficulties. In the summer of 1519, the
Elector Frederick the Wise of Saxony (1462–1525)
fell gravely ill, and his secretary Georg Spalatin
(1484–1545) asked Martin Luther (1483–1546) to
write a word of spiritual consolation for their prince.
It was an extremely trying season for young Luther
himself, whose Ninety-Five Theses were shaking the
foundations of Christendom. In accepting the task,
Luther tried to transform the traditional appeal to
the 14 saints into a scripturally grounded meditation
upon 14 themes of spiritual cure: the seven aspects
of evil and the seven symmetrical benedictions of a
merciful God.

Although Luther set no great store on this work
that was composed as well for his own comfort in
crisis as for Frederick's, the "Fourteen Comforts for
the Weary and Heavy Laden" were published in
1520 in both Latin and German editions, and they
have remained through the centuries a favorite

Luther writing. The topics for meditation are quite simple. Seven aspects of evil are matched by seven goods: internal, future, past, infernal, sinister, dexter, supernal. Thus, the writing makes a formal scheme of spiritual exercise designed to re-unite souls, estranged by anxiety, to their gracious God. The evils appear overwhelming in themselves, but flimsy when measured against the goods, and the crowning comfort is found in the suffering, death, and resurrection of Christ, who conquered all evils and distributed all divine mercies. Satan's terrible assaults on the human spirit could not win against the reconciliation of man with a benign God through the mediation of Christ.

Luther believed that the wrath of God was displayed through plague, pestilence, sword, famine, and sickness; but God's wrath was also God's love, as it drove the sinner into the arms of the loving and forgiving Christ. Sickness, therefore, was to be seen by the sufferer in two ways: on the one hand, for what it was, a painful and debilitating event which the believer wished to be ended; but on the other hand, sickness had a meaning for faith, an inside meaning, as it were, for which the believer was to raise his voice in thanksgiving. By sickness he was being driven to participate in the grace of God which in this world was still the *via passionis* of Christ.

As the Christian should understand his own misery as an opportunity to participate in God's grace, so he should take the misery of others as an opportunity to minister to Christ, who became somehow incarnated in the sufferer's need. Luther wrote, "For I cannot pretend to be deaf to the voice of Christ crying to me out of your Lordship's flesh and blood, 'Behold, here I am sick.' For such ills as sickness and the like are endured not by us Christians, but by Christ Himself, our Lord and Saviour, in Whom we live." The latter notion, however curious to moderns, lay at the heart of Luther's pastoral concern for Frederick.

Luther's lengthy book is represented here by the prefaces and by the meditations on the first two evils and the first two goods.

# CONSOLING
# AN ANXIOUS MAN

From: *The Fourteen of Consolation* (1520),
by Martin Luther.

## DEDICATORY EPISTLE

*To the Most Illustrious Prince and Lord, Frederick,*
*Duke of Saxony, Arch-marshal and Elector of the Holy Roman Empire,*
*Landgrave of Thuringia, Margrave of Meissen,*
*his most gracious Lord.*

Our Lord and Saviour Jesus hath left us a commandment, which concerns all Christians alike,—that we should render the duties of humanity, or (as the Scriptures call them) the works of mercy, to such as are afflicted and under calamity; that we should visit the sick, endeavor to set free the prisoners, and perform other like acts of kindness to our neighbor, whereby the evils of this present time may in some measure be lightened. And of this command our Lord Jesus Christ hath Himself given us the brightest example, in that, out of infinite love to the race of men, He descended out of the bosom of the Father into our misery and prison-cell, that is, our flesh and life so full of ills, and took upon Him the penalty of our sins, in order that we might be saved; as He saith in Isaiah xliii, "Thou hast made Me to serve with thy sins, and wearied Me with thine iniquities."

Whoever is not moved by so bright an example, and driven by the authority of the divine command, to show forth such works of mercy, he will deservedly hear, in the last judgment, the voice of the angry Judge saying: "Depart from me, thou cursed, into everlasting fire! For I was sick, and thou didst not visit Me; but, basely ungrateful for the many blessings I bestowed on thee and on all the world, thou wouldest not so much as lift a finger to succor thy brethren, nay Me, Christ, thy God and Saviour, in thy brethren."

Since, then, most noble Prince, I perceive that your Lordship has been smitten with a dangerous malady, and that Christ has thus fallen sick in you, I have counted it my duty to visit your Lordship with a little writing of mine. For I cannot pretend to be deaf to the voice of Christ crying to me out of your Lordship's flesh and blood, "Behold, here am I sick." For such ills as sickness and the like are endured, not by us Christians, but by Christ Himself, our Lord and Saviour, in Whom we live. Even as He plainly testifies in the Gospel, "Whatsoever ye have done unto one of the least of these My brethren, ye have done it unto Me." And while we should visit and console all who are afflicted with sickness, yet we owe this duty specially to those who are of the household of faith. For Paul clearly distinguishes between strangers and those of the household, or those who are bound to us by intimate ties, Galatians vi.

But I have yet other reasons for performing this my duty. For I consider that, as one of your Lordship's subjects, I must needs share in your Lordship's illness, together with the remainder of your many subjects, and suffer with you as a member with the Head, on which all our fortunes, our safety, and our happiness depend. For we recognize in your Lordship another Naaman, by whom God is now giving deliverance to Germany, as in times past He gave deliverance to Syria. Wherefore the whole Roman Empire turns its eyes to your Lordship alone, and venerates and receives you as the Father of the Fatherland, and the bright ornament and protector of the whole Empire, but of the German nation in particular.

Nor are we bound only to console your Lordship as much as in us lies, and to make your present sorrow our own, but much more to pray God for your health and safety; which I trust your Lordship's subjects are doing with all diligence and devotion. But as for me, whom your Lordship's many and signal benefactions have made your debtor above all others, I count it my duty to express my gratitude by rendering you some special service. But now, by reason of my poverty both of mind and fortune, it is not possible for me to offer anything of value; therefore I gladly welcomed the suggestion of Doctor George Spalatin, one of your Lordship's court chaplains, that I should prepare a kind of spiritual consolation and present it to your Lordship, to whom, he said, it would be most acceptable. Being unwilling to reject this friendly counsel, I have put together the following fourteen chapters, after the fashion of an altar tablet, and have called them, "The Fourteen." They are to take the place of the fourteen saints whom our superstition has invented and called, "The Defenders against all evil." But this is a tablet not of silver, but of a spiritual sort; nor is it intended to adorn the walls of a church, but to uplift and strengthen a pious heart. I trust it will stand your Lordship in good stead in your present condition. It consists of two divisions; the former containing the images of seven evils, in the contemplation of which your present troubles will grow light; the latter presenting the images of seven blessings, brought together for the same purpose.

May it please your Lordship graciously to accept this little work of mine, and to make such use of it that the diligent reading and contemplation of these "images" may minister some small comfort. Your Lordship's humble servant, MARTIN LUTHER, DOCTOR.

## PREFACE

The Apostle Paul, treating in Romans xv. of the consolations of Christians, writes, "Whatsoever things were written aforetime were written for our learning, that we through patience and comfort of the scriptures might have hope." In these words he plainly teaches that our consolations are to be drawn from the Holy Scriptures. Now the Holy Scriptures administer comfort after a twofold fashion, by presenting to our view blessings and evils, most wholesomely intermingled; as the wise Preacher saith, "In the day of evil be mindful of the good, and in the day of good be mindful of the evil." For the Holy Spirit knows that a thing has only such meaning and value for a man as he assigns to it in his thoughts; for what he holds common and of no value will move him but little, either to pleasure when he obtains it, or to grief when he loses it. Therefore He endeavors with all His might to draw us away from thinking about things and from being moved by them; and when He has effected this, then all things whatsoever are alike to us. Now this drawing away is best accomplished by means of the Word, whereby our thoughts are turned from the thing that moves us at the present moment to that which either is absent or does not at the moment move us. Therefore it is true that we shall attain to this state of mind only through the comfort of the Scriptures, which call us, in the day of evil, to the contemplation of good things, either present or to come, and, in the day of good, to the contemplation of evil things.

But let us, for our better understanding of these two series of pictures or images, divide each of them into seven parts. The first series will treat of the evils, and we shall consider (1) the evil within us, (2) the evil before us, (3) the evil behind us, (4) the evil on our left hand, (5) the evil on our right hand, (6) the evil beneath us, and (7) the evil above us.

## CHAPTER I
### THE FIRST IMAGE
### THE EVIL WITHIN US

This is most certain and true—we may believe it or not—that no suffering in a man's experience, be it never so severe, can be the greatest of the evils that are within him. So many more and far greater evils are there within him than any that he feels. And if he were to feel those evils, he would feel the pains of hell; for he holds a hell within himself. Do you ask how this can be? The Prophet says, "All men are liars"; and again,

"Every man at his best state is altogether vanity." But to be a liar and
vanity, is to be without truth and reality; and to be without truth and
reality, is to be without God and to be nothing; and this is to be in hell
and damned. Therefore, when God in His mercy chastens us, He reveals
to us and lays upon us only the lighter evils; for if He were to lead us
to the full knowledge of our evil, we should straightway perish. Yet even
this He has given some to taste, and of them it is written, "He bringeth
down to hell, and bringeth up." Therefore they say well who call our
bodily sufferings the monitors of the evil within. And the Apostle, in
Hebrews xii, calls them God's fatherly chastenings, when he says, "He
scourgeth every son whom He receiveth." And He does this, in order
by such scourgings and lesser evils to drive out those great evils, that we
may never need to feel them; as it is written, "Foolishness is bound in
the heart of a child; but the rod of correction shall drive it far from him."
Do not loving parents grieve more for their sons when they turn out
thieves and evil-doers than when they receive a wound? Nay, they themselves beat them until the blood flows, to keep them from becoming
evil-doers.

What is it, then, that prevents us from feeling this our true evil?
It is, as I have said, so ordered by God, that we may not perish on
seeing the evils hidden in the depths of our hearts. For God keeps them
hidden, and would have us discern them only by faith, when He points
them out to us by means of the evil that we feel. Therefore, "In the day
of evil be mindful of the good." Behold, how great a good it is, not to
know the whole of our evil! Be mindful of this good, and the evil that
you feel will press you less cruelly. Again, "In the day of good be mindful
of the evil." That is to say, Whilst you do not feel your true evil, be
grateful for this respite; then will the evil that you feel sit lightly upon
you. It is clear, then, that in this life a man's freedom from pain is
always greater than his pain. Not that his whole evil is not present with
him, but he does not think about it and is not moved by it, through
the goodness of God, Who keeps it hidden.

How furiously do those men rage against themselves, to whom their
true evil has been revealed! How they count as nothing whatever sufferings life may bring, if only they might not feel the hell within! Even
so would every one do, who felt or truly believed in the evil within him.
Gladly would he call down all external evils on his head, and count them
mere child's play; nay, he would never be more sorrowful than when
he had no evils to bear, after the manner of certain of the saints, such
as David in Psalm vi.

Therefore, this is our first image of consolation, that a man should
say to himself: "Not yet, O man, dost thou feel thine evil. Rejoice and
give thanks that thou dost not need to feel it!" And so the lesser evil
grows light by comparison with the greatest evil. That is what others

mean when they say, "I have deserved far worse things, yea, hell itself"
—a thing easy to say, but horrible to contemplate.

And this evil, though never so deeply hidden, yet puts forth fruits
that are plainly enough perceived. These are the dread and uncertainty
of a trembling conscience, when faith is assailed, and a man is not sure,
or doubts, whether he have a gracious God. And this fruit is bitter in
proportion to the weakness of one's faith. Nay, when rightly considered,
this weakness alone, being spiritual, far outweighs every weakness of the
body, and renders it, in comparison, light as a feather.

Moreover, to the evils within us belong all those tragic experiences
described by the Preacher, when he refers again and again to "vanity and
vexation of spirit." How many of our plans come to naught! How oft our
hopes are deceived! How many things that are not to our liking must we
see and hear! And the very things that fall out according to our wish fall
out also against our wish! So that there is nothing perfect and complete.
Finally, all these things are so much greater, the higher one rises in rank
and station; for such a one will of necessity be driven about by far more
and greater billows, floods, and tempests, than others who labor in a like
case. As it is truly said in Psalm ciii, "In the sea of this world there are
things creeping innumerable, both small and great beasts," that is, an
infinite number of trials. And Job, for this reason, calls the life of man a
"trial."

These evils do not, indeed, cease to be evils because they are less
sharply felt by us; but we have grown accustomed to them from having
them constantly with us, and through the goodness of God our thoughts
and feelings concerning them have become blunted. That is why they
move us the more deeply when we do feel them now and then, since we
have not learned through familiarity to despise them. So true is it, therefore, that we feel scarce a thousandth part of our evils, and also that we
estimate them and feel them or do not feel them, not as they are in
themselves, but only as they exist in our thoughts and feelings.

## CHAPTER II
### THE SECOND IMAGE
### THE FUTURE EVIL, OR THE EVIL BEFORE US

It will tend in no small degree to lighten any present evil if a man
turn his mind to the evils to come. These are so many, so diverse, and so
great, that out of them has arisen one of the strongest emotions of the
soul; namely, fear. For fear has been defined by some as the emotion
caused by coming evil. Even as the Apostle says in Romans xi, "Be not
high-minded, but fear." This evil is all the greater because of our uncertainty in what form and with what force it may come; so that there

goes a popular saying, "No age is proof against the itch," although this is but a little children's disease. Even so, no man is safe from the evils that befall any other; for what one has suffered another may suffer also. Here belong all the tragic histories of the ages, and all the lamentations of the world. Here belong the more than three hundred diseases—which some have observed—with which the human body may be vexed. And if there be so many diseases, how great will be the number of other misfortunes that may befall our possessions, our friends, and even our mind itself, that target of all evils, and trysting-place of sorrow and every ill!

And these evils increase in power and intensity as a man rises to higher rank and dignity; in which estate he must needs dread every moment the coming of poverty, disgrace, and every indignity, which may indeed swiftly overtake him, for they all hang by but a slender thread, not unlike the sword which the tyrant Dionysius suspended above the head of the guest at his table.

And if none of these evils befall us, we should count it our gain, and no small comfort in the evil that does befall us; so that we should feel constrained to say with Jeremiah, "It is of the Lord's mercies that we are not consumed." For when none of them befall us, it is because they have been kept from us by the right hand of the Most High that compasses us about with such mighty power (as we see in Job) that Satan and all evils can but gnash their teeth in helpless rage. From this we see how sweetly we ought to love our Lord, whenever any evil comes upon us. For our most loving Father would by that one evil have us see how many evils threaten us and would fall on us, if He did not Himself stand in the way, as though He said, "Satan and the host of evils have desired to have thee, to sift thee as wheat; but I have marked out bounds for the sea, and have said, Hitherto shalt thou come, and here shall thy proud waves be stayed," as He saith in Job xxxviii.

And, granted that perchance, if God please, none of these things will come upon you; nevertheless, that which is known as the greatest of terrors, death, is certain to come, and nothing is less certain than the hour of its coming. Truly, this is so great an evil that there are many who would rather live on amid all the above-named evils than to die once and have them ended. With this one thing the Scriptures, which hold all others in contempt, associate fear, saying, "Remember thy end, and thou shalt never do amiss." Behold, how many meditations, how many books, how many rules and remedies have been brought together, in order, by calling to men's minds this one evil, to keep them from sin, to render the world contemptible, to lighten suffering, to comfort the afflicted,—all by a comparison with this great and terrible, and yet so inevitable, evil of death. This evil even the saints dreaded, and Christ submitted to it with trembling and bloody sweat. So that the divine Mercy hath been nowhere more concerned to comfort our little faith than in the matter of this evil, as we shall see below.

But all these things are common to all men, even as the blessings of salvation under these evils are common to all. For Christians, however, there is another and a particular reason for dreading the evils to come, which easily surpasses all the evils that have been mentioned. It is that which the Apostle portrays in I. Corinthians x, when he says, "He that standeth, let him take heed lest he fall." So unstable is our footing, and so powerful our foe, armed with our own strength (that is, the weapons of our flesh and all our evil lusts), attended by the countless armies of the world, its delights and pleasures on the right hand, its hardships and the plots of wicked men on the left, and, besides all this, master himself of the art of doing us harm, seducing us, and bringing us down to destruction by a thousand different ways. Such is our life that we are not safe for one moment in our good intentions. Cyprian, who in his *De Mortalitate* touches on many of these matters, teaches that death is to be desired as a swift means of escape from these evils. And truly, wherever there have been high-hearted men, who brought their minds steadily to bear on these infinite perils of hell, we find them, with contempt of life and death (that is, all the aforesaid evils), desiring to die, that so they might be delivered at one and the same time from this evil of the sins in which they now are (of which we spoke in the previous chapter), and of the sins into which they might fall (of which we are treating now). And these are, indeed, two most weighty reasons why we should not only desire death, but also despise all evils, to say nothing of lightly bearing a single evil; if the Lord grant us to be moved thereby. For it is God's gift that we are moved thereby. For what true Christian will not even desire to die, and much more to bear sickness, seeing that, so long as he lives and is in health, he is in sin, and is constantly prone to fall, yea, is falling every day, into more sins; and is thus constantly thwarting the most loving will of his most loving Father! To such a heat of indignation was St. Paul moved, in Romans vii, when after complaining that he did not the good that he would, but the evil that he would not, he cried out, "O wretched man that I am! who shall deliver me from the body of this death? The grace of God," he answers, "through Jesus Christ."

That man loves God his Father but little, who does not prefer the evil of dying to this evil of sinning. For God has appointed death, that this evil might come to an end, and that death might be the minister of life and righteousness, of which more below.

\* \* \* \* \*

## PART II

The second part also consists of seven images, answering to the first; the first representing the internal blessing, the second the future blessing, the third the past blessing, the fourth the infernal blessing, the fifth the blessing on the left hand, the sixth the blessing on the right hand, and the seventh the supernal blessing.

## CHAPTER I
### THE FIRST IMAGE
### THE BLESSING WITHIN US

Who can recount only those blessings which every one hath in his own person? How great are, first, the gifts and endowments of the body; such as beauty, strength, health, and the lively play of the senses! To these there comes, in the case of the male, a greater mobility of sex, that fits him for the doing of many things both in public and in private life, and for many splendid achievements, to which woman is a stranger. And if, by the grace of God, you enjoy these excellent gifts for ten, twenty, or thirty years, and in all this time endure suffering for a few days now and then, what great matter is that? There is a proverb among knaves, *Es ist umb ein bose stund zuthun*, and, *Ein gutt stund ist eyner posen werdt*. What shall be said of us, who have seen so many good hours, yet are not willing to endure evil for a single hour! We see, therefore, how many blessings God showers upon us, and how few evils barely touch us. This is true at least of the most of us.

But not content with these blessings, our gracious God adds to them riches and an abundance of all things; if not in the case of all, certainly in the case of many, and of those especially who are too frail to bear the evil. For as I said before, when He grants fewer bodily gifts and possessions, He gives greater mental gifts; so that all things may be equal, and He the just Judge of all. For a cheerful mind is a greater comfort than much riches. Moreover, to some He grants offspring, and, as men say, the highest pleasure, influence, rank, honor, fame, glory, favor, and the like. And if these be enjoyed for a long or even for a short season, they will soon teach men how they ought to conduct themselves under some small evil.

But more excellent than all these are the blessings of the mind; such as reason, knowledge, judgment, eloquence, prudence. And, here again, God tempers the justice of His dealing, so that when He bestows more of these gifts on some men, He does not therefore prefer them to others, since on these again He confers greater peace and cheerfulness of mind. In all these things we should gratefully mark the bountiful hand of God, and take comfort in our infirmity. For we should feel no surprise if among so many and great blessings there be some intermingling of bitterness; since even for epicures no meat is savory without salt, nor scarce any dish palatable that has not a certain bitter savor, either native or produced by seasoning. So intolerable is a continual and unrelieved sweetness, that it has been truly said, "Every pleasure too long continued begets disgust";

and again, "Pleasure itself turns at length to loathing." That is to say, this life is incapable of enjoying only good things without a tempering of evil, because of the too great abundance of good things. Whence has arisen also this proverb, "It needs sturdy bones to bear good days"; which proverb I have often pondered and much admired for its excellent true sense, namely, that the wishes of men are contrary to one another; they seek none but good days, and, when these arrive, are less able to bear them than evil days.

What, then, would God have us here lay to heart but this, that the cross is held in honor even among the enemies of the cross! For all things must needs be tempered and sanctified with the relics of the cross, lest they decay; even as the meat must be seasoned with salt, that it may not breed worms. And why will we not gladly accept this tempering which God sends, and which, if He did not send it, our own life, weakened with pleasures and blessings, would of itself demand? Hence we see with what truth the Book of Wisdom says of God, "He reacheth from end to end mightily, and ordereth all things sweetly." And if we examine these blessings, the truth of Moses' words, in Deuteronomy xxxii, will become plain, "He bore him on His shoulders, He led him about, and kept him as the apple of His eye." With these words we may stop the mouths of those ungrateful praters who hold that there is in this life more of evil than of good. For there is no lack of good things and endless sweet blessings, but they are lacking who are of the same mind with him who said, "The earth is full of the mercy of the Lord"; and again, "The earth is full of His praise"; and in Psalm ciii, "The earth is full of Thy riches"; "Thou, Lord, hast made me glad through Thy work." Hence we sing every day in the Mass: "Heaven and earth are full of Thy glory." Why do we sing this? Because there are many blessings for which God may be praised, but it is done only by those who see the fulness of them. Even as we said concerning the evils of the first image, that a man's evils are only so great as he in his thoughts acknowledges them to be, so it is also with the blessings. Though they crowd upon us from every side, yet they are only so great as we acknowledge them to be. For all things that God made are very good, but they are not acknowledged as very good by all. Such were they of whom it is said in Psalm lxxvii, "They despised the pleasant land."

The most beautiful and instructive example of this image is furnished by Job, who when he had lost all said, "Shall we receive good at the hand of God, and shall we not receive evil?" Truly, that is a golden saying, and a mighty comfort in temptation. For Job not only suffered, but was tempted to impatience by his wife, who said to him, "Dost thou still retain thine integrity? curse God, and die." As who should say, "It is plain that he is not God who is thus forsaking thee. Why, then, dost thou trust in him, and not rather, renouncing him, and thus cursing him, acknowledge thyself a mortal man, for whom naught remains after this life?" These things and the like are suggested to each one of us by his wife (i.e., his carnal mind) in time of temptation; for the carnal mind savoreth not the things that be of God.

But these are all bodily blessings, and common to all men. A Christian has other and far better blessings within, namely, faith in Christ; of which it is said in Psalm xliv, "The king's daughter is all glorious within; her clothing is of wrought gold." For, as we said concerning the evil of the first image, that no evil in a man can be so great as to be the worst of the evils within him; so too the greatest of the blessings which are in the Christian, he himself is unable to see. Could he perceive it, he would forthwith be in heaven; since the kingdom of heaven, as Christ says, is within us. For to have faith is to have the Word and truth of God; and to have the Word of God is to have God Himself, the Maker of all. If these blessings, in all their fulness, were discovered to the soul, straightway it would be released from the body, for the exceeding abundance of sweet pleasure. Wherefore, of a truth, all the other blessings which we have mentioned are but as the monitors of those blessings which we have within, and which God would by them commend unto us. For this life of ours could not endure to have them revealed, but God mercifully keeps them hidden, until they have reached their full measure. Even so loving parents give their children foolish little toys, in order thereby to lead them on to look for better things.

Nevertheless, these blessings show themselves at times, and break out of doors, when the happy conscience rejoices in its trust to Godward, is fain to speak of Him, hears His Word with pleasure, and is quick to serve Him, to do good and suffer evil. All these are the evidence of that infinite and incomparable blessing hidden within, which sends forth such little drops and tiny rills. Still, it is sometimes more fully revealed to contemplative souls, who then are rapt away thereby, and know not where they are; as is confessed by St. Augustine and his mother, and by many others.

## CHAPTER II
## THE SECOND IMAGE
## THE FUTURE BLESSING, OR THE BLESSING BEFORE US

Those who are not Christians will find small comfort, amid their evils, in the contemplation of future blessings; since for them all these things are uncertain. Although much ado is made here by that famous emotion called hope, by which we call on each other, in words of human comfort, to look for better times, and continually plan greater things for the uncertain future, yet are always deceived. Even as Christ teaches concerning the man in the Gospel, Luke xii, who said to his soul, "I will pull down my barns, and build greater; and will say to my soul, Soul, thou hast much goods laid up for many years; take thine ease, eat, drink, and be merry. But God said unto him, Thou fool, this night thy soul shall be required of thee; and then whose shall those things be which thou hast provided? So is he that layeth up treasure for himself, and is not rich toward God."

Nevertheless, God has not so utterly forsaken the sons of men that He will not grant them some measure of comfort in this hope of the passing of evil and the coming of good things. Though they are uncertain of the future, yet they hope with certain hope, and hereby they are meanwhile buoyed up, lest falling into the further evil of despair, they should break down under their present evil, and do some worse thing. Hence, even this sort of hope is the gift of God; not that He would have them lean on it, but that He would turn their attention to that firm hope, which is in Him alone. For He is so long-suffering that He leadeth them to repentance, as it is said in Romans ii, and suffers none to be straightway deceived by this deceitful hope, if haply they may "return to the heart," and come to the true hope.

But Christians have, beside this twofold blessing, the very greatest future blessings certainly awaiting them; yet only through death and suffering. Although they, too, rejoice in that common and uncertain hope that the evil of the present will come to an end, and that its opposite, the blessing, will increase; still, that is not their chief concern, but rather this, that their own particular blessing should increase, which is the truth as it is in Christ, in which they grow from day to day, and for which they both live and hope. But beside this they have, as I have said, the two greatest future blessings in their death. The first, in that through death the whole tragedy of this world's ills is brought to a close; as it is written, "Precious in the sight of the Lord is the death of His saints"; and again, "I will lay me down in peace and sleep"; and, "Though the righteous be prevented with death, yet shall he be at rest." But to the ungodly death is the beginning of evils; as it is said, "The death of the wicked is very evil," and, "Evil shall catch the unjust man unto destruction." Even so Lazarus, who received his evil things in his lifetime, is comforted, while the rich glutton is tormented, because he received his good things here. So that it is always well with the Christian, whether he die or live; so blessed a thing is it to be a Christian and to believe in Christ. Wherefore Paul says, "To me to live is Christ, and to die is gain," and, in Romans xiv, "Whether we live, we live unto the Lord; and whether we die, we die unto the Lord; whether we live therefore, or die, we are the Lord's." This security Christ hath won for us by His death and rising again, that He might be Lord of both the living and dead, able to keep us safe in life and in death; as Psalm xxii. saith, "Though I walk through the valley of the shadow of death, I will fear no evil, for Thou art with me." If this gain of death move us but little, it is proof that our faith in Christ is feeble, and does not prize highly enough the reward

and gain of a blessed death, or does not yet believe that death is a blessing; because the old man is still too much alive in us, and the wisdom of
the flesh too strong. We should, therefore, endeavor to attain to the
knowledge and the love of this blessing of death. It is a great thing that
death, which is to others the greatest of evils, is made to us the greatest
gain. And unless Christ had obtained this for us, what had He done that
was worthy of the great price He paid, namely, His own self? It is indeed
a divine work that He wrought, and none need wonder, therefore, that
He made the evil of death to be something that is very good.

Death, then, to believers is already dead, and hath nothing terrible
behind its grinning mask. Like unto a slain serpent, it hath indeed its
former terrifying appearance, but it is only the appearance; in truth it is
a dead evil, and harmless enough. Nay, as God commanded Moses to
lift up a serpent of brass, at sight of which the living serpents perished,
even so our death dies in the believing contemplation of the death of
Christ, and now hath but the outward appearance of death. With such
fine similitudes the mercy of God prefigures to us, in our infirmity, this
truth, that though death should not be taken away, He yet has reduced
its power to a mere shadow. For this reason it is called in the Scriptures
a "sleep" rather than death.

The other blessing of death is this, that it not only concludes the
pains and evils of this life, but (which is more excellent) makes an end
of sins and vices. And this renders death far more desirable to believing
souls, as I have said above, than the former blessing; since the evils of
the soul, which are its sins, are beyond comparison worse evils than those
of the body. This alone, did we but know it, should make death most
desirable. But if it does not, it is a sign that we neither feel nor hate our
sin as we should. For this our life is so full of perils—sin, like a serpent,
besetting us on every side—and it is impossible for us to live without
sinning; but fairest death delivers us from these perils, and cuts our sin
clean away from us. Therefore, the praise of the just man, in Wisdom iv,
concludes on this wise: "He pleased God, and was taken away, and was
beloved of Him: so that living among sinners he was translated. Yea,
speedily was he taken away, lest that wickedness should alter his understanding, or deceit beguile his soul. For the bewitching of naughtiness
doth obscure things that are honest; and the wandering of concupiscence
doth undermine the simple mind (O how constantly true is this!). He,
being made perfect in a short time, fulfilled a long time; for his soul
pleased the Lord: therefore hasted He to take him away from the
wicked."

Thus, by the mercy of God, death, which was to man the punishment for his sin, is made unto the Christian the end of sin, and the
beginning of life and righteousness. Wherefore, he that loves life and
righteousness must not hate, but love sin, their minister and workshop;
else he will never attain to either life or righteousness. But he that is not

able to do this, let him pray God to enable him. For to this end are we taught to pray, "Thy will be done," because we cannot do it of ourselves, since through fear of death we love death and sin rather than life and righteousness. And that God appointed death for the putting to death of sin, may be gathered also from the fact that He imposed death upon Adam immediately after his sin; and that before He drove him out of paradise; in order to show us that death should bring us no evil, but every blessing, since it was imposed in paradise, as a penance and satisfaction. For it is true that, through the envy of the devil, death entered into the world; but it is of the Lord's surpassing goodness that, after having thus entered in, it is not permitted to harm us very much, but is taken captive from the very beginning, and set to be the punishment and death of sin.

This He signified when, after having in His commandment foretold the death of Adam, He did not afterward hold His peace, but imposed death anew, and tempered the severity of His commandment, nay, He did not so much as mention death with a single syllable, but said only, "Dust thou art, and unto dust shalt thou return"; and, "Until thou return unto the ground, from whence thou wast taken"—as if He then so bitterly hated death that He would not deign to call it by its name, according to the word, "Wrath is in His indignation; and life in His good will." Thus He seemed to say that, unless death had been necessary to the abolishing of sin, He would not have been willing to know it nor to name it, much less to impose it. And so, against sin, which wrought death, the zeal of God arms none other than this very death again; so that you may here see exemplified the poet's line.

By his own art the artist perisheth.

Even so sin is destroyed by its own fruit, and is slain by the death which it brought forth; as a viper is slain by its own offspring. This is a brave spectacle, to see how death is destroyed, not by another's work, but by its own; is stabbed with its own weapon, and, like Goliath, is beheaded with its own sword. For Goliath also was a type of sin, a giant terrible to all save the young lad David,—that is Christ,—who single-handed laid him low, and having cut off his head with his own sword, said afterward that there was no better sword than the sword of Goliath (I. Samuel xxi.).

Therefore, if we meditate on these joys of the power of Christ, and these gifts of His grace, how can any small evil distress us, the while we see such blessings in this great evil that is to come!

---

"The Fourteen of Consolation (1520)," tr. A. T. W. Steinhaeuser, *Works of Martin Luther With Introductions and Notes* (The Philadelphia Edition; 6 vols., Philadelphia: Muhlenberg Press, 1943), vol. I, pp. 110–122, 141–151. By permission.

# Exhibit Thirteen

## DEATH:
## MOMENT OF TRUTH
*JOHN CALVIN*

### Introduction

John Calvin (1509–1564) is justly famous for devising and establishing in Reformation Geneva a system of pastoral supervision of daily life that aimed to reconcile every aspect of human affairs with the sovereign God's revealed law. By borrowing certain ecclesiological notions from Martin Bucer of Strassburg during his brief career in that city (1538–1541), Calvin, when he became chief leader of the Genevan Reformation, brought private and public morality alike under the surveillance of the ministers of Geneva, meeting in a "consistory" with certain designated lay leaders. This rigorous system of ecclesiastical supervision of the common life spread during the sixteenth century through Switzerland, much of Germany, the Low Countries, and Scotland and into England.

In his own voluminous correspondence, however, a more tender side of Calvin as pastor comes to the fore. Here he appears, not as a rigoristic regulator of morality, but as a wise, gentle, masterful, and persuasive pastor, anxious to help his correspondents live out their personal affairs in that reconciliation with God and neighbor which he was so confident had been achieved for mankind by Jesus Christ.

These letters deal kindly with persons troubled by illness, religious oppression, derelict servants, family disagreements, poverty, wealth, and every imaginable difficulty.

Three of Calvin's letters have been selected for their occupation with a common predicament—death. Like all medieval Christian writers, Calvin saw death as ordained for men in order that they might feel God's curse on their alienation from His kingdom. At the same time he saw death as agony for the believer who died "in Christ," and for whom destruction became not only pain but the deepest blessing; faith also found in death at once a sign of God's wrath and a gift of communion with Christ. These three letters show Calvin's attachment to ancient traditions of soul care and also his own unique insights and contributions.

These letters recount in detail Calvin's own pastoral actions on behalf of dying persons: a dear friend, a civic leader of Geneva, and his own wife. The last-mentioned illustrates the difficulties of exercising pastoral care for a member of the pastor's own family. While Stoic and traditional Christian themes and expressions show themselves in these letters as well, so also does a quality of soul care that is distinctive and creative. The Christian believer's encounter with death, grim as it might be from one perspective, becomes an eloquent sermon. Not only do the dying person's friends sustain and nourish him with exhortation and prayer, but the dying believer in approaching his end makes a moving witness to the grace that reconciles man to God. Calvin saw not only his moribund friends but his own wife as increasing in spiritual strength as the end drew nearer: Amy Porral's spirit became "animated and vivid" and his words "luminous"; Calvin's wife exhibited an increased "magnanimity"; the profound obedience to God's word that Mme. de Normandie displayed in dying was deeply touching. So Calvin saw in the act of dying a crisis in the Christian's career—a moment in which he might become most fully what he was called to be: an obedient servant to the God whom he glorified and enjoyed. And at this "moment of truth" the believer made his truest witness to his fellows. Death became not so much an occasion demanding sustenance or guidance as an opportunity for a double reconciliation: the faithful man's reconciliation with God, attested and exhorted by his friends in faith; and, even more than that, mankind's reconciliation under God, attested and exhorted by the dying Christian himself as his last bequest.

# DEATH:
# MOMENT OF TRUTH

From: *Letters* (1541–1549), by John Calvin.

## TO WILLIAM FAREL[81]

Geneva, *16th June* 1542.

Would that I might attain to that discipline in contempt of this present life, and in the meditation of a holy death, as the experience of the past year, in the deaths of many pious persons, may well have brought me. Porral, the chief magistrate of the city, has departed to the Lord; his death, which could not be other than occasion of sadness to us, has been bitterly lamented. The manner of his decease, as it was in some respects consolatory to me, so, on the other hand, it increased my sorrow when I considered how great has been our loss in the bereavement of that one man. The day after he became unwell, when we were calling upon him, that is, Viret and myself, he told us that he considered himself in danger, for that the disease with which he was afflicted had been fatal in his family. Thereupon we had a long conversation on a variety of matters: he talked about them just as though he had been in sound and perfect health. During the two following days his sufferings were more acute, but, notwithstanding, his intellect was stronger, and he exhibited more fluency of speech than he had ever manifested in his life hitherto. Whoever called to see him, heard some suitable exhortation; and that you may not suppose it to have been mere talkative vanity, as far as was possible he applied to each individual what was best adapted to his circumstances, and most likely to be of use to him. Afterward he began to feel somewhat better, so that very much hope was entertained that he would be forthwith restored to health. In this state he continued for three days; at length, however, the disease began to grow more severe, so that it was evident that he was in the greatest danger. The more he was afflicted in body, the more animated and vivid was the spirit. I say nought about the intermediate period; but upon the day of his death, about nine in the morning, we went thither, I and Viret. When I had spoken a few words, to set before him the cross, the grace of

---

[81] Amy Porral, whose death Calvin recounted to his friend and former fellow-worker at Geneva, Farel, was first Syndic of the Republic of Geneva at the time of his death in 1542. Porral had supported Calvin's Ecclesiastical Ordinances, adopted by the Republic in 1541; but in 1540 he had sharply disagreed with two Genevan ministers to whom Calvin refers in this letter as "our two colleagues."

Christ, and the hope of eternal life,—for we were unwilling to weary him with tedious addresses,—he replied, that he received God's message as became him; that he knew the efficacy of the power of Christ for confirming the consciences of true believers. Thereupon he spoke in such a luminous manner on the work of the ministry, and all the benefits which accompany or flow from it as the means of grace, that we were both of us in a sort of stupor of astonishment; and whenever it recurs to my memory, even yet I grow bewildered. For he spoke in such a way, that it seemed to reflect some discourse by one of ourselves after long and careful meditation. He concluded this part of his address by declaring, that the remission of sins which we promised on the authority of Christ, he received just the same as if an angel had appeared to him from heaven. After that he spoke of the unity of the Church, which he commended with marvellous praise; he bore testimony that, in his own experience, he had found no better or more certain source of consolation, in the struggle of death, than from having already been confirmed in the assurance of this unity. He had summoned, a little before, our two colleagues, and had been reconciled with them, lest, having persisted in that dispute, others might make a bad use of it in following his example. And he had, moreover, said to ourselves, Since the public edification of the Church compels you to bear with them as brethren, why might not I acknowledge them as pastors? He had previously, however, seriously admonished them, and reminded them of their sins. But I return to that last address. Turning himself to those who stood around, he exhorted every one to prize very highly the communion of the Church; such of them as are superstitious in the observance of days and ceremonies, he advised to lay aside their perverse opposition, and to agree with us, for that we better understood, and saw more clearly what was the prudent course than they did; that he had himself, also, been rather obstinate in these things, but that his eyes were at length opened to perceive how injurious contention might become. After that he made a short, serious, as well as sincere and luculent confession. Thence he proceeded to exhort us both, as well regarding the other departments of our charge as ministers, as also to constancy and firmness; and when he discoursed at some length on the future difficulties of the ministers of the Gospel, he seemed inspired with the foresight of a prophet. It was wonderful how wisely he spoke to purpose on what concerned the public weal. He recommended, as a most important step, that we ought to lose no time in devoting our utmost attention to bring about a reconciliation among the cities in alliance with us. "However some noisy people may clamour loudly," he said, "don't trouble yourselves about it, and do not be discouraged." My time will not admit of my relating everything. After we had submitted a few observations we engaged in prayer, and then took our leave and departed.

On the second afternoon, when my wife arrived, he told her to be of good courage whatever might happen, that she ought to consider that she had not been rashly led hither, but brought by the wonderful counsel of God, that she also might serve in the Gospel. A little while after he signified that his voice was gone; but even when his speech entirely failed he intimated that he retained a perfect consciousness of the confession which he had previously made, and in that same he would die. At the same time, having repeated the song of Simeon, with application of it to himself, "I have seen," he said, "and have touched with my hand, that saving merciful Redeemer." He then composed himself to rest. From that time he was speechless, but indicated at times, by a nod, that he had lost nothing of his strength of mind. About four o'clock I went thither with the Syndics; when, as often as he attempted to speak, and was hindered by obstruction in the throat, I requested that he would not further disturb himself, for that his confession was abundantly satisfactory. At length I began to speak as well as I could: he hearkened with a very composed and tranquil countenance. Scarcely had we left when he gave up his pious soul to Christ. This narrative, when you weigh the character of the man, will hardly appear credible to you; but I would have you understand that he had been thoroughly renewed in the spirit of his mind.

We are at present very much occupied in the choice of new colleagues, and the more so because, when we thought that we had fallen upon a very suitable one, we afterwards discovered that he did not answer our expectation. When we fix anything definitely you shall receive information. There is no reason, although you may be absent, why you may not aid us with your counsel.—Adieu.

## TO FAREL[82]

Geneva, *11th April* 1549.

Intelligence of my wife's death has perhaps reached you before now. I do what I can to keep myself from being overwhelmed with grief. My friends also leave nothing undone that may administer relief to my mental suffering. When your brother left, her life was all but despaired of. When the brethren were assembled on Tuesday, they thought it best that we should join together in prayer. This was done. When Abel, in the name of the rest, exhorted her to faith and patience, she briefly (for she was now greatly worn) stated her frame of mind. I afterwards added an exhortation, which seemed to me appropriate to the occasion. And then, as she had made no allusion to her children, I, fearing that, restrained by modesty, she might be feeling an anxiety concerning them, which would cause her greater suffering than the disease itself, de-

---

[82] Shortly after the death of Calvin's wife, Idelette de Bure, in 1549, he described her last hours in a letter to Farel.

clared in the presence of the brethren, that I should henceforth care for them as if they were my own. She replied, "I have already committed them to the Lord." When I replied, that that was not to hinder me from doing my duty, she immediately answered, "If the Lord shall care for them, I know they will be commended to you." Her magnanimity was so great, that she seemed to have already left the world. About the sixth hour of the day, on which she yielded up her soul to the Lord, our brother Bourgouin addressed some pious words to her, and while he was doing so, she spoke aloud, so that all saw that her heart was raised far above the world. For these were her words: "O glorious resurrection! O God of Abraham, and of all our fathers, in thee have the faithful trusted during so many past ages, and none of them have trusted in vain. I also will hope." These short sentences were rather ejaculated than distinctly spoken. This did not come from the suggestion of others, but from our own reflections, so that she made it obvious in few words what were her own meditations. I had to go out at six o'clock. Having been removed to another apartment after seven, she immediately began to decline. When she felt her voice suddenly failing her, she said: "Let us pray: let us pray. All pray for me." I had now returned. She was unable to speak, and her mind seemed to be troubled. I, having spoken a few words about the love of Christ, the hope of eternal life, concerning our married life, and her departure, engaged in prayer. In full possession of her mind, she both heard the prayer, and attended to it. Before eight she expired, so calmly, that those present could scarcely distinguish between her life and her death. I at present control my sorrow so that my duties may not be interfered with. But in the mean while the Lord has sent other trials upon me. Adieu, brother, and very excellent friend. May the Lord Jesus strengthen you by his Spirit; and may he support me also under this heavy affliction, which would certainly have overcome me, had not he, who raises up the prostrate, strengthens the weak, and refreshes the weary, stretched forth his hand from heaven to me. Salute all the brethren and your whole family.—Yours,

JOHN CALVIN

## TO MADAME DE CANY[83]

*This 29th of April* 1549.

MADAME,—Although the news which I communicate is sad, and must also sadden the person to whom I beg you to impart it, nevertheless I hope that my letter will not be unwelcome to you. It has pleased

[83] Peronne de Pisseleu was wife of Michel de Barbançon, Seigneur de Cany, an important personage in Picardy. She had been instructed in Reformed religion by Laurent de Normandie, whose wife died two years after their removal from Picardy to Geneva. Calvin's letter recounting Mme. de Normandie's death bore a favorite pseudonym, "Charles d'Espeville."

my God to withdraw from this world the wife of my kind brother, M. de Normandie. Our consolation is, that he has gathered her unto himself; for he has guided her even to the last sigh, as if visibly he had held out the hand to her. Now, forasmuch as her father must needs be informed, we have thought there was no way more suitable than to request that you would please take the trouble to request him to call on you, that the painful intelligence may be broken to him by your communication of it. What the gentleman has written to us who lately presented our letter to you, has emboldened us to take this step, viz., that you had introduced the good man in question to the right way of salvation, and that you had given him understanding of the pure and sound doctrine which we must maintain. We do not doubt, therefore, that you are willing to continue your good offices, and that even in this present need. For we cannot employ ourselves better, than in carrying this message in the name of God, to comfort him to whom you have already done so much good, that he may not be beyond measure disconsolate. Therefore, Madame, I leave you to set before him the arguments and reasons which you know to be suitable for exhorting to submission. Only I shall shortly relate to you the history, which will furnish you with ample matter for showing him that he has reason to be thankful. And, according to the grace and wisdom that God has given you, you will draw thence for his comfort as opportunity shall require.

Having heard of the illness of the good woman, we were amazed how she could have been able to bear so well the fatigue of the journey, for she arrived quite fresh, and without showing any sign of weariness. Indeed she acknowledged that God had singularly supported her during that time. Weak as she was, she kept well enough until a little before Christmas. The eager desire which she had to hear the word of God, upheld her until the month of January. She then began to take to bed, not because the complaint was as yet thought to be mortal, but to prevent the danger which might arise. Although expecting a favourable termination, and hoping to recover her health, she nevertheless prepared for death, saying often, that if this was not the finishing blow, it could not be long delayed. As for remedies, all was done that could be. And if her bodily comfort was provided for, that which she prized most highly was nowise wanting, to wit, pious admonitions to confirm her in the fear of God, in the faith of Jesus Christ, in patience, in the hope of salvation. On her part she always gave clear evidence that the labour was not in vain, for in her discourse you could see that she had the whole deeply imprinted upon her heart. In short, throughout the course of her sickness, she proved herself to be a true sheep of our Lord Jesus, letting herself be quietly led by the Great Shepherd. Two or three days before death, as her heart was more raised to God, she also spoke with more earnest affection than ever. Even the day before, while she was exhorting her people, she said to her attendant, that he must take good heed never to return thither where he had polluted himself with idolatry; and that since God had led him to a Christian Church, he should be careful to live therein a holy life. The night following, she was oppressed with great and continued pain. Yet never did one hear any other cry from her, than the prayer to God that he would have pity upon her, and that he would deliver her out of the world, vouchsafing grace to persevere always in the faith which he had bestowed. Toward five o'clock in the morning I went to her. After she had listened very patiently to the doctrine which I set before her, such as the occasion called for, she said: "The hour draws near, I must needs depart from the world; this flesh asks only to go away into corruption; but I feel certain that my God is withdrawing my soul into his kingdom. I know what a poor sinful woman I am, but my confidence is in his goodness, and in the death and passion of his Son. Therefore, I do not doubt of my salvation, since he has assured me of it. I go to him as to a Father." While she was thus discoursing, a considerable number of persons came in. I threw in from time to time some words, such as seemed suitable; and we also made supplication to God as the exigency of her need required. After once more declaring the sense she had of her sins, to ask the pardon of them from God, and the certainty which she entertained of her salvation, putting her sole confidence in Jesus, and having her whole trust in him,—without being invited by any one to do so, she began to pronounce the *Miserere* as we sing it in church, and continued with a loud and strong voice, not without great difficulty, but she entreated that we would allow her to continue. Whereupon, I made her a short recapitulation of the whole argument of the psalm, seeing the pleasure she took in it. Afterwards, taking me by the hand, she said to me, "How happy I am, and how am I beholden to God, for having brought me here to die! Had I been in that wretched prison, I could not have ventured to open my mouth to make confession of my Christianity. Here I have not only liberty to glorify God, but I have so many sound arguments to confirm me in my salvation." Sometimes, indeed, she said, "I am not able for more." When I answered her, "God is able to help you; he has, indeed, shown you how he is a present aid to his own;" she said immediately, "I do believe so, and he makes me feel his help." Her husband was there, striving to keep up in such sort that we were all sorry for him, while he made us wonder in amazement at his fortitude. For while possessed with such grief as I know it to have been, and weighed down by extremity of sorrow, he had so far gained the mastery over self, as to exhort his better part as freely as if they were going to make a most joyful journey together. The conversation I have related took place in the midst of the great torment she endured from pains in her stomach. Towards nine or ten o'clock they abated. Availing herself of this relaxation, she never ceased to glorify God, humbly seeking her salvation and all her wellbeing in Jesus Christ. When speech failed her, her countenance told how intently she was interested, as well in the prayers as in the exhortations which were made. Otherwise she was so motionless, that sight alone gave indication of life. Towards the end, considering that she was gone, I said, "Now let us pray God that he would give us grace to follow her." As I rose, she turned her eyes upon us, as if charging us to persevere in prayer and consolation; after that, we perceived no motion, and she passed away so gracefully, that it was as if she had fallen asleep.

I pray you, Madame, to excuse me if I have been too tedious. But I thought that the father would be well pleased to be fully informed of the whole, as if he himself had been upon the spot. And I hope that in so good a work you will find nothing troublesome. St. Paul, in treating of charity, does not forget that we ought to weep with those who weep; that is to say, that if we are Christians, we ought to have such compassion and sorrow for our neighbours, that we should willingly take part in their tears, and thus comfort them. It cannot otherwise be but the good man must, at the first, be wrung with grief. Howbeit he must already have been long prepared to receive the news, considering that his daughter's sickness had increased so much, that her recovery was despaired of. But the great consolation is, the example which she had afforded to him and to all of us, of bowing to the will of God. And thus, seeing that she has presented herself so peaceably to death, let us herein follow her, willingly complying with the disposal of God; and if her father loved her, let him show his love in conforming himself to the desire which she exhibited of submitting herself to God. And seeing that her dismissal has been so happy, let him rejoice in the grace of God vouchsafed to her, which far surpasses all the comforts we can possess in this world.

In conclusion, Madame, having humbly commended me to your kind favour, I beseech our good Lord to be always your protector, to increase you with all spiritual blessing, and to cause you to glorify his name even to the end.

Your humble servitor and brother,

CHARLES D'ESPEVILLE.

John Calvin, *Letters of John Calvin Compiled from the Original Manuscripts and Edited with Historical Notes by Jules Bonnet*, tr. David Constable *et al.* (3 vols., Philadelphia: Presbyterian Board of Publication, 1858); letters numbered LXXXVI, CCXXXIX, CCXL; I, 331–335; II, 217–223.

# Exhibit Fourteen

## CALISTHENICS OF THE SPIRIT

*IGNATIUS LOYOLA*

### Introduction

Psychologically the most penetrating, and pastorally the most effective, scheme of spiritual transformation ever devised in the Christian tradition is a brief, straightforward book by Ignatius Loyola entitled *The Spiritual Exercises*. Devised to occupy four weeks of strenuous effort under the direction of a spiritual master, the Exercises can be accomplished by a virtuoso in a ten-day span of time. Four movements carry the subject, or "retreatant," from a condition of severe alienation from God to a condition of complete—but, of course, by no means permanent—reconciliation. First, the soul that has been deformed by sin is *reformed* by meditating upon the awful consequences of sin. Next, the reformed soul is *conformed* in all its yearnings to the Kingdom of Christ. Third, by reflecting upon Christ's passion, the retreatant is *confirmed* or established in his conformity to the spiritual kingdom. Finally, the soul thus confirmed, by means of meditation upon the glory of the risen and exalted Christ, is *transformed* by union with God.

At each step in this graduated process, the retreatant under Ignatius' rule is examined by his director; the entire being of the retreatant—his bodily

233

senses, his mind, and his will—must be simultaneously transfixed by each object of meditation before he progresses to another.

The following selection from the Exercises gives the prescriptions for spiritual transformation only for the first week, but from the "Rules for Thinking With the Church" that stand at the end of Ignatius' book, one perceives the completeness of the entire scheme.

Ignatius Loyola, born Ignacio de Recalde of Loyola in Spain in the year 1491 or 1495, lived through the turmoil between papal catholicism and the Protestant Reformation, and died in 1556; he was canonized in 1622. His early military career was cut short in 1521 by a nasty wound in his right leg. Ignatius turned a lengthy convalescence into a time of spiritual preparation for his career as a soldier of the church. In the midst of this preparation, he first drafted the Exercises in 1523, but refined and revised the book through the rest of his life as he directed the preparation of others for membership in the Society of Jesus, of which he was founder and first general. This remarkable group he organized in 1534 as a small band of men utterly dedicated both to protecting the papal church against further incursions by the Protestant Reformation, and to a counteroffensive against that movement. The Society was chartered as such by Pope Paul III in 1540 in a bull entitled *Regimini militantis Ecclesiae*. The order expanded rapidly and by Ignatius' death was the most powerful entity within the Roman Catholic Church. One symbol of Ignatius' inestimable influence upon modern Roman catholicism is the fact that his Exercises are prescribed for all candidates for ordination in that church.

Many schemes for spiritual transformation and reconciliation had been developed in the medieval and Renaissance periods. Broadly speaking, those that built upon the work of Bernard of Clairvaux emphasized visual or sensory perceptions of mystical phenomena, and those that built upon the mysticism of Hugo of St. Victor (c. 1096–1141) emphasized intellectual perceptions. The genius of Ignatius' Exercises lies in the fact that they focus upon the totality of human experience, sensory, mental, and voluntary. Body, mind, and will must focus at once upon objects of meditation. Ignatius felt keenly the need of his times for persons of absolute and unhesitating obedience, lest the Reformation should increase its depredations of the church ruled by Christ's vicar on earth. Ignatius interpreted Christian duty as the kind of obedience commanded of soldiers, one that brooked no personal scruples or dubieties. Through the sudden and immense growth in influence of the Jesuits, the whole

Roman Catholic Church was transformed into a spiritual militia that demanded, and in the name of God received, such obedience.

Ignatius' Exercises, primarily devised for applicants for membership in the Society of Jesus, have proved their applicability not only to monks and clergy but to lay people as well. Superb in their thoroughness, the Exercises deserve the superiority over all other schemes of spiritual development which they enjoy in Roman Catholic piety.

# CALISTHENICS
# OF THE SPIRIT

From: *Spiritual Exercises* (1523–1556),
by Ignatius Loyola.

## I H S
## ANNOTATIONS
TO GIVE SOME UNDERSTANDING OF THE SPIRITUAL
EXERCISES WHICH FOLLOW, AND TO ENABLE HIM
WHO IS TO GIVE AND HIM WHO IS TO RECEIVE
THEM TO HELP THEMSELVES

*First Annotation.* The first Annotation is that by this name of Spiritual Exercises is meant every way of examining one's conscience, of meditating, of contemplating, of praying vocally and mentally, and of performing other spiritual actions, as will be said later. For as strolling, walking and running are bodily exercises, so every way of preparing and disposing the soul to rid itself of all the disordered tendencies, and, after it is rid, to seek and find the Divine Will as to the management of one's life for the salvation of the soul, is called a Spiritual Exercise.

*Second Annotation.* The second is that the person who gives to another the way and order in which to meditate or contemplate, ought to relate faithfully the events of such Contemplation or Meditation, going over the Points with only a short or summary development. For, if the person who is making the Contemplation, takes the true groundwork of the narrative, and, discussing and considering for himself, finds something which makes the events a little clearer or brings them a little more home to him—whether this comes through his own reasoning, or because his intellect is enlightened by the Divine power—he will get more spiritual relish and fruit, than if he who is giving the Exercises had much explained and amplified the meaning of the events. For it is not knowing much, but realising and relishing things interiorly, that contents and satisfies the soul.

*Third Annotation.* The third: As in all the following Spiritual Exercises, we use acts of the intellect in reasoning, and acts of the will in movements of the feelings: let us remark that, in the acts of the will, when we are speaking vocally or mentally with God our Lord, or with His Saints, greater reverence is required on our part than when we are using the intellect in understanding.

*Fourth Annotation.* The fourth: The following Exercises are divided into four parts:

First, the consideration and contemplation on the sins;

Second, the life of Christ our Lord up to Palm Sunday inclusively;

Third, the Passion of Christ our Lord;

Fourth, the Resurrection and Ascension, with the three Methods of Prayer.

Though four weeks, to correspond to this division, are spent in the Exercises, it is not to be understood that each Week has, of necessity, seven or eight days. For, as it happens that in the First Week some are slower to find what they seek—namely, contrition, sorrow and tears for their sins—and in the same way some are more diligent than others, and more acted on or tried by different spirits; it is necessary sometimes to shorten the Week, and at other times to lengthen it. The same is true of all the other subsequent Weeks, seeking out the things according to the subject matter. However, the Exercises will be finished in thirty days, a little more or less.

*Fifth Annotation.* The fifth: It is very helpful to him who is receiving the Exercises to enter into them with great courage and generosity towards his Creator and Lord, offering Him all his will and liberty, that His Divine Majesty may make use of his person and of all he has according to His most Holy Will.

*Sixth Annotation.* The sixth: When he who is giving the Exercises sees that no spiritual movements, such as consolations or desolations, come to the soul of him who is exercising himself, and that he is not moved by different spirits, he ought to inquire carefully of him about the Exercises, whether he does them at their appointed times, and how. So too of the Additions, whether he observes them with diligence. Let him ask in detail about each of these things. . . .

*Seventh Annotation.* The seventh: If he who is giving the Exercises sees that he who is receiving them is in desolation and tempted, let him not be hard or dissatisfied with him, but gentle and indulgent, giving him courage and strength for the future, and laying bare to him the wiles of the enemy of human nature, and getting him to prepare and dispose himself for the consolation coming.

*Eighth Annotation.* The eighth: If he who is giving the Exercises sees that he who is receiving them is in need of instruction about the

desolations and wiles of the enemy—and the same of consolations—
he may explain to him, as far as he needs them, the Rules of the First
and Second Weeks for recognising different spirits.

* * * * *

*Eleventh Annotation.* The eleventh: It is helpful to him who is
receiving the Exercises in the First Week, not to know anything of
what he is to do in the Second, but so to labor in the First to attain
the object he is seeking as if he did not hope to find in the Second any
good.

*Twelfth Annotation.* The twelfth: As he who is receiving the Exercises is to give an hour to each of the five Exercises or Contemplations
which will be made every day, he who is giving the Exercises has to
warn him carefully to always see that his soul remains content in the
consciousness of having been a full hour in the Exercise, and rather
more than less. For the enemy is not a little used to try and make one
cut short the hour of such contemplation, meditation or prayer.

* * * * *

*Fourteenth Annotation.* The fourteenth: If he who is giving the
Exercises sees that he who is receiving them is going on in consolation
and with much fervor, he ought to warn him not to make any incon-
siderate and hasty promise or vow: and the more light of character he
knows him to be, the more he ought to warn and admonish him. For,
though one may justly influence another to embrace the religious life,
in which he is understood to make vows of obedience, poverty and
chastity, and, although a good work done under vow is more meritorious
than one done without it, one should carefully consider the circumstances and personal qualities of the individual and how much help or
hindrance he is likely to find in fulfilling the thing he would want to
promise.

*Fifteenth Annotation.* The fifteenth: He who is giving the Exercises ought not to influence him who is receiving them more to poverty
or to a promise, than to their opposites, nor more to one state or way of
life than to another. For though, outside the Exercises, we can lawfully
and with merit influence every one who is probably fit to choose continence, virginity, the religious life and all manner of evangelical perfection, still in the Spiritual Exercises, when seeking the Divine Will, it
is more fitting and much better, that the Creator and Lord Himself
should communicate Himself to His devout soul, inflaming it with His
love and praise, and disposing it for the way in which it will be better
able to serve Him in future. So, he who is giving the Exercises should not
turn or incline to one side or the other, but standing in the centre like
a balance, leave the Creator to act immediately with the creature, and
the creature with its Creator and Lord.

* * * * *

*Eighteenth Annotation.* The eighteenth: The Spiritual Exercises have to be adapted to the dispositions of the persons who wish to receive them, that is, to their age, education or ability, in order not to give to one who is uneducated or of little intelligence things he cannot easily bear and profit by.

Again, that should be given to each one by which, according to his wish to dispose himself, he may be better able to help himself and to profit.

\*    \*    \*    \*    \*

*Nineteenth Annotation.* The nineteenth: A person of education or ability who is taken up with public affairs or suitable business, may take an hour and a half daily to exercise himself.

\*    \*    \*    \*    \*

*Twentieth Annotation.* The twentieth: To him who is more disengaged, and who desires to get all the profit he can, let all the Spiritual Exercises be given in the order in which they follow.

In these he will, ordinarily, more benefit himself, the more he separates himself from all friends and acquaintances and from all earthly care, as by changing from the house where he was dwelling, and taking another house or room to live in, in as much privacy as he can, so that it be in his power to go each day to Mass and to Vespers, without fear that his acquaintances will put obstacles in his way.

From this isolation three chief benefits, among many others, follow.

The first is that a man, by separating himself from many friends and acquaintances, and likewise from many not well-ordered affairs, to serve and praise God our Lord, merits no little in the sight of His Divine Majesty.

The second is, that being thus isolated, and not having his understanding divided on many things, but concentrating his care on one only, namely, on serving his Creator and benefiting his own soul, he uses with greater freedom his natural powers, in seeking with diligence what he so much desires.

The third: the more our soul finds itself alone and isolated, the more apt it makes itself to approach and to reach its Creator and Lord, and the more it so approaches Him, the more it disposes itself to receive graces and gifts from His Divine and Sovereign Goodness.

## SPIRITUAL EXERCISES
## TO CONQUER ONESELF AND REGULATE ONE'S LIFE
## WITHOUT DETERMINING ONESELF THROUGH
## ANY TENDENCY THAT IS DISORDERED

### PRESUPPOSITION

In order that both he who is giving the Spiritual Exercises, and he who is receiving them, may more help and benefit themselves, let it be presupposed that every good Christian is to be more ready to save his neighbor's proposition than to condemn it. If he cannot save it, let him inquire how he means it; and if he means it badly, let him correct him with charity. If that is not enough, let him seek all the suitable means to bring him to mean it well, and save himself.

### FIRST WEEK
### PRINCIPLE AND FOUNDATION

Man is created to praise, reverence, and serve God our Lord, and by this means to save his soul.

And the other things on the face of the earth are created for man and that they may help him in prosecuting the end for which he is created.

From this it follows that man is to use them as much as they help him on to his end, and ought to rid himself of them so far as they hinder him as to it.

For this it is necessary to make ourselves indifferent to all created things in all that is allowed to the choice of our free will and is not prohibited to it; so that, on our part, we want not health rather than sickness, riches rather than poverty, honor rather than dishonor, long rather than short life, and so in all the rest; desiring and choosing only what is most conducive for us to the end for which we are created.

### PARTICULAR AND DAILY EXAMEN

It contains in it three times, and two to examine oneself.

The first time is in the morning, immediately on rising, when one ought to propose to guard himself with diligence against that particular sin or defect which he wants to correct and amend.

The second time is after dinner, when one is to ask of God our Lord what one wants, namely, grace to remember how many times he has fallen into that particular sin or defect, and to amend himself in the future. Then let him make the first Examen, asking account of his soul of that particular thing proposed, which he wants to correct and amend. Let him go over hour by hour, or period by period, commencing at the hour he rose, and continuing up to the hour and instant of the present examen, and let him make in the first line of the G as⸺ many dots as were the times he has fallen into that particular sin or defect. Then let him resolve anew to amend himself up to the second Examen which he will make.

The third time: After supper, the second Examen will be made, in the same way, hour by hour, commencing at the first Examen and continuing up to the present (second) one, and let him make in the second line of the same G ⸺ as many dots as were the times he has fallen into that particular sin or defect.

## FOUR ADDITIONS
### FOLLOW TO RID ONESELF SOONER OF THAT PARTICULAR SIN OR DEFECT

*First Addition.* The first Addition is that each time one falls into that particular sin or defect, let him put his hand on his breast, grieving for having fallen: which can be done even in the presence of many, without their perceiving what he is doing.

*Second Addition.* The second: As the first line of the G ⸺ means the first Examen, and the second line the second Examen, let him look at night if there is amendment from the first line to the second, that is, from the first Examen to the second.

*Third Addition.* The third: To compare the second day with the first; that is, the two Examens of the present day with the other two Examens of the previous day, and see if he has amended himself from one day to the other.

*Fourth Addition.* The fourth Addition: To compare one week with another, and see if he has amended himself in the present week over the week past.

*Note.* It is to be noted that the first (large) G ⸺ which follows means the Sunday: the second (smaller), the Monday: the third, the Tuesday, and so on.

G ⸻

G ⸻

G ⸻

G ⸻

G ═══════════════════════════════

G ═══════════════════════════════

G ═══════════════════════════════

* * * * *

## FIRST EXERCISE
## IT IS A MEDITATION WITH THE THREE POWERS
## ON THE FIRST, THE SECOND AND THE THIRD SIN

It contains in it, after one Preparatory Prayer and two Preludes, three chief Points and one Colloquy.

*Prayer.* The Preparatory Prayer is to ask grace of God our Lord that all my intentions, actions and operations may be directed purely to the service and praise of His Divine Majesty.

*First Prelude.* The First Prelude is a composition, seeing the place.

Here it is to be noted that, in a visible contemplation or meditation—as, for instance, when one contemplates Christ our Lord, Who is visible—the composition will be to see with the sight of the imagination the corporeal place where the thing is found which I want to contemplate. I say the corporeal place, as for instance, a Temple or Mountain where Jesus Christ or Our Lady is found, according to what I want to contemplate. In an invisible contemplation or meditation—as here on the Sins—the composition will be to see with the sight of the imagination and consider that my soul is imprisoned in this corruptible body, and all the compound in this valley, as exiled among brute beasts: I say all the compound of soul and body.

*Second Prelude.* The second is to ask God our Lord for what I want and desire.

The petition has to be according to the subject matter; that is, if the contemplation is on the Resurrection, one is to ask for joy with Christ in joy; if it is on the Passion, he is to ask for pain, tears and torment with Christ in torment.

Here it will be to ask shame and confusion at myself, seeing how many have been damned for only one mortal sin, and how many times I deserved to be condemned forever for my so many sins.

*Note.* Before all Contemplations or Meditations, there ought always to be made the Preparatory Prayer, which is not changed, and the two Preludes already mentioned, which are sometimes changed, according to the subject matter.

*First Point.*  The first Point will be to bring the memory on the First Sin, which was that of the Angels, and then to bring the intellect on the same, discussing it; then the will, wanting to recall and understand all this in order to make me more ashamed and confound me more, bringing into comparison with the one sin of the Angels my so many sins, and reflecting, while they for one sin were cast into Hell, how often I have deserved it for so many.

I say to bring to memory the sin of the Angels, how they, being created in grace, not wanting to help themselves with their liberty to reverence and obey their Creator and Lord, coming to pride, were changed from grace to malice, and hurled from Heaven to Hell; and so then to discuss more in detail with the intellect: and then to move the feelings more with the will.

*Second Point.*  The second is to do the same—that is, to bring the Three Powers—on the sin of Adam and Eve, bringing to memory how on account of that sin they did penance for so long a time, and how much corruption came on the human race, so many people going the way to Hell.

I say to bring to memory the Second Sin, that of our First Parents; how after Adam was created in the field of Damascus and placed in the Terrestrial Paradise, and Eve was created from his rib, being forbidden to eat of the Tree of Knowledge, they ate and so sinned, and afterwards clothed in tunics of skins and cast from Paradise, they lived, all their life, without the original justice which they had lost, and in many labors and much penance. And then to discuss with the understanding more in detail; and to use the will as has been said.

*Third Point.*  The third is likewise to do the same on the Third particular Sin of any one who for one mortal sin is gone to Hell—and many others without number, for fewer sins than I have committed.

I say to do the same on the Third particular Sin, bringing to memory the gravity and malice of the sin against one's Creator and Lord; to discuss with the understanding how in sinning and acting against the Infinite Goodness, he has been justly condemned forever; and to finish with the will as has been said.

*Colloquy.*  Imagining Christ our Lord present and placed on the Cross, let me make a Colloquy, how from Creator He is come to making Himself man, and from life eternal is come to temporal death, and so to die for my sins.

Likewise, looking at myself, what I have done for Christ, what I am doing for Christ, what I ought to do for Christ.

And so, seeing Him such, and so nailed on the Cross, to go over that which will present itself.

The Colloquy is made, properly speaking, as one friend speaks to another, or as a servant to his master; now asking some grace, now blaming oneself for some misdeed, now communicating one's affairs, and asking advice in them.

And let me say an OUR FATHER.


## SECOND EXERCISE
### IT IS A MEDITATION ON THE SINS AND CONTAINS IN IT AFTER THE PREPARATORY PRAYER AND TWO PRELUDES, FIVE POINTS AND ONE COLLOQUY

*Prayer.*   Let the Preparatory Prayer be the same.

*First Prelude.*   The First Prelude will be the same composition.

*Second Prelude.*   The second is to ask for what I want. It will be here to beg a great and intense sorrow and tears for my sins.

*First Point.*   The first Point is the statement of the sins; that is to say, to bring to memory all the sins of life, looking from year to year, or from period to period. For this three things are helpful: first, to look at the place and the house where I have lived; second, the relations I have had with others; third, the occupation in which I have lived.

*Second Point.*   The second, to weigh the sins, looking at the foulness and the malice which any mortal sin committed has in it, even supposing it were not forbidden.

*Third Point.*   The third, to look at who I am, lessening myself by examples:

First, how much I am in comparison to all men;

Second, what men are in comparison to all the Angels and Saints of Paradise;

Third, what all Creation is in comparison to God: (—Then I alone, what can I be?)

Fourth, to see all my bodily corruption and foulness;

Fifth, to look at myself as a sore and ulcer, from which have sprung so many sins and so many iniquities and so very vile poison.

*Fourth Point.*   The fourth, to consider what God is, against Whom I have sinned, according to His attributes; comparing them with their contraries in me—His Wisdom with my ignorance; His Omnipotence with my weakness; His Justice with my iniquity; His Goodness with my malice.

*Fifth Point.*   The fifth, an exclamation of wonder with deep feeling, going through all creatures, how they have left me in life and preserved me in it; the Angels, how, though they are the sword of the Divine Justice, they have endured me, and guarded me, and prayed for me; the Saints, how they have been engaged in interceding and praying for me; and the heavens, sun, moon, stars, and elements, fruits, birds, fishes and animals—and the earth, how it has not opened to swallow me up, creating new Hells for me to suffer in them forever!

*Colloquy.* Let me finish with a Colloquy of mercy, pondering and giving thanks to God our Lord that He has given me life up to now, proposing amendment, with His grace, for the future.

OUR FATHER.

\*    \*    \*    \*    \*

## FIFTH EXERCISE
## IT IS A MEDITATION ON HELL

It contains in it, after the Preparatory Prayer and two Preludes, five Points and one Colloquy:

*Prayer.* Let the Preparatory Prayer be the usual one.

*First Prelude.* The first Prelude is the composition, which is here to see with the sight of the imagination the length, breadth and depth of Hell.

*Second Prelude.* The second, to ask for what I want: it will be here to ask for interior sense of the pain which the damned suffer, in order that, if, through my faults, I should forget the love of the Eternal Lord, at least the fear of the pains may help me not to come into sin.

*First Point.* The first Point will be to see with the sight of the imagination the great fires, and the souls as in bodies of fire.

*Second Point.* The second, to hear with the ears wailings, howlings, cries, blasphemies against Christ our Lord and against all His Saints.

*Third Point.* The third, to smell with the smell smoke, sulphur, dregs and putrid things.

*Fourth Point.* The fourth, to taste with the taste bitter things, like tears, sadness and the worm of conscience.

*Fifth Point.* The fifth, to touch with the touch; that is to say, how the fires touch and burn the souls.

*Colloquy.* Making a Colloquy to Christ our Lord, I will bring to memory the souls that are in Hell, some because they did not believe the Coming, others because, believing, they did not act according to His Commandments; making three divisions:

*First, Second, and Third Divisions.* The first, before the Coming; the second, during His life; the third, after His life in this world; and with this I will give Him thanks that He has not let me fall into any of these divisions, ending my life.

Likewise, I will consider how up to now He has always had so great pity and mercy on me.

I will end with an OUR FATHER.

*Note.* The first Exercise will be made at midnight; the second immediately on rising in the morning; the third, before or after

Mass; in any case, before dinner; the fourth at the hour of Vespers; the fifth, an hour before supper.

This arrangement of hours, more or less, I always mean in all the four Weeks, according as his age, disposition and physical condition help the person who is exercising himself to make five Exercises or fewer.

## ADDITIONS
## TO MAKE THE EXERCISES BETTER AND TO FIND BETTER WHAT ONE DESIRES

*First Addition.* The first Addition is, after going to bed, just when I want to go to asleep, to think, for the space of a HAIL MARY, of the hour that I have to rise and for what, making a résumé of the Exercise which I have to make.

*Second Addition.* The second: When I wake up, not giving place to any other thought, to turn my attention immediately to what I am going to contemplate in the first Exercise, at midnight, bringing myself to confusion for my so many sins, setting examples, as, for instance, if a knight found himself before his king and all his court, ashamed and confused at having much offended him, from whom he had first received many gifts and many favors: in the same way, in the second Exercise, making myself a great sinner and in chains; that is to say going to appear bound as in chains before the Supreme Eternal Judge; taking for an example how prisoners in chains and already deserving death, appear before their temporal judge. And I will dress with these thoughts or with others, according to the subject matter.

*Third Addition.* The third: A step or two before the place where I have to contemplate or meditate, I will put myself standing for the space of an OUR FATHER, my intellect raised on high, considering how God our Lord is looking at me, etc.; and will make an act of reverence or humility.

*Fourth Addition.* The fourth: To enter on the contemplation now on my knees, now prostrate on the earth, now lying face upwards, now seated, now standing, always intent on seeking what I want.

We will attend to two things. The first is, that if I find what I want kneeling, I will not pass on; and if prostrate, likewise, etc. The second; in the Point in which I find what I want, there I will rest, without being anxious to pass on, until I content myself.

*Fifth Addition.* The fifth: After finishing the Exercise, I will, during the space of a quarter of an hour, seated or walking leisurely, look how it went with me in the Contemplation or Meditation; and if badly, I will look for the cause from which it proceeds, and having so seen it, will be sorry, in order to correct myself in future; and if well, I will give thanks to God our Lord, and will do in like manner another time.

*Sixth Addition.* The sixth: Not to want to think on things of pleasure or joy, such as heavenly glory, the Resurrection, etc. Because whatever consideration of joy and gladness hinders our feeling pain and grief and shedding tears for our sins: but to keep before me that I want to grieve and feel pain, bringing to memory rather Death and Judgment.

*Seventh Addition.* The seventh: For the same end, to deprive myself of all light, closing the blinds and doors while I am in the room, if it be not to recite prayers, to read and eat.

*Eighth Addition.* The eighth: Not to laugh nor say a thing provocative of laughter.

*Ninth Addition.* The ninth: To restrain my sight, except in receiving or dismissing the person with whom I have spoken.

*Tenth Addition.* The tenth Addition is penance.

This is divided into interior and exterior. The interior is to grieve for one's sins, with a firm purpose of not committing them nor any others. The exterior, or fruit of the first, is chastisement for the sins committed, and is chiefly taken in three ways.

*First Way.* The first is as to eating. That is to say, when we leave off the superfluous, it is not penance, but temperance. It is penance when we leave off from the suitable; and the more and more, the greater and better—provided that the person does not injure himself, and that no notable illness follows.

*Second Way.* The second, as to the manner of sleeping. Here too it is not penance to leave off the superfluous of delicate or soft things, but it is penance when one leaves off from the suitable in the manner: and the more and more, the better—provided that the person does not injure himself and no notable illness follows. Besides, let not anything of the suitable sleep be left off, unless in order to come to the mean, if one has a bad habit of sleeping too much.

*Third Way.* The third, to chastise the flesh, that is, giving it sensible pain, which is given by wearing haircloth or cords or iron chains next to the flesh, by scourging or wounding oneself, and by other kinds of austerity.

*Note.* What appears most suitable and most secure with regard to penance is that the pain should be sensible in the flesh and not enter within the bones, so that it give pain and not illness. For this it appears to be more suitable to scourge oneself with thin cords, which give pain exteriorly, rather than in another way which would cause notable illness within.

*First Note.* The first Note is that the exterior penances are done chiefly for three ends:

First, as satisfaction for the sins committed;

Second, to conquer oneself—that is, to make sensuality obey reason and all inferior parts be more subject to the superior;

Third, to seek and find some grace or gift which the person wants and desires; as, for instance, if he desires to have interior contrition for his sins, or to weep much over them, or over the pains and sufferings which Christ our Lord suffered in His Passion, or to settle some doubt in which the person finds himself.

*Second Note.* The second: It is to be noted that the first and second Addition have to be made for the Exercises of midnight and at daybreak, but not for those which will be made at other times; and the fourth Addition will never be made in church in the presence of others, but in private, as at home, etc.

*Third Note.* The third: When the person who is exercising himself does not yet find what he desires—as tears, consolations, etc.,—it often helps for him to make a change in food, in sleep and in other ways of doing penance, so that he change himself, doing penance two or three days, and two or three others not. For it suits some to do more penance and others less, and we often omit doing penance from sensual love and from an erroneous judgment that the human system will not be able to bear it without notable illness; and sometimes, on the contrary, we do too much, thinking that the body can bear it; and as God our Lord knows our nature infinitely better, often in such changes He gives each one to perceive what is suitable for him.

*Fourth Note.* The fourth: Let the Particular Examen be made to rid oneself of defects and negligences on the Exercises and Additions. And so in the SECOND, THIRD and FOURTH WEEKS.

\* \* \* \* \*

## RULES
### FOR PERCEIVING AND KNOWING IN SOME MANNER THE DIFFERENT MOVEMENTS WHICH ARE CAUSED IN THE SOUL THE GOOD, TO RECEIVE THEM, AND THE BAD TO REJECT THEM. AND THEY ARE MORE PROPER FOR THE FIRST WEEK

*First Rule.* The first Rule: In the persons who go from mortal sin to mortal sin, the enemy is commonly used to propose to them apparent pleasures, making them imagine sensual delights and pleasures in order to hold them more and make them grow in their vices and sins. In these persons the good spirit uses the opposite method, pricking them and biting their consciences through the process of reason.

*Second Rule.* The second: In the persons who are going on intensely cleansing their sins and rising from good to better in the service of God our Lord, it is the method contrary to that in the first Rule, for then it is the way of the evil spirit to bite, sadden and put obstacles, disquieting with false reasons, that one may not go on; and it is proper to the good to give courage and strength, consolations, tears, inspirations and quiet, easing, and putting away all obstacles, that one may go on in well doing.

*Third Rule.* The third: OF SPIRITUAL CONSOLATION. I call it consolation when some interior movement in the soul is caused, through which the soul comes to be inflamed with love of its Creator and Lord; and when it can in consequence love no created thing on the face of the earth in itself, but in the Creator of them all.

Likewise, when it sheds tears that move to love of its Lord, whether out of sorrow for one's sins, or for the Passion of Christ our Lord, or because of other things directly connected with His service and praise.

Finally, I call consolation every increase of hope, faith and charity, and all interior joy which calls and attracts to heavenly things and to the salvation of one's soul, quieting it and giving it peace in its Creator and Lord.

*Fourth Rule.* The fourth: OF SPIRITUAL DESOLATION. I call desolation all the contrary of the third rule, such as darkness of soul, disturbance in it, movement to things low and earthly, the unquiet of different agitations and temptations, moving to want of confidence, without hope, without love, when one finds oneself all lazy, tepid, sad, and as if separated from his Creator and Lord. Because, as consolation is contrary to desolation, in the same way the thoughts which come from consolation are contrary to the thoughts which come from desolation.

*Fifth Rule.* The fifth: In time of desolation never to make a change; but to be firm and constant in the resolutions and determination in which one was the day preceding such desolation, or in the determination in which he was in the preceding consolation. Because, as in consolation it is rather the good spirit who guides and counsels us, so in desolation it is the bad, with whose counsels we cannot take a course to decide rightly.

*Sixth Rule.* The sixth: Although in desolation we ought not to change our first resolutions, it is very helpful intensely to change ourselves against the same desolation, as by insisting more on prayer, meditation, on much examination, and by giving ourselves more scope in some suitable way of doing penance.

*Seventh Rule.* The seventh: Let him who is in desolation consider how the Lord has left him in trial in his natural powers, in order to resist the different agitations and temptations of the enemy; since he can with the Divine help, which always remains to him, though he does not clearly perceive it: because the Lord has taken from him his great fervor, great love and intense grace, leaving him, however, grace enough for eternal salvation.

*Eighth Rule.* The eighth: Let him who is in desolation labor to be in patience, which is contrary to the vexations which come to him:

and let him think that he will soon be consoled, employing against the desolation the devices, as is said in the sixth Rule.

*Ninth Rule.* The ninth: There are three principal reasons why we find ourselves desolate.

The first is, because of our being tepid, lazy or negligent in our spiritual exercises; and so through our faults, spiritual consolation withdraws from us.

The second, to try us and see how much we are and how much we let ourselves out in His service and praise without such great pay of consolation and great graces.

The third, to give us true acquaintance and knowledge, that we may interiorly feel that it is not ours to get or keep great devotion, intense love, tears, or any other spiritual consolation, but that all is the gift and grace of God our Lord, and that we may not build a nest in a thing not ours, raising our intellect into some pride or vainglory, attributing to us devotion or the other things of the spiritual consolation.

*Tenth Rule.* The tenth: Let him who is in consolation think how he will be in the desolation which will come after, taking new strength for them.

*Eleventh Rule.* The eleventh: Let him who is consoled see to humbling himself and lowering himself as much as he can, thinking how little he is able for in the time of desolation without such grace or consolation.

On the contrary, let him who is in desolation think that he can do much with the grace sufficient to resist all his enemies, taking strength in his Creator and Lord.

*Twelfth Rule.* The twelfth: The enemy acts like a woman, in being weak against vigor and strong of will. Because, as it is the way of the woman when she is quarrelling with some man to lose heart, taking flight when the man shows her much courage: and on the contrary, if the man, losing heart, begins to fly, the wrath, revenge, and ferocity of the woman is very great, and so without bounds; in the same manner, it is the way of the enemy to weaken and lose heart, his temptations taking flight, when the person who is exercising himself in spiritual things opposes a bold front against the temptations of the enemy, doing diametrically the opposite. And on the contrary, if the person who is exercising himself commences to have fear and lose heart in suffering the temptations, there is no beast so wild on the face of the earth as the enemy of human nature in following out his damnable intention with so great malice.

*Thirteenth Rule.* The thirteenth: Likewise, he acts as a licentious lover in wanting to be secret and not revealed. For, as the licentious man who, speaking for an evil purpose, solicits a daughter of a good father or a wife of a good husband, wants his words and persuasions to be secret, and the contrary displeases him much, when the daughter reveals to her father or the wife to her husband his licentious words and depraved intention, because he easily gathers that he will not be able to succeed with the undertaking begun: in the same way, when the enemy of human nature brings his wiles and persuasions to the just soul, he wants and desires that they be received and kept in secret; but when one reveals them to his good Confessor or to another spiritual person that knows his deceits and evil ends, it is very grievous to him, because he gathers, from his manifest deceits being discovered, that he will not be able to succeed with his wickedness begun.

*Fourteenth Rule.* The fourteenth: Likewise, he behaves as a chief bent on conquering and robbing what he desires: for, as a captain and chief of the army, pitching his camp, and looking at the forces or defences of a stronghold, attacks it on the weakest side, in like manner the enemy of human nature, roaming about, looks in turn at all our virtues, theological, cardinal and moral; and where he finds us weakest and most in need for our eternal salvation, there he attacks us and aims at taking us.

*    *    *    *    *

## [RULES FOR THINKING WITH THE CHURCH]

Let the following Rules be observed.

*First Rule.* The first: All judgment laid aside, we ought to have our mind ready and prompt to obey, in all, the true Spouse of Christ our Lord, which is our holy Mother the Church Hierarchical.

*Second Rule.* The second: To praise confession to a Priest, and the reception of the most Holy Sacrament of the Altar once in the year, and much more each month, and much better from week to week, with the conditions required and due.

*Third Rule.* The third: To praise the hearing of Mass often, likewise hymns, psalms, and long prayers, in the church and out of it; likewise the hours set at the time fixed for each Divine Office and for all prayer and all Canonical Hours.

*Fourth Rule.* The fourth: To praise much Religious Orders, virginity and continence, and not so much marriage as any of these.

*Fifth Rule.* The fifth: To praise vows of Religion, of obedience, of poverty, of chastity and of other perfections of supererogation. And it is to be noted that as the vow is about the things which approach to Evangelical perfection, a vow ought not to be made in the things which withdraw from it, such as to be a merchant, or to be married, etc.

*Sixth Rule.* To praise relics of the Saints, giving veneration to them and praying to the Saints; and to praise Stations, pilgrimages, Indulgences, pardons, Cruzadas [*i.e.*, indults; exemptions], and candles lighted in the churches.

*Seventh Rule.* To praise Constitutions about fasts and abstinence, as of Lent, Ember Days, Vigils, Friday and Saturday; likewise penances, not only interior, but also exterior.

*Eighth Rule.* To praise the ornaments and the buildings of churches; likewise images, and to venerate them according to what they represent.

*Ninth Rule.* Finally, to praise all precepts of the Church, keeping the mind prompt to find reasons in their defence and in no manner against them.

*Tenth Rule.* We ought to be more prompt to find good and praise as well the Constitutions and recommendations as the ways of our Superiors. Because, although some are not or have not been such, to speak against them, whether preaching in public or discoursing before the common people, would rather give rise to fault-finding and scandal than profit; and so the people would be incensed against their Superiors, whether temporal or spiritual. So that, as it does harm to speak evil to the common people of Superiors in their absence, so it can make profit to speak of the evil ways to the persons themselves who can remedy them.

*Eleventh Rule.* To praise positive and scholastic learning. Because, as it is more proper to the Positive Doctors, as St. Jerome, St. Augustine and St. Gregory, etc., to move the heart to love and serve God our Lord in everything; so it is more proper to the Scholastics, as St. Thomas, St. Bonaventure, and to the Master of the Sentences, etc., to define or explain for our times the things necessary for eternal salvation; and to combat and explain better all errors and all fallacies. For the Scholastic Doctors, as they are more modern, not only help themselves with the true understanding of the Sacred Scripture and of the Positive and holy Doctors, but also, they being enlightened and clarified by the Divine virtue, help themselves by the Councils, Canons and Constitutions of our holy Mother the Church.

*Twelfth Rule.* We ought to be on our guard in making comparison of those of us who are alive to the blessed passed away, because error is committed not a little in this; that is to say, in saying, this one knows more than St. Augustine; he is another, or greater than, St. Francis; he is another St. Paul in goodness, holiness, etc.

*Thirteenth Rule.* To be right in everything, we ought always to hold that the white which I see, is black, if the Hierarchical Church so decides it, believing that between Christ our Lord, the Bridegroom, ˄nd the Church, His Bride, there is the same Spirit which governs and directs us for the salvation of our souls. Because by the same Spirit and our Lord Who gave the ten Commandments, our holy Mother the Church is directed and governed.

*Fourteenth Rule.* Although there is much truth in the assertion that no one can save himself without being predestined and without having faith and grace; we must be very cautious in the manner of speaking and communicating with others about all these things.

*Fifteenth Rule.*  We ought not, by way of custom, to speak much of predestination; but if in some way and at some times one speaks, let him so speak that the common people may not come into any error, as sometimes happens, saying: Whether I have to be saved or condemned is already determined, and no other thing can now be, through my doing well or ill; and with this, growing lazy, they become negligent in the works which lead to the salvation and the spiritual profit of their souls.

*Sixteenth Rule.*  In the same way, we must be on our guard that by talking much and with much insistence of faith, without any distinction and explanation, occasion be not given to the people to be lazy and slothful in works, whether before faith is formed in charity or after.

*Seventeenth Rule.*  Likewise, we ought not to speak so much with insistence on grace that the poison of discarding liberty be engendered.

So that of faith and grace one can speak as much as is possible with the Divine help for the greater praise of His Divine Majesty, but not in such way, nor in such manners, especially in our so dangerous times, that works and free will receive any harm, or be held for nothing.

*Eighteenth Rule.*  Although serving God our Lord much out of pure love is to be esteemed above all; we ought to praise much the fear of His Divine Majesty, because not only filial fear is a thing pious and most holy, but even servile fear—when the man reaches nothing else better or more useful—helps much to get out of mortal sin. And when he is out, he easily comes to filial fear, which is all acceptable and grateful to God our Lord, as being at one with the Divine Love.

---

*The Spiritual Exercises of St. Ignatius of Loyola,* tr. Father Elder Mullan, S.J. (New York: P. J. Kenedy & Sons, 1914), pp. 3–11, 13–23, 35–42, 44–52, 169–175, 189–194. By permission.

# Exhibit Fifteen

## A LITURGY
## FOR RECONCILIATION
*JOHN KNOX*

## Introduction

Calvinist church order, employing the pastoral office
for maintaining the cohesion of the church as well
as a strict public and private morality, was transported to Scotland by that formidable leader and
chronicler of the Reformation, John Knox (c. 1505–
1572). Knox first came into prominence as a Protestant when in the mid-1540's he embraced the Lutheran teachings of the earliest Reformation leaders
in Scotland, Patrick Hamilton and George Wishart.
In 1551 he became a chaplain to England's young
King Edward VI, and he played an important part
in drafting the 1552 *Book of Common Prayer* of the
Church of England. During the Catholic reaction
under Mary Tudor, Knox fled to Geneva, then Frank-
furt, returning to Scotland briefly in 1555 and per-
manently in 1559. After the latter date, he led Scottish Christianity along the paths of Calvin's Geneva,
and after his death this program won complete
victory in his native land.

For use by English exiles in Geneva, Knox
devised a liturgy which became the Church of Scotland's *Book of Common Order*, in force from its
adoption in 1564 until superseded by the *Westminster Directory* of 1645. That the work was defi-

nitely oriented toward the exercise of pastoral discipline is seen
clearly in the portion here reproduced, the Form of Public Repentance. The liturgy contained "The Confession of Faith";
rules for the work and election of ministers; forms for public
congregational worship, The Lord's Supper, and Baptism; "The
Ordoure of The Generall Fast"; prayers for use in private houses;
and pastoral offices for excommunication, public repentance, the
reinstatement of excommunicates, and the visitation of the sick.
No liturgy in the English language has surpassed its pastoral
richness and its disciplinary precision.

The Form of Public Repentance was designed to reconcile
to the congregation and to God persons guilty of the severer sins
that constituted deep offense to the congregation, but Knox also
provided detailed procedures for the discipline, forgiveness, and
reconciliation of persons convicted of minor sins. In the latter
case, members of the congregation might carry out the function
of pastoral discipline without recourse to the chief minister of
the congregation. But if the sinner proved obstinate in refusing
either to acknowledge his sin or to remove the offense, this transmuted his error into a major matter calling for action by the
official pastor. Even in dealing with the more serious crimes, however, the congregation was involved heavily with the pronounce-
ment of divine forgiveness both upon the errant brother and
upon itself, and with the re-acceptance of the sinner into the
fellowship of the church.

Some of Knox's more colorful and quaint expressions have
changed their meanings so drastically over the years that, in the
following pages, they have been modernized; while these changes
gain clarity, they unfortunately sacrifice pungency.


# A LITURGY
# FOR RECONCILIATION

From: *The Book of Common Order* (1564),
by John Knox.

### Offenses that deserve Public Repentance,
### and Order to proceed thereinto

Such offenses as fall not under the civil sword, and yet are slanderous
and offensive in the Church, deserve Public Repentance: and of these
some are more heinous than others—fornication, [habitual] drunkenness . . . , swearing, cursed speaking, chiding, fighting, brawling, . . .
common contempt of the order of the Church, breaking of the Sabbath,
and such like, ought to be in no person suffered: but the slander being

known, the offender should be called before the [assembly of] Ministers, his crime . . . [tried], accused, rebuked, and he commanded publicly to satisfy the Church; which if the offender refuse, they may proceed to Excommunication, as after shall be declared. If the offender appear not, summons ought to pass to the third time; and then in case he appear not, the Church may . . . [decide] the sentence to be pronounced.

Others be less heinous and yet deserve admonition, as wanton and vain words, uncomely gestures, negligence in hearing the preachings or abstaining from the Lord's Table when it is publicly ministered, suspicion of avarice or of pride, superfluity or riotousness in . . . [expression of the face] or raiment; these, we say, and such others that of the world are not regarded, deserve admonition among the members of Christ's body: first, secretly, by one or two of those that first espy the offense, which if the person suspected hear, and give declaration of amendment, then there need [be] no further process.

But if he contemn and despise admonition, then should the former admonishers take to themselves two or three faithful and honest witnesses, in whose presence the suspected offender should be admonished, and the causes of their suspicion declared; to whom if then he give signification of repentance and promise of amendment, they may cut off all further accusation: but if he obstinately contemn both the said admonitions, then ought the first and second brethren to signify the matter to the Ministers and Elders in their Session, who ought to call the offender, and, before the complainers, accuse him as well of the crime as of the contempt of the admonition. If then he acknowledge his offense, and be willing to satisfy the brethren before offended and the Session then present, there need [be] no further publication of the offense.

But if he declare himself inobedient to the Session, then without delay the next Sunday ought the crime, and the order of admonitions passed before, be publicly declared to the Church, and the person (without specification of his name) be admonished to satisfy in public that which he refused to do in secret: and that for the first. If he offers himself to the Church before the next Sunday, the discretion of the Ministry may take such order, as may satisfy as well the private persons that first were offended, as the Church, declaring the repentance and submission of that brother that before appeared stubborn and incorrigible.

But if he abide the second public admonition, when his name shall be expressed and his offenses and stubbornness declared, then can no satisfaction be received but in public; yea, it may not be received before he has humbly . . . [asked] the same of the Ministry and Session of the Church in their appointed Assembly.

If he continue stubborn, then the third Sunday ought he to be charged publicly to satisfy the Church for his offense and contempt, under the pain of Excommunication; the Order wherof shall [here]-

after be declared. And thus a small offense or slander may justly deserve Excommunication, by reason of the contempt and disobedience of the offender. If the offender show himself penitent between the first admonition and the second, and satisfy the Ministry of the Church and the brethren that were before offended in their Assembly, then it may suffice that the Minister, at the commandment of the Session, declare the next Sunday (without [the] appearing or expressing of the person) his repentance and submission in this or other words:—

It was signified unto you before, dearly beloved, that one certain brother (or brethren) was noted, or at least suspected of some offense whereof he, being admonished by one or two, appeared lightly to regard the same; and therefore was he and his offense notified unto the Ministry in their Assembly, who, according to their duty and charge, accused him of the same; and not finding in him such obedience as the profession of a Christian requires, fearing that such offenses and stubbornness should engender contempt and infect others, they were compelled to notify unto you the crime and the proceedings of the Session, minding to have sought the uttermost remedy in case the offender had continued obstinate. But seeing that it has pleased God to mollify the heart of our brother, whose name we need not express, so that he has not only acknowledged his offense, but also has fully satisfied the brethren that first were offended, and us the Ministry, and has promised to abstain from all appearance of such evil as whereof he was suspected and admonished, we have no just cause to proceed to any further extremity, but rather to glorify God for the submission of our brother, and unfeignedly pray unto Him that in the like case we and every one of us may give the like obedience.

## THE FORM OF PUBLIC REPENTANCE

*It is first to be observed, that none may be admitted to Public Repentance except first they be admitted thereto by the Session and Assembly of the Minister and Elders; in which they ought sharply to be examined, what fear and terror they have of God's judgments, what hatred of sin and dolor for the same, and what sense and feeling they have of God's mercies: in which if they be ignorant, they ought diligently to be instructed; for it is but a mocking to present such to public repentance as neither understand what sin is, what repentance is, what grace is, nor by whom God's favor and mercy is purchased. After . . . the offender . . . [has been] instructed in the Assembly, so as to have some taste of God's judgments, but chiefly of God's mercies in Christ Jesus, he may be presented before the public Church upon a Sunday after the sermon, and before the Prayers and Psalm, and then the Minister shall say:—*

Beloved and dearest Brethren, we, by reason of our charge and Ministry, present before you this brother, that, by the infirmity of the flesh and craft of Satan, has fearfully fallen from the obedience of his God, by committing N. of a crime, etc. (let the sin be expressed); by which he has not only offended against the Majesty of God, but also by the same has given great slander and offense to His holy congregation; and therefore does, to his own confusion (but to the glory of God and our great comfort), present himself here before you, to witness and declare his unfeigned repentance, the thirst and the care that he has to be reconciled with God through Jesus Christ and with you his brethren whom he has offended: and therefore it is requisite that you and he understand what assurance we have to require such public satisfaction of him, what profit we ought to learn in the same, and what profit and utility redounds to both, . . . [from] this his humiliation.

That Public Repentance is the institution of God, and not man's invention, may be plainly gathered out of the words of our Master, commanding "that if one has offended his brother, in what sort soever it be, that he shall go to him and be reconciled unto his brother." If the offense committed against one brother requires reconciliation, the offense committed against many brethren requires the same. And if a man be charged by Christ Jesus to go to a man whom he has offended, and there by confession of his offense . . . [ask] reconciliation, much more is he bound to seek a whole multitude whom he has offended, and before them with all humility . . . [ask] the same; for that woe which our Master Christ Jesus pronounces against every man that has offended the least one within his Church, remains upon every public offender until such time as he declare himself willing to remove the same, which he can never do until such time as he let the multitude whom he has offended understand his unfeigned repentance.

But because . . . all men of upright judgment agree in this, that public offenses require public repentance, we pass to the second head, which is, what it is that we have to consider in the fall and sin of this our brother. If we consider his fall and sin in him only, without having consideration of ourselves and of our own corruption, we shall profit nothing, for so shall we both despise our brother and flatter ourselves. But if we shall earnestly consider what nature we bear, what corruption lurks in it, how prone and ready every one of us is to such and greater impiety, then shall we in the sin of this our brother accuse and damn our own sins, in his fall shall we consider and lament our sinful nature; also shall we join our repentance, tears, and prayers with him and his, knowing that no flesh can be justified before God's presence if the judgment proceed without mercy. The profit which this our brother and we have of this his humiliation, is, that we and he may be assured that our God is more ready to receive us to mercy, through Jesus Christ his only Son, than we are to crave it. It is not sin, be it never so grievous, that shall debar us from his favor, if we seek . . . [out] his mercy; for as all have sinned and are by themselves destitute of God's grace, so is He ready to show mercy unto all that unfeignedly call for the same; yea, He does not only receive such as come, but He, by the mouth of His dear Son, calls upon such as be burdened and laden with sin, and solemnly promises that He will refresh them.

We have besides another commodity, to wit, that if we shall hereafter fall into the like or greater [sin] (for we stand not by our own power, but by grace only), . . . we be not ashamed in this same . . . [way] to humble ourselves and confess our offense. Now, therefore, brother, as we all praise God in this your humiliation, beseeching Him that it be without hypocrisy, so it becomes you earnestly to consider of what mind and with what heart you present yourself here before this Assembly. It is not your sin that shall separate you from your God, nor from His mercy in Jesus Christ, if you repent the same; but hypocrisy and impenitence, which, God remove from you and us, is nowise tolerable before His presence.

*The Offender ought to protest before God that he is sorry for his sin and unfeignedly desires God to be merciful unto him, and that for the obedience of His dear Son our Lord Jesus Christ.*

### The Minister

We can only see that which is without, and according to your confession [we] judge, leaving the secrets of the heart to God, who only can try and search the same. But because unfeigned repentance for sin, and simple confession of the same, are the mere gifts of God, we will join our prayers with yours, that the one and the other may be granted to you and to us.

### The Prayer

Eternal and everliving God, Father of our Lord Jesus Christ, thou that by the mouth of thy holy Prophets and Apostles has plainly pronounced, that thou desirest not the death of a sinner, but rather that he may convert and live; who also has sent thy only Son to suffer the cruel death of the cross, not for the just, but for such as find themselves oppressed with the burden of sin, that by Him and His advocacy they may have access to the throne of thy grace, being assured that before thee they shall find favor and mercy: We are convened, O Lord, in thy presence, and that in the Name of this same our Lord Jesus thy dear Son, to accuse before thee our sins, and before the feet of thy Majesty to crave mercy for the same. We most humbly beseech thee, O Father of Mercies, first that thou wilt touch and move our hearts by the power of thy Holy Spirit, in such sort that we may come to a true knowledge of our sins; but chiefly, O Lord, it will please thee to move the heart of this our brother N., etc., who as he has offended thy Majesty and a great number of this thy holy congregation, by his grievous and public sin, so does he not refuse publicly to acknowledge and confess the same, as . . . this his humiliation given to the glory of thy Name presently does witness. But because, O Lord, the external confession, without the dolor of the heart, avails nothing in thy presence, we most humbly beseech thee, that thou wilt so effectually move his heart, and ours also, that he and we without hypocrisy, damning that which thy law pronounces unjust, may attain to some sense and feeling of thy mercy, which thou hast abundantly shown unto mankind in Jesus Christ our Lord.

Grant, O Lord, unto this our brother, the repentance of the heart and sincere confession of the mouth, to the praise of thy Name, to the comfort of thy Church, and to the confusion of Satan. And unto us grant, O Lord, that albeit we cannot live altogether clean of our sin, yet that we fall not in horrible crimes to the dishonor of thy holy Name, to the slander of our brethren, and infamy of thy holy Evangel, which we profess. Let thy godly power, O Lord, so strengthen our weakness that neither the craft of Satan nor the tyranny of sin draw us utterly from thy obedience. Give us grace, O Lord, that by holiness and innocency of life we may declare to this wicked generation what difference there is between the sons of light and the sons of darkness; that men seeing our good works may glorify thee and thy Son Jesus Christ, our only Saviour and Redeemer, to whom with Thee and the Holy Spirit be all honor, praise and glory, now and ever. Amen.

*The Prayer finished, the Minister shall turn . . . to the Penitent brother, and in full audience shall say:—*

You have heard, brother, what is your duty towards the Church which you have offended, to wit, that willingly you confess that crime that you have committed, asking God mercy for the same, so that you may reconcile yourself to the Church which you have offended. You have heard also the affection and care of the Church towards you their penitent brother, notwithstanding your grievous fall, to wit, that we all here present join our sins with your sin; we all repute and esteem your fall to be our own; we accuse ourselves no less than we accuse you. Now, finally, we join our prayers with yours that we and you may obtain mercy and that by the means of our Lord Jesus Christ. Let us, therefore, brother, have this comfort of you, that you will openly and simply confess your crime, and give to us attestation of your unfeigned repentance.

*The Penitent shall then openly confess the crime, whatsoever it be, and shall desire God's mercy, and pray the Church to call to God for*

*mercy with him, and unfeignedly desire that he may be joined again
to their society and number.*

*If the Penitent be confounded with shame, or such a one as cannot
distinctly speak to the comfort and instruction of the Church, the Minister shall make repetition, that every head may be understood by itself,
and thereafter shall ask the Penitent if that be his confession, and if so
he believes. His answer affirmative being received, the Minister shall ask
the congregation if they judge any further to be required for their satisfaction and reconciliation of that brother. No contradiction being made,
the Minister shall say to the Penitent:—*

We have heard, dear brother, your confession, for . . . which we
from our hearts praise God; for in it the Spirit of Jesus Christ has confounded the Devil, and broken down his head and power, in that . . .
you, to the glory of God, have openly damned yourself and your impiety, imploring grace and mercy for Christ Jesus His Son's sake. This
strength, submission and obedience cannot proceed from flesh and blood,
but is the singular gift of the Holy Ghost: acknowledge therefore it
to be given unto you by Jesus Christ our Lord; and now take heed lest at
any time you be unmindful of this great benefit, which no doubt Satan
does envy and will assail by all means possible that you may abuse it. He
will not cease to tempt you to fall again in such, or crimes more horrible; but resist the devil and he shall flee from you. Live in sobriety,
be instant in prayer, commend yourself unfeignedly to God, who
as He is faithful so shall He give to us victory over sin, death and Satan,
and that by means of our Head and sovereign champion Jesus Christ,
to whom be all praise, glory and honor, now and ever. Amen.

### An Admonition to the Church

It is your duty, Brethren, to take example of this our penitent
brother: first, that you be unfeignedly displeased in your own hearts
for your sins; second, that with this our brother you . . . [disclose] them
in the sight of God, imploring grace and mercy for your offenses committed; and last, if any of you shall after this publicly offend, that you
refuse not with the like reverence to satisfy the Church of God, offended
in you. Now only rests, that you remit and forget all offenses which you
have conceived heretofore by the sin and fall of this our brother; accept and embrace him as a member of Christ's body; let none take upon
him[self] to reproach or accuse him for any offenses that before this
hour he has committed. And that he may have the better assurance of
your good will and reconciliation, prostrate yourselves before God and
render Him thanks for the conversion and repentance of this our brother.

## The Thanksgiving

Heavenly Father, Fountain of all mercy and consolation, we confess ourselves unworthy to be counted amongst thy children, if thou have respect to the corruption of our nature; but seeing it has pleased thy Fatherly goodness not only freely to choose us in thy dear Son our Lord Jesus Christ, by His death to redeem us, by His Evangel to call us, and by His Holy Spirit (which both are thine) to illuminate us; but also that thou hast committed thy Word and holy Evangel to be preached, to the end that the penitent shall have an assurance of the remission of their sins, not only for a time but even as oft as men from sorrowful hearts shall call for thy grace and mercy. In consideration of this thy Fatherly adoption and ineffable clemency shown upon us, we cannot but praise and magnify thy Fatherly mercy, a testimony whereof we not only feel in ourselves but also see the same evidently in the conversion of this our brother, whom Satan for a time held in bondage, but now is set at freedom by the power of our Lord Jesus Christ, and is returned again to the society of His body. Grant unto us, heavenly Father, that he and we may more and more be displeased for our sins, and proceed in all manner of good works to the praise of thy holy Name and edification of thy Church, by Jesus Christ our Lord and only Saviour. So be it.

*The Thanksgiving being finished, the Minister shall ask the Penitent if he will be subject to the Discipline of the Church in case . . . he after[wards] offend: Who answering that he will, the Minister shall say, in manner of Absolution:—*

If thou unfeignedly repent thy former iniquity and believe in the Lord Jesus, then I, in His Name, pronounce and affirm that thy sins are forgiven not only on earth but also in heaven, according to the promises annexed with the preaching of His Word and to the power put in the Ministry of His Church.

*Then shall the Elders and Deacons, with Ministers (if any be), in the name of the whole Church take the reconciled brother by the hand and embrace him in sign of full reconciliation.*

*Then after [that] shall the Church sing the CIII Psalm, so much as they think expedient; and so shall the Assembly, with the benediction, be dismissed.*

John Knox, *The Liturgy of John Knox Received by the Church of Scotland in 1564* (Glasgow: Printed at the University Press, 1886), pp. 46–60 (spelling and punctuation modernized).

# Exhibit Sixteen

## MAKING THE MOST
## OF SICKNESS
### JEREMY TAYLOR

### Introduction

English literature of Christian devotion flowered during the stormiest decades of English religious strife,
the middle years of the seventeenth century. The era
that produced John Bunyan's books and John Milton's poems was the time that evoked Jeremy Taylor's
(1613–1667) memorable pastoral treatises on spiritual
growth through a holy approach to the vicissitudes of
living, being ill, and dying.

Taylor, Church of England clergyman, teacher,
preacher, and eventually bishop, had been promoted
to an Oxford fellowship by Archbishop William Laud
(1573–1645) and soon became chaplain to the ill-
fated King Charles I. After brief service in the royalist
army during the civil war, and after his monarch had
been murdered, Taylor withdrew to Wales, where he
spent the years of England's interregnum under
Oliver Cromwell. From this retirement Taylor wrote
in 1650 *The Rule and Exercise of Holy Living* and,
in the following year, the companion volume, *The
Rule and Exercise of Holy Dying*, the two works for
which he is most widely known. In these, as in more
scholarly and polemical works, Taylor furnished
guides to Christian action amidst the natural crises
of human existence. The source and authority for this

guidance Taylor found in the traditional church, whose experience through the ages made it a depository of pastoral and moral wisdom. By codifying the ways in which past Christians had lived and died holy, he sought to convey to his troubled times prescriptions by which to wrest opportunities for spiritual advancement from the temptations of living and dying.

*Holy Dying* was written as a ministry to Church of England folk who found themselves during the interregnum bereft of priestly counsel, but the work quickly became a classic for less exigent days. Unlike the late medieval *Ars moriendi* literature, the book was meant to be used chiefly by persons in full health in order to prepare themselves for the inevitabilities of sickness and death. Taylor sketched out some general principles regarding illness, but also gave quite detailed advices for comporting oneself in the face of particular aspects of ill health.

Taylor was confident that sickness was sent by God for the edification and growth of the sufferer; the God who did nothing in vain meant illness to be a school of faith and virtue. Specific burdens and pains of disease taught their special lessons. The sick man's helplessness inculcated humility of spirit. As the illness ran its own course, the sufferer learned patience by having to await those who nursed him and by being unable to hurry his own recovery. Most important of all, illness revealed the precariousness of life and taught faith: the threat of the end of life reminded one that life was God's gracious gift. Thus, the Christian during illness, like an attentive pupil before his teacher, learned much about himself and about the human predicament.

In the following selections from this long work, Taylor gives helps and hints how the sufferer can take advantage of his spiritual opportunities. He is told how to enter illness quietly and in a spirit ready to listen. He must refrain from making any important decisions before he hears the message of his own sickness. He is advised how to regard those who care for him, and how to wait patiently for death if dying seems probable. Enough of Taylor's writing is provided to indicate that it is perhaps the most detailed Christian philosophy of illness yet to appear in the English language.

# MAKING THE MOST
# OF SICKNESS

From: *The Rule and Exercise of Holy Dying* (1651),
by Jeremy Taylor.

## OF THE PRACTICE OF THE GRACES PROPER TO THE STATE OF SICKNESS, WHICH A SICK MAN MAY PRACTISE ALONE.

*Of the Practice of Patience.*

Now we suppose the man entering upon his scene of sorrows and passive graces. It may be, he went yesterday to a wedding, merry and brisk, and there he felt his sentence, that he must return home and die (for men very commonly enter into the snare singing, and consider not whither their fate leads them): nor feared, that then the angel was to strike his stroke till his knees kissed the earth, and his head trembled with the weight of the rod which God put into the hand of an exterminating angel. But whatsoever the ingress was, when the man feels his blood boil, or his bones weary, or his flesh diseased with a load of a dispersed and disordered humour, or his head to ache, or his faculties discomposed, then he must consider, that all those discourses he hath heard concerning patience and resignation, and conformity to Christ's sufferings, and the melancholy lectures of the cross, must, all of them, now be reduced to practice, and pass from an ineffective contemplation to such an exercise as will really try whether we were true disciples of the cross, or only believe the doctrines of religion, when we were at ease, and that they never passed through the ear to the heart, and dwelt not in our spirits. But every man should consider God does nothing in vain; that he would not to no purpose, send us preachers, and give us rules, and furnish us with discourse, and lend us books, and provide sermons, and make examples, and promise his Spirit, and describe the blessedness of holy sufferings, and prepare us with daily alarms, if he did not really purpose to order our affairs so that we should need all this, and use it all. There were no such thing as the grace of patience, if we were not to feel a sickness, or enter into a state of sufferings: whither, when we are entered, we are to practise by the following rules.

*The Practice and Acts of Patience, by way of Rule.*

At the first address and presence of sickness, stand still and arrest thy spirit, that it may, without amazement or affright, consider, that this was that thou lookedst for, and wert always certain should happen:

and that now thou art to enter into the actions of a new religion, the agony of a strange constitution; but at no hand suffer thy spirits to be dispersed with fear, or wildness of thought, but stay their looseness and dispersion by a serious consideration of the present and future employment. For so doth the Libyan lion, spying the fierce huntsman, first beats himself with the strokes of his tail, and curls up his spirits, making them strong with union and recollection, till, being struck with a Mauritanian spear, he rushes forth into his defence and noblest contention; and either escapes into the secrets of his own dwelling, or else dies the bravest of the forest. Every man, when shot with an arrow from God's quiver, must then draw in all the auxiliaries of reason, and know, that then is the time to try his strength, and to reduce the words of his religion into action, and consider, that if he behaves himself weakly and timorously, he suffers nevertheless of sickness; but if he returns to health, he carries along with him the mark of a coward and a fool; and if he descends into his grave, he enters into the state of the faithless and unbelievers. Let him set his heart firm upon this resolution; "I must bear it inevitably, and I will, by God's grace, do it nobly."

Bear in thy sickness all along the same thoughts, propositions, and discourses, concerning thy person, thy life and death, thy soul and religion, which thou hadst in the best days of thy health: and when thou didst discourse wisely concerning things spiritual. For it is to be supposed (and if it be not yet done, let this rule remind thee of it, and direct thee) that thou hast cast about in thy health and considered concerning thy change and the evil day, that thou must be sick and die, that thou must need a comforter, and that it was certain, thou shouldst fall into a state in which all the cords of thy anchor should be stretched, and the very rock and foundation of faith should be attempted; and whatsoever fancies may disturb you, or whatsoever weaknesses may invade you, yet consider, when you were better able to judge and govern the accidents of your life, you concluded it necessary to trust in God, and possess your souls with patience. Think of things as they think that stand by you, and as you did, when you stood by others; that it is a blessed thing to be patient; that a quietness of spirit hath a certain reward: that still there is infinite truth and reality in the promises of the Gospel; that still thou art in the care of God, in the condition of a son, and working out thy salvation with labour and pain, with fear and trembling; that now the sun is under a cloud, but it still sends forth the same influence: and be sure to make no new principles, upon the stock of a quick and an impatient sense, or too busy an apprehension: keep your old principles, and upon their stock, discourse and practise on towards your conclusion.

Resolve to bear your sickness like a child, that is, without considering the evils and the pains, the sorrows and the danger; but go straight forward, and let thy thoughts cast about for nothing, but how to make advantages of it by the instrument of religion. He that from a high tower looks down upon the precipice, and measures the space through which he must descend, and considers what a huge fall he shall have, shall feel more by the horror of it than by the last dash on the pavement: and he that tells his groans and numbers his sighs, and reckons one for every gripe of his belly or throb of his distempered pulse, will make an artificial sickness greater than the natural. And if thou beest ashamed that a child should bear an evil better than thou, then take his instrument, and allay thy spirit with it; reflect not upon thy evil, but contrive as much as you can for duty, and, in all the rest, inconsideration will ease your pain.

If thou fearest thou shalt need, observe and draw together all such things as are apt to charm thy spirit, and ease thy fancy in the sufferance. It is the counsel of Socrates: "It is (said he) a great danger, and you must, by discourse and arts of reasoning, enchant it into slumber and some rest." It may be, thou wert moved much to see a person of honour to die untimely; or thou didst love the religion of that death-bed, and it was dressed up in circumstances fitted to thy needs, and hit thee on that part where thou wert most sensible; or some little saying in a sermon or passage of a book was chosen and singled out by a peculiar apprehension, and made consent to lodge awhile in thy spirit, even then, when thou didst place death in thy meditation, and didst view it in all its dress of fancy. Whatsoever that was, which at any time did please thee in thy most passionate and fantastic part, let not that go, but bring it home at that time especially: because when thou art in thy weakness, such little things will easier move thee than a more severe discourse and a better reason. For a sick man is like a scrupulous: his case is gone beyond the cure of arguments, and it is a trouble that can only be helped by chance, or a lucky saying: and Ludovico Corbinelli was moved at the death of Henry the Second, more than if he had read the saddest elegy of all the unfortunate princes in Christendom, or all the sad sayings of Scripture, or the threnes [*i.e.*, dirges] of the funeral prophets. I deny not but this course is most proper to weak persons; but it is a state of weakness, for which we are now providing remedies and instruction: a strong man will not need it; but when our sickness hath rendered us weak in all senses, it is not good to refuse a remedy, because it supposes us to be sick. But then, if to the catalogue of weak persons we add all those who are ruled by fancy, we shall find, that many persons in their health, and more in their sickness, are under the dominion of fancy, and apt to be helped by those little things which themselves have found fitted to their apprehension, and which no other man can minister to their needs, unless by chance, or in a heap of other things. But, therefore, every man should remember, by what instruments he was at any time much moved, and try them upon his spirit in the day of his calamity.

Do not choose the kind of thy sickness, or the manner of thy death;

but let it be what God please, so it be no greater than thy spirit or thy patience: and for that you are to rely upon the promise of God, and to secure thyself by prayer and industry; but in all things else let God be thy chooser, and let it be thy work to submit indifferently, and attend thy duty. It is lawful to beg of God, that thy sickness may not be sharp or noisome, infectious or unusual, because these are circumstances of evil, which are also proper instruments of temptation; and though it may well concern the prudence of thy religion to fear thyself, and keep thee from violent temptations, who hast so often fallen in little ones; yet even in these things, be sure to keep some degrees of indifference; that is, if God will not be entreated to ease thee, or to change thy trial, then be importunate, that thy spirit and its interest be secured, and let him do what seemeth good in his eyes. But as in the degrees of sickness, thou art to submit to God, so in the kind of it (supposing equal degrees) thou art to be altogether incurious, whether God call thee by a consumption or an asthma, by a dropsy or a palsy, by a fever in thy humours, or a fever in thy spirits; because all such nicety of choice is nothing but a colour to a legitimate impatience, and to make an excuse to murmur privately, and for circumstances, when in the sum of affairs we durst not own impatience. I have known some persons vehemently wish that they might die of a consumption, and some of these had a plot upon heaven, and hoped by that means to secure it after a careless life; as thinking a lingering sickness would certainly infer a lingering and a protracted repentance; and by that means, they thought they should be safest: others of them dreamed it would be an easier death; and have found themselves deceived, and their patience hath been tired with a weary spirit, and a useless body, by often conversing with healthful persons and vigorous neighbours, by uneasiness of the flesh and the sharpness of their bones, by want of spirits and a dying life; and, in conclusion, have been directly debauched by peevishness and a fretful sickness; and these men had better have left it to the wisdom and goodness of God; for they both are infinite.

Be patient in the desires of religion; and take care that the forwardness of exterior actions do not discompose thy spirit; while thou fearest, that by less serving God in thy disability, thou runnest backward in the accounts of pardon and the favour of God. Be content, that the time which was formerly spent in prayer, be now spent in vomiting, and carefulness, and attendances; since God hath pleased it should be so, it does not become us to think hard thoughts concerning it. Do not think, that God is only to be found in great prayer, or a solemn office: he is moved by a sigh, by a groan, by an act of love; and therefore, when your pain is great and pungent, lay all your strength upon it, to bear it patiently: when the evil is something more tolerable, let your mind think some pious, though short, meditation: let it not be very busy, and full of attention; for that will be but a new temptation to your patience, and render your religion tedious and hateful. But record your desires, and present yourself to God by general acts of will and understanding, and by habitual remembrances of your former vigorousness, and by verification of the same grace, rather than proper exercises. If you can do more, do it; but if you cannot, let it not become a scruple to thee. We must not think man is tied to the forms of health, or that he who swoons and faints is obliged to his usual forms and hours of prayer: if we cannot labour, yet let us love. Nothing can hinder us from that, but our own uncharitableness.

Be obedient to thy physician in those things that concern him, if he be a person fit to minister unto thee. God is he only that needs no help, and God hath created the physician for thine; therefore use him temperately, without violent confidences, and sweetly, without uncivil distrustings, or refusing his prescriptions upon humours or impotent fear. A man may refuse to have his arm or leg cut off, or to suffer the pains of Marius's incision: and if he believes that to die is the less evil, he may compose himself to it without hazarding his patience, or introducing that which he thinks a worse evil; but that which in this article is to be reproved and avoided, is, that some men will choose to die out of fear of death, and send for physicians, and do what themselves list, and call for counsel, and follow none. When there is reason they should decline him, it is not to be accounted to the stock of a sin; but where there is no just cause, there is a direct impatience.

Hither is to be reduced, that we be not too confident of the physician, or drain our hopes of recovery from the fountain through so imperfect channels; laying the wells of God dry, and digging to ourselves broken cisterns. Physicians are the ministers of God's mercies and providence, in the matter of health and ease, of restitution or death; and when God shall enable their judgments, and direct their counsels, and prosper their medicines, they shall do thee good, for which you must give God thanks, and to the physician the honour of a blessed instrument. But this cannot always be done: and Lucius Cornelius, the lieutenant in Portugal under Favius the consul, boasted in the inscription of his monument, that he had lived a healthful and vegete age till his last sickness, but then complained he was forsaken by his physician, and railed upon Æsculapius, for not accepting his vow and passionate desire of preserving his life longer; and all the effect of that impatience and folly was, that it is recorded to following ages, that he died without reason and without religion. But it was a sad sight to see the favour of all France confined to a physician and a barber, and the king (Louis XI.) to be so much their servant, that he should acknowledge and own his life from them, and all his ease to their gentle dressing of his gout and friendly ministries; for the king thought himself undone and robbed, if he should die: his portion here was fair; and he was loath to exchange his possession for the interest of a bigger hope.

Treat thy nurses and servants sweetly, and as it becomes an obliged and a necessitous person. Remember, that thou art very troublesome to them; that they trouble not thee willingly; that they strive to do thee ease and benefit, that they wish it, and sigh and pray for it, and are glad, if thou likest their attendance: that whatsoever is amiss, is thy disease, and the uneasiness of thy head or thy side, thy distemper or thy dis-affections; and it will be an unhandsome injustice to be troublesome to them, because thou art so to thyself; to make them feel a part of thy sorrows, that thou mayest not bear them alone; evilly to requite their care by thy too curious and impatient wrangling and fretful spirit. That tenderness is vicious and unnatural, that shrieks out under the weight of a gentle cataplasm [*i.e.*, poultice]; and he will ill comply with God's rod that cannot endure his friend's greatest kindness; and he will be very angry (if he durst) with God's smiting him, that is peevish with his servants that go about to ease him.

Let not the smart of your sickness make you to call violently for death: you are not patient, unless you be content to live; God hath wisely ordered that we may be the better reconciled with death, because it is the period of many calamities; but wherever the general hath placed thee, stir not from thy station, until thou beest called off, but abide so, that death may come to thee by the design of him who intends it to be thy advantage. God hath made sufferance to be thy work; and do not impatiently long for evening, lest, at night, thou findest the reward of him that was weary of his work: for he that is weary before his time is an unprofitable servant, and is either idle or diseased.

That which remains in the practice of this grace, is, that the sick man should do acts of patience by way of prayer and ejaculations: in which he may serve himself of the following collection.

\*     \*     \*     \*     \*

### The Prayer to be said in the beginning of a Sickness.

O Almighty God, merciful and gracious, who, in thy justice, didst send sorrow and tears, sickness and death, into the world, as a punish-ment for man's sins, and hast comprehended all under sin, and this sad covenant of sufferings, not to destroy us, but that thou mightest have mercy upon all, making thy justice to minister to mercy, short afflictions to an eternal weight of glory; as thou hast turned my sins into sickness, so turn my sickness to the advantages of holiness and religion, of mercy and pardon, of faith and hope, of grace and glory. Thou hast now called me to the fellowship of sufferings: Lord, by the instrument of religion let my present condition be so sanctified, that my sufferings may be united to the sufferings of my Lord, that so thou mayest pity and assist me. Relieve my sorrow, and support my spirit: direct my thoughts, and sanctify the accidents of my sickness, and that the punishment of my sin may be the school of virtue: in which, since thou hast now entered me, Lord, make me a holy proficient; that I may behave myself as a son under discipline, humbly and obediently, evenly and penitently, that I may come by this means nearer unto thee; that if I shall go forth of this sickness by the gate of life and health, I may return to the world with great strengths of spirit, to run a new race of a stricter holiness and a more severe religion: or if I pass from hence with the outlet of death, I may enter into the bosom of my Lord, and may feel the present joys of a certain hope of that sea of pleasures, in which all thy saints and servants shall be comprehended to eternal ages. Grant this for Jesus Christ's sake, our dearest Lord and Saviour. Amen.

*   *   *   *   *

## A Prayer to be said when the Sick Man takes Physic.

O most blessed and eternal Jesus, thou, who art the great physician of our souls, and the Sun of Righteousness arising with healing in thy wings, to thee is given by thy heavenly Father the government of all the world, and thou disposest every great and little accident to thy Father's honour, and to the good and comfort of them that love and serve thee: be pleased to bless the ministry of thy servant in order to my ease and health, direct his judgment, prosper the medicines, and dispose the chances of my sickness fortunately, that I may feel the blessing and loving-kindness of the Lord in the ease of my pain and the restitution of my health: that I, being restored to the society of the living, and to thy solemn assemblies, may praise thee and thy goodness, secretly among the faithful, and in the congregation of thy redeemed ones, here in the outer-courts of the Lord, and hereafter in thy eternal temple for ever and ever. Amen.

*   *   *   *   *

## ADVANTAGES OF SICKNESS

But for the sickness itself; if all the calumnies were true concerning it with which it is aspersed, yet it is far to be preferred before the most pleasant sin, and before a great secular business and a temporal care: and some men wake as much in the foldings of the softest beds as others on the cross: and sometimes the very weight of sorrow and the weariness of a sickness press the spirit into slumbers and the images of rest, when the intemperate or the lustful person rolls upon his uneasy thorns, and sleep is departed from his eyes. Certain it is some sickness is a blessing. Indeed, blindness were a most accursed thing, if no man were ever blind but he whose eyes were pulled out with tortures or burning basins: and if sickness were always a testimony of God's anger, and a violence to a man's whole condition, then it were a huge calamity: but because God sends it to his servants, to his children, to little infants, to apostles and saints, with designs of mercy, to preserve their innocence, to overcome temptation, to try their virtue, to fit them for rewards; it is certain that sickness never is an evil but by our own faults; and if we will do our duty, we shall be sure to turn it into a blessing. If the sickness be great, it may end in death; and the greater it is the sooner: and if it be very little, it hath great intervals of rest: if it be between both, we may be masters of it, and, by serving the ends of Providence, serve also the perfective end of human nature, and enter into the possession of everlasting mercies.

The sum is this: He that is afraid of pain is afraid of his own nature; and if his fear be violent, it is a sign his patience is none at all; and an impatient person is not ready-dressed for heaven. None but suffering, humble, and patient persons can go to heaven; and when God hath given us the whole stage of our life to exercise all the active virtues of religion, it is necessary in the state of virtues, that some portion and period of our lives be assigned to passive graces; for patience, for Christian fortitude, for resignation, or conformity to the Divine will. But as the violent fear of sickness makes us impatient, so it will make our death without comfort and without religion; and we shall go off from our stage of actions and sufferings with an unhandsome exit, because we were willing to receive the kindness of God, when he expressed it as we listed; but we would not suffer him to be kind and gracious to us in his own method, nor were willing to exercise and improve our virtues at the charge of a sharp fever, or a lingering consumption. "Wo be to the man that hath lost patience; for what will he do when the Lord shall visit him?"

---

Jeremy Taylor, *The Rule and Exercise of Holy Dying,* from *The Whole Works of the Right Rev. Jeremy Taylor, D.D.* . . . , ed. Reginald Heber (Third Edition of the Collected Works, 15 vols., London: printed for Longman, Orme, Brown, Green, and Longmans, etc., 1839), IV, 445–452, 456–457, 422–423.

# Exhibit Seventeen

## THE SHIELD
## OF SCRIPTURE
### JOHN BUNYAN

### Introduction

The author of the most influential modern Protestant manual of personal piety was neither theologian nor scholar but a man educated almost wholly
by his own religious experience and by the King
James Bible—John Bunyan. Born near Bedford, England, in 1628, the son of a mender of pots and kettles,
Bunyan became a boisterous and gay young fellow
reputed for his proficiency at swearing before he met
and married a devout young woman whose books on
religion he read with interest and alarm. Having
fought for the parliamentary cause in the English
civil war, Bunyan's marriage in 1648 led swiftly to
a personal reform that made him outwardly an upright and religious man.

When it dawned upon him that this reform
rooted in no deep inner conviction, Bunyan found
himself thrust upon a lifelong, soul-shaking spiritual
battle against the devil, a battle in which his best
weapon was always the Bible. His own struggle Bunyan poignantly narrated in the book *Grace Abounding to the Chief of Sinners* (1666). The same spiritual warfare he generalized as the plight of everyman
—"Christian"—in the classic writing *The Pilgrim's
Progress* (published 1678), a work that has appeared

in innumerable English editions and has been translated into more than 100 languages.

Bunyan's own pilgrimage led to inner peace during the interregnum, but outward enemies arose again at the restoration of Charles II, when Bunyan was arrested for his illegal activities as a Nonconformist minister and lodged in the county jail at Bedford for a dozen years. Here he found scope for a ministry amongst fellow prisoners that would have been illegal outside; here he studied the Bible and John Foxe's stories of England's evangelical martyrs; here he wrote many of his 59 literary works.

Pardoned in 1672 and licensed as a preacher, Bunyan yet refused to conform to the established church. His long imprisonment added to the depth and the impact of his preaching until he died in 1688—shortly before the Glorious Revolution that secured the religious toleration for which he had valiantly stood throughout his career.

A life filled with various oppressions gave Bunyan profound insight into spiritual trouble, and especially into the malady of obsession by demons. Before accumulating its modern psychological connotations, "obsession" had long been distinguished in the Christian pastoral tradition from "possession," in which demons were thought to have gained entrance into and to have occupied a man. In obsession (Latin: *ob-sedere*, to sit outside) the demon remained outside the afflicted person and laid siege to his spirit. In noting the power of and remedies against obsessive demons, Bunyan renewed a tradition of pastoral care whose *locus classicus* in the New Testament was the temptation of Jesus in the wilderness (Mark 1:12–13; Matthew 4:1–11; Luke 4:1–13), as in the early church it was the story of the temptation of St. Antony (251?–356) in the Egyptian desert.

In the following passage from *Grace Abounding*, Bunyan recounts his own perilous obsession by Satan, as in the later and more famous book he showed how Satan exteriorly attacks every Christian. The devil assailed Bunyan with the thought that perhaps he was not one of the saved, and Satan's most devastating attack put doubts into his mind as to the validity of the Scriptures. These attacks came in definite waves, punctuated by short periods of relative calm before the action mounted again to dramatic intensity. Bunyan's own personal resources he summoned in vain to ward off the onslaughts, but occasionally God, the ardent spectator, broke into the struggle with succor. For Bunyan the shield that most effectively warded off Satan's thrusts was Scripture, whose verses came to mind as God's helping action.

Bunyan's depiction of Scripture as the effective shield

against obsession furnished protestantism with yet another reason for the necessity of each believer's possession and knowledge
of the Bible, and made this book an inexhaustible mine from
which pastors might mint weapons for spiritual battle.


# THE SHIELD
# OF SCRIPTURE

From: *Grace Abounding to the Chief of Sinners* (1666),
by John Bunyan.

Wherefore while I was thus considering, and being put to a plunge
about it, (for you must know, that as yet I had not in this matter broken
my mind to any one, only did hear and consider,) the tempter came in
with this delusion, "that there was no way for me to know I had faith,
but by trying to work some miracle["]; urging those Scriptures that seem
to look that way, for the enforcing and strengthening his temptation.
Nay, one day, as I was between Elstow and Bedford, the temptation
was hot upon me, to try if I had faith, by doing some miracle; which
miracle at this time was this, I must say to the puddles that were in the
horsepads, be dry; and to the dry places, be you puddles: and truly one
time I was going to say so indeed; but just as I was about to speak, this
thought came into my mind; "but go under yonder hedge and pray first,
that God will make you able." But when I had concluded to pray, this
came hot upon me; that if I prayed, and came again, and tried to do it,
and yet did nothing notwithstanding, then to be sure I had no faith, but
was a castaway, and lost, nay thought I, if it be so, I will not try yet, but
will stay a little longer.

So I continued at a great loss; for I thought, if they only had faith,
which could do so wonderful things, then I concluded, that for the
present I neither had it, nor yet for the time to come, were ever like to
have it. Thus I was tossed betwixt the devil and mine own ignorance,
and so perplexed, especially at some times, that I could not tell what
to do.

About this time, the state and happiness of those poor people at
Bedford was thus, in a kind of a vision, presented to me. I saw as if they
were on the sunny side of some high mountain, there refreshing themselves with the pleasant beams of the sun, while I was shivering and
shrinking in the cold, afflicted with frost, snow, and dark clouds: methought also, betwixt me and them, I saw a wall that did compass about
this mountain, now through this wall, my soul did greatly desire to pass;
concluding, that if I could, I would even go into the very midst of them,
and there also comfort myself with the heat of their sun.

About this wall I bethought myself, to go again and again, still praying as I went, to see if I could find some way or passage, by which I might enter therein; but none could I find for some time; at the last, I saw, as it were, a narrow gap, like a little door-way in the wall, .hrough which I attempted to pass: now the passage being very straight and narrow, I made many offers to get in, but all in vain, even until I was well nigh quite beat out, by striving to get in; at last, with great striving, methought I at first did get in my head, and after that, by a sideling striving, my shoulders, and my whole body: then I was exceeding glad, went and sat down in the midst of them, and so was comforted with the light and heat of their sun.

Now this mountain, and wall, &c., was thus made out to me: the mountain signified the church of the living God; the sun that shone thereon, the comfortable shining of his merciful face on them that were therein; the wall I thought was the world, that did make separation between the Christians and the world; and the gap which was in the wall, I thought, was Jesus Christ, who is the way to God the Father. (John xiv. 6. Matt. vii. 14.) But forasmuch as the passage was wonderfully narrow, even so narrow, that I could not, but with great difficulty enter in thereat, it showed me, that none could enter into life, but those that were in downright earnest, and unless also they left that wicked world behind them; for here was only room for body and soul, but not for body and soul, and sin.

This resemblance abode upon my spirit many days: all which time I saw myself in a forlorn and sad condition, but yet was provoked to a vehement hunger and desire to be one of that number that did sit in the sunshine: now also would I pray wherever I was; whether at home or abroad; in house or field; and would also often, with lifting up of heart sing that of the fifty-first Psalm, "O Lord, consider my distress," for as yet I knew not where I was.

Neither as yet could I attain to any comfortable persuasion that I had faith in Christ; but instead of having satisfaction here I began to find my soul to be assaulted with fresh doubts about my future happiness; especially with such as these, "whether I was elected; but how if the day of grace should be past and gone?"

By these two temptations I was very much afflicted and disquieted; sometimes by one and sometimes by the other of them. And first, to speak of that about my questioning my election, I found at this time, that though I was in a flame to find the way to heaven and glory, and thought nothing could beat me off from this, yet this question did so offend and discourage me, that I was, especially sometimes, as if the very strength of my body also had been taken away by the force and power thereof. This Scripture did also seem to me to trample upon all my desires: "it is neither in him that willeth, nor in him that runneth; but in God that showeth mercy."

With this Scripture I could not tell what to do; for I evidently saw, unless that the great God, of his infinite grace and bounty, had voluntarily chosen me to be a vessel of mercy, though I should desire, and long, and labour until my heart did break, no good could come of it. Therefore this would stick with me, "How can you tell that you are elected? And what if you should not? How then?"

O Lord, thought I, what if I should not indeed? It may be you are not, said the tempter; it may be so indeed, thought I. Why then, said Satan, you had as good leave off, and strive no farther; for if indeed, you should not be elected and chosen of God, there is no hope of your being saved: "For it is neither in him that willeth, nor in him that runneth; but in God that showeth mercy."

\*     \*     \*     \*     \*

For, about the space of a month after, a very great storm came down upon me, which handled me twenty times worse than all I had met with before; it came stealing upon me, now by one piece, then by another; first, all my comfort was taken from me; then darkness seized upon me; after which, whole floods of blasphemies, both against God, Christ, and the Scriptures were poured upon my spirit, to my great confusion and astonishment. These blasphemous thoughts were such as stirred up questions in me against the very being of God, and of his only beloved Son; as whether there were in truth a God, or Christ? and whether the holy Scriptures were not rather a fable and cunning story, than the holy and pure word of God.

The tempter would also much assault me with this, "How can you tell but that the Turks had as good Scriptures to prove their Mahomet the Saviour as we have to prove our Jesus? And, could I think, that so many ten thousands in so many countries and kingdoms, should be without the knowledge of the right way to heaven, (if there were indeed a heaven,) and that we only, who live in a corner of the earth, should alone be blessed therewith? Every one doth think his own religion rightest, both Jews and Moors, and Pagans; and how if all our faith, and Christ, and Scriptures, should be but a think so too?"

Sometimes I have endeavoured to argue against these suggestions, and to set some of the sentences of blessed Paul against them; but alas! I quickly felt, when I thus did, such arguings as these would return again upon me, "Though we made so great a matter of Paul and of his words, yet how could I tell, that in very deed, he being a subtle and cunning man, may give himself up to deceive with strong delusions; and also take the pains and travel, to undo and destroy his fellows."

These suggestions (with many other which at this time I may not nor dare not utter, neither by word or pen) did make such a seizure upon my spirit, and did so overweigh my heart, both with their number, continuance, and fiery force, that I felt as if there were nothing else but these from morning to night within me; and as though indeed there could be room for nothing else: and also concluded, that God had, in very wrath to my soul, given me up to them, to be carried away with them, as with a mighty whirlwind.

Only by the distaste that they gave unto my spirit, I felt there was something in me that refused to embrace me. But this consideration I then only had, when God gave me leave to swallow my spittle; otherwise the noise, and strength, and force of these temptations would drown and overflow, and as it were, bury all such thoughts, or the remembrance of any such thing. While I was in this temptation, I found my mind suddenly put upon it to curse and swear, or to speak some grievous thing against God, or Christ his Son, and of the Scriptures.

Now I thought, surely I am possessed of the devil; at other times, again I thought I should be bereft of my wits; for instead of lauding and magnifying God the Lord, with others, if I have heard him spoken of, presently some most horrible blasphemous thought or other would bolt out of my heart against him; so that whether I did think that God was, or again did think there was no such thing, no love, nor peace, nor gracious disposition could I feel within me.

These things did sink me into very great despair; for I concluded that such things could not possibly be found amongst them that loved God. I often, when these temptations had been with force upon me, did compare myself to the case of such a child, whom some gipsy hath by force took up in her arms, and is carrying from friend and country; kick sometimes I did, and also shriek and cry; but yet I was bound in the wings of temptation, and the wind would carry me away. I thought also of Saul, and of the evil spirit that did possess him; and did greatly fear that my condition was the same with that of his.

In those days, when I have heard others talk of what was the sin against the Holy Ghost, then would the tempter so provoke me to desire to sin that sin, that I was as if I could not, must not, neither should be quiet until I had committed it; now no sin would serve but that: if it were to be committed by speaking of such a word, then I have been as if my mouth would have spoken that word, whether I would or no; and in so strong a measure was this temptation upon me, that often I have been ready to clap my hands under my chin, to hold my mouth from opening; and to that end also I have had thoughts at other times, to leap with my head downward, into some muck hole or other, to keep my mouth from speaking.

Now again I beheld the condition of the dog and toad, and counted the estate of everything that God had made, far better than this dreadful state of mine, and such as my companions was. Yea, gladly would I have been in the condition of a dog or horse; for I knew they had no souls to perish under the everlasting weight of hell, or sin, as mine was like to do. Nay, and though I saw this, felt this, and was broken to pieces with it, yet that which added to my sorrow was that I could not find, that with all my soul I did desire, deliverance. That Scripture did also tear and rend my soul in the midst of these distractions, "The wicked are like the troubled sea, which cannot rest, whose waters cast up mire and dirt. There is no peace to the wicked, saith my God."

And now my heart was, at times, exceeding hard; if I would have given a thousand pounds for a tear, I could not shed one; no nor sometimes scarce desire to shed one. I was much dejected, to think that this would be my lot. I saw some could mourn and lament their sin, and others again, could rejoice and bless God for Christ; and others again, could quietly talk of, and with gladness remember the word of God, while I only was in a storm or tempest. This much sunk me. I thought my condition was alone, I should therefore much bewail my hard hap, but get out of, or get rid of these things, I could not.

While this temptation lasted, which was about a year, I could attend upon none of the ordinances of God, but with sore and great affliction. Yea, then was I most distressed with blasphemies; if I had been hearing the word, then uncleanness, blasphemies and despair would hold me a captive there; if I have been reading, then sometimes I had sudden thoughts to question all I read; sometimes again, my mind would be so strangely snatched away, and possessed with other things, that I have neither known, nor regarded, nor remembered so much as the sentence that but now I have heard.

In prayer also I have been greatly troubled at this time; sometimes I have thought I have felt him behind me, pull my clothes; he would be also continually at me in time of prayer, to have done, break off, make haste, you have prayed enough, and stay no longer; still drawing my mind away. Sometimes also he would cast in such wicked thoughts as these, that I must pray to him, or for him; I have thought sometimes of that, "Fall down; or, if thou wilt fall down and worship me."

Also, when because I have had wandering thoughts in the time of this duty, I have laboured to compose my mind, and fix it upon God; then with great force hath the tempter laboured to distract me, and confound me, and to turn away my mind, by presenting to my heart and fancy, the form of a bush, a bull, a besom, or the like, as if I should pray to these; to these he would also (at sometimes especially) so hold my mind, that I was as if I could think of nothing else, or pray to nothing else but to these, or such as they.

Yet at times I should have some strong and heart-affecting apprehensions of God, and reality of the truth of his Gospel; but, oh! how would my heart, at such times, put forth itself with inexpressible groanings. My whole soul was then in every word; I should cry with pangs after God, that he would be merciful unto me; but then I should be daunted again with such conceits as these; I should think that God did mock at these my prayers, saying, and that in the audience of the holy angels, "This poor simple wretch doth hanker after me, as if I had nothing to do with my mercy but to bestow it on such as he. Alas, poor soul, how art thou deceived! It is not for such as thee to have favour with the Highest."

Then hath the tempter come upon me also with such discouragements as these: "You are very hot after mercy, but I will cool you; this frame shall not last always; many have been as hot as you for a spirit, but I have quenched their zeal," (and with this, such and such who were fallen off would be set before mine eyes.) Then I would be afraid that I should do so too; but thought I, I am glad this comes into my mind; well, I will watch, and take what care I can. "Though you do, (said Satan,) I shall be too hard for you; I will cool you insensibly, by degrees, by little and little. What care I, (saith he,) though I be seven years in chilling your heart if I can do it at last? Continual rocking will lull a crying child asleep; I will ply it close, but I will have my end accomplished. Though you be burning hot at present, yet I can pull you from this fire; I shall have you cold before it be long."

These things brought me into great straits; for as I at present could not find myself fit for present death, so I thought, to live long, would make me yet more unfit; for time would make me forget all, and wear even the remembrance of the evil of sin, the worth of heaven, and the need I had of the blood of Christ to wash me, both out of mind and thought; but I thank Christ Jesus, these things did not at present make me slack my crying, but rather did put me more upon it, (like her who met with the adulterer, Deut. xxii. 26.) In which days that was a good word to me, after I had suffered these things a while: "I am persuaded that neither height, nor death, nor life, shall separate us from the love of God, which is in Christ Jesus." And now I hoped long life would not destroy me, nor make me miss of heaven.

Yet I had some supports in this temptation, though they were then all questioned by me. That in Jer. iii. at the first was something to me; and so was the consideration of verse 5 of that chapter; that though we have spoken and done all the evil things as we could, yet we should cry unto God, "My Father, thou art the guide of my youth;" and shall return unto him.

I had also once a sweet glance from that, "For he hath made him to be sin for us who knew no sin, that we might be made the righteousness of God in him." I remember that one day, as I was sitting in a neighbour's house, and there very sad at the consideration of my many blasphemies; and as I was saying in my mind, What ground have I to think that I, who have been so vile and abominable, should ever inherit eternal life? That word came suddenly upon me, "What shall we say to these things? If God be for us, who can be against us?" That also was an help unto me, "Because I live, ye shall live also." But these words were but hints, touches, and short visits, though very sweet when present; only they lasted not; but like to Peter's sheet, of a sudden were caught up from me to heaven again.

But afterwards the Lord did more fully and graciously discover himself unto me, and indeed did quite, not only deliver me from the guilt, that by these things was laid upon my conscience, but also from the very filth thereof; for the temptation was removed and I was put into my right mind again, as other Christians were.

I remember that one day, as I was travelling into the country, and musing on the wickedness and blasphemy of my heart, and considering the enmity that was in me to God, that Scripture came into my mind, "He hath made peace by the blood of his cross." By which I was made to see, both again, and again, that day, that God and my soul were friends by his blood; yea, I saw that the justice of God and my sinful soul could embrace and kiss each other through his blood. This was a good day to me; I hope I shall never forget it.

At another time, as I sat by the fire in my house, and musing on my wretchedness, the Lord made that also a precious word unto me, "Forasmuch then as children are partakers of flesh and blood, he also himself likewise took part of the same, that through death he might destroy him that had the power of death, that is, the devil; and deliver those who through the fear of death, were all their life subject to bondage." I thought that the glory of these words was then so weighty on me, that I was both once and twice ready to swoon as I sat; yet not with grief and trouble, but with solid joy and peace.

At this time also I sat under the ministry of holy Mr. Gifford, whose doctrine, by God's grace, was much for my stability. This man made it much his business to deliver the people of God from all those hard and unsound tests, that by nature we are prone to. He would bid us take special heed that we took not up any truth upon trust; as from this, or that, or any other man or men; but cry mightily to God, that he would convince us of the reality thereof, and set us down therein by his own Spirit in the holy word; for, said he, if you do otherwise, when temptation comes, if strongly upon you, you not having received them with evidence from heaven, will find you want that help and strength now to resist, that once you thought you had.

This was as seasonable to my soul as the former and latter rain in their season; for I had found, and that by sad experience, the truth of his words: (for I had felt "no man can say," especially when tempted by the devil, "that Jesus Christ is Lord, but by the Holy Ghost.") Wherefore I found my soul, through grace, very apt to drink in this doctrine, and to incline to pray to God, that in nothing that pertained to God's glory, and my own eternal happiness, he would suffer me to be without the confirmation thereof from heaven; for now I saw clearly, there was an exceeding difference betwixt the notion of the flesh and blood, and the revelation of God in heaven; also a great difference betwixt that faith that is feigned, and according to man's wisdom, and of that which comes by a man's being born thereto of God.

But, oh! now how was my soul led from truth to truth by God! Even from the birth and cradle of the Son of God, to his ascension, and second coming from heaven to judge the world.

Truly, I then found upon this account, the great God was very good unto me; for, to my remembrance, there was not any thing that I then cried unto God to make known, and reveal unto me, but he was pleased to do it for me; I mean, not one part of the gospel of the Lord Jesus, but I was orderly led into it; methought I saw with great evidence, from the four evangelists, the wonderful words of God, in giving Jesus Christ to save us, from his conception and birth, even to his second coming to judgment; methought I was as if I had seen him born, as if I had seen him grow up; as if I had seen him walk through the world, from the cradle to the cross; to which also, when he came, I saw how gently he gave himself to be hanged, and nailed on it for my sins and wicked doing. Also as I was musing on this his progress, that dropped on my spirit, "He was ordained for the slaughter."

When I have considered also the truth of his resurrection, and have remembered that word, "Touch me not, Mary," &c., I have seen as if he had leaped out of the grave's mouth, for joy that he had risen again, and had got the conquest over our dreadful foes. (John xx. 17.) I have also, in the spirit, seen him a man, on the right hand of God the Father for me; and have seen the manner of his coming from heaven, to judge the world with glory, and have been confirmed in these things by these Scriptures. (Acts i. 9, 10, and vii. 56, and x. 42. Heb. vii. 24, and viii. 3, 8. Rev. i. 18. 1 Thess. iv. 17, 18.)

---

John Bunyan, *Grace Abounding to the Chief of Sinners*, paragraphs 51–60, 96–120, from *The Complete Works of John Bunyan*, with an introduction by John P. Gulliver (Illustrated Edition, Philadelphia: Bradley, Garretson & Co., etc., 1872), pp. 35–36, 40–44.

# Exhibit Eighteen

## THE THERAPEUTICS
## OF REVIVAL RELIGION
### JOHN WALSH

### Introduction

Eighteenth-century pastoral literature abounds with stories of the conversion experiences of persons peculiarly moved by the fervent preaching of the Pietists on the Continent, the evangelicals in Britain, and the "Great Awakeners" in the American colonies. The *Journal* of John Wesley (1703–1791), which records the career of that charismatic man, is replete with stories of strange behavior that attended conversions under the preaching of the early Methodists. Into his diary for 1759 Wesley inserted several accounts of what he called "the work of God in and near Everton," a village in Bedfordshire. On 18 December 1758 Wesley himself had preached in Everton to great effect, and during the ensuing year several awakenings occurred there and in neighboring villages under the preaching of the Rev. John Berridge (1716–1793).

One of the most fascinating narratives of the Everton revival, though presented by Wesley as anonymous, is apparently from the pen of one John Walsh, a former deist who after conversion became a frequent correspondent of Wesley's. Walsh's account paid meticulous attention to various behavioral phenomena accompanying the religious experience of

conversion. As an observer of these phenomena, Walsh rivals
some of the writings of the great American preacher, philosopher, and psychologist of religion, Jonathan Edwards (1703–
1758).

Bodily symptoms of various sorts have attended Christian
religious experience, and especially conversion, in every age; St.
Paul went blind and Martin Luther fell down dumb. The particular interest of the eighteenth-century writings on conversion
experiences arises from the fact that such experiences were regarded as important opportunities for soul care. Somatic symptoms were analyzed as indicating various states of the soul, and
particular religious exercises, such as exhortation, prayer, and
especially hymn singing, were thought to aid in transforming
these frightening physical manifestations into valuable spiritual
episodes.

The seemingly strange expressions of piety depicted by John
Walsh's account of the Everton revivals were not, of course,
peculiar to Protestant evangelical religion, for every epoch of
Christian literature yields its stories of mystical experiences similar in form and content to those here described. Two centuries
before the episodes recounted by Walsh, St. Teresa of Avila
(1515–1582) described autobiographically the raptures of religion in words which, with a few changes in language, might have
told about an early Methodist meeting. During her agony over
deciding to enter a convent, she suffered from various pains and
a rash of fits which she recorded, in part, as follows:

And now the August festival of Our Lady came round: I had
been in torment ever since April, though the last three months were
the worst. . . . That night I had a fit, which left me unconscious
for nearly four days. During that time they gave me the Sacrament
of Unction, and from hour to hour, from moment to moment,
thought I was dying; they did nothing but repeat the Creed to
me. . . .[84]

On another occasion, when about to receive Communion,
Teresa tells that she felt herself about to be "enraptured" by
God so that she ordered other nuns to hold her on the ground
to prevent her bodily movements from indicating that she was
seized by God. Again, she described stupors that would weaken
her body or make it rigid, as God granted her visions or was

[84] From *The Complete Works of Saint Teresa of Jesus*, Volume I, Translated and edited by E. Allison Peers from the critical edition of P. Silverio
de Santa Teresa, C.D., Published by Sheed & Ward, Inc., New York (3
vols., 1957), I, 30–31. By permission.

about to speak with her. These dramatic or violent seizures made Teresa's pastors wonder whether she was experiencing God or Satan, as she herself confided.[85] John Walsh tells that a Mr. John Keeling doubted seriously whether similar behavior among the Methodists "was the work of God or of the devil. . . ."

In both the Protestant and Catholic instances of somatic manifestations of religious experience which we have cited, pastors sought to know whether the behavior was from God or Satan. In both cases it was thought that a danger to be avoided at all costs was isolation, with its temptation to self-diagnosis; only in the company of other Christian people might a person so seized expose himself to scrutiny and evaluation by which the source of his rapture might be identified. The following paragraphs indicate an emphatic interest in hymn singing, an important expression of Christian solidarity, as a clear diagnostic sign; if the seized person awakened wanting to sing with other Christians then surely his experience was from God. Catholics, on the other hand, found diagnosis by submitting to the direction of a spiritual advisor.

Diagnosis and pastoral support of those, whose life in faith was characterized by the religious expression of a Teresa or an early Methodist convert, placed no mean burden on the cure of souls. The following pages ring with the Everton Methodists' sensitivity to that burden, as they portray revival religion as spiritual therapy.

# THE THERAPEUTICS
# OF REVIVAL RELIGION

From: *The Journal of John Wesley* (1759),
by John Walsh.

I shall easily be excused for adding here a farther account of the work of God in and near Everton:

On Monday, July 9, I set out, and on Wednesday noon reached Potton, where I rejoiced at the account given by John Keeling of himself and others. He was justified, it seems, on that memorable Sabbath, but had not a clear witness of it till ten days after; about which time his sister (who was, on that day, in great distress) was also set at liberty. I discoursed also with Ann Thorn, who told me of much heaviness fol-

---

[85] *Ibid.*, pp. 120–127, 151.

lowing the visions with which she had been favoured; but said she was at intervals visited still with such overpowering love and joy, especially at the Lord's Supper, that she often lay in a trance for many hours. She is twenty-one years old. We were soon after called into the garden, where Patty Jenkins (one of the same age) was so overwhelmed with the love of God that she sunk down, and appeared as one in a pleasant sleep, only with her eyes open; yet she had often just strength to utter, with a low voice, ejaculations of joy and praise; but, no words coming up to what she felt, she frequently laughed while she saw His glory. This is quite unintelligible to many; for a stranger intermeddleth not with our joy. So it was to Mr. M[adan], who doubted whether God or the devil had filled her with love and praise. Oh the depth of human wisdom! Mr. R[omaine], the meantime, was filled with a solemn awe. I no sooner sat down by her than the Spirit of God poured the same blessedness into my soul. Hers continued till the time we were to set out for Cockaigne-Hatley. Then her strength was restored in a moment, and we walked together, sixteen in number, singing to the Lord as we went along.

Mr. Hicks preached an excellent sermon on the Strait Gate. The next morning, Thursday, 12, he gave me leave to take an extract from his Journal; but I had only time to write the occurrences of one morning, as follows:

*June* 6, 1759.—I spoke this morning, at Orwell, on Isa. lv I. One who had been before convinced of sin fell down in a kind of fit, and broke out, in great anguish of soul, calling on the Lord Jesus for salvation. He wrought as in the agonies of death, and was quite bathed in sweat. He beat the chair against which he kneeled, as one whose soul drew nigh unto hell. His countenance then cleared up at once: we hoped he would be presently set at liberty; but on a sudden he was more distressed than ever, being in the sharpest conflict. Every muscle of his body was in strong agitation, as if nature was just dissolving. I never saw any convulsion fit so violent. But in a moment God dispelled the cloud. His face was again covered with smiles, and he spake as seeing the Lord near him. He cried unto Him, and, the Lord hearing, pronounced him freely forgiven. At that instant he clapped his hands and cried aloud, "Jesus is mine! He is *my* Saviour!" His soul was in peace; neither did he find the least bodily pain or soreness. I asked, "For what would you undergo this again?" He said, "Not for all the world; but I would suffer more rather than be without Christ; yea, for His sake, I would suffer all things." "An unwise man doth not consider this; a fool doth not understand it."

This morning, Ann Simpson, aged sixteen or seventeen, lay near an hour in the utmost distress, shrieking out, "Christ! Christ!" and no other word, her face all the time being violently distorted. I left her awhile, but could scarce sit down before I heard the voice of praise. I went, and found her heaviness turned into joy, even the joyful assurance that her sins were pardoned. She sprang by me to a young woman who lay in a kind of trance, and clasped her in her arms, breathing forth praise to God. I retired again, but had not been long seated ere she came in, running to me in a transport of praise. I asked her why she cried out continually, "Christ! Christ!" She answered, "I thought myself at that time on a little island, and saw Satan, in a hideous form, just ready to devour me, hell all around open to receive me, and myself ready to drop in; while no help appeared, nor any way to escape. But, just as I was dropping in, the Lord appeared between me and the great gulf, and would not let me fall into it. As soon as I saw Him all my trouble was gone, and all the pain I felt before; and ever since I have been light and joyful, and filled with the love of God."

So far Mr. Hicks, who told me he was first convinced of sin August 1, 1758, and, finding peace in about six weeks, first preached the gospel on September 17. From that time he was accounted a fool and a madman. About two thousand souls seem to have been awakened by Mr. B[erridge] and him within this twelvemonth.

*Fri.* 13.—Mr. R[omaine], as well as Mr. M[adan], was in doubt concerning the work of God here. But this morning they were both fully convinced, while Alice Miller, the little pale girl, justified May 20, who is in the sixteenth, and Molly Raymond, who is in the twelfth, year of her age, related their experience, their artless confidence confirming all their words. We walked this forenoon to Tadlow, in Cambridgeshire, to hear Mr. B[erridge], but came too late for the sermon. However, the account we received of the wonderful works of God in this and the neighbouring places was matter of great rejoicing to me, as are all manifestations of the world to come.

*Sat.* 14.—Mr. B[erridge], being ill, desired me to exhort a few people in his house, which the Lord enabled me to do with such ease and power that I was quite amazed. The next morning, at seven, his servant, Caleb Price, spoke to about two hundred people. The Lord was wonderfully present, more than twenty persons feeling the arrows of conviction. Several fell to the ground, some of whom seemed dead, others in the agonies of death, the violence of their bodily convulsions exceeding all description. There was also great crying and agonizing in prayer, mixed with deep and deadly groans on every side.

When sermon was ended, one brought good tidings to Mr. B[erridge] from Grantchester, that God had there broken down seventeen persons last week by the singing of hymns only; and that a child, seven years old, sees many visions and astonishes the neighbours with her innocent, awful manner of declaring them.

While Mr. B[erridge] preached in the church, I stood with many in the churchyard, to make room for those who came from far; therefore I *saw* little, but *heard* the agonizing of many, panting and gasping after eternal life. In the afternoon Mr. B[erridge] was constrained, by the multitude of people, to come out of the church and preach in his own close. Some of those who were here pricked to the heart were affected in an astonishing manner. The first man I saw wounded would have dropped, but others, catching him in their arms, did, indeed, prop him up, but were so far from keeping him still that he caused all of them to totter and tremble. His own shaking exceeded that of a cloth in the wind. It seemed as if the Lord came upon him like a giant, taking him by the neck and shaking all his bones in pieces. One woman tore up the ground with her hands, filling them with dust and with the hard-trodden grass, on which I saw her lie, with her hands clinched, as one dead, when the multitude dispersed. Another roared and screamed in a more dreadful agony than ever I heard before. I omitted the rejoicing of believers, because of their number, and the frequency thereof, though the manner was strange; some of them being quite overpowered with divine love, and only showing enough of natural life to let us know they were overwhelmed with joy and life eternal. Some continued long as if they were dead, but with a calm sweetness in their looks. I saw one who lay two or three hours in the open air, and, being then carried into the house, continued insensible another hour, as if actually dead. The first sign of life she showed was a rapture of praise intermixed with a small, joyous laughter.

*Mon.* 16.—Mr. B[erridge] this evening preached in his house, where I observed Molly Raymond leaning all the while as if asleep; but an hour or two after she desired to speak with him. I wondered she was not gone home, and was concerned that so little a girl should have so far to go in the dark without company. Mr. B[erridge] told me neither she nor the other justified children were afraid of anything.

*Tues.* 17.—We walked toward Harlston, near which Mr. B[erridge] overtook us. He was greatly fatigued and dejected, and said, "I am now so weak, I must leave off field-preaching." Nevertheless, he cast himself on the Lord, and stood up to preach, having near three thousand hearers. He was very weak at first, and scarce able to speak; but God soon performed His promise, imparting new strength to him, and causing him to speak with mighty power. A great shaking was among the dry bones. Incessant were the cries, groans, wringing of hands, and prayers of sinners, now first convinced of their deplorable state. After preaching he was lively and strong, so that the closeness of a crowded room neither affected his breath nor hindered his rejoicing over two children, one about eight, and the other about six years old, who were crying aloud to God for mercy.

Not only Harlston, but Stapleford and Triplow, to which Mr. B[erridge] was now going, were places in which he had never preached the gospel, and probably never would have done had it not been for the thundering sermons made against him from their several pulpits. So does Satan frequently overshoot himself, and occasion the downfall of his own kingdom.

I had been very ill the preceding week. Wherefore, last night I had recourse to God in prayer, and this morning, instead of rising with difficulty at eight or nine, as I had usually done, I rose with ease at five; and, instead of losing my strength in a mile or two, I walked eighteen without any weakness or weariness.

*Wed.* 18.—We called at the house where Mr. B[erridge] had been preaching in the morning, and found several there rejoicing in God and several mourning after Him. While I prayed with them many crowded into the house, some of whom burst into a strange, involuntary laughter, so that my voice could scarce be heard, and when I strove to speak louder a sudden hoarseness seized me. Then the laughter increased. I perceived it was Satan, and resolved to pray on. Immediately the Lord rebuked him that laughter was at an end, and so was my hoarseness. A vehement wrestling with God ran through the whole company, whether sorrowful or rejoicing, till, beside the three young women of the house, one young man and a girl about eleven years old, who had been counted one of the wickedest in Harlston, were exceedingly blessed with the consolations of God.

Among those under conviction was an elderly woman, who had been a scoffer at the gospel, and a keen ridiculer of all that cried out; but she now cried louder than any present. Another I observed who had known the Lord about five-and-twenty years. When Mr. B[erridge] first brought the gospel to her ears she was filled with gladness, knowing this was the same salvation which God had long ago brought to her heart.

We walked hence to the middle of Shelford Moor, and, seeing no person but a young woman who kept sheep, the solitude invited us to stop and sing a hymn, the sound thereof reached her. She came up slowly, weeping as she came, and then stood by a brook of water over against us with the tears running down her cheeks apace. We sang another hymn for this mourner in Sion, and wrestled for her with God in prayer. But He did not yet comfort her. And indeed I have observed of the people in general who hear Mr. B[erridge], their convictions are not only deep and violent, but last a long time. Wherefore those that are offended at them who rejoice should consider how terrible a cup they received first. Now they are all light; but they well remember the darkness and misery, the wormwood and the gall.

We met Mr. B[erridge] at Stapleford, five miles from Cambridge. His heart was particularly set on this people, because he was curate here five or six years; but never preached a gospel sermon among them till this evening. About one thousand five hundred persons met in a close to hear him, great part of whom were laughers and mockers. The work of God, however, quickly began among them that were serious, while not a few endeavoured to make sport by mimicking the gestures of them that were wounded. Both these and those who rejoiced in God gave great offence to some stern-looking men, who vehemently demanded to have those wretches horse-whipped out of the close. Need we wonder at this, when several of His own people are unwilling to let God work in His own way? And well may Satan be enraged at the cries of the people, and the prayers they make in the bitterness of their souls, seeing we know these are the chief times at which Satan is cast out.

However, in a while, many of the scoffers were weary, and went away; the rest continued as insensible as before. I had long been walking round the multitude, feeling a jealousy for my God, and praying Him to make the place of His feet glorious. My patience at last began to fail, and I prayed, "O King of glory, break some of them in pieces; but let it be to the saving of their souls!" I had but just spoke when I heard a dreadful noise on the farther side of the congregation, and, turning thither, saw one Thomas Skinner coming forward, the most horrible human figure I ever saw. His large wig and hair were coal black; his face distorted beyond all description. He roared incessantly, throwing and clapping his hands together with his whole force. Several were terrified, and hasted out of his way. I was glad to hear him, after a while, pray aloud. Not a few of the triflers grew serious, while his kindred and acquaintance were very unwilling to believe even their own eyes and ears. They would fain have got him away, but he fell to the earth, crying, "My burden! My burden! I cannot bear it!" Some of his brother scoffers were calling for horse-whips, till they saw him extended on his back at full length. They then said he was dead. And, indeed, the only sign of life was the working of his breast and the distortions of his face, while the veins of his neck were swelled as if ready to burst. He was just before the chief captain of Satan's forces. None was by nature more fitted for mockery; none could swear more heroically to whip out of the close all who were affected by the preaching. His agonies lasted some hours; then his body and soul were eased.

When Mr. B[erridge] had refreshed himself a little he returned to the close and bid the multitude take warning by Skinner, who still lay roaring and tormented on the ground. All the people were now deeply serious, and several hundreds, instead of going when Mr. B[erridge] dismissed them, stayed in Mr. Jennings's yard. Many of these, especially men, were truly broken in heart. Mr. B[erridge] talked with as many as could come into the house, and, seeing what numbers stood hungering without, sent me word to pray with them. This was a grievous cross! I knew it was the Lord's will, but felt such weakness of body and sinking of spirit, and was withal so hoarse, that I supposed few could hear out of some hundreds who stood before me. However, I attempted, and in a moment the Lord poured upon me such a spirit of supplication, and gave me so clear and strong an utterance, that it seemed I was another man—a further instance that the servants of God are not sent a warfare on their own charge.

No sooner had I finished than we were called to see John Dennis, aged twenty years, who lay on a table. His body was stiff and motionless as a statue; his very neck seemed as if made of iron. He was looking steadfastly up to heaven, and praying aloud with a melodious voice. His words surprised Mr. B[erridge] as well as me, who said to the assembly, "You need no better preacher; none can tell you the truths of the gospel more clearly." And, indeed, his prayer unfolded the whole Christian system with the greatest accuracy. When he came out of the fit he was in perfect health, but declared he knew not a word of all he had spoken. His mother then informed us he had had these fits for two years, at least once a day, but he never spoke in any fit till three weeks ago; ever since he prays in them as to-night, but he is himself as ignorant of the matter as if he had been dead all the time.

It was late when I went to lodge about half a mile off, where I found a young woman reading hymns, and the power of the Lord falling on the hearers, especially one young man, who cried aloud in such bitter anguish that I soon desired we might join in prayer. This was the seventh time of my praying in public that day, and had I been faithful I should probably have prayed seven more.

*Thur.* 19.—I returned to Mr. J[ennin]gs's, who had set out at four in the morning to hear Mr. B[erridge] at Grantchester. He came soon after me, but was scarce able to speak. I never saw a man sweat in such a manner—the large drops seeming fixed all over his face, just like beads of glass. The congregation at Grantchester this morning consisted of about one thousand persons, among whom the Lord was wonderfully present, convincing a far greater number now than even last night. Mr. J[ennin]gs was a mild, good-natured Pharisee, who never had been awakened; but he was now thoroughly convinced of his lost estate, and stood for a time in utter despair, with his mouth wide open, his eyes staring, and full of huge dismay. When he found power to speak he cried out, "I thought I had led a good life; I thought I was not so bad as others; but I am the vilest creature upon earth; I am dropping into hell! Now, now; this very moment!" He then saw hell open to receive him, and Satan ready to cast him in; but it was not long before he saw the Lord Jesus, and knew He had accepted him. He then cried aloud in an unspeakable rapture, "I have got Christ! I have got Christ!" For two hours he was in the visions of God; then the joy, though not the peace, abated.

I had left Mr. J[ennin]gs but a little while when I heard John Dennis loudly praising God. I no sooner kneeled by him than the consolations of God came upon me, so that I trembled and wept much. Nor was the Spirit poured out upon us alone; all in the house were partakers of it. J[ohn] D[ennis] was kneeling when his fit came. We laid him on the ground, where he soon became stiff as last night, and prayed in like manner. Afterwards his body grew flexible by degrees, but was convulsed from head to foot. When he was quite recovered he said he was quite resigned to the will of God, who gave him such strength in the inner man that he did not find any of these things grievous, neither could ask to be delivered from them.

I walked from Stapleford with twenty persons to hear Mr. B[erridge] at Triplow, and saw many other companies, some before, some behind, some on either hand, going the same way. This brought to my mind the words of Zechariah, "And the inhabitants of one city shall go to another, saying, Let us go speedily to pray before the Lord, and to seek the Lord of hosts; I wi^ll go also."

Fifteen hundred or two thousand were assembled in the close at Triplow. The only unpolished part of the audience were a few gentlemen on horseback. They were much offended at the cries of those in conviction, but much more at the rejoicing of others, even to laughter; but they were not able to look them in the face for half a minute together. I looked after service at every ring which the people made about those that fell under the word. Here and there was a place with only one, but there were generally two or three together, and on one spot no less than seven who lay on the ground as if slain in battle. I soon followed Mr. B[erridge] to the house, and found both it and the orchard filled with serious people, to whom he spake till his strength failed, and then, seeing them unwilling to depart, desired me to dismiss them with a prayer. I felt great reluctance; but so mightily, when I began, came the Spirit upon me that I found no want of utterance while I was praying with about two hundred persons. I thought they had then gone away, but perceived, an hour after, most of them were still in the house or orchard—sighs and groans, prayers, tears, and joyful praise being intermixed on every side.

*Fri.* 20.—I was wakeful before five; but, conferring with flesh and blood, I slept again. Mr. B[erridge] sent for me at seven; but I was then so weak I could not go till the people were dispersed. Three times more persons were struck with convictions this morning than had been last night. Mr. B[erridge] had prayed with them till near fainting, who then sent for me to come; and who knows what God might have done, even by me, if I had not been indulging my vile body? I was glad to see a woman, supposed the chief sinner in the town, now rolling on the earth, screaming and roaring in strong convictions. The man of the house informed us of her having had nine or ten children by whoredom; and that, being at last married, her husband was more angry with her for hearing the word than he would probably have been for committing adultery. Nor was her minister displeased that she never came to church, but mightily strove to prevent both her and all the sinners of his parish from going to hear the gospel. I observed also a beggar-girl, seven or eight years old, who had scarce any clothes but a ragged piece of old rug. She too had felt the word of God as a two-edged sword, and mourned to be covered with Christ's righteousness.

From Triplow I walked to Orwell, and thence to Everton, in weakness of body and heaviness of spirit. Mr. B[erridge] was preaching when I came in. Here God again refreshed my soul. I shook from head to foot, while tears of joy ran down my face, and my distress was at an end.

*Sat.* 21.—I was troubled for some of our brethren, who began to doubt whether this was a work of God or of the devil; John Keeling in particular, who, instead of his frank, lively zeal, and happiness in God, was now filled with gloomy discontent, and grown dark, sullen, and reserved. As we were walking together, he told me it was his resolution to keep himself to himself; to let them who struggled so struggle as they would, and leave all those to themselves whom Satan cast into visions or trances till Satan brought them out again. "But," he added, "I am so uneasy, I don't know what to do; and most of our people begin to shun one another." The snare was now broken. He saw the delusion he had been in, and I trust will hereafter shun the troublers of Israel.

*Sun.* 22.—The church was quite filled, and hundreds were without. And now the arrows of God flew abroad. The inexpressible groans, the lamenting, praying, roaring, were so loud, almost without intermission, that we who stood without could scarce help thinking all in the church were cut to the heart. But, upon inquiry, we found about two hundred persons, chiefly men, cried aloud for mercy; but many more were affected, perhaps as deeply, though in a calmer way.

I rejoiced to see many from Cambridgeshire, particularly John Dennis, Thomas Skinner, and the sorrowful young woman with whom we had prayer on Shelford Moor. Now, too, came good news from several parts, especially Grantchester, where ten more persons were cut to the heart in singing hymns among themselves, and the little child beforementioned continues to astonish all the neighbourhood. A noted physician came some time ago and closely examined her. The result was, he confessed it was no distemper of mind, but the hand of God.

I sought for Thomas Skinner after morning service, and found him, with many more, singing hymns under a tree. When they stopped, I asked, "How do you find your mind now?" Instead of speaking he looked upon me with great steadiness, fetched a deep sigh, burst out into tears and prayers, and, throwing himself along on the ground, fell into more and more agony, till he roared aloud. I told him how great a sinner I had been; but the more I spoke, the more was he distressed. Wherefore John Dennis and I went to prayer for him; but his deliverance was not yet. Make him, O Lord, a greater champion for Thy truth than ever he was against it!

Mr. B[erridge] preached in his close this afternoon, though in great bodily weakness; but when he is weakest, God so strengthens him that it is surprising to what a distance his voice reaches. I have heard Mr.

Whitefield speak as loud, but not with such a continued, strong, un-broken tenor.

*Mon. 23.*—Mr. Keeling and I walked to Bedford. I was relating there how God had plucked such a brand as me out of the burning, but my voice was quickly stopped by rejoicing; and I have often found that nothing I can say makes so much impression on myself or others as thus repeating my own conversion.

The first time I saw Mr. B[erridge] was June 2, 1758. But I scarce thought of him again till June 7, as I was walking up to Luton Down. There an awful sense of God's presence fell upon me, and my voice grew louder and louder, in proportion to the joy of my soul, with a strong im-pulse to pray for the success of Mr. B[erridge]'s labours. And such a fore-sight did the Lord give me of what He was bringing to pass through his ministry that I was quite overwhelmed for near an hour; till my voice was lost, and only tears remained. And oh, how graciously has the God of truth accomplished all those things! With what delight hast Thou since caused me to walk round the walls of Thy Sion, to mark well her bulwarks, and count the towers thereof!

*The Journal of the Rev. John Wesley*, A.M., ed. by Nehemiah Curnock, (A Bicentenary Issue 1938, London: The Epworth Press, 1913, 1938), Vol. IV, pp. 333–343. By permission.

# Exhibit Nineteen

## HOW TO HEAR CONFESSIONS

### JEAN JOSEPH GAUME

## Introduction

Pastoral care in modern Roman Catholic Christianity since the Counter Reformation has centered on inductive guidance by means of auricular confession. That mode of spiritual direction flourished in France during the eighteenth and nineteenth centuries and became the subject of diligent study by Abbé Jean Joseph Gaume (1802–1879), whose *Le Manuel des confesseurs* first appeared when he was 35 years old and entered its eleventh revised edition the year after his death. Ordained in 1825, Gaume became a teacher and pastor in Nevers and later vicar-general of Reims and of Montauban. His book was particularly admired by Church of England clergy of the Tractarian party, who yearned to recover auricular confession as a traditionally Catholic pastoral practice. Thus, one of their leaders, Edward Bouverie Pusey (1800–1882) translated and adapted Gaume's book in 1877 as *Advice for Those Who Exercise the Ministry of Reconciliation Through Confession and Absolution.*

*Le Manuel des confesseurs* drew heavily from the great Catholic masters of spiritual direction—such noted pastors as St. Francis of Sales (1567–1622), St. Charles Borromeo (1538–1584), St. Philip

Neri (1515–1595), St. Francis Xavier (1506–1552), and St. Alphonsus Liguori (1696–1787). Thus, it represents not only a nineteenth-century insight into pastoral guidance, but gathers up the wisdom of the confessional accumulated from Reformation to modern times. Since that particular means of pastoring guarantees the strictest confidence, practitioners of auricular confession have resorted to abstracting rules from their experience because they have been unable in conscience to hand on actual case records to those who learn and advance this particular art of spiritual direction.

These selections from Pusey's translation of Gaume's book exemplify a prescriptive type of counseling in which the helper becomes a spiritual "Father" to the troubled person or "child" whom he helps. The confessor represents a definitely superior wisdom and viewpoint about moral action and spiritual perplexities. By virtue of ordination the confessor becomes the master whose task is to locate the person under his tutelage in his natural family, the family of the church, and finally the family of mankind. The "Father" identifies desirable goals for the "child," prescribes the ways in which these goals are to be pursued, and names the errant attitudes and acts that are to be eschewed. Imparting information, exhorting, admonishing, and even threatening become appropriate parts of pastoring in the confessional.

In part, these selections emphasize a particular difficulty that has repeatedly presented itself to confessors—the spiritual condition of scrupulosity. "Scrupulosity" refers to the client's inability to come to a creative decision as to right and wrong, an inability that is heightened by the fear of sinning no matter which course of action is chosen. Traditionally, scrupulosity has been treated by confessors through insisting that the penitent put total confidence in the confessor's advice, even to the point of believing the confessor against his own conscience. Abbé Gaume quotes St. Philip Neri as requiring scrupulous persons to "put themselves wholly and irrevocably into the hands of their . . . Confessor, obeying him as GOD Himself, laying all their concerns freely and simply before him, and never coming to any determination without his advice." Certainly prescriptive counseling, as contrasted with client-centered guidance, invites the counselee's dependence upon the counselor—a posture which might become the harbinger of scrupulosity. The classical remedies for the difficulty, centering upon ever more strict obedience to the confessor, perhaps compounded the basic problem.

On the other hand, however, it must be noted that the very authority and prescriptiveness that might abet scrupulosity do furnish for the penitent a secure, understandable, and manageable structure of values in which to live. In such a way a person in dire trouble can be relieved of the compounding perplexity of finding for himself sound sets of values and effective means of pursuing them.

The following paragraphs deal with a number of features of the art of spiritual direction by means of the confessional, such as interrogations, penances, relapses, and so forth, as well as with the high professional qualifications necessary to the effective administration of sacramental penance.

# HOW TO HEAR
# CONFESSIONS

From: *Le Manuel des confesseurs* (1837),
by Jean Joseph Gaume.

## On Interrogations

On all subjects, as well as that of purity, you should avoid beginning interrogations, unless circumstances give you some just cause for supposing that the penitent has omitted anything he ought to confess, through shame or ignorance. If you mean to question a penitent concerning all the sins he might possibly commit, there will be no end to it, and you will make the Sacrament [of Penance] odious both to him and yourself, wearying him with a string of useless queries, of which you would be the first to complain, if they were put to you when making your own confession. Do not go beyond necessary things or what have probably occurred to your penitent. If for instance you know who the penitent is, and that he or she has lately been to confession, and you believe him to be good and well-instructed, you should let him accuse himself, and afterwards, if you think it necessary, you can put questions which seem to you necessary. In order not to confuse the penitent and make him forget what he had prepared in his self-examination, do not interrupt him; but defer your questions till the end, when you foresee that the confession will be short, judging by the short time elapsed since his last confession. In longer ones, if you are afraid of forgetting, you should only interrupt him to ask briefly what may be necessary, reserving all else for the end.

\*    \*    \*    \*    \*

But if it be clear that the penitent is ignorant of that which is necessary in order to receive sanctifying grace, you have two courses open to you; 1) to explain to him the duty of learning, recommending or obliging him as a penance to attend instructions and catechisings, and to read or listen to books concerning Christian doctrine. 2) The second course is quicker. Teach him briefly yourself, and, without waiting till he can learn these things by heart, make him repeat slowly and devoutly after you these formulas, so that he should *actually* believe, hope, love, and repent rightly; and then, if there be no other difficulty, give him absolution. This is the best course to take with grown-up people of a certain position, who would be ashamed to be asked if they knew the first truths of the Faith, while yet the confession leads you to believe that they are ignorant. Help such persons gently and effectually by making them repeat these acts, after which you can inquire if they habitually do repeat these or similar formulas, and according to what you ascertain, you can then make use of the first remedy. Combined with the fatal ignorance which makes people unfit for absolution, we too often find ignorance of that true contrition which is necessary for this Sacrament. How many there are who, while they are scrupulous in examining themselves, yet hardly bestow a thought on their repentance! Some content themselves with an attempt at contrition after leaving the tribunal of penance; others wait to be helped to make some such act by their Confessor; or they make one while he says the short prayers which precede absolution. Therefore, let one of the points you press most upon your penitents be repentance and firm resolution of amendment. Teach them the extreme importance thereof, suggest the means of obtaining it, i.e. prayer to God, weighing their own motives, and earnest desire for it; advise them to make acts of attrition and perfect contrition from time to time, not as an obligation, but as an useful practice. Strengthened by such precautions, they need entertain no doubts as to their contrition, and that they have dispositions requisite for approaching the Sacraments.

\* \* \* \* \*

### Interrogation of Uneducated Penitents

Ask children, 1) if they have nourished hatred towards their parents, which is a double sin against charity and piety; 2) if they have disobeyed them in serious and just matters, such as going out at night, gambling, frequenting bad society, &c. I say in *just* matters, because as regards the choice of a state of life, children are not bound to obey their parents. In truth parents sin grievously when they force their children to marry, or to take Orders or monastic vows; or when they deter them by unjust means from the state of life they seek to follow. 3) Ask if they have been wanting in respect to their parents, either by act or by word, calling them names or mocking them. If children have been thus wanting, they are bound to make reparation, by asking pardon, if possible in the presence of those who witnessed the fault; and it is better this reparation be made before you give absolution.

Ask of parents whether they have attended to their children's education, instructing them in the Faith, and taking them to Church and the Sacraments; keeping them from evil company. Ask if they have given scandal to their children by blasphemy; if they have neglected to correct them for sin; if they have exposed them to any temptation through care[-]lessness; or neglected to give them proper support, or forced them to marry, or take Holy Orders. Such are mortal sins. Ask masters, if they have reproved their servants for blasphemy, or for neglecting the public worship; or for any indecent behaviour, especially in harvest and similar times, when masters are bound to take whatever precautions they can against evil. Ask husbands, if they have duly supplied the wants of the families; and wives, if they have angered their husbands, or neglected their duties as wives. Many men are led into sin by their wives' neglect of home duties.

*   *   *   *   *

## Treatment of Difficult Cases

When the scrupulous torment themselves about their past confessions, fearing that they did not fully explain all their sins or the attending circumstances; or that they made their general confession without fitting contrition, going on for a length of time dwelling upon their past life; you must forbid them ever deliberately to dwell upon it, or to confess their past sins, unless they are morally certain that they were mortal sins, and that they were never confessed. In fact the doctors [of the Church] teach, that even if through inadvertence they have omitted some mortal sin, scrupulous persons are not obliged to return to the subject . . . unless they are quite certain, that it is essential to the integrity of the confession. Less grave inconvenience would dispense with it. Be resolute in enforcing obedience on this point, and if the penitent disobeys, reprove him sharply, deprive him of Communion, and mortify him as severely as you can. Scrupulous people ought to be treated with great severity, for if they lose the anchor of obedience they are lost; they will either go mad, or plunge into sin.

There are others who are afraid of sinning in every action. It is necessary to desire these to act freely without heeding their scruples, as indeed they are bound to do when there is no plain evidence that such an action is sinful. That is what the doctors teach. It does not matter that they will act with fear, that is, without getting rid of their scruple (one can rarely hope for this in scrupulous people), because that fear is not . . . a true practical doubt. Neither does it hinder the first judgment, which virtually exists, although the fear hinders them from noticing it. That judgment is, that when performing any action which they do not certainly know to be bad, they are not sinning. In fact in such a case, they are not opposing conscience, but an idle fear. You must insist with a penitent of this character, that he shall conquer his scruple by boldly doing that which the scruple forbids; and also forbid his returning to the subject in confession.

S. Philip Neri [1515–1595] used to say that those scrupulous persons who desire to advance in perfection, must put themselves wholly and irrevocably into the hands of their superiors. Those who do not live under a Rule must voluntarily submit themselves to a learned and wise Confessor, obeying him as God Himself, laying all their concerns freely and simply before him, and never coming to any determination without his advice. Such an one, S. Philip said, need not fear being called to account by God. He used to add however, that it was necessary to reflect deliberately and pray before choosing a Confessor: and, that once done, not to change without very good cause; to put entire trust in him, confiding everything to him, and to be certain that the Lord will not allow him to be mistaken in anything concerning the soul's salvation. When the devil has exhausted his other wiles, and cannot make a man fall into great sins, he will use every wile to set up mistrust between the penitent and Confessor, and thus he will lead by degrees to great evils. S. Philip used further to say that obedience is the most direct road, by which to obtain perfection quickly. He had a greater esteem for persons who led an ordinary life in obedience, than for such as practised great austerities according to their own fancy, saying that there was nothing more dangerous in the spiritual life than seeking to be guided by one's own judgment, while on the other hand, nothing gave greater strength or went farther to defeat our enemy than obedience to the will of another in the practice of what is good. Obedience, he was wont to repeat, Obedience to God, that is the true sacrifice which we ought to offer upon the altar of our heart.

\* \* \* \* \*

## Treatment of Bad Habits and Relapses

One of your hardest and most important duties is the dealing with habitual and relapsing sinners; nor can their faults, constantly recurring and unexpected as they are, be dealt with summarily on one system, but by a prolonged and arduous course of treatment: for the passions, which seemed to be conquered to-day, spring forth afresh to-morrow, and when defeated on one side, take us by surprise on the other. It is in dealing with such sick souls as these above all others, that you require the balm composed of the oil of compassion and encouragement, so that they may not despair, and of the wine of paternal authority, so that they may not be careless and flag in their earnest efforts to amend. They are exposed to two opposite and yet simultaneous perils; despair, because of the difficulty of their position; and presumption, which urges them to regard their want of purpose and perseverance as a real impossibility.

Such persons should not be absolved unless you can satisfy yourself as to the fitness of their disposition; and the proofs that this is lacking are; 1) If the penitent has used none or few of the means prescribed for conquering his faults: 2) If his faults have not diminished: 3) If he gives no sign of more than ordinary contrition. In such case, you have no indication of any resolute and effectual intention to amend; you can but mistrust his protestations of repentance. But while you defer giving absolution, do all in your power to lead him to amendment, by suggesting the most likely inducements and means thereto; and urge him to return speedily to confession, . . . [but] do not leave so long an interval as a week or ten days in such a case; the sick man will derive great benefit from frequent visits on the part of his physician, who can thus watch his symptoms, and apply the fittest remedies; but rare visits from the doctor will be very prejudicial to him.

If at the end of a week your penitent comes back without having made any improvement, send him away for a shorter time. S. Bernard, when dealing with a young man who lapsed into habitual sins of impurity, bade him return after three days, during which he was to abstain from sin, in honour of the Three Divine Persons of the Trinity to whom we owe so much. The penitent returns, without having fallen. S. Bernard then intreated him to keep watch over himself for three days more, in honour of the purity of the B[lessed] Virgin. Once again the young man returns without a relapse. "My son," the Saint said, "give me three days more, in honour of your guardian Angel, to whom you already owe so much, and after that I will absolve you." At the end of the triduum, the youth returned and said, "Now I promise you to abstain from this sin, not for three days but for always. I see thus it was no want of grace or power, but of real will, which has hitherto been wanting to me: to him who sincerely wills, nothing is impossible with the grace of God." Happy young man to have fallen into the hands of so experienced a father and physician, who knew how to win him by motives at once so sweet and so powerful, and who, by skilfully lessening the difficulties and duration of the trials, dividing, so to speak, the medicine into small portions, could adapt it to his want of strength and restore him to health!

It is a great mistake to dismiss for a fortnight or a month a penitent who has failed to abstain from sin during a week; or to tell him that it is useless to come either to you or any one else, unless he corrects himself. Perhaps he would find some S. Bernard who would succeed in curing him by the very opposite treatment. Beware lest you are misled by false zeal or ignorance of the right treatment to adopt, or by your own impatience and dislike of trouble. Doubtless at times your paternal tenderness or your medical skill will be sorely tried by the negligence of some relapsers in using the appointed remedies; or even if they do use these, by the strength of their bad habits, their weakness or perversity, you may scarcely know how to deal with them, and then you may be tempted to send them away, not only unabsolved, but with harshness; which at the moment may seem to you justifiable, or even necessary. But in order to convince yourself that this impulse is not from God, but rather impatience cloaked with a pharisaical zeal, quite unlike that of Jesus Christ, I would ask you to think about this backsliding penitent, who appears to you so unworthy of compassion. God bore with him yesterday and bears with him to-day; this very day He so surrounded and urged the sinner with His grace, as to bring him to you in spite of his own reluctance: it is God alone Whom he has offended, and yet you, against whom he has not sinned, cannot bear with him! Do you affect to know your Master's interests better than He Himself? or do you think that this zeal, so easy to yourself, so harmful to the penitent, comes from a healthier source than the very different zeal of God? Never, I intreat you, let fall any words which may lead the relapsed sinner to despair, to which he is tempted already by the difficulty of correcting himself; but rather keep God's patience and goodness towards him ever before you as your example. Maintain a firm confidence in God, that, if you persevere in your care and your remedies, the evil will be subdued and the penitent will be cured; and thus you will be able to inspire him with earnest desires to amend, and courage to persevere. Such a hope will not be in vain: experience teaches us that with, it may be a month, or it may be a year of patience on the part of both confessor and penitent, a thorough lasting cure may be effected. Even after very serious relapses, God has granted it, when both priest and penitent have gone on praying and toiling. Urge him to come very often, that he may diminish the power of temptation, take breath and receive fresh counsel. . . .

Always receive such penitents with open arms, never betraying the slightest sign of weariness or surprise at their having fallen again so soon and so grievously: if you do, it may prevent their coming back another time. Rather commend them for coming at once, and earnestly strive to find the cause of relapse; examine what precautions they have neglected, and how and when the temptation came and got the mastery over them; you may require to know these details, better to understand the cause and remedy of the evil. Ask God to teach you suitable remedies, and among others press the necessity of frequent confession. In the Life of S. Philip Neri, by the P. Baccia, we read, "A penitent who fell almost daily into sin came to the Saint, who gave him no other penance than bidding him come to confession directly that he fell into sin, without waiting for the chance of a second fall. The penitent obeyed, and S. Philip absolved him, continuing to give the same penance. By this means he was entirely reclaimed in a few months . . . and in a short time led a holy life." Of course you cannot judge from this instance exactly, what should be the test of fitness for absolution; but it shows that a penitent may not be wholly devoid of such fitness, because he cannot overcome his bad habits after his first confession; his ultimate restoration will be the proof that those repeated special confessions have borne good fruit. Moreover, you must remember that it is no light penance to such a penitent to be obliged to come and make confession directly that he falls: while it is certainly a most useful penance. It is not light, because the relapsed penitent has even greater repugnance than other sinners to accuse himself of his faithlessness to his repeated promises. . . . Thus confession is not only a light penance, but is, for the relapsers, the most salutary, because of the help given by the Sacrament "ex opere operato," if the penitent comes worthily, even when the priest does not feel it right to give him absolution. The humility he exercises, and the victory he wins by returning to his confessor after each fall, and the counsel which he will then receive, will be more profitable to him than fasting and other austerities. Therefore, however often he relapses, never rebuff him; and do not impose heavy penances on him, that you may the better enforce that of immediate confession, which will become both harder to him and more necessary. Think how terrible it would be, were the unhappy sinner (who perhaps is striving to resist his bad habits more than you imagine) to give in, either from his inward misery, or from the weight that you have laid upon him; and fall into the most common snare of first delaying, and finally forsaking confession, so that he becomes like a sick man, whose illness increases and who has no doctor, or a sheep without a shepherd, with fresh wounds from the wolf.

*       *       *       *       *

## Of Penances and Absolution

With respect to the penances which you must impose as a judge, they must be modified as to quality and quantity by your skill as a physician; not considering the illness alone, but the strength or weakness of the patient's constitution. A good physician does not give the same remedies to a weak person, even in a great fever, as to one who is strong. In complicated maladies, he adjusts his treatment carefully, so as not to aggravate one while curing another. A physician who neglects to heed these varying circumstances, might do more harm than good. The wise doctor prefers to administer cautiously and by degrees, such powerful treatment as the weak patient cannot bear all at once; preparing him and strengthening him, till he can use stronger remedies with benefit.

So also it would be very unwise to lay heavy penances upon a newly converted sinner, whose sorrow for sin is but ordinary though sufficient; in so doing you would run the risk of driving him from devotion. Your object should be not only to punish his past sins, but to win him to the Sacraments and to piety, so that, through your gentleness and moderation, he may be induced to return frequently and so obtain fresh spiritual strength. Then you may be sure that he will be the first to accept or even to ask for severer penances. By such a course you will secure God's glory more effectually than by premature stringency. Such moderation is not laxity, but rather a wise combination of the judge's and physician's skill. S. Thomas [Aquinas] says, "As a small fire is put out, if much fuel is heaped upon it, so it may happen, that a slight feeling of contrition in the penitent may give way under the weight of penance. It is better that the priest should tell the penitent what penance ought to be enjoined, and yet only enjoin what the penitent may cheerfully bear." S. Chrysostom teaches us what is the consequence of undue severity;—"I could recount many, who were brought to the extremest ills, because a penance was required of them equal to their sins. For a penance is not to be hastily adapted to the measure of the sins, but the mind of the sinner has to be ascertained; lest, while you would mend the rent, you make a worse; while you would amend the fallen, you occasion a greater fall. For those who are weak and remiss and entangled with the pleasures of the world, and who from their birth or power may be highminded, may be gradually withdrawn from the practice of sin, and may be freed, if not altogether yet in part, from the ills with which they are held; whereas if you rebuke them with severity at first, you will deprive them of that lesser amendment. For the soul put suddenly to shame, sinks into impassiveness, and then neither obeys gentle words, nor is moved by threats, nor is touched by benefits."

If then, you confess a penitent who is seriously ill, although his many sins may deserve a long and heavy penance, yet have regard to his condition, and do not overwhelm him by imposing the penance he deserves. Be satisfied with giving him some brief prayer to say, and bidding him offer his illness resignedly to God; telling him that if he recovers, he is to come to you, and then you will give him some further penance in acquittal of the repentance; or if he be unable to do so, he must confess frequently, do good works, and bear his trials patiently, in amends for his faults. But if you prescribe penances of months and years, you may, as has happened, diminish his confidence in you so much, that perhaps if he were to remember some grave hitherto forgotten sin, he would be afraid to turn to you for absolution, and so might be in peril of dying a bad death. The actual and very grave peril outweighs your fear, that he may not come to you when recovered.

Be equally cautious as to the nature of the penances you impose. Never impose as obligations, difficult things which may be left undone; but suggest such by way of counsel. For instance, you may counsel children to beg pardon of their parents for disobedience, but do not order them to do so; do not forbid a drunkard to drink anything at all on a certain day, but fix a discreet limit beyond which he may not go. Various other penances may be given, subject to certain conditions, rather than absolutely; such as giving alms, coming on a certain day to confession, saying certain prayers, in the event of the penitent's being guilty of a particular fault within a certain time.

Still less ought you to inflict penances which expose your penitent's faults to others: e.g. you may impose a day of fasting upon the head of a household, who is independent of others, but not upon his child, whose parents might easily guess the cause. When you give easy penances, such as saying five *Our Fathers*, you may prescribe them daily for some time. But it is not well to do so with less easy penances. In these cases it is better to leave a certain amount of liberty, lest the penitent be embarrassed, and perhaps incur guilt by omitting what he is bound to do. If you impose several different things, keep to the same number in each, to avoid confusion; e.g. five fasts, five litanies &c. When you are doubtful if you ought to impose a more severe penance, bid your penitent specially offer all the good he is able to do throughout the week, to God; thus sanctifying what he does, without overburdening him. S. Thomas de Villeneuve [1488–1555] says, "So temper the rigour of penance, that neither its lightness should lessen the sense of the gravity of the sin, nor the severity risk its omission. This you will secure, if you enjoin an easy one, and counsel the sinner a sharper one; yet so that the efficacy of the Sacrament should apply to all his voluntary and spontaneous penance."

You should take especial care that, while a penance is borne to make amends to God, it be also profitable as to the penitent's future preservation from sin. Thus you should always give the preference (especially when dealing with delicate people,) to such as encourage holy thoughts and affections, rather than to bodily penances. Many a soul has made great progress in sanctification through meditations, spiritual readings, and devotions, especially to the Passion of our Lord, practised as penances. [Giovanni] Clericato [1633–1717] mentions having seen several sinners who were gifted with unusual contrition in their last hours; and when he investigated what had won so great a grace for such sinful men, he found that they had taken great pains to be present at Holy Communion and been very devout thereat. Thus the Sacrifice, pleaded there, worked Its result, and though late, the Divine Blood demanded their salvation, and obtained it.

No penance is more useful than frequenting the Sacraments. It is certain that among those who have the power of frequenting them, and have not done it, very few have been able to keep in the right way by means of all other aids. On the other hand, you will generally find that those who do come constantly to the Sacraments, whatever their bad habits, rarely grow worse, gradually gain the victory over their sins, and end by entire amendment; and that, because the Sacraments are the most powerful means of grace set before men. But they are useless to such as do not receive them with fitting dispositions. Consequently do you leave nothing undone to inspire men with reverence and love for them, that so they may with all possible diligence prepare for them.

Above all, employ your utmost skill and charity in dealing with backsliders, who both urgently need to come to confession, and at the same time have great difficulty in so doing. Tell them that should they relapse it will be a great consolation to you, if they would come to confess at once, not, in regard to the evil, but for the Christian humility and good will which they would shew by having recourse at once to the remedy. Tell them that it matters not that they are not prepared for confession; let them anyhow come and say that the fever has returned. Such speedy humility weakens the devil's power not a little; encourages the penitent, and God gives him fresh grace. By persevering in such a course, his own humility, and your salutary counsels will, by the blessing of God, soon gain the victory over his own temptations.

But if he delays his humiliation and confession, he runs a great risk of falling rapidly and of losing all desire and energy in self-correction. Your manner of receiving such persons should encourage them; never seeming astonished at their relapses, never treating them with any contempt, never sending them back with harshness. Any one of these faults might discourage them altogether from ever coming to you again. Yet, as a general rule, it is desirable for all penitents, and especially for backsliders, to go habitually to the same Confessor. When they come to you, always shew that you are glad to see them, always sympathise with them, and, above all, always help them. . . .

\* \* \* \* \*

One of the most important obligations to lay upon a penitent, is that of making a general confession. Sometimes you must oblige him to make it, at other times you need only advise him to do so. But, as a spiritual physician, you ought to render it as easy to him as you can, by shewing him how to examine himself, and excite his contrition. Teach him to keep the sins committed since his last special confession apart, and to confess them before or after his general confession; which will enable you better to apply the remedies, by setting before you the present actual condition of his soul, as well as the past. With regard to ignorant people, P. Seigneri [1624–1694] says, that, if the penitent in former confessions has accused himself confusedly, it is not necessary to make him repeat every thing exactly, inasmuch as such sins have been remitted, notwithstanding their confused explanation. Generally, persons of this sort are confused, and you can for the most part gain a clearer understanding of their sins, both as to number and circumstances, by judicious questioning, than they could ever give you after the longest self-examination. Do not therefore be alarmed, if they come ill-prepared; if you send them away they will often be troubled and never return: rather question them. But to make general confessions really useful to those who make them, besides instructing them and inducing them to prepare with special care, persuade them for some days to render thanks to God for His help hitherto, that their gratitude may obtain for them the grace of perseverance. It is well to recommend this practice for particular confessions also, which are always acts of great importance, needing special grace.

\*      \*      \*      \*      \*

## General Summary

To sum up all my instructions, I will specially point out some of the chief things, to which you should give most heed in the exercise of your sacred ministry.

1. Above all things, use the greatest charity towards sinners, both in receiving them, and inspiring them with confidence in God's mercy. But never let any human respect hinder you from warning them earnestly, or pointing out their evil condition, and the most suitable means for breaking the chains of their evil habits. Be firm in refusing absolution, when it is necessary to do so.

2. Examine the ignorant concerning the chief mysteries of the faith.

3. Do not fail to question ignorant and careless persons as to the faults, to which they are most liable, if they do not accuse themselves.

4. [Be reserved in questions concerning purity, especially with women and children, so that you may run no risk of teaching them what they do not know.] If you feel any temptations yourself, in interrogating on these subjects, lift your heart frequently to God; keep some sacred image before your eyes, and be sure always to purify your intentions before entering the confessional.

5. Do not be content with questioning parents generally as to the education of their children, but go into particulars—such as, whether they take pains to correct their faults, to give them religious instruction, to keep them from bad company, &c.

6. When dealing with penitents whom you suspect of having kept something back through shame, refer to their past lives, asking if they are troubled about anything in it, and encouraging them to tell every thing. Such a course has saved many a soul.

7. However many penitents may want you, do not be in a hurry, or prefer confessing a number of people to giving fit care and attention to a few, or advising and warning them, as they have need.

8. When a penitent accuses himself of a mortal sin, especially if he has committed it several times, do not be satisfied with asking the number and kind, ascertain if it has been an habitual sin: and enquire as to the place, and the [sort of] person with whom he has sinned, so as to know whether there is a habit or an occasion to be broken through. Many Confessors fail in this point, to the great loss of souls, as, without such knowledge, it is not possible to teach the penitent how to conquer bad habits or get rid of occasions of sin.

9. Do not give absolution to any candidate for Holy Orders, who is in the habit of any vice, until you are satisfied that he has acquired that holiness, which is positively necessary for the holy office to which he aspires.

10. Beware of dissuading any one from a religious vocation through human respect. S. Thomas says that to do so involves mortal sin. Some Confessors, in order to please their parents, do not scruple to dissuade young people from such a vocation, telling the children that they are bound to obey their fathers and mothers. But the universal opinion of theologians, founded on S. Thomas's authority, is that every one is free to choose their state in life, and ought rather to obey God, if He calls them, than their parents. On the other hand, remember that you must not absolve such as intend to take Holy Orders, without having a vocation.

11. When you confess priests, be respectful, but firm in admonishing them duly, and in withholding absolution, if it be necessary. Do not fail to urge them to fit themselves more and more to labour for the salvation of souls, according to the talents God may have given them, as also to be diligent in preparation before, and thanksgiving after celebrating, and in mental prayer, without which it is not easy to be a good priest.

12. In matters of restitution, enforce it, if possible, before giving absolution.

13. If the penitent has received some offence, for which his enemy is publicly prosecuted, do not ordinarily absolve him, unless he remit it.

15. [sic] Cause every one to make an act of contrition, unless you are certain that they have already done so duly. Do not fail to teach the motives to attrition and contrition; and remember that, if the penitent comes without fit dispositions, it is your part, to try and lead him to them, before giving absolution.

16. Do not give absolution to penitents, whose sins, though venial, are habitual, unless they shew true contrition and a firm intention of amendment.

17. Only impose such penances as you know your penitent can fulfil, and give heed that they be medicinal and remedial.

18. Inculcate the practice of mental prayer on those who frequent the Sacraments, and require them to give an account, at all events, as to whether they have performed it. This is a powerful means for the salvation of souls. Do not hesitate to allow frequent Communion, whenever you think it will be profitable to your penitent.

19. When dealing with scrupulous people, above all things urge obedience upon them, and shew them the great danger of disobedience. Be firm and severe in exacting obedience; be decided and resolute in what you say; if you speak hesitatingly, you will only add to their disquietude. Give them general rules for the removal of their doubts, according to each person's wants; e.g. where a penitent has continual scruples as to his past confessions, forbid him to return to the consideration of any past faults, unless he is certain that they were mortal sins, and unconfessed; and be firm in refusing to hear any more about them. If you once yield, your penitent will always be restless. Some Confessors do great harm to souls in this way. In dealing with such as imagine everything they do to be a sin, enjoin a victory over scruples, and a free action in whatever is not plainly sin.

20. As to the choice of opinions, if it is a question of removing the penitent from danger of formal sin, do not follow indulgent opinions beyond the limits of Christian prudence.

21. In confessing women, deal with them as austerely as prudence permits; refuse presents, avoid familiarity, and whatever may lead to attachment.

22. Be humble, and do not presume upon your knowledge. Ask continually of God the light, needful to guide you through difficulties through the merits of Jesus Christ. "I prayed, and the spirit of wisdom came unto me." No Confessor can be wise and discreet, who is not given to prayer. In serious or perplexing cases, always consult those who are more learned and experienced than yourself; and that especially, where you have to direct a very advanced soul, to whom God grants any supernatural gifts, you yourself being unpractised in such matters. Some men, with scarcely a pretence of any knowledge of asceticism, are yet too proud to consult others; but no really humble priest can act thus. A humble mind will not only take counsel with others, but if it seems desirable, will readily commit the guidance of souls beyond his powers of handling to more experienced directors.

Jean Joseph Gaume, *Advice for Those Who Exercise the Ministry of Reconciliation through Confession and Absolution* . . . , abridged, condensed, and adapted to the use of the English Church by E. B. Pusey (Second Edition, Oxford: James Parker & Co., 1878), pp. 119–120, 123–124, 131–132, 179–181, 279–285, 353–359, 372–373, 404–408.

# Exhibit Twenty

## DEAR JOHN KEBLE...
*JOHN KEBLE*

### Introduction

John Keble (1792–1866), poet, hymn-writer, scholar, and pastor, is outstanding amongst a multitude of well-known mid-Victorian clergymen of the Church of England. The sensitive and sensible pastor that he was is portrayed in a number of advice-giving letters coming from every phase of his long career.

During a brief but brilliant time as an Oxford don at Oriel College—a fellowship to which he was elected at the age of 19—he joined a group of men who soon became prominent figures in ecclesiastical controversy. Keble's famous sermon on "National Apostasy," preached in July 1833 against Parliament's suppression of certain Irish bishoprics, is generally regarded as having touched off the Oxford Movement in the Church of England, and he wrote nine of the important *Tracts for the Times*, by which the movement announced its effort toward a Catholic revival within the established church. For the remainder of his life, Keble shared leadership of the Anglo-Catholic party.

Soon after the Oxford Movement began, however, Keble left academic pursuits for a pastorate in Hursley near Winchester, where, during the last thirty years of his life, he engaged in an assiduous

pastoral ministry and was much sought after as a spiritual director both personally and through correspondence. From his numerous letters have been selected a few representative ones
which reveal his keen pastoral abilities.

Keble's intense practical interest in personal religion was
early reflected by a collection of poems, first published in 1827,
entitled "The Christian Year," and by numerous hymns, the
most familiar of which is "Sun of my soul, thou Saviour dear,/
It is not night if thou be near . . ." (1820). Scholarly work,
such as preparing and publishing in 1836 a definitive edition of
the writings of Richard Hooker (c. 1554–1600), did not distract
Keble's constant interest in religious poetry, piety, and pastoring. Only four years after death, his memory was honored by
the foundation of Keble College at Oxford.

Of Keble's many letters to troubled correspondents, even
the few selected for inclusion in this exhibit show him as a
considerate and sensitive pastor, and have about them a distinctive ring of modernity. Almost completely gone is any indication
that man stands as the prize and locus of spiritual warfare between the forces of God and Satan. Nowhere does Keble give
advice that is posited on the notion that his troubled friends'
miseries spring from or are influenced by demons. On the other
hand, however, Keble does not belong to our own times, by
virtue of the very simplicity of his view of human troubles. His
understandings were formed before Freud, Dostoyevsky, the appreciation of Kierkegaard, and the advent of the social sciences.
Therefore, perplexed and distraught souls he saw as victimized
neither by demons nor by pathogenic environmental and bio-
graphical forces, but rather as free, open, rational entities ready
to submit to the decrees of their resolute and intelligent wills.
We share with Keble a distance from the literalism of medieval
ideas of possession and obsession, but we rest uneasily with what
sometimes seems a determination to ignore elements of the
human situation which limit freedom or which weigh otherwise
against constructive solutions. Perhaps Keble's "demonology" is
modern, but his psychology remains that of the Enlightenment
—a confident appraisal of human "faculties" able to operate effi-
ciently apart from hidden influences and mixtures of motives.
If it is obvious that Keble had been emancipated from the
theological thought-forms of *Malleus Maleficarum*, it is also
obvious that he has not entered the anthropological world of
Dostoyevsky, where human decisions are formed first in the dark
subconsciousness of man.

With his reliance upon the ability of the conscience to
direct human action, Keble appeals in these letters to the re-

sponsibility and religious common-sense of the sufferer, all the while exhorting a vigorous exercise of freedom: one should examine his duty, resolve to perform it, and then do it. Yet the counselor is kindly tolerant of failure and remains in a warm and empathic relationship with his troubled clients. Keble's letters form a picture of counseling by moral exhortation at its best—if not a fully modern, certainly not an unattractive picture.

# DEAR JOHN KEBLE...

From: *Letters* (1820–c. 1860), by John Keble.

## TO ONE IN DISTRESS FOR PAST SIN, AND ON REMEDIES AGAINST TEMPTATION.

My dear _____,

If you knew my real history, you would know how little it would become such an one to turn away from a frail and erring brother; and were I, indeed, such as you mistakenly imagine, it would be the very joy of my heart to welcome and encourage the penitent. I do not mean to make light of the sad account you sent me: the fall, no doubt, has been grievous, and you do well to judge and condemn yourself for it, but do not for a moment despond. Set yourself to the work of penitence as you would to the cure of any bodily illness: judge and punish yourself secretly and soberly for the fault, and watch with all your might against every degree of relapse, especially guarding (as our Lord Himself directed) the eyes. I suppose no words can express the importance of that one caution.

If evil thoughts occur in the night, rise and pray on your knees for a few moments: say, e.g. the 51st Psalm. Some *slight* bodily hardship is often useful, I believe, at such times. Be very careful about your fasting, whether in the way of penitence or precaution; it causes sometimes, especially when persons are unused to it, a kind of reaction very distressing. If you have reason to fear that, you had better use hard and unpleasant diet, instead of actually going without.

If you find that your mind is still oppressed, and especially if your enemy still haunts you, make use of the Church's motherly direction about confession. You will find directions for it, and for the conduct of your repentance altogether, in a little book lately republished, Kettlewell's "Companion for the Penitent."

Pray do not give up your intention of coming to see us; there is one person in the house, at any rate, who ought to be very thankful to be allowed to kneel down and ask pardon with you; one who has need of all the help he can find for himself, and to whom, therefore, it is the greatest charity to shew him how he may be of some little help to others. I quite depend upon making your acquaintance some day. God grant we may meet in peace; and we shall do so, if we meet as true penitents.

Ever yours affec<sup>ly</sup>,
J. KEBLE.

## REMEDIES AND HELPS UNDER TEMPTATION.

My dear _____,

It was a great relief to hear from you again, sad as your report is in some respects: for I had begun to fear that I had lost you quite: I mean, that I was to give up the hope which I had entertained, and in which I found a peculiar sort of comfort, that I, unworthy as I know myself to be, might be permitted to do you good. Your writing again is a merciful token, that both you and I may have hope for ourselves and for one another; I trust I am not wrong in saying this with entire confidence.

If the Great Judge had already sentenced you, He would not put it into your mind to have such misgivings, and to write so of yourself to one, to whom you are drawn no otherwise than as to His (supposed) instrument for your good. No, my dear young friend, be sure you are very very dear to Him. He is but waiting to see you stand manfully in His strength (which you will have if you pray for it) against the next assault of your enemy: you know you *can* do it, if you will—you have that power, for how would it be if some one were by who stood in some very dear and sacred relation to you, a parent for example, or a sister? Should you not of course keep *then* from outward excess at least, such as they could take notice of? Only in this case you must not wait for outward excess: the time to think of God's eye being upon you is when your own eyes are tempted to look the wrong way, or your ears to listen to what you know will prove near occasions of sin; it is there, where the battle of purity must be fought, and where the purity of Repentance must begin to be recovered, even if that of innocency is lost.

In other words, the only safety in temptations, properly called carnal, is in *flight*; when that can be had, it is vain trusting to resistance. This you will find strongly put in a little book called the "Spiritual Combat," which has been translated, and edited by Dr. Pusey; there are many things in it which I think may be useful to you.

I cannot but hope something from your being called home just now; family anxiety (for I will hope it may not amount to affliction) and absence for a while from the scene of your usual temptations, seem providential calls, of which a good use may be made. I would beg of you to watch every thing of that sort, every thing that tends to recall you to your better self, however trifling or merely accidental it may seem.

You are, if I do not guess wrongly, sensitive and quick in your imaginations, and able, therefore, to catch up and to interpret every hint of that kind which your ever-present Friend may vouchsafe you. The mere exercise of watching for such hints will do you good, by God's blessing, in many ways.

Do you know La Motte Fouqué's "Sintram and his Companions?" if you do not, I would beg you to get it and read it; it will explain what I mean in these last sentences, which perhaps may be rather obscure.

I should repeat to you now, more earnestly than ever, the advice I gave, about avoiding disputes and mere conversations on sacred subjects. You seem yourself quite aware of the danger, and perhaps it behoves you more than ever to think of others, who might be injured by one's conversing on such subjects, without earnest preparation of the heart and conduct.

In the mean time, be of good courage, I beseech you, in this respect also; make it specially matter of your prayers, and assure yourself that here, as in the other equally painful subject, it is not having a bad thought suggested to you, but consenting to it, which makes guilt before God.

If the worst comes to the worst, and you find yourself so tempted in your present situation that you cannot *fight*, you have still the chance of *flying*, that is, of sacrificing your present prospects; if you could so do it as to punish yourself only, it might be an acceptable offering, and obtain a great blessing. But I say this, of course, in great ignorance, and in much doubt whether I ought to say it at all; only that this, or indeed anything would be better than going on in a bad way, in a kind of reckless despondency.

If anything more occurs to me, I will write to you again, for, indeed, I think of you daily: but I deeply wish you had some one at hand whom you might trust in these matters. Yet, again, you have such an One at hand; only fear not to trust Him. And never, never give way to despair. Think of the good Angels and Saints praying for you, and of your friends who are gone; and think of one most unworthy, who depends partly on you, to "cover the" sad "multitude of his sins."

Ever anxiously and affectionately yours,

J. KEBLE.

## TO THE SAME, ON CONFESSION.

My dear young friend,

Indeed I am very sorry for you, but I must not lose a moment in beseeching you not to despair, but to go on courageously in the way of penitence, on which, by God's grace, you have entered. I feel sure that as the evil spirit must have rejoiced in your fall (no doubt he was especially busy with you, those who are making any kind of effort in the way of goodness must always expect to find him so), so the good Angels rejoiced, and I trust are still rejoicing, at your having the heart to confess. May He, who put that good mind into you, strengthen you more and more by His grace, that you may feel more and more the shame and horror of so dealing with the members of Christ, and resolve more and more earnestly, to avoid not only the sin, but all temptations and near occasions of it, however dull and wearisome the time may seem to pass to you. The dulness and weariness, as far as they go, will be useful in the way of penance.

I forget whether I mentioned to you, in talking of this kind of subject, that some people had found it useful to associate the idea of dirt, of bodily foulness and loathsomeness, with temptations of that sort. But I am persuaded that in most cases (and yours seems no exception) *regular* confession, and not occasional only, will be found the best help, by way both of precaution and remedy. It was partly with this view that I mentioned to you Mr. _____, whom I suppose to be a most discreet and charitable director. But I hope you will understand that I am quite at your service, should you prefer "opening your grief" to me, Providence having somehow brought us together.

I think you had better begin immediately to prepare for what is called General Confession, by reviewing your whole history, and setting down your sins as well as you can; any book of preparation for the Holy Communion will help you to do so. And, having this paper by you, you may add to it from time to time, as new faults occur, or old ones are remembered; and then when a good opportunity comes, you may pour it all out into your loving Lord's ear, through some one of His unworthy Priests, and be by Him, through the Priest's mouth, so fully absolved, that the sins, if not returned to, shall be no more mentioned unto you, and you may with humble confidence communicate as often as ever you can reverently draw near. In the meantime, I should rather recommend your abstaining from Holy Communion, unless the time, from circumstances, were too long, in which case you should make your earnest purpose of special confession, when it may be had, part of your preparation for the Sacrament.

Pray consider this, and with earnest prayer. I cannot but hope that courage will be given you to try this remedy, bitter as it must be, and to persevere in it. You need not have to wait long, as, if you prefer Mr. _____ (which, on many accounts, I should be glad of), you might go to him at any time. The practice once begun, I trust in His great goodness would go on, and do you great good. The general confession need not be repeated, though you changed your director, unless you wished it.

May He, who can, forgive and bless you,

And believe me always,<br>Your affectionate Friend,<br>J. Keble.

## THE SAME SUBJECT CONTINUED.

Your letter was a great comfort to me, and I earnestly hope and pray that you may not suffer anything to move you from the course which you have marked out for yourself. I am so sure it is the right one. If I had plenty of time, I might, perhaps, have much more to say on the best way of discharging the duty you have now undertaken of special confession. At present I will only just say, be not too scrupulous in setting down things, nor yet too general, but take some one or more as specimens in any kind which may have become habitual, and describe the frequency of the habit, if you can, by the number of sins in a given time, and the degree, by some aggravating circumstances, such as your conscience most reproaches you for, and He who is merciful will accept it, if fairly so intended, for a full confession. What you write is best written in some kind of cypher or abbreviation, lest it be lost, and do harm. Do it all as a religious exercise, as in God's presence, and a good deal on your knees. Being thus set down as you may remember it, it will save you the trouble of recollection when you come to confess, and you will be more at leisure for pure contrition.

On the whole matter you will find good directions in Bishop Taylor's "Holy Dying," and "Golden Grove;" and also in Kettlewell's "Companion to the Penitent."

May God and all good angels be with you in the good work.


## TO A PERSON UNDER SPECIAL TEMPTATION.

I think it probable that some of your worst falls arise in some measure from your getting into an excited and irregular state of body and mind by sitting up late, whether for study or amusement, and that if you could set yourself a moderately strict rule in that matter, and keep to it, besides the little self-denial, it would be a help to you, in more ways than one. At the same time you know very well that there is one who will make it his particular business to put this sort of temptation in your way. . . . Therefore you must not be too much cast down, nor think all is going wrong, should you find yourself for a long time haunted in the way I mean: only do not lend yourself to it in the least degree, do not wait to fight, but fly; and perhaps it may help if you use yourself to consider it as specially a work of the devil, which no doubt it often is. If you can get your hours of sleeping and waking properly arranged, might you not, do you think, find time to say the fifty-first Psalm *before* your other prayers, the first thing on waking in the morning: and then if you *should* happen to wake in the night, it would suggest itself. Especially when the enemy seems near, it would be almost sure help, if you got up and prayed.

As to the bitter and scornful words, might it not be a good help against them to make a rule of trying to remember at such times something that you are most ashamed of. The very effort would do much good, though the thought were ever so rapid and superficial, and might scarce seem to amount to contrition.

I shall, I hope, pray for you, that your earnest wish for a like-minded companion may be granted, and that it may prove an effectual help in the way you wish. I think you should be aware that some of your trials are of that subtle nature that no society, nor state of life, nor anything else but the grace of God blessing one's sincere endeavours, can overcome them. So that, even if you had such a friend, some of the gravest of your trials might still continue: and by His gracious help you may be completely delivered without such an outward advantage. Only be resolute in guarding your thoughts and senses, and cleanness of heart will, by God's blessing, return; and if I am not mistaken, this will help more than you might think in checking the bitter and angry thoughts and words which you complain of. For few things, I suppose, put a person more out of tune, than the feeling of continually yielding to what he is ashamed of, and what, in his better mind, he detests.

Ever yours very affectionately,

J. KEBLE.

## TO A LADY, ON THE ABSENCE OF CONSCIOUS LOVE AND DEVOTION.

My dear _____,

I am much confirmed in my opinion, that your distress is, in a great measure, what may be called "morbid feeling," and that the way to deal with it is, not so much by direct opposition as by refusing to attend to it, and turning the mind another way. This, therefore, with such authority as I have, I enjoin you to do to the best of your power, at least until I see you again. Pray against it beforehand, but do not brood over it when it comes. I have no doubt that, if another person were to come to you with the same kind of trouble in heart, you would say to him, "If you had no kind of love for God, you would not be troubled at your want of love for Him;" and this at once makes an unspeakable difference between your case and such as was supposed in that Sermon. I say this (which I am sure is true) for the chance of its being useful, but you are not to go on thinking about it, but to turn away from the subject entirely, and let your self-examination for the present rather turn upon the government of your thoughts, ways, and tempers, towards your fellow-creatures. This, I trust, by the blessing of God, will be an effectual help to you in all respects. May that blessing be on you for ever, dear daughter, is the sincere prayer of

Your affec<sup>te</sup> friend,

J. KEBLE.

## TO THE SAME, ON THE SAME.

My dear child in our Lord,

I am truly sorry for your distress: yet in substance I fear I can say little to help you that I have not said before. It is a trouble to be borne, this consciousness of being so dull and dry when you least wish to be so: only take care that you do not grow impatient, as though you were hardly used in its being allowed: neither be too minute in searching out the reason of it, only let it make you more and more watchful of your general conduct, especially against the infirmities of your temper. Take care that you do not ask angrily, "Must I continue to serve God in slavish fear?" Of course you must, if it be His will. Is it not infinitely better than not serving Him at all? Do not dwell upon this subject; do not allow yourself to be worked up into any bitter feelings about it. Every morning, as earnestly as you can, commit yourself in prayer concerning it to our loving Saviour, and then dismiss it. Do not fret about it between whiles; you cannot help being grieved at it when it occurs in private or public devotion, but then also dismiss it as well as you can at the end, by an earnest wish before God, which wish will be in His ears a prayer, that He would forgive you what in it may be due to any fault of your own, and enable you to mend it: and for the rest, that He would either relieve it, or enable you to bear it as He knows to be best for you, and especially pray against all bitterness.

For reading I do not think anything so likely to do good as "Meditations on the Life and Death of our Lord." Do you know Isaac Williams' books on that subject? if you have not studied them, you might try them.

God be with you.

Y<sup>r</sup> affec<sup>te</sup> Father in X<sup>t</sup>,

J. K.

. . . . I think you ought not to indulge the somewhat morbid feeling which you express about our Lord's own words, but neither need you violently overbear it. There is danger lest under the guise of humility, (and not I daresay without a mixture of true humility in it,) it may have a touch of the old danger—ill temper (so to speak) towards God. Might you not draw up for yourself a very short prayer to be used some time every morning, for grace to derive comfort for that day from His own words?

## TO THE SAME.

My dear child,

I am grieved to the heart at your distress, and the more as I cannot help fearing that it may be greatly owing to insufficiency in one who ought to know better how to help you.

It seems to me so entirely a matter of dreamy morbid imagination, that I could sometimes wish myself a physician as my only chance of being able to deal with it. This plainly shews that praying for you is at least one thing which one is bound never to neglect, and I hope not to do so.

In the meantime, what if you were calmly to consider (and set down?) what thoughts and ways have done you good in previous attacks of this sort, and what you would say to another person who should describe to you such feelings as his or her own? May He, who only can, effectually relieve you.

Ever y$^{rs}$ affec$^{tly}$,

J. KEBLE.

## TO THE SAME.

My dear child,

I am truly sorry to hear of your distress continuing, but I must put it to your own conscience, whether there is not in it somewhat of self-tormenting and wilful pe[e]vishness; and whether, *so far*, the remedy is not, by God's mercy, in your own power. I must beg you to ask yourself whether you are really endeavouring to shake off the morbid feelings which haunt you, as sincerely as you would endeavour to cure a toothache. You refer to some similar trials in times past. Perhaps it might be well if you would tell me what was Mr. _____'s course, which you seem to say prospered then. May God bless and relieve you! and He surely will if you are not wanting to yourself. In Him

I am ever y$^{rs}$ most truly,

J. KEBLE.

## AGAINST SEARCHING TOO CLOSELY INTO MOTIVES.

My dear child,

My entire conviction is that your anxiety about your *motive* for what you do in the way of penitence is carried too far. *He*, on purpose, for the most part hides that point from us; so that few, if any, shall be able to say in what measure they are influenced by love, in what by fear, and shame, and indignation, and such inferior, yet legitimate motives. You, my child, must learn to bear this painful doubt, and to be thankful that He releases and keeps you from wilful sin *anyhow.* You must pray and strive for love, but not be violently grieved, nor angry with yourself, should you still feel as if the lower motives alone, or nearly alone, were yours. . . .

Do not allow yourself, if you can help it, to sit for many minutes, moody and dreaming. Your judgments, your conduct, your feelings towards others—*that* is where your minute watchfulness should be, *there* will be the proof of your grief being accepted as real contrition, much more than in any consciousness you may seem to have of it at the time.

Your loving Father in Christ,

J. K.

## TO THE FATHER OF AN ILLEGITIMATE CHILD.

Dear Sir,

I wish to say a few words to you on a very painful matter. . . . I fear it is impossible for you to deny that you are the father of _____'s child, and I do beseech you to consider what a heavy burden this ought to be on your mind. You are not like an ignorant person, brought up amongst unprincipled people; you cannot but know that, however lightly the world may treat such sins as these, the Bible speaks plainly, and says, they who do such things, cannot inherit the kingdom of God; and that these are the very sinful lusts which you renounced in your Baptism and Confirmation, so that now you have, by indulging them, cast away the blessing of your Baptism, and ought not to have a moment's peace of mind until you have some good ground to believe that you are in God's sight a true penitent. S. Matt. vii. 7–10; S. Luke xi. 5–13; S. Matt. xviii. 1–14.

You ought not to be easy for this plain reason, that if you should die before such a change has taken place in you, you are sure to be lost for ever. You cannot deny this without contradicting a great many plain words of God. Then, besides the danger of your own soul, what a burthen it is to have to answer for the souls of others, unhappy partners in such sins; innocent, perhaps, until corrupted by you; or if they had gone wrong before, plunged by you into deeper wickedness.

Remember our Lord Himself says, "Whoso shall be the cause of sin to one of these little ones, it were better," &c. Think what it must be to meet them at the last day, and to feel that you are the cause of their ruin—the devil's agent to prepare them for his kingdom, and not only them, but all others whom such bad example tends to corrupt.

Now I do not at all suppose that you ever intended all this mischief; nor do I doubt that, as a good-natured young man, you are sorry for the present misery of this poor young woman; but the mischief you see is done: you were carried away by your passion in spite of good instruction; and however sorry you may be now, surely experience must have taught you to mistrust yourself for the future. Surely you must feel that if you do not now turn over a new leaf entirely, and seek God's pardon and help in a truer and better way than you have hitherto done, there is no chance, but you will go on from bad to worse: and what will the end be? For the sake of your parents, and for your own sake, I beseech you to think on these things now: you know as well as I do that the time will soon come when you will wish you had thought on them. If, according to our Saviour's and the Church's direction, you make use of me or any other clergyman to advise you in the difficult work of steady repentance, you are aware, of course, that any clergyman is bound to keep people's secrets so applying to him.

But, in any case, repentance after such things must be a long and painful business, and particularly it will be quite necessary to make up your mind not to care for the foolish laughter of those who make a mock at sin. . . . Do let me have the comfort of knowing that you intend to repent in earnest. . . .

*Letters of Spiritual Counsel and Guidance, by the Late Rev. J. Keble, M.A. Vicar of Hursley,* ed. R. F. Wilson (Oxford and London: printed by James Parker and Co.; New York: for Messrs. Pott and Amery, 1870), pp. 86–91, 95–99, 102–103, 126–131, 133, 138–140.

# Exhibit Twenty-One

## REMEDIAL RELIGION

### WILLIAM JAMES

Introduction

William James, noted American philosopher and psychologist, was born in 1842, the son of a Sweden-borgian theologian and the brother of the famed novelist Henry James. His career was spent as a professor at Harvard University, first in medicine, then in psychology, finally in philosophy. As a pragmatic philosopher, he sought to describe the usefulness of religious belief for the psycho-physical well-being of the believer, grounding there a "right to believe" in God. As a psychologist, he acknowledged how the endless variety of human types and conditions gave rise to quite plural religious attitudes and activities. These variations James described and classified in his classic Gifford Lectures on *The Varieties of Religious Experience* (1902), from which this exhibit is drawn. In other books, he defined and defended the validity of religious experiences, always pointing to "the faith-state" as closer to reality than the religious dogma and ceremony that tried to express it.

In the Gifford Lectures, James made the now famous distinction between "the healthy-minded" or "once-born" and "the sick soul" or "twice-born" personalities, viewing the latter's vision of life as more profound because it reckoned seriously with the

321

power of evil. Classifying himself philosophically as a "piece-meal" supernaturalist against monistic, universalistic theism, James contended that religious experience "unequivocally testifies . . . that we can experience union with *something* larger than ourselves and in that union find our greatest peace."[86]

James' researches and deliberations have stirred interest in a modern psychology of religion and have directed much religious thought and practice toward utilitarianism, perhaps especially in America. His contribution to the reassessment of the therapeutic value of religious experience has been summarized by a contemporary scholar who noted James' importance for an understanding of

> . . . the application of the ideas of health and disease to those types of experience which had been conceived exclusively in terms of sin and salvation. James was more prophetic than he knew when he described religious types as "healthy" or "sick." And he was very subtly prophetic in contrasting healthy *mind* with sick *soul*. For the basic aim of modern pastoral counseling as also of modern psychiatry is to provide even a sick *soul* with a healthy *mind*; that is, psychological analysis and psychiatric diagnosis have provided the means (to some extent, at least) for enabling a broken spirit to have a critical and clinical understanding of his own condition. Thus the general and traditional judgments passed on man's sinfulness by the word of God, by which a sinner becomes "convicted," can now be supplemented by detailed diagnosis and prescriptions. The sharp lines that used to be drawn between crimes and diseases, morals and religion, eternal and temporal welfare have become shadowy. Some distinctions no doubt will remain, but as the body-mind-soul complex is unified in the concept of the person or self, so the health-righteousness-salvation complex becomes a unified though complicated problem.[87]

Thus, along with philosophical achievements, James made immense contributions to modern pastoral theology. His two-volume work, *The Principles of Psychology* (1890), was clearly the most exhaustive book on general psychology of its time, and after its appearance James' thought was inescapable wherever psychology was seriously studied. His studies of religion and religious belief were part and parcel of his empirical and scientific psychology, and his *Varieties* virtually founded the modern study of religious psychology.

---

86 *The Varieties of Religious Experience* (New York: Longmans, Green, and Co., 1902), pp. 521, 525.
87 Herbert Wallace Schneider, *Religion in 20th Century America* (Cambridge, Mass.: Harvard University Press, 1952), p. 186. By permission.

In that germinal work James concluded that, while certain religious questions like that of the existence of God must be decided without benefit of empirical data, the religious hypothesis itself might be tested by careful psychological study. Hence these lectures argued that religious belief made a significant difference to human life, and that the effects of religious devotion were on the whole good. He saw religious conversion as beneficial, since it subordinated previously conflicting tendencies to a new group of ideals that became the focus for a new integration of a personality on a higher and more efficient level. In discussing the religion of "the healthy-minded," James soberly and appreciatively analyzed what has come to be known as the power of positive thinking. And he saw the religion of the "sick soul" as making possible a fundamental optimism in the midst of sensitivity to evil and pain. Although at present the psychology of religion is a more confused subject than it was when James left it, the accents of his discussion ring clearly in modern ears. His analysis of the nineteenth-century mind-cure movement reminds us that our generation has bought more than two million copies of Norman Vincent Peale's book on *The Power of Positive Thinking*. His explanation of an anti-moralistic therapy of relaxation which he perceived in the Lutheran and Wesleyan movements still lives in the advices of countless religious counselors today, and to good effect.[88]

The following pages from James' seminal study of religion make an appropriate final exhibit, for they at once re-interpret familiar data about religion in the past and speak directly to pastoral care in the modern world.

## REMEDIAL RELIGION

From: *The Varieties of Religious Experience*
(1901–1902), by William James.

If, then, we give the name of healthy-mindedness to the tendency which looks on all things and sees that they are good, we find that we must distinguish between a more involuntary and a more voluntary or systematic way of being healthy-minded. In its involuntary variety, healthy-mindedness is a way of feeling happy about things immediately. In its systematical variety, it is an abstract way of conceiving things as

---

[88] See, for example, Smiley Blanton, M.D., "The Best Prescription I Know," *The Reader's Digest*, December 1962.

good. Every abstract way of conceiving things selects some one aspect of them as their essence for the time being, and disregards the other aspects. Systematic healthy-mindedness, conceiving good as the essential and universal aspect of being, deliberately excludes evil from its field of vision; and although, when thus nakedly stated, this might seem a difficult feat to perform for one who is intellectually sincere with himself and honest about facts, a little reflection shows that the situation is too complex to lie open to so simple a criticism.

In the first place, happiness, like every other emotional state, has blindness and insensibility to opposing facts given it as its instinctive weapon for self-protection against disturbance. When happiness is actually in possession, the thought of evil can no more acquire the feeling of reality than the thought of good can gain reality when melancholy rules. To the man actively happy, from whatever cause, evil simply cannot then and there be believed in. He must ignore it; and to the bystander he may then seem perversely to shut his eyes to it and hush it up.

But more than this: the hushing of it up may, in a perfectly candid and honest mind, grow into a deliberate religious policy, or *parti pris* [*i.e.*, prejudice]. Much of what we call evil is due entirely to the way men take the phenomenon. It can so often be converted into a bracing and tonic good by a simple change of the sufferer's inner attitude from one of fear to one of fight; its sting so often departs and turns into a relish when, after vainly seeking to shun it, we agree to face about and bear it cheerfully, that a man is simply bound in honor, with reference to many of the facts that seem at first to disconcert his peace, to adopt this way of escape. Refuse to admit their badness; despise their power; ignore their presence; turn your attention the other way; and so far as you yourself are concerned at any rate, though the facts may still exist, their evil character exists no longer. Since you make them evil or good by your own thoughts about them, it is the ruling of your thoughts which proves to be your principal concern.

The deliberate adoption of an optimistic turn of mind thus makes its entrance into philosophy. And once in, it is hard to trace its lawful bounds. Not only does the human instinct for happiness, bent on self-protection by ignoring, keep working in its favor, but higher inner ideals have weighty words to say. The attitude of unhappiness is not only painful, it is mean and ugly. What can be more base and unworthy than the pining, puling, mumping mood, no matter by what outward ills it may have been engendered? What is more injurious to others? What less helpful as a way out of the difficulty? It but fastens and perpetuates the trouble which occasioned it, and increases the total evil of the situation. At all costs, then, we ought to reduce the sway of that mood; we ought to scout it in ourselves and others, and never show it tolerance. But it is impossible to carry on this discipline in the subjective sphere without zealously emphasizing the brighter and minimizing the darker aspects of the objective sphere of things at the same time. And thus our resolution not to indulge in misery, beginning at a comparatively small point within ourselves, may not stop until it has brought the entire frame of reality under a systematic conception optimistic enough to be congenial with its needs.

In all this I say nothing of any mystical insight or persuasion that the total frame of things absolutely must be good. Such mystical persuasion plays an enormous part in the history of the religious consciousness, and we must look at it later with some care. But we need not go so far at present. More ordinary non-mystical conditions of rapture suffice for my immediate contention. All invasive moral states and passionate enthusiasms make one feelingless to evil in some direction. The common penalties cease to deter the patriot, the usual prudences are flung by the lover to the winds. When the passion is extreme, suffering may actually be gloried in, provided it be for the ideal cause, death may lose its sting, the grave its victory. In these states, the ordinary contrast of good and ill seems to be swallowed up in a higher denomination, an omnipotent excitement which engulfs the evil, and which the human being welcomes as the crowning experience of his life. This, he says, is truly to live, and I exult in the heroic opportunity and adventure.

The systematic cultivation of healthy-mindedness as a religious attitude is therefore consonant with important currents in human nature, and is anything but absurd. In fact, we all do cultivate it more or less, even when our professed theology should in consistency forbid it. We divert our attention from disease and death as much as we can; and the slaughter-houses and indecencies without end on which our life is founded are huddled out of sight and never mentioned, so that the world we recognize officially in literature and in society is a poetic fiction far handsomer and cleaner and better than the world that really is.

*  *  *  *  *

Here is another case, more concrete, also that of a woman. I read you these cases without comment,—they express so many varieties of the state of mind we are studying.

"I had been a sufferer from my childhood till my fortieth year. [Details of ill-health are given which I omit.] I had been in Vermont several months hoping for good from the change of air, but steadily growing weaker, when one day during the latter part of October, while resting in the afternoon, I suddenly heard as it were these words: 'You will be healed and do a work you never dreamed of.' These words were impressed upon my mind with such power I said at once that only God could have put them there. I believed them in spite of myself and of my suffering and weakness, which continued until Christmas, when I returned to Boston. Within two days a young friend offered to take me to a mental healer (this was January 7, 1881). The healer said: 'There is nothing but Mind; we are expressions of the One Mind; body is only a mortal belief; as a man thinketh so is he.' I could not accept all she said, but I translated all that was there for *me* in this way: 'There is nothing but God; I am created by Him, and am absolutely dependent upon Him; mind is given me to use; and by just so much of it as I will put upon the thought of right action in body I shall be lifted out of bondage to my ignorance and fear and past experience.' That day I commenced accordingly to take a little of every food provided for the family, constantly saying to myself: 'The Power that created the stomach must take care of what I have eaten.' By holding these suggestions through the evening I went to bed and fell asleep, saying: 'I am soul, spirit, just one with God's Thought of me,' and slept all night without waking, for the first time in several years [the distress-turns had usually recurred about two o'clock in the night]. I felt the next day like an escaped prisoner, and believed I had found the secret that would in time give me perfect health. Within ten days I was able to eat anything provided for others, and after two weeks I began to have my own positive mental suggestions of Truth, which were to me like stepping-stones. I will note a few of them; they came about two weeks apart.

"1st. I am Soul, therefore it is well with me.

"2d. I am soul, therefore I *am* well.

"3d. A sort of inner vision of myself as a four-footed beast with a protuberance on every part of my body where I had suffering, with my own face, begging me to acknowledge it as myself. I resolutely fixed my attention on being well, and refused to even look at my old self in this form.

"4th. Again the vision of the beast far in the background, with faint voice. Again refusal to acknowledge.

"5th. Once more the vision, but only of my eyes with the longing look; and again the refusal. Then came the conviction, the inner consciousness, that I was perfectly well and always had been, for I was Soul, an expression of God's Perfect Thought. That was to me the perfect and completed separation between what I was and what I appeared to be. I succeeded in never losing sight after this of my real being, by constantly affirming this truth, and by degrees (though it took me two years of hard work to get there) *I expressed health continuously throughout my whole body*.

"In my subsequent nineteen years' experience I have never known this Truth to fail when I applied it, though in my ignorance I have often failed to apply it, but through my failures I have learned the simplicity and trustfulness of the little child."

But I fear that I risk tiring you by so many examples, and I must lead you back to philosophic generalities again. You see already by such records of experience how impossible it is not to class mind-cure as primarily a religious movement. Its doctrine of the oneness of our life with God's life is in fact quite indistinguishable from an interpretation of Christ's message which in these very Gifford lectures has been defended by some of your very ablest Scottish religious philosophers.

\*     \*     \*     \*     \*

On the whole, one is struck by a psychological similarity between the mind-cure movement and the Lutheran and Wesleyan movements. To the believer in moralism and works, with his anxious query, "What shall I do to be saved?" Luther and Wesley replied: "You are saved now, if you would but believe it." And the mind-curers come with precisely similar words of emancipation. They speak, it is true, to persons for whom the conception of salvation has lost its ancient theological meaning, but who labor nevertheless with the same eternal human difficulty. *Things are wrong with them*; and "What shall I do to be clear, right, sound, whole, well?" is the form of their question. And the answer is: "You *are* well, sound, and clear already, if you did but know it." "The whole matter may be summed up in one sentence," says one of the authors whom I have already quoted, "*God is well, and so are you.* You must awaken to the knowledge of your real being."

The adequacy of their message to the mental needs of a large fraction of mankind is what gave force to those earlier gospels. Exactly the same adequacy holds in the case of the mind-cure message, foolish as it may sound upon its surface; and seeing its rapid growth in influence, and its therapeutic triumphs, one is tempted to ask whether it may not be destined (probably by very reason of the crudity and extravagance of many of its manifestations) to play a part almost as great in the evolution of the popular religion of the future as did those earlier movements in their day.

But I here fear that I may begin to "jar upon the nerves" of some of the members of this academic audience. Such contemporary vagaries, you may think, should hardly take so large a place in dignified Gifford lectures. I can only beseech you to have patience. The whole outcome of these lectures will, I imagine, be the emphasizing to your mind of the enormous diversities which the spiritual lives of different men exhibit. Their wants, their susceptibilities, and their capacities all vary and must be classed under different heads. The result is that we have really different types of religious experience; and, seeking in these lectures closer acquaintance with the healthy-minded type, we must take it where we find it in most radical form. The psychology of individual types of character has hardly begun even to be sketched as yet—our lectures may possibly serve as a crumb-like contribution to the structure. The first thing to bear in mind (especially if we ourselves belong to the clerico-academic-scientific type, the officially and conventionally "correct" type, "the deadly respectable" type, for which to ignore others is a besetting temptation) is that nothing can be more stupid than to bar out phenomena from our notice, merely because we are incapable of taking part in any-thing like them ourselves.

Now the history of Lutheran salvation by faith, of methodistic con-versions, and of what I call the mind-cure movement seems to prove the existence of numerous persons in whom—at any rate at a certain stage in their development—a change of character for the better, so far from being facilitated by the rules laid down by official moralists, will take place all the more successfully if those rules be exactly reversed. Official moralists advise us never to relax our strenuousness. "Be vigilant, day and night," they adjure us; "hold your passive tendencies in check; shrink from no effort; keep your will like a bow always bent." But the persons I speak of find that all this conscious effort leads to nothing but failure and vexation in their hands, and only makes them twofold more the children of hell they were before. The tense and voluntary attitude be-comes in them an impossible fever and torment. Their machinery re-fuses to run at all when the bearings are made so hot and the belts are so tightened.

Under these circumstances the way to success, as vouched for by innumerable authentic personal narrations, is by an anti-moralistic method, by the "surrender" of which I spoke in my second lecture. Pas-sivity, not activity; relaxation, not intentness, should be now the rule. Give up the feeling of responsibility, let go your hold, resign the care of your destiny to higher powers, be genuinely indifferent as to what becomes of it all, and you will find not only that you gain a perfect inward relief, but often also, in addition, the particular goods you sincerely thought you were renouncing. This is the salvation through self-despair, the dying to be truly born, of Lutheran theology, the passage into *nothing* of which Jacob Behmen [Jakob Boehme, 1575–1624] writes. To get to it, a critical point must usually be passed, a corner turned within one. Something must give way, a native hardness must break down and liquefy; and this event (as we shall abundantly see hereafter) is frequently sudden and automatic, and leaves on the Subject an im-pression that he has been wrought on by an external power.

Whatever its ultimate significance may prove to be, this is certainly one fundamental form of human experience. Some say that the capacity or incapacity for it is what divides the religious from the merely moral-istic character. With those who undergo it in its fullness, no criticism avails to cast doubt on its reality. They *know*; for they have actually *felt* the higher powers, in giving up the tension of their personal will.

A story which revivalist preachers often tell is that of a man who found himself at night slipping down the side of a precipice. At last he caught a branch which stopped his fall, and remained clinging to it in misery for hours. But finally his fingers had to loose their hold, and with a despairing farewell to life, he let himself drop. He fell just six inches. If he have given up the struggle earlier, his agony would have been spared. As the mother earth received him, so, the preachers tell us, will the everlasting arms receive *us* if we confide absolutely in them, and give up the hereditary habit of relying on our personal strength, with its precautions that cannot shelter and safeguards that never save.

The mind-curers have given the widest scope to this sort of experience. They have demonstrated that a form of regeneration by relaxing, by letting go, psychologically indistinguishable from the Lutheran justification by faith and the Wesleyan acceptance of free grace, is within the reach of persons who have no conviction of sin and care nothing for the Lutheran theology. It is but giving your little private convulsive self a rest, and finding that a greater Self is there. The results, slow or sudden, or great or small, of the combined optimism and expectancy, the regenerative phenomena which ensue on the abandonment of effort, remain firm facts of human nature, no matter whether we adopt a theistic, a pantheistic-idealistic, or a medical-materialistic view of their ultimate causal explanation.

When we take up the phenomena of revivalistic conversion, we shall learn something more about all this. Meanwhile I will say a brief word about the mind-curer's *methods*.

They are of course largely suggestive. The suggestive influence of environment plays an enormous part in all spiritual education. But the word "suggestion," having acquired official status, is unfortunately already beginning to play in many quarters the part of a wet blanket upon investigation, being used to fend off all inquiry into the varying susceptibilities of individual cases. "Suggestion" is only another name for the power of ideas, *so far as they prove efficacious over belief and conduct.* Ideas efficacious over some people prove inefficacious over others. Ideas efficacious at some times and in some human surroundings are not so at other times and elsewhere. The ideas of Christian churches are not efficacious in the therapeutic direction to-day, whatever they may have been in earlier centuries; and when the whole question is as to why the salt has lost its savor here or gained it there, the mere blank waving of the word "suggestion" as if it were a banner gives no light. Dr. Goddard, whose candid psychological essay on Faith Cures ascribes them to nothing but ordinary suggestion, concludes by saying that "Religion [and by this he seems to mean our popular Christianity] has in it all there is in mental therapeutics, and has it in its best form. Living up to [our religious] ideas will do anything for us that can be done." And this in spite of the actual fact that the popular Christianity does absolutely *nothing*, or did nothing until mind-cure came to the rescue.

An idea, to be suggestive, must come to the individual with the force of a revelation. The mind-cure with its gospel of healthy-mindedness has come as a revelation to many whose hearts the church Christianity had left hardened. It has let loose their springs of higher life. In what can the originality of any religious movement consist, save in finding a channel, until then sealed up, through which those springs may be set free in some group of human beings?

The force of personal faith, enthusiasm, and example, and above all the force of novelty, are always the prime suggestive agency in this kind of success. If mind-cure should ever become official, respectable, and intrenched, these elements of suggestive efficacy will be lost. In its acuter stages every religion must be a homeless Arab of the desert. The church knows this well enough, with its everlasting inner struggle of the acute religion of the few against the chronic religion of the many, indurated into an obstructiveness worse than that which irreligion opposes to the movings of the Spirit. "We may pray," says Jonathan Edwards [1703–1758], "concerning all those saints that are not lively Christians, that they may either be enlivened, or taken away; if that be true that is often said by some at this day, that these cold dead saints do more hurt than natural men, and lead more souls to hell, and that it would be well for mankind if they were all dead."

The next condition of success is the apparent existence, in large numbers, of minds who unite healthy-mindedness with readiness for regeneration by letting go. Protestantism has been too pessimistic as regards the natural man, Catholicism has been too legalistic and moralistic, for either the one or the other to appeal in any generous way to the type of character formed of this peculiar mingling of elements. However few of us here present may belong to such a type, it is now evident that it forms a specific moral combination, well represented in the world.

Finally, mind-cure has made what in our protestant countries is an unprecedentedly great use of the subconscious life. To their reasoned advice and dogmatic assertion, its founders have added systematic exercise in passive relaxation, concentration, and meditation, and have even invoked something like hypnotic practice.

\* \* \* \* \*

## [THE SICK SOUL]

Let us now say good-by for a while to all this way of thinking, and turn towards those persons who cannot so swiftly throw off the burden of the consciousness of evil, but are congenitally fated to suffer from its presence. Just as we saw that in healthy-mindedness there are shallower and profounder levels, happiness like that of the mere animal, and more regenerate sorts of happiness, so also are there different levels of the morbid mind, and the one is much more formidable than the other. There are people for whom evil means only a mal-adjustment with *things*, a wrong correspondence of one's life with the environment. Such evil as this is curable, in principle at least, upon the natural plane, for merely by modifying either the self or the things, or both at once, the two terms may be made to fit, and all go merry as a marriage bell again. But there are others for whom evil is no mere relation of the subject to particular outer things, but something more radical and general, a wrongness or vice in his essential nature, which no alteration of the environment, or any superficial rearrangement of the inner self, can cure, and which requires a supernatural remedy. On the whole, the Latin races have leaned more towards the former way of looking upon evil, as made up of ills and sins in the plural, removable in detail; while the Germanic races have tended rather to think of Sin in the singular, and with a capital S, as of something ineradicably ingrained in our natural subjectivity, and never to be removed by any superficial piecemeal operations. These comparisons of races are always open to exception, but undoubtedly the northern tone in religion has inclined to the more intimately pessimistic persuasion, and this way of feeling, being the more extreme, we shall find by far the more instructive for our study.

Recent psychology has found great use for the word "threshold" as a symbolic designation for the point at which one state of mind passes into another. Thus we speak of the threshold of a man's consciousness in general, to indicate the amount of noise, pressure, or other outer stimulus which it takes to arouse his attention at all. One with a high threshold will doze through an amount of racket by which one with a low threshold would be immediately waked. Similarly, when one is sensitive to small differences in any order of sensation, we say he has a low "difference-threshold"—his mind easily steps over it into the consciousness of the differences in question. And just so we might speak of a "pain-threshold," a "fear-threshold," a "misery-threshold," and find it quickly overpassed by the consciousness of some individuals, but lying too high in others to be often reached by their consciousness. The sanguine and healthy-minded live habitually on the sunny side of their misery-line, the depressed and melancholy live beyond it, in darkness and apprehension. There are men who seem to have started in life with a bottle or two of champagne inscribed to their credit; whilst others seem to have been born close to the pain-threshold, which the slightest irritants fatally send them over.

Does it not appear as if one who lived more habitually on one side of the pain-threshold might need a different sort of religion from one who habitually lived on the other? This question, of the relativity of different types of religion to different types of need, arises naturally at this point, and will become a serious problem ere we have done. But before we confront it in general terms, we must address ourselves to the unpleasant task of hearing what the sick souls, as we may call them in contrast to the healthy-minded, have to say of the secrets of their prison-house, their own peculiar form of consciousness. Let us then resolutely turn our backs on the once-born and their sky-blue optimistic gospel;

let us not simply cry out in spite of all appearances, "Hurrah for the Universe!—God's in his Heaven, all's right with the world." Let us see rather whether pity, pain, and fear, and the sentiment of human helplessness may not open a profounder view and put into our hands a more complicated key to the meaning of the situation.

* * * * *

The worst kind of melancholy is that which takes the form of panic fear. Here is an excellent example, for permission to print which I have to thank the sufferer. The original is in French, and though the subject was evidently in a bad nervous condition at the time of which he writes, his case has otherwise the merit of extreme simplicity. I translate freely.

"Whilst in this state of philosophic pessimism and general depression of spirits about my prospects, I went one evening into a dressing-room in the twilight to procure some article that was there; when suddenly there fell upon me without any warning, just as if it came out of the darkness, a horrible fear of my own existence. Simultaneously there arose in my mind the image of an epileptic patient whom I had seen in the asylum, a black-haired youth with greenish skin, entirely idiotic, who used to sit all day on one of the benches, or rather shelves against the wall, with his knees drawn up against his chin, and the coarse gray undershirt, which was his only garment, drawn over them inclosing his entire figure. He sat there like a sort of sculptured Egyptian cat or Peruvian mummy, moving nothing but his black eyes and looking absolutely non-human. This image and my fear entered into a species of combination with each other. *That shape am I*, I felt, potentially. Nothing that I possess can defend me against that fate, if the hour for it should strike for me as it struck for him. There was such a horror of him, and such a perception of my own merely momentary discrepancy from him, that it was as if something hitherto solid within my breast gave way entirely, and I became a mass of quivering fear. After this the universe was changed for me altogether. I awoke morning after morning with a horrible dread at the pit of my stomach, and with a sense of the insecurity of life that I never knew before, and that I have never felt since. It was like a revelation; and although the immediate feelings passed away, the experience has made me sympathetic with the morbid feelings of others ever since. It gradually faded, but for months I was unable to go out into the dark alone.

"In general I dreaded to be left alone. I remember wondering how other people could live, how I myself had ever lived, so unconscious of that pit of insecurity beneath the surface of life. My mother in particular, a very cheerful person, seemed to me a perfect paradox in her unconsciousness of danger, which you may well believe I was very careful not to disturb by revelations of my own state of mind. I have always thought that this experience of melancholia of mine had a religious bearing."

On asking this correspondent to explain more fully what he meant by these last words, the answer he wrote was this:—

"I mean that the fear was so invasive and powerful that if I had not clung to scripture-texts like 'The eternal God is my refuge,' etc., 'Come unto me, all ye that labor and are heavy-laden,' etc., 'I am the resurrection and the life,' etc., I think I should have grown really insane."

There is no need of more examples. The cases we have looked at are enough. One of them gives us the vanity of mortal things; another the sense of sin; and the remaining one describes the fear of the universe;— and in one or other of these three ways it always is that man's original optimism and self-satisfaction get leveled with the dust.

In none of these cases was there any intellectual insanity or delusion about matters of fact; but were we disposed to open the chapter of really insane melancholia, with its hallucinations and delusions, it would be a worse story still—desperation absolute and complete, the whole universe coagulating about the sufferer into a material of overwhelming horror, surrounding him without opening or end. Not the conception or intellectual perception of evil, but the grisly blood-freezing heart-palsying sensation of it close upon one, and no other conception or sensation able to live for a moment in its presence. How irrelevantly remote seem all our usual refined optimisms and intellectual and moral consolations in presence of a need of help like this! Here is the real core of the religious problem: Help! help! No prophet can claim to bring a final message unless he says things that will have a sound of reality in the ears of victims such as these. But the deliverance must come in as strong a form as the complaint, if it is to take effect; and that seems a reason why the coarser religions, revivalistic, orgiastic, with blood and miracles and supernatural operations, may possibly never be displaced. Some constitutions need them too much.

Arrived at this point, we can see how great an antagonism may naturally arise between the healthy-minded way of viewing life and the way that takes all this experience of evil as something essential. To this latter way, the morbid-minded way, as we might call it, healthy-mindedness pure and simple seems unspeakably blind and shallow. To the healthy-minded way, on the other hand, the way of the sick soul seems unmanly and diseased. With their grubbing in rat-holes instead of living in the light; with their manufacture of fears, and preoccupation with every unwholesome kind of misery, there is something almost obscene about these children of wrath and cravers of a second birth. If religious intolerance and hanging and burning could again become the order of the day, there is little doubt that, however it may have been in the past, the healthy-minded would at present show themselves the less indulgent party of the two.

In our own attitude, not yet abandoned, of impartial onlookers, what are we to say of this quarrel? It seems to me that we are bound to say that morbid-mindedness ranges over the wider scale of experience, and that its survey is the one that overlaps. The method of averting one's attention from evil, and living simply in the light of good is splendid as long as it will work. It will work with many persons; it will work far more generally than most of us are ready to suppose; and within the sphere of its successful operation there is nothing to be said against it as a religious solution. But it breaks down impotently as soon as melancholy comes; and even though one be quite free from melancholy one's self, there is no doubt that healthy-mindedness is inadequate as a philosophical doctrine, because the evil facts which it refuses positively to account for are a genuine portion of reality; and they may after all be the best key to life's significance, and possibly the only openers of our eyes to the deepest levels of truth.

The normal process of life contains moments as bad as any of those which insane melancholy is filled with, moments in which radical evil gets its innings and takes its solid turn. The lunatic's visions of horror are all drawn from the material of daily fact. Our civilization is founded on the shambles, and every individual existence goes out in a lonely spasm of helpless agony. If you protest, my friend, wait till you arrive there yourself! To believe in the carnivorous reptiles of geologic times is hard for our imagination—they seem too much like mere museum specimens. Yet there is no tooth in any one of those museum-skulls that did not daily through long years of the foretime hold fast to the body struggling in despair of some fated living victim. Forms of horror just as dreadful to their victims, if on a smaller spatial scale, fill the world about us today. Here on our very hearths and in our gardens the infernal cat plays with the panting mouse, or holds the hot bird fluttering in her jaws. Crocodiles and rattlesnakes and pythons are at this moment vessels of life as real as we are; their loathsome existence fills every minute of every day that drags its length along; and whenever they or other wild beasts clutch their living prey, the deadly horror which an agitated melancholiac feels is the literally right reaction on the situation.

It may indeed be that no religious reconcilation with the absolute totality of things is possible. Some evils, indeed, are ministerial to higher forms of good; but it may be that there are forms of evil so extreme as to enter into no good system whatsoever, and that, in respect of such evil, dumb submission or neglect to notice is the only practical resource. This question must confront us on a later day. But provisionally, and as a mere matter of program and method, since the evil facts are as genuine parts of nature as the good ones, the philosophic presumption should be that they have some rational significance, and that systematic healthy-mindedness, failing as it does to accord to sorrow, pain, and death any positive and active attention whatever, is formally less complete than systems that try at least to include these elements in their scope.

The completest religions would therefore seem to be those in which the pessimistic elements are best developed. Buddhism, of course, and Christianity are the best known to us of these. They are essentially religions of deliverance: the man must die to an unreal life before he can be born into the real life. In my next lecture, I will try to discuss some of the psychological conditions of this second birth. Fortunately from now onward we shall have to deal with more cheerful subjects than those which we have recently been dwelling on.

---

William James, *The Varieties of Religious Experience* (New York: Longmans, Green, and Co., reprinted, with revisions, August, 1902), pp. 87–90, 104–105, 107–115, 133–136, 159–165.

# Index

336